THE PRACTICE OF DZOGCHEN

THE PRACTICE OF DZOGCHEN

by

Longchen Rabjam

Introduced, translated and annotated by

Tulku Thondup

Edited by

Harold Talbott

Snow Lion Publications
Ithaca, New York
Boulder, Colorado

Snow Lion Publications
P.O. Box 6483
Ithaca, New York 14851 USA
(607) 273-8519
www.snowlionpub.com

Buddhayana Series: III

Third Edition USA 2002

Printed in USA on acid-free, recycled paper.

This edition ISBN 1-55939-179-0

The Library of Congress catalogued the previous edition of this book as follows:

Kloṅ-chen-pa Dri-med'od-zer, 1308-1363.
The practice of Dzogchen / by Longchen Rabjampa ; introduced, translated, and annotated by Tulku Thondup ; edited by Harold Talbott.
p. cm.
Includes bibliographical references and index.
ISBN 1-55939-054-9
1. Rdzogs-chen (Rñiṅ-ma-pa) – Early works to 1800. I. Thondup, Tulku. II. Talbott, Harold. III. Title.
BQ7662.4.K54357 1993
294.3'4—dc20 95-50004
CIP

CONTENTS

THREE DIVISIONS OF ATIYOGA
(*Dzogpa Chenpo*)

Abbreviations of Cited Texts: TD: *Tshig-Don Rin-Po-Ch'e'i mDzod.* SC: *Shing-Ta Ch'en-Po, the Commentary on Sems-Nyid Ngal-gSo.* GD: *dGe-Ba gSum-Gyi Don-Khrid. Instructions on Three Stages of Training of Sems-Nyid Ngal-gSo.* SR: *Sems-Nyid Rang-Grol, Naturally Liberated Mind.* LN: *Lam-Rim sNying-Po'i Don-Khrid, the Instructional Commentary on Sems-Nyid Rang-Grol.* PK: *Padma dKar-Po, the commentary on Yid-bZhin mDzod.* CD: *Ch'os-dByings Rin-Po-Ch'e'i mDzod.* NKC: *gNyis-Ga'i Yang-Yig Nam-mKha' Klong-Ch'en* from *Bla-Ma Yang-Tig.* NKS: *Thod-Gal Gyi Yang-Yig Nam-mKha' Klong-gSal* from *Bla-Ma Yang-Tig.*

Epigraphs

(*Dzogpa Chenpo*) is the path of luminous absorption, the
essence of the ultimate definitive meaning,
And the summit of the teachings of *sūtras* and *tantras:*
This is the meaning of the instructions on the direct
approach
To the ultimate nature, the Buddha-essence as it is.
—Longchen Rabjam[NKC 13a/4]

The essence of the discourses on the Three Doors of
Liberation
Given by the Victorious One in the Second Turning of the
Dharma Wheel is the very Discriminative Self-awareness
Which is present naturally in the nature of beings as the
Buddha-essence,
And that is known as *Dzogpa Chenpo.*
The entire meaning of the vast, excellent paths (of
Buddhism)
Is only for cleansing the mind.
So the three precepts, six perfections, development and
perfection stages, etc.
Are the steps to the path of *Dzogpa Chenpo.*
—Jigmed Lingpa[YTD 40b/1]

The appearances are free from objective (entity), the intrinsic awareness is the liberation from primordial (time),
The view and meditation are action-free and the six consciousnesses are self-free;
There is no need of apprehending with recollections (for) or antidotes (against):
The action-free *Dzogpa Chenpo* is the cessation of phenomena.

—Jigmed Lingpa[KZD 12b/1]

Note on the Structure of the Book

This book has two parts. Part I is an introduction which includes extensive quotations from various *sūtras*, *tantras*, and writings of great Buddhist scholars, notably of the *Nyingma* school of Tibet. The introduction is followed by an account of the life of Longchen Rabjam.

Part II has thirteen sections. It is an anthology of translations of Longchen Rabjam's writings on *Dzogpa Chenpo* and on *sūtras* and *tantras* as the basis of *Dzogpa Chenpo* and the steps leading to it. The translations are preceded by a summary of the thirteen sections. Each section is preceded by a few lines of my own in smaller type to introduce it. At many places in the translations I have added lines to make the meaning clear, and they are printed in smaller type.

Throughout both sections of the book I have added words in parenthesis for clarification. I have also put some synonyms in square brackets. The letter S. in parenthesis means Sanskrit.

The titles of texts quoted are indicated by abbreviations, for example NKC meaning *gNyis-Ka'i Yang-Yig* Nam-*mKha'* *Klong*-*Ch'en* by Longchen Rabjam. They are listed alphabetically in the bibliography. When a text is quoted, the letters signifying the title are followed by the folio number, then the letters a or b meaning the front or back side of the folio, and then the line number. For example, NKC 13a/4.

Sometimes in this book the same Tibetan term is translated in several different ways according to the context. For example *A'od-gSal* or *gSal* is variously translated as "luminous absorption," "luminescence," "luminescent," "clarity," or "clear." In some instances, when I was not sure of the proper English equivalent, I have put the Tibetan term in parenthesis.

In this book the ordinary mind (*Sems, S. citta*) is translated as "mind" and the essential nature of mind (*Sems-Nyid, S. cittatā*) is translated as "Mind."

I have capitalized the root-letters (*Ming-gZhi*) of each word in the transliterated Tibetan in order to ensure a correct reading. When the root letters are not capitalized, it is possible to confuse two entirely different words. For example, "Gyang" means "wall," while the meaning of "gYang" is "luck."

Preface

In the emptiness, ultimate sphere, the essence-mother,
Dwells the clarity,intrinsic awareness,the nature-father.
To the union of the primordial mother and father, the continuum of Great Perfection,
I pay homage in the state of naturally liberated Buddha Mind.

This book contains an anthology of the writings of Longchen Rabjam (*Klong-Ch'en Rab-'Byams*, 1308-1363) on *Dzogpa Chenpo* (*rDzogs-Pa Ch'en-Po, S. mahāsandhi*). The translations are preceded by a detailed introduction based strictly on the scriptures and traditional interpretations of the innermost esoteric aspect of Buddhism.

The teachings of *Dzogpa Chenpo* (or *Dzogchen*), the Great Perfection, are the innermost esoteric Buddhist training preserved and practiced to this day by the followers of the *Nyingma* (*rNying-Ma*) school of Tibet. The main emphasis of *Dzogpa Chenpo* is to attain and perfect the realization of the true nature of the mind, the Intrinsic Awareness (*Rig-Pa*), which is the Buddha Mind or Buddha-essence. Thereby one attains and perfects the realization of the true nature of all phenomenal existents, all of which are the same in their essence.

According to *Dzogpa Chenpo* scriptures, all forms of Buddhist training lead to the same goal, the realization of the Intrinsic Awareness, which is taught in *Dzogpa Chenpo*; and further, that the essence of all the Buddhist teachings is completed in *Dzogpa Chenpo* meditation and its results. Many accomplished *Dzogpa Chenpo* meditators, in addition to their attainment of the utmost mental peace and enlightenment in this very lifetime, physically display signs of extraordinary accomplishments at the time of death. For example, they dissolve their gross bodies without remainder or transform their mortal bodies into subtle light bodies.

Dzogpa Chenpo meditation is the method of training of utmost simplicity in order to reach the most simple state free from conceptual elaborations. But for ordinary people like us, to attain the state of utmost simplicity and ease is the hardest goal to accomplish. Thus, to prepare for the *Dzogpa Chenpo* training, one has to do various preliminary studies and training in order to learn the path and purify the stains of negative emotions with their traces; to generate positive energy through the force of virtues; and to realize, refine and perfect the ordinary meditative attainments taught in the common Buddhist paths. When one is ready, in accordance with the strength of one's spiritual experiences, one should be instructed in the *Dzogpa Chenpo* meditation by a qualified master.

For the happiness and enlightenment of beings, Buddhism works with the root, the root of gaining joy and dispelling misery, which lies in individuals; for society is a collection of individuals. For an individual, the mind is the main factor and the forerunner of all activities. So the improvement and perfection of the mental state is the primary emphasis of Buddhist training. If one has improved and perfected one's mind, all one's physical activities will be naturally perfect and one's presence and activities will become a source of true happiness and enlightenment for others. From the moment of becoming a *Mahāyāna* Buddhist, one is expected to exert oneself in the service of others. The whole aspiration in spiritual training is for the sake of others. But at the beginning, the emphasis will be on the spiritual progress of oneself, deriving from one's own mind. Without spiritual strength within oneself, trying to serve others will be as a Tibetan proverb says: "A falling person cannot give his shoulder to another falling person to rely on."

The meditations of *tantra* and of *Dzogpa Chenpo* taught and transmitted by Guru Padmasambhava are a training on the balanced path of the view of primordial wisdom and the activities of meritorious applications. They are neither a contemplation on mere view, although some interpret them thus, nor training on just meritorious activities. Guru Padmasambhava said to King Thrisong Deutsen (790-858):[YM 34a/2]

> Please do not lose the view in favor of activities. If you do, being tied to existential characteristics, you will not attain liberation. Please do not lose activities in favor of the view. If you do, there arises (a situation of) absence of both virtues and vices (and one falls into the extreme of) nihilism, and (one's spiritual life) becomes irreparable. O great king, as my *tantras* possess extensive (teachings on) view, in the future many people who know the words [textual expression] of the view but lack the confidence of the view in their mental continuum could stray into inferior realms.

In *Dzogpa Chenpo* meditation itself there are numerous stages of training which must be taught and practiced step by step. Each step is taken only when the trainee is ready for it. In *Dzogpa Chenpo,* a subtle and esoteric meditation which transcends intellectual and mental fabrications, one doesn't study or read the teachings on a particular aspect until one is ready for that particular step of experience and for training on it. And one is definitely excluded from "instructions on experiential meditation" (*Nyams-Khrid* or *dMar-Khrid*). If, without being ready for the particular meditative experiences, one reads about or studies them, one could just build up fabricated images of intellectual understanding about a particular meditative experience. Thereby, before having any true experience or pure realization, one could fall into the pit of mental creations. Then the trainee will find it hard even to distinguish whether it is a true experience of realization or a mentally created image. This way of introduction applies not only to *Dzogpa Chenpo*, but also to general *tantric* training. In *sūtric* teaching, first you study and then enter into the training. But in the *tantras*, when you have matured through the common preparatory virtues and are ready for the esoteric training, you will receive the transmission of the realization through an Empowerment (*dBang, S.,abhiṣekha*) ceremony. Only then will you be introduced to the course of study and training in the *tantra* by using the Primordial Wisdom, the meaning of the empowerment(*dBang-Don Gyi Ye-Shes*), which is realized during the transmission of empowerment, as the means and the basis of meditation.

Some people do not need to undergo any common training but are ready for higher training such as *Dzogpa Chenpo*. But such people are a bare possibility in this world of ours.

Therefore, in this book I have tried to avoid including any "instructions on the stages of experiential meditation," since one should get them individually from a true master in person, stage by stage, according to one's own experiential abilities. I have tried to present here only, or at least mainly, the teachings on view, the outline of the meditation, and the result of *Dzogpa Chenpo*.

Nowadays, as the cultural context of the traditional teachings is changing, the *tantric* teachings and even the *Dzogpa Chenpo* teachings are being given in public to many people who may have little belief, who have done no preliminary training or have received no introductory empowerments. The main focus of attraction and the goal of many so-called masters and disciples unfortunately have become worldly or sensual attributes. On the other hand, there are many serious Dharma people who wish to study *Dzogpa Chenpo* teachings out of pure Dharma interest, and who are prepared for such teachings through preliminary study and training. But the lack of instruction and reading material in Western languages is preventing them from making much progress on this path. In this situation, it is a serious decision whether or not to write and translate such teachings and to make them public. Realistically, in this modern age, there is no way that these teachings could be preserved and practiced traditionally only by those who are ready for them. So the alternative is to consider what will be the best possible way to present the teachings to the public so that they will be of most benefit to the people whom they will reach.

After all these considerations, I reached the conclusion that I would attempt to translate and present these original scriptures, the very words which came from the wisdom minds of the Enlightened Ones, unstained by the contemporary intellectual thought of this modern materialistic world of ours.

I have translated and written this book not because I am an authority on such an esoteric teaching as *Dzogpa Chenpo.* I feel proud of having the courage to admit it without trying to create stories that I was born with wisdom or that I absorbed an ocean of scriptures in no time. But as a Tibetan proverb says: "The behavior of a servant of a cultured family will be better than that of the head of an uncultured family." I was fortunate to grow up at Dodrup Chen (*rDo Grub-Ch'en*) monastery, a famous institution of learning and enlightenment drawing upon hundreds of years of spiritual tradition. There, although I became neither a scholar nor a sage, I lived with the wisest and most peaceful spiritual masters, such as Kyala Khenpo Chochog (*Kya-La mKhan-Po Ch'os-mCh'og*, 1893-1957), and I heard the true Dharma words that came from the depth of their most pure and enlightened minds. As the blessing of having been at such a great institution, I always feel traces of the strength of courage and the light of wisdom which enable me to see and respect the pure teachings and their true traditions as they are, without any need of adjusting them to the dimensions of my own intellectual judgment or using them as tools to glorify my ego. It doesn't matter where I go or live, in the academic, materialistic or spiritual worlds.

For *Dzogpa Chenpo* teachings,first there are many original

scriptures, called the *tantras* of *Dzogpa Chenpo.* Unfortunately, they are very difficult to understand, and most of them do not have any commentaries and are in need of interpretation. So, if I were to translate such texts, it would become unavoidable for me to indulge my own interpretations, and these could be very wrong.

After the *tantras*, there are the texts and commentaries on *Dzogpa Chenpo tantras* written or discovered by great adepts of the *Dzogpa Chenpo* lineage. Of these the writings and discovered texts and commentaries of Longchen Rabjam are respected as the most detailed, much clearer than the *tantras*, and as authentic as the *tantras* without any dispute throughout the *Nyingma* world since the fourteenth century. For all these reasons, I have produced this book, an anthology of Longchen Rabjam's writings on *Dzogpa Chenpo.*

This book has two parts. The first part is the introduction, and in it I have tried to present the whole scope of Buddhism in such a way as to show that the common Buddhist teachings are the basis of *Dzogpa Chenpo* doctrine and that *Dzogpa Chenpo* is their essence. I have also tried to explain the similarities of *Dzogpa Chenpo* to some other Buddhist schools of thought as well as its unique distinction from them. For each point I have extensively quoted *tantras*, texts, and commentaries written by the greatest *Nyingma* writers to present the true traditional views and values.

The second part provides a complete structure of *Dzogpa Chenpo* teachings in the words of the Omniscient Master Longchen Rabjam, from the delusions leading to *Saṃsāra* through the attainment of liberation. It is organized in three sections: view, meditation, and result. There are thirteen sections which contain excerpts from *Shingta Chenpo* (SC), *Pema Karpo* (PK), *Tshigdon Rinpoch'e'i Dzod* (TD), *Gewa Sumgyi Donthrid* (GD), *Ch'oying Dzod* (CD), *Namkha Longch'en* (NCK), *Namkha Longsal* (NKS) and the complete texts of *Sem-nyid Rangtrol* (SR) and its commentary (*LN*) by Longchen Rabjam.

To develop trust and inspiration in the teachings, it is important to know about the author, his scholarship, and his realization of the teachings on which he is writing. So I have written a detailed life of Longchen Rabjam gathered from his various biographies. I have also quoted his writings extensively to illustrate his view of nature. As a poet he depicts nature in images of beauty, joy, and peace; as a common trainee of Buddhism, he sees them as the demonstration of impermanence and as false reflections; and as a *Dzogpa Chenpo* philosopher, he views all in the sameness of utmost peace, the Primordial Awareness.

My main aim in preparing this book is to provide the following clarifications: (a) The common *Mahāyāna* Buddhist views are the basis of *Dzogpa Chenpo* teachings. (b) All the essential aspects of Buddhist training are condensed in *Dzogpa Chenpo*, and *Dzogpa Chenpo* is the essence of Buddhist teachings. (c) To become a *Dzogpa Chenpo* trainee one needs to train through the common preparatory studies and meditations. As *Dzogpa Chenpo* is the highest and the most simple training, it requires earnest preparation and meditation.

Until a few years ago, I was against being involved in publishing or presenting any *tantric* texts to the uninitiated public. Then one day I saw a manuscript of a *tantric* ritual text translated by a scholar who intended to publish it. To my surprise, I was convinced that my own translation of the same text was a little more accurate. It encouraged me to send my translation for publication to preserve the sacred text in a better form. Since then, my view of translating and publishing scriptures has changed.

For translating and publishing this book, I received the blessings of the two highest living authorities on *Dzogpa Chenpo* in the world today. Kyabje Dodrup Chen Rinpoche said: "In my view, it seems that ours is most probably the last generation in which there are people who really have the opportunity to have direct realization or understanding of real *Dzogpa Chenpo* and to receive the training and transmissions from a true *Dzogpa Chenpo* master in the light of traditional wisdom. Therefore, as I have kept saying, the most important task for people like you is to propagate this tradition through teaching or writing, in whatever way you can, whenever there are appropriate circumstances for preserving this tradition purely and making it available to future generations." Kyabje Dilgo Khyentse Rinpoche said: "I think that it is not only permissible but very important to publish your work on Kunkhyen Longchen Rabjam's writings on *Dzogpa Chenpo* as you will make sure to present them as they are. I truly think so." And so I worked hard on this book to provide a sense of the scope of *Dzogpa Chenpo* teaching in the realm of Buddhism for the sincere Dharma friends in the West.

I pray to the Buddhas, the lineal masters, and the Dharma protectors and Dharma protectresses for their forgiveness of any mistakes of omission and commission and of the improper disclosure of the secret essence of the teachings which have been committed in preparing this book. May all the merits accumulated from this work cause happiness and enlightenment for all mother beings, and may it spread the pure Dharma in the world.

I would like to express my thankfulness to Harold Talbott for his wisdom and patience in editing every line of this work, to Michael Baldwin for taking care of all the needs of life, providing the golden opportunity for me to work on these expressions of *Dzogpa Chenpo* wisdom, to the members and patrons of the Buddhayana, U.S.A., under whose sponsorship I have been able to work on my scholarly projects for the last many years, and to the Center for the Study of World Religions, Harvard University, where I started my work on this book when I was a visiting scholar there. I am highly grateful to Kyabje Khyentse Rinpoche for providing many important clarifications and to Kyabje Dodrup Chen Rinpoche for conferring the transmission of the teachings of Longchen Rabjam. I am also thankful to Khenpo Palden Sherab and Lama Golok Jigtshe (*d. 1987*) for their scholarly interpretations of many points. Thanks also to Helena Hughes and Linas Vytuvis for preparing the index, and to John Cochran for the cover photograph. I would like to thank Jeanne Astor of Snow Lion Publications for her thorough editorial work. I am deeply indebted to Victor and Ruby Lam for providing me with a lovely apartment in which to live and work on this book.

Tulku Thondup
Cambridge
December, 1987

PART I

INTRODUCTION

INTRODUCTION

In Tibetan *Mahāyāna* Buddhism there are four major schools. The *Nyingma* (*rNying-Ma*) began in the seventh century A.D. and was fully established in the ninth century by Guru Padmasambhava, Śāntarakṣita, and King Thrisong Deutsen. The *Kagyud* (*bKa'-rGyud*) and *Sakya* (*Sa-sKya*) schools were founded in the eleventh century A.D. respectively by Marpa Chokyi Lodro (*Mar-Pa Ch'os-Kyi Blo-Gros*, 1012-1099) and Khon Konchog Gyalpo (*'Khon dKon-mCh'og rGYal-Po*, 1034-1102). The *Gelug* (*dGe-Lugs*) was founded by Je Tsongkhapa (*rJe Tsong-Kha-Pa*, 1357-1419) in the fourteenth century A.D. The differences in the *sūtra* (*mDo*, exoteric scriptures) aspect of the four schools are mainly a matter of emphasis on particular scriptures and ways of interpretation. In regard to *tantra* (*rGyud*, esoteric scriptures), the *Nyingma* school has unique teachings which were brought to Tibet, translated, and propagated mainly between the ninth and eleventh centuries. They are known as the "Old *Tantras*" (*sNgags rNying-Ma*). The other three schools have common *tantric* scriptures which reached Tibet in and after the eleventh century, and those *tantras* are known as the "New *Tantras*" (*sNgags gSar-Ma*). The *Nyingma* is the oldest school and the mother of the other schools. According to *Nyingma* tradition the entire Buddhist *sūtric* and *tantric* teachings are classified as "Nine *Yānas*" (*Theg-Pa dGu*):

The Three *Sūtric Yānas*:
a. *Śrāvakayāna* (*Nyan-Thos*), *Hīnayāna*
b. *Pratyekabuddhayāna* (*Rang-Sangs-rGyas*), *Hīnayāna*
c. *Bodhisattvayāna* (*Byang-Ch'ub Sems-dPa'*), *Mahāyāna*
The Three Outer *Tantric Yānas* (*Phyi-rGyud sDe-gSum*):
a. *Kriyāyoga* (*Bya-rGyud*)
b. *Caryāyoga* (*sPyod-rGyud*)
c. *Yogatantra* (*rNal-'Byor rGyud*)
The Three Inner *Tantric Yānas* (*Nang-rGyud*):
a. *Mahāyoga* (*rNal-'Byor Ch'en-Po*)

b. *Anuyoga (rJes-Su rNal-'Byor)*
c. *Atiyoga (Shin-Tu rNal-'Byor)*

The unique teachings of *Nyingma* are the three Inner *Tantras*, especially *Atiyoga*. The various levels of *yānas* are not a system that presents contradictory theories or leads to different goals: the *yānas* are all processes for growing in the same path of training. They lead, directly or indirectly, to the ultimate goal and awaken the enlightened state, which is Buddhahood. Because of the differences in intellectual sharpness and predispositions of trainees, some may start from the lower *yānas* and progress according to the strength of their experiences. A common follower practices a lower *yāna* and continues to practice it until he is ready to move to a higher training. People who have exceptionally brilliant minds and strong *karmic* foundations from the past may directly enter the highest *yānas*, such as *Atiyoga*, and may even attain the result instantly. To introduce a gifted person into a common training is a waste of life, energy and opportunity, but, equally, to start from a higher training is not only unproductive but an error. So, to be realistic or to have a wise guide is most essential for entering into different types of training.

In *Śrāvakayāna* the view is the realization of selflessness of persons. The main goal of attainment is the achievement of cessation, the peace and happiness of oneself. The practice is to observe any of "the eight categories of precepts of individual emancipation" (*So-Thar Ris-brGyad*). The meditation is to maintain one's mind in tranquillity (*Zhi-gNas*) and to realize the insight (*Lhag-mThong*) of "the four noble truths" (*'Phags-Pa'i bDen-Pa bZhi*) with their "sixteen aspects" (*Khyad-Ch'os bChu-Drug*). The result is the attainment of "the eight stages of levels" (*sKyes-Bu Zung-bZhi Ya-brGyad*), the eighth being the attainment of the state of the *Arhat* [Subduer of Foes or Worthy One].

In *Pratyekabuddhayāna* the view is the realization of the selflessness of persons and phenomena, but the shortest, indivisible moment of mind is held to be real. The main goal is the attainment of the *Arhathood* of a *Pratyekabuddha* for oneself through one's own efforts. The practice is to observe any one of the eight categories of precepts. The practitioners meditate on tranquil abiding and on the "four noble truths with their sixteen aspects," and especially on "the twelve links in the chain of interdependent causation" (*rTen-'Brel Yan-Lag bChu-gNyis*) sucessively and in reverse order (*Lugs-'Byung-lDog*). The result that is attained is *Arhathood.*

In *Bodhisattvayāna* the view is the realization of the selflessness of all phenomenal existents. The main goal is to lead all living beings to the fully enlightened state or Buddhahood. The main practice is training on the six perfections: generosity, ethical discipline, patience, diligence, contemplation, and wisdom. The practitioners meditate on the "twofold selflessness" (*bDag-Med gNyis*) and "fourfold path of training" (*Lam-bZhi*) with "thirty-seven wings of enlightenment" (*Byang-Phogs Kyi Ch'os Sum-bChu rTsa-bDun*). The result is that they attain Buddhahood with "two bodies" (*sKu-gNyis*), the formless body for themselves and form-bodies for the sake of others.

DISTINCTIONS BETWEEN SŪTRA AND TANTRA

Pema Ledrel Tsal explains the distinctions between *sūtra* and *tantra* in the following lines:[KZZ 21a/4]

> In *Tshulsum Dronme* (*Tshul-gSum sGron-Me, Nayatraya-pradīpa*[TG 6B/3]) it is said:
>
> "(Although) the goal is the same (as in *Mahāyāna sūtra*),
> (in *tantra*) there is no ignorance,
> There are many skillful means and less hardship.
> It is for people of sharp intellect.
> Hence, the *tantrayāna* is superior."*
>
> Both *sūtric* and *tantric* traditions have the same goal of final attainment, the state of fully perfected enlightenment. (However, the *tantra*) is distinctive for superior means of attaining (that goal).They are the superiority of view free

*See also RT page 278/2/3

from ignorance, the superiority of meditation with many skillful means, the superiority of activities of no hardship, and the person of sharp intellect. . . .
(1) The Characteristic Causation (*sūtric*) Yāna ascertains that (a) the ultimate nature, the absolute truth (is) free from elaborations of eight extremes, but it does not realize the nature of the union of the ultimate sphere and primordial wisdom, as it is. (*Tantra*,) having dispelled (that ignorance), realizes the nature of the union of the ultimate sphere and primordial wisdom; so the *tantra* is not ignorant of the view of the ultimate nature. (b) The Characteristic Causation Yāna ascertains phenomena, the things of relative truth, as the nature of interdependent arising like a magical apparition (*māyā*), but it is ignorant because of not yet having ascertained (phenomena) as the (Buddha-) bodies and primordial wisdoms, (but having ascertained them as just) impure (like) magical apparitions. *Vajrayāna tantra* ascertains (that all are): the play of the (Buddha-) bodies and primordial wisdoms, the meaning of non-duality of the ultimate sphere and primordial wisdom, the non-duality of the two truths and the supreme ultimate body. So (*tantra*) is superior in being free from ignorance. (2) The meditation (of *tantra*) is superior because of the two stages: the skillful means of the development stage and the wisdom of the perfection stage. (3) Superiority of activities with no hardship: In the Characteristic Causation *Yāna* there is no path to attain enlightenment which does not abandon the objects of desire. Whereas in this (*tantra*), having taken the objects of desire, without abandoning, as the path (of training) which protects the mind-consciousness easily and blissfully, one becomes able to attain the state of *Vajradhara* in this very lifetime with this single body. (4) The superiority of the person of sharp intellect: *Tantra* is the training for exceptional persons who possess superior qualities. The general (quality is) the superiority of having special fivefold powers (*dBang-Po*) which generate enlightenment; and the special (quality is) the wisdom of

realizing the profound view of *Vajrayāna tantra* as well as a strong power of faith with "no fear in the heavy activities" (of *tantra*).

The goal in both *Mahāyāna sūtra* and *tantra* is the attainment of enlightenment. The differences are the means that lead to the goal directly. In *tantric* teachings, the view is indivisibility of cause and result. The appearances of the five external elements are five female Buddha consorts, the appearances of the five inner aggregates are five male Buddha consorts, the hosts of thoughts are five primordial wisdoms, and the world and beings are equally as pure as the Buddhas and Buddha-fields.

Since the practitioners of *tantra* realize all phenomena as totally pure, they enjoy everything in the indivisible nature of the two truths. Since the practitioners of *sūtra* perceive things as good and bad, they are unable to take every aspect of phenomena as the support of training, whereas *tantrists* can transform everything as the means of training.

The view of the inner *tantras*, and particularly of *Atiyoga*, is the actual indivisibility of cause and result. While the outer *tantras* are more concerned with indivisibility than the *sūtric* teachings, the inner *tantric yānas* are superior to the outer ones in this respect. Therefore, the *sūtric yānas* are known as the *yānas* of causation, since the practitioners train in the path as the cause to attain the goal as the result. The *tantric yānas* are called the resultant *yānas* because by using the realization of primordial wisdom, which is the significance of empowerment (*dBang-Don*) and which is transmitted at the time of empowerment, tantrists perceive the world and beings as the Buddhas and Buddha-fields, and they develop and perfect the realization. *Tantra* perfects the result in a short time by using the state of the three *kāyas* as the path of training by profound skillful means.

Tantra is a path of transformation of unenlightenment and emotions as the Buddha-essence and Buddha-virtues. But this is not a transformation of something into something else, like iron into gold, as some recent scholars have understood; it is transforming, purifying, or perfecting (*gNas-Su Dag-Pa*) something which is stained into its own true state.

The *tantric* teachings are to be understood and followed by people of high intellect and excellent *karma*. Longchen Rabjam summarizes the distinctions between *sūtric* and *tantric* teachings as follows:[PK II, 79b/4]

> The *sūtric* teachings of *Bodhisattvayāna* (*or Mahāyāna*) assert that (beings) possess the Buddha-essence (*Tathāgatagarbha*). With the Buddha-essence as the seed and with training on the two accumulations, the accumulations of merits and primordial wisdom, as the conditions during numerous lives, the Buddha-essence will blossom, and (as a result) fully enlightened Buddhahood will be achieved. It is called "the *yāna* of causation" since it asserts that cause and result are successive.
>
> In the *tantric* view (wherein cause and result are indivisible, *dByer-Med*) the Buddha-essence is naturally present in all living beings with its virtues complete, like the sun with its lights, and that is the "basis of purification." The eight consciousnesses with appearances [percepts], like clouds, the obscurations of the Buddha-essence, are the things "to be purified." Empowerment and meditation on the "development and perfection stages" (*bsKyed-Rim and rDzogs-Rim*) causing, as clouds are dispelled by air, the obscurations to be purified and the light of virtues to shine forth, are the "means of purification." Thereby, the attainment of the absolute universal ground (*Don-Gyi Kun-gZhi*) shining forth, as it is, like the sun, is the "result of purification." At that time, since there are no longer the previous defilements, although the names and habituations of the universal ground have been transformed (as Buddhahood and its virtues), in reality they manifest without differentiation or succession. In *Tag-nyee* (*brTags-gNyis* of *Hevajratantra*) it is said:
>
> > "Beings are the very Buddha (in their true nature),

> But their (nature) is obscured by adventitious
> obscurations.
> When the obscurations are cleansed, they themselves
> are the very Buddha."

Do-ngag Tenpa'i Nyima explains that according to *Nyingma* scholars, the *sūtras* and *tantras* do not differ regarding the view of emptiness, the absolute truth, but that their differences lie in the view of appearances, the relative truth:JG 11a/5

> According to the view of *Ngagyur Nyingma*, there are no differences between the *sūtras* and *tantras* in respect to (their views of) emptiness, the ultimate sphere. Because the absolute great emptiness of the great *Madhyamaka*, the absolute great equalness of the great *Mahāyoga*, the absolute *Samantabhadrī, the maṇḍala* of "as it is" (*Ji-bZhin-Pa*), and the absolute great primordial purity (*Ka-Dag*) of *Atiyoga* are synonyms for the same truth. In the general canonical and commentarial scriptures of *Ngagyur* (*Nyingma*) and especially in *Ngeshey Dronme Rinpoche* (*Nges-Shes sGron-Me Rin-Po-Ch'e* by Mipham) it is said:
>
> > "Both Glorious Candra(kīrti) of the Noble Land [India]
> > And Rongzom Chozang of Tibet
> > In one voice and mind
> > Prove that the primordial purity (*Ka-Dag*) is the great
> > emptiness."
>
> However, if you analyze from the standpoint of appearances: according to the view of the glorious *Mahāyoga* tradition, the aspect of appearances is the luminous nature, the relative truth of great purity (*Dag-Pa Che'n-Po*). (According to the view of) *Anuyoga*, the aspect of appearances is *Samantabhadra*, the *maṇḍala* of the three divine seats (*gDan-gSum*). (*According to*) the view of *Atiyoga*, (the appearances) are the profound "appearances of the basis" (*gZhi-sNang*), the spontaneously accomplished *maṇḍala*. These views are unknown, even the terms for them being absent, in the Characteristic [*sūtric*] *yānas*. So there are great

differences between the views of *sūtras* and *tantras* (comparable to the distance between the) sky and the earth.

DEFINITION OF *TANTRAS* (*rGyud*)

The meaning of *tantra* is continuum. Sogpo Tentar gives the definition in the following lines:[ST 165a/1]

> In *Dorje Tsemo* (*rDo-rJe rTse-Mo tantra*) it is said:
>
> "*Tantra* means continuum.
> *Saṃsāra* is the *tantra*,
> And *nirvāṇa* is the later *tantra* (*rGyud Phyi-Ma*)."
>
> *Tantra* has three aspects, which depend on the connection between *saṃsāra* and *nirvāṇa*, a continuum like the strings of a lute: (a) The Buddha-essence is the *tantra* of basis, (b) the union of the view and meditation is the *tantra* of path and (c) the bodies and primordial wisdoms are the *tantra* of result. As (*tantric* teaching) is union of skillful means and primordial wisdom by means of the development and perfection stages, its entrance is wide. Unlike *sūtric* training it is without the hardship of asceticism, and it is a training (that produces its result) extremely swiftly for trainees of sharp intellect."

Jigmed Tenpa'i Nyima defines the *tantras*:[RDD 22b/5]

> The (attainments which) are to be realized are the *tantra* of cause or basis. That by which one realizes and proceeds (along the path) is the *tantra* of skillful means or path. The (goal) which one perfects is the *tantra* of result.... In this way the basis, path and result are linked in the same continuum. So it is called *tantra* [continuum]. In *Gyud Chima* (*rGyu-Phyi-Ma*) it is said:
>
> "*Tantra* means continuum of
> The cause (*basis*), skillful means (*path*) and result."

DIVISIONS OF *TANTRA*

According to the *Nyingma* lineage there are six classes of *tan-*

tras. *Kriyāyoga*, *Caryāyoga* or *Upayoga*, and *Yogatantra* are the three Outer *Tantras* and *Mahāyoga*, *Anuyoga*, and *Atiyoga* or *Mahāsandhiyoga* are the three Inner *Tantras*. In *Rigpa Rangshar tantra* it is said:[RR 45b/1]

> *Vajrayāna* has two (*divisions*):
> Outer *Tantra* of discipline and
> Inner *Tantra* of skillful means....
> Outer (*Tantra*) has three (*sub-divisions*):
> *Kriyā*, *Upa*, and *Yoga*....
> Inner (*Tantra*) has three (sub-divisions):
> *Mahā*, *Anu*, and *Ati*.

DIFFERENT CLASSES OF TEACHINGS ON TANTRA

There are different classes of scriptures that discourse on the *tantras*:[RDD-8b/6]

> The *tantras* are expounded by scriptures (*Lung*), instructions (*Man-Ngag*) and reasoning (*Rigs-Pa*). (a) Scriptures: (In the case of *Guhyagarbhamāyājāla-tantra*) they include the four "explanatory *tantras*" (*bShad-rGyud*) and the "later *tantras*." (Among the four explanatory *tantras*, the first two) on gradual and instant ways of "the liberation path" (*Grol-Lam*) are *Yeshey Nyingpo* (*Ye-Shes sNying-Po*) and *Dorje Melong* (*rDo-rJe Me-Long*). The other two *tantras* on gradual and instant ways of "the path of skillful means" (*Thabs-Lam*) are *Gyatsho* (*rGya-mTsho*) and *Thalwa* (*Thal-Ba*). Although there are many interpretations of "root" (*rTsa-rGyud*) and "explanatory *tantras*" (*bShad-rGyud*), according to Rog Desheg Nyingpo (*Rog bDe-gShegs sNying-Po*) the *tantras* which were expounded earlier and have become the matter to be explained (by other *tantras*) are the "root *tantras*" and the *tantras* which appeared later and which explain (the root *tantras*) are the "explanatory *tantras*".... (b) Instruction: The commentaries and miscellaneous writings (*Thor-Bu*), either of superior writers who have the ability to teach through foreknowledge as a result of attainment of (the realization) of the noble path of

anuttaratantra, or of mediocre writers who are able to interpret the *tantras* because they are blessed by the tutelary deities directly, or by lesser writers who possess the authentic transmission of the lineage of the instructions of earlier knowledge-holders. Examples of these texts (in the case of *Guhyagarbha*) are *Parkhab* (*sPar-Khab*) and the brief commentary called *Piṇḍārtha*, etc., as well as *Lamrim* (*Lam-Rim*), *Thugthig* (*Thugs-Thig*), and *Tathreng* (*lTa-'Phreng*). (c) Reasoning: Interpreters of the profound vajra-subjects of the *tantras* who are reckless, and who arrogantly rely on logical knowledge, succeed only in mixing their own fabrications with the doctrine. Although in those interpretations there may be much dry understanding in the form of quotations—"This is said in such and such a text"—they do not show with any certainty that they are not twisting the meanings of the *tantras* into something that they are not. So, it is very important to have certainty (of the meaning of the *tantras*) in oneself and the ability to teach the "root *tantras*" with proper and pure reasoning by relying on the "explanatory *tantras*" and the instructions of adepts.

DEVELOPMENT AND PERFECTION STAGES OF TANTRA

The *Yānas of tantra* differ from each other in respect to their view and techniques of practice, but the practice of two stages is essential to each of them. Longchen Rabjam explains:[SC-II, 21a/4]

Development Stage: By meditating (or visualizing) the external world as the mansions (etc. of the deities), one purifies the ordinary apprehension of the appearances as (truly existing) in their own nature (or reality) as stones and earth. By meditating on beings as male and female deities, one purifies attachment to beings as (truly existing) in their own nature (or reality) and abandons attachment to and hatred of them. By visualizing one's own aggregates

> (*Phung-Po*), elements (*Khams*) and sources (*sKye-mCh'ed*) as the deities, which is what they are from the primordial state, one obtains many benefits. These include purification of the obscurations to the form-body (S. *rūpakāya*), perfection of the accumulation of merits (*bSod-Nams*) and generation of the contemplation of tranquillity (*Zhi-gNas*). . . .
>
> Perfection Stage: It purifies even the aspect of slight clinging to the meditation of the development stage as well as that of seeing phenomena as illusions. As it is free from all perception as and concept of "this is this," it purifies the obscurations of the ultimate body (S. *Dharmakāya*) and perfects the inconceivable contemplation and the accumulation of primordial wisdom (*Ye-Shes*). By concentrating the mind one-pointedly on any contemplation (*dMigs-Pa*), one remains in the state of bliss, clarity and no-thought, and this leads to the realization of the meaning of innate wisdom, the *mahāmudrā* that is the essence (*Ngo-Bo*) of the perfection stage. In order to view the true nature as it is, having realized the nature of the primordial basis, the nature of the vajrabody, and the ultimate nature of the Mind, one then meditates on it. There are two ways of (training in the perfection stage, which rely respectively on) one's own body and on another's. (The training by means of) one's own body is mental effort such as the *yogas* of heat, illusory-body, dream, luminous absorption, intermediate state, and transference of consciousness. Those are the trainings in the perfection stage which bring enlightenment without relying on others. (The training by means of) another's body is the way of taking bliss as the path by a *yogi* who is skilled in (the *yogas* that use the) channels, air [energy], and essence.

Gyurmed Tshewang Chogdrub summarizes the meaning of the Development Stage and the Perfection Stage:[LNT-1, 92b/3]

> To meditate [visualize and perceive] all the appearances without differentiation as the Buddha-bodies of the dei-

> ties, (in form or structure) similar to the phenomena of the three existents [worlds], combined with great compassion and contemplation of the bliss of melting, which causes the three Buddha-bodies to mature (within oneself) is the essence (*Ngo-Bo*) of the development stage.... To merge the energy/air, mind and thoughts (*rLung Sems Yid*) into the central channel and to actualize the blissful and empty primordial wisdom directly is the essence of the perfection stage.... The stage of the training [*yoga*] on channels, energies and subtle essence and the stage of (training in using) consorts (S. *mudrā*) which cause the energies to enter, be maintained and dissolve into the central channel is not the actual perfection stage, but since it causes one to achieve it, it is (also) called the perfection stage.

Training in the Two Stages applies to all six levels of *tantras*. But in comparison to the higher *tantras*, the lower ones are lacking in the perfection stage, and especially in the union or indivisibility of the Two Stages. Longchen Rabjam writes as follows on this matter:[SC-II,4b/3]

> (In the *Yoga Tantra* of Outer *Tantra*) one meditates on skillful means and wisdom successively. So one (practices) the stages of development and perfection separately.

The Three Outer Tantras

(A) *KRIYĀ YOGA* (*Bya-rGyud*)

Longchen Rabjam describes *Kriyāyoga*:[LG 34b/4]

> In the *tantras* of *Kriyāyoga* one realizes that all the phenomena of aggregates (*Phung-Po*), elements (*Khams*), and sources (*sKye-mCh'ed*) which appeared in the relative level are subject to being purified. The ultimate sphere, naturally pure Mind, is the basis of purification. One lives in pure livelihood and meditates, as the path, on the suchness of the deities by means of seeing the deity as the lord and oneself as the servant, and one wishes for the attainments (as the blessings).

Mipham summarizes the view and meditation of *Kriyāyoga* as follows:[YDGD 32a/2]

> View (*lTa-Ba*)
>
> It asserts that in absolute truth all phenomenal existents are equal in the indivisible nature of the two truths, appearances and emptiness. But in relative truth, it views the tutelary deities as lords, who are free from all faults, are perfect in all the virtues, are the manifestation of the clarity of the ultimate sphere as the form of the primor-

dial wisdom and who grant the temporary and final attainments. It views oneself as the devotee to be blessed, as one who has still not reached the goal and who has coverings. So, in absolute truth all are equal and in relative truth the interdependent causation is incontrovertible. Therefore, its view is to believe that through practicing and accepting all (phenomena) as signs of the body, speech, and mind of the deities themselves, for the time being one achieves the power of numerous activities, and finally one attains the essence of the deities itself.

Meditation (*bsGom-Pa*)

By one-pointed contemplation on the six divine powers (or deities) of *Kriyā(yoga)* (*Kri-Ya Lha-Drug*)—the gestures of the body (of the deity), syllables of speech, implements of the mind, the mansions and the projections and withdrawals of lights, etc.—and by invoking the deities by reciting their heart-essences (*mantras*) one receives the blessings (and perfects oneself as the deities as) iron is transmuted into gold through alchemical skills.

Longchen Rabjam explains the six divine powers of *Kriyā-yoga*:[GD 157b/2]

(a) Having seen the appearances as the illusory divine bodies, one transcends the extremes of singularity and plurality, and the appearances are liberated as the divine body. (b) Having seen the syllables (*Yig-'Bru*) as divine sound, the wheel of recitation of (the union of) sound and emptiness continues and the syllables are liberated as divine syllables. (c) Having contemplated on the implements (signifying) the divine mind, the recollections and thoughts arise as contemplation and the concepts are liberated as divine contemplation. (d) Having seen the projections and withdrawals as the colors of the deities, they are liberated as divine lights, and the letters are liberated as divine, as the primordial wisdom-nature. (e) Having seen the clarity as divine postures, seats, thrones, and costumes, whatever

> appears is liberated as divine mansions. (f) Having seen the phenomenal existents as *Dharmakāya*, the divine liberation of primordial wisdom (emptiness), the (things) to be abandoned are liberated as the primordial wisdom. Likewise, having liberated the six attachments to the six objects and having realized the six aspects, such as seeing appearances as the divine body (or bodies of deities), one purifies the defilements.

According to Sogpo Tentar:[ST 169a/6]

> (The six *Kriyā* divine powers) are the divine powers of emptiness, letters, sound, form, gestures, and signs: In *Naljor Kyi Guyd* (*rNal-'Byor Gyi rGyud*) it is said: "They are emptiness, letters, sound, form, gestures and signs." In common *Kriyāyoga* there is no visualization of oneself as the deities, but in the uncommon (or higher) *Kriyāyoga* practices there are visualizations of oneself as the deities.

Mipham summarizes the practice and result of *Kriyāyoga* as follows:[YDGD 32b/2]

> Practice (*sPyod-Pa*)
>
> *Kriyāyoga* asserts that the practice of *tantra* will only be accomplished if all parts of the ritual (*Ch'o-Ga*) are observed completely. Otherwise it will not produce any result, as it will be like sowing a seed without water and manure. So it emphasizes the performance of ritual actions of body and speech and living a clean and pure life by bathing and changing clothes three times a day (etc.), making offerings and performing fire ceremony (*sByin-bSreg*, S. *Homa*) as instructed by the *tantras*.
>
> Result (*'Bras-Bu*)
>
> For the time being one achieves many common accomplishments such as the life of a knowledge-holder whose fortune is comparable to that of the beings in the form and formless realms, and finally one attains the *Vajradharahood* of the three Buddha families [*Tathāgata*, *Vajra*,

and *Padma* families, which are endowed with three Buddha-bodies and five primordial wisdoms] within sixteen lives.

(B) *CARYĀ YOGA* OR *UPAYOGA* (*sPyod-rGyud*)

Caryāyoga is also known as the "dual *tantra*" since its practice is similar to *Kriyāyoga*'s and its view is similar to *Yogatantra*'s. Mipham summarizes *Caryāyoga* as follows:[YDGD 32b/5]

> *Caryāyoga* emphasizes equally outer [physical] cleaning such as bathing and inner [mental] contemplation. It relies on receiving attainments by seeing the deities as friends and siblings.
>
> View
>
> In absolute truth all phenomena are equalness. In relative truth, because of unceasing appearances through interdependent causation, *Caryāyoga* believes in relying on the deities for temporary and final attainments. As it is more advanced than *Kriyāyoga*, it sees the deities as a friend. It has the view of believing in the two profound truths.
>
> Meditation
>
> One visualizes the deities in front of oneself and with recitation concentrates on the turning of the chain of *mantras*, and that is called the meditation with signs. At the end of the meditation period one bids farewell to the deities and contemplates on the ultimate state, free from conceptualization, and that is called the meditation without signs.
>
> Practice
>
> (As in *Kriyāyoga*) it is to lead a pure and clean life.
>
> Result
>
> It actualizes infinite attainments for the time being and finally attains the state of *Vajradharahood* of the four Buddha-families [*Tathāgata*, *Vajra*, *Ratna* (*Karma* is combined with *Ratna*) and Padma families] with the endowment of

three Buddha-bodies and five primordial wisdoms in seven lifetimes.

(C) *YOGATANTRA (rNal-'Byor rGyud)*

Yogatantra emphasizes mental contemplation and uses physical training such as pure and clean living only as a secondary support. Mipham summarizes *Yogatantra* as follows:[YDGD 33b/1]

> As its strength of realization of equalness is superior to that of the two previous *yānas,* one gains certainty in the realization of equalness of oneself and the deities in their true nature. As the blessing of that (realization), in relative truth, by meditating oneself as inseparable from the deities like water into water, one accomplishes oneself as the deities. As all phenomena are mere perceptions of mind, if one uses the contemplative power, one will become the visualized deity oneself. *Yogatantra* has the view of extraordinary certainty that by practicing the fourfold signs *(Phyag-rGya),* which are the nature of the divine body, speech, mind, and actions of the deities, one actualizes oneself as the deities.
>
> Meditation
>
> After taking refuge and developing the mind of enlightenment, from the emptiness state one visualizes oneself as the *maṇḍala* of deities with five actualizations (*mNgon-Byang*) and (then invites and merges the primordial wisdom deities or actual deities into the visualized form, and) one seals (*rGya-bTab*) them by meditating one's body, speech, mind, and action as the divine body, speech, mind, and actions of the deities, the four signs (*Phyag-rGya*). The five actualizations are:
>
> 1. Seat of lotus and moon (and sun), the seed or cause of auspicious dwelling and Buddha-field.
> 2. Syllables [vowels and consonants] of speech, the seed of auspicious teachings.
> 3. Signs [*vajra,* jewel, etc.] of mind, the seed of auspi-

cious presence for eternal and inconceivable time.
4. Wheel of *Maṇḍala* [*Vairocana*, etc.] of body, the seed of auspicious retinues and teachers.
5. Primordial Wisdom Deity (*Jñānasattva*), the seed of auspicious essence of the body and primordial wisdom (of the deities).

The four signs are:

1. Great sign (*mahāmudrā*), the gestures of body.
2. Teaching (*Dharma*) sign, the form of speech.
3. Esoteric link (*samaya*) sign, the form of mind.
4. Action (*Karma*) sign, perfecting actions through such means as emanation of lights.

Practice

Occasionally it carries on the practice of cleaning, etc., but mainly it is more relaxed about physical disciplines than the previous two *yānas*, and it emphasizes the inner *yoga*.

Result

For the time being it develops the virtues of experiences and realizations, and ultimately the five aggregates, five senses, and five defilements will be purified and the Buddhas of five families, the nature of five primordial wisdoms, will be achieved in three lifetimes.

DISTINCTIONS BETWEEN OUTER *TANTRAS* AND INNER *TANTRAS*

The following is a summary of explanations given by Longchen Rabjam and Mipham.[GD 151a/2 & YDGD 34a/5]

Concerning view, the outer *tantras* view the two truths alternately or separately. In most of the outer *tantras* one meditates the appearances, the relative truth, as deities and at the end, when one dissolves the appearances of the deities, one contemplates on the absolute truth, free from conceptualizations and elaborations. Whereas in inner *tantras*, one views the two truths as union and meditates on them simultaneously. In inner *tantras*, the basis is the sphere of realization of total purity without discrimination, knowing all phenomenal existents as the three *maṇḍalas*, the *maṇḍala* of body, speech, and mind of the Buddhas from primordial time. For outer *tantras* this is not the basis. Regarding the two stages, in inner *tantras* one meditates on the development and perfection stages in union, as one sees all as total purity without discrimination; but in outer *tantras* one meditates on them separately. Regarding empowerments (*dBang*), in outer *tantras* the "vase empowerment" (*Bum-dBang*) is the main one and in the inner *tantras* the "secret empowerment" (*gSang-dBang*), "wisdom empowerment" (*Sher-dBang*), and "verbal empowerment" (*Tshig-dBang*) are the main ones. In practice, in outer *tantras* one enjoys purity and cleanness of food, clothing, dwelling, and so on, but in inner *tantras* one enjoys all with equalness. For visualizations, in inner *tantras* the deities are in union with their consorts and in outer *tantras* they are not.

For place, in outer *tantras* one perceives clean and beautiful places such as palaces and the top of Mt. Sumeru, etc, and in inner *tantras* one perceives cemeteries, the land of Oḍḍiyāna, and so on. For vessels, outer *tantras* use clean vessels made of precious metals and inner *tantras* mainly use skulls. For substances of enjoyment, in outer *tantras* one enjoys three white or pure substances, milk, butter, and curd, and three sweet substances, molasses, honey, and sugar. In inner *tantras* one enjoys five meats—the flesh of man, cow, dog, horse, and elephant—and five nectars: excrement, semen, brain, blood (seminal fluid of female), and urine. For result, through inner *tantras* one will be able to attain Buddhahood in this very lifetime and through outer *tantras* in the next lives.

The scriptures of the three outer *tantras* are common to both Old and New Translated Tantric (*gSang-sNgags sNga-'Gyur Dang Phyi-'Gyur*) traditions of Tibetan Buddhism. But the scriptures of the three inner *tantras*, *Mahāyoga*, *Anuyoga*, and *Atiyoga*, are unique to the Nyingma school, while most of the three divisions of *Anuttaratantra*, the *Matṛtantra*, *Pitṛtantra*, and *Advitīyatantra*, are unique to the Kagyud, Sakya, and Gelug schools of Tibet.

DISTINCTIONS BETWEEN THE THREE INNER *TANTRAS*

In *Dorje Sempa Nying-gi Melong Tantra* it is said:[DNM 270b/1]

> *Mahāyoga*, the developing stage, is like the foundation of all the Dharmas. *Anuyoga*, the perfection stage, is like the path of all the Dharmas. *Atiyoga*, the great perfection, is like the quintessence (*gNad*) of all the Dharmas.

Texts and scholars have different ways of distinguishing the three inner *tantras*. Lochen Dharmaśrī summarizes some of the different interpretations:[ZL 34b/6]

> In an answer to the questions of Lenchab Parpa (*Glan-Ch'ab Bar-Pa*), Je Zurchung (*rJe Zur-Ch'ung*) said: "(Realizing all phenomena to be appearing as the miracles (*Ch'o-'Phrul (Yul?)*) of intrinsic awareness is *Anuyoga* and to be appearing as the self-appearances of intrinsic awareness is *Atiyoga*. Because Ru Garab Dorje (*Ru dGa'-Rab rDo-rJe*) said, "They are appearing as miracles, power, and self-appearances."
>
> The meaning is that in *Mahāyoga* one realizes all phenomena as the miraculous display of the Mind, the indivisibility of appearances and emptiness (*sNang-sTong*). In *Anuyoga* one realizes all phenomena as the power of the Mind, the indivisibility of the ultimate sphere and primordial wisdom (*dByings-Ye*). In *Atiyoga* one realizes all phenomena as the self-appearances of the Mind, the primordially self-arisen primordial wisdom, free from birth and cessation. Da (*mDa'*) and Len (*Glan*) both cherish this view.
>
> According to Kyo Kongbupa (*sKyo Gong-Bu-Pa*), *Ma-*

> *hāyoga* puts more emphasis on practice, *Anuyoga* on contemplation, and *Atiyoga* on view. According to Lhaje Rog (*Lha-rJe Rog*), *Mahāyoga* (which emphasizes the) development stage, visualizes the deities gradually through three contemplations (*Ting-Nge 'Dzin gSum*; emptiness, all-pervading compassion and seed letters), *Anuyoga* (which emphasizes the) perfection stage, does not rely on gradual visualization but on instant contemplation of deities, and *Atiyoga* or great perfection has no visualization as it transcends both stages. . . .
>
> Menyag Jungtrag (*Me-Nyag 'Byung-Grags*) says: "Although in all the three inner *tantras* one trains on the two stages, *Mahāyoga* emphasizes the development stage, *Anuyoga* the perfection stage, and *Atiyoga* freedom from efforts." Challo (*dPyal-Lo*) and Kundor (*Kun-rDor*) both think that this is the best definition. The Great Omniscient One (*Kun-mKhyen Ch'en-Po*, i.e., Longchen Rabjam) asserts that *Mahāyoga* is the father *tantra*. It concerns appearances and skillful means and is for the trainees who possess more concepts and emotions of anger. *Anuyoga* is the mother *tantra*. It concerns emptiness and primordial wisdom and is for the trainees who possess more stable mind and emotions of desire. *Atiyoga* concerns non-duality and is for the trainees who possess more ignorant emotions. . . .

In *Semnyid Ngalso*, Longchen Rabjam writes:[SN 38a/4]

> *Mahāyoga* is mainly concerned with air, the development stage and skillful means.
> *Anuyoga* is mainly concerned with essence, the perfection stage and wisdom.
> *Atiyoga* is concerned with everything, non-duality and primordial wisdom.

Do-ngag Tenpa'i Nyima briefly explains how the view of the three Inner *Tantras* is based on the *Mahāyāna* view of the two truths:[JG 30a/1]

> *Mahāyoga* presents the appearances and emptiness as the two truths: the aspect of appearances as the relative truth of great purity (*Dag-Pa Ch'en-Po*) and the aspect of emptiness as the absolute truth of great equalness (*mNyam-Pa Ch'en-Po*). Likewise, *Anuyoga* presents the two truths: the aspect of appearances as the relative truth, *Samantabhadra*, the *maṇḍala* of the three divine seats (*gDan-gSum*), and the aspect of emptiness as the absolute truth, *Samantabhadrī*, the *maṇḍala* of primordial suchness (*Ye Ji-bZhin-Pa*). In Ati also, the aspect of appearances is the relative truth, "appearances of the basis" (*gZhi-sNang*), the spontaneous accomplishment, and the aspect of emptiness is the absolute truth, ultimate sphere at the basis (*gZhi-dByings*), the primordial pure essence. In all the *tantras*) there is no other way (of presenting the philosophical views) except in terms of the two truths of appearances and emptiness.

In *Shingta Chenpo* Longchen Rabjam describes the unique character of the three inner *tantras* in the following lines:[SC 11, 6b/3]

> In *Mahāyoga,* the father *tantras* of skillful means, one achieves the common and supreme attainments mainly by training on the two means. They are skillful means, the development stage of the *maṇḍalas* of the deities; and primordial wisdom means, the freedom from thoughts, which is (the union of) clarity and emptiness (that produces the result of) purifying the air (*rLung*) of five elements. In *Anuyoga,* which is the mother *tantra,* the primordial wisdom means, there is little training on the development stage. In it the great blissful essence (*Khams*) reaches enlightenment through the (training on the) great bliss of the primordial wisdom of fourfold joy (*dGa'-Ba bZhi'i Ye-Shes*) by means of syllables and the *Bhaga maṇḍala,* through the stages of enlightened womb, relying on a consort, another's body, and on skillful means, one's own body. In *Advitīyayoga,* one achieves enlightenment by em-

phasizing (the union of) the two stages, and especially the great primordial wisdom, the ultimate nature with clarity, which is tied to (the postulations neither of) singularity nor plurality.

In *Palchen Zhalung* Jigmed Lingpa writes:[PZ 2a/2]

Dzogpa Chenpo is for the supreme,
Anuyoga is for the mediocre,
And *Mahāyoga* is for those of lesser intellect.
(*Mahāyoga*) develops (the *maṇḍala*) gradually.
It is like the basis of all the *tantras*.
(*Anuyoga*) perfects (the *maṇḍala*) instantly.
It is like the path of all *tantras*.
Dzogpa Chenpo, which is free from mental phenomena,
Is said to be the result of all the *tantras*.
In *Mahāyoga:*
Through the miracles of the three contemplations,
The power of ultimate nature, the unborn absolute truth.
To purify clinging to the world and beings,
It [the power] arises as the *maṇḍala* of the basis [Buddha-fields] and the based [deities].

Jigmed Lingpa continues:[PZ 4b/1]

In the great teachings of *Anuyoga:*
From the pure vast womb
Of *Samantabhadrī,* the absolute ultimate sphere,
Arises *Samantabhadra,* the intrinsic awareness.
Without relying on words,
In the state of spontaneously accomplished view
Of indivisibility of the ultimate sphere and intrinsic awareness,
Through the power of recollecting awareness,
The conventional *maṇḍala* of the deities develops.
By means of spontaneously perfected profound contemplations,
The two obscurational defilements are purified
And the four Buddha-bodies develop. . . .

In the absolute *Dzogpa Chenpo*:
It is the realization that the deities are the enlightened mind
And the Mind is the Buddha.
There is nothing to develop, as they are (Buddhas) from primordial time.
Whatever uncertain (phenomena) arise,
Dzogpa Chenpo does not prevent or create them. In the natural clarity,
The natural glow (*mDangs*) which is free from conceptions and expressions,
Appear all the signs of the major and minor characteristics (of the Buddhas).
They are emptiness, at the very moment of their arising.

Jigmed Tenpa'i Nyima gives a brief outline of the three Inner *tantras*:[RDD 7b/6]

> In *Anuttaratantra*, there are the *tantras* of the divisions of *Mahā, Anu,* and *Ati.* The ultimate essential meaning of all those *tantras* is the sole suchness of the luminous innate (nature), which has the characteristics of non-duality of profundity [emptiness] and clarity. There are three entrances to that practice: (a) the elaborate ritual of the development stage for taking the three *kāyas* as the path, (b) the ritual of the development stage which is not elaborate but trains in the two aspects of taking the intrinsic wisdom and the ultimate sphere gradually as the path, and (c) actualization of the intrinsic wisdom by means of natural contemplation without effort and without reliance on fabricated rituals of the development stage. These *tantras* which mainly emphasize the first, second, and third entrances are identified respectively as *Mahā, Anu,* and *Ati.*

Jigmed Tenpa'i Nyima explains the main emphasis of training in the three Inner *Tantras*:[DC 16b/1]

> (a) In father *tantra* (or *Mahāyoga*) by the power of con-

trol over the air/energy (*rLung*), one brings about the clarity [luminous absorption] (*A'od-gSal*) nakedly or empowers oneself with the clarity. To the extent that one controls and increases the air, the clarity will become stable. (b) In Mother *tantra* (or *Anuyoga*), by the power of perfecting the essence (*Thig-Le*), one controls the *yoga* of clarity. To the extent that (the bliss) of blazing up and flowing down of the essence increases, the force of arising and increasing of the radiance of clarity grows. To the extent that one gains control over the air and that the bliss blazes up, concepts will be eliminated and the clarity will become clearer. Both (the father and mother *tantras*) possess (the practice) on both (air and essence), but (the difference lies) in which one is emphasized. (c) In *Atiyoga*, in the clarity, one maintains the aspect of intrinsic awareness or the knowledge which ascertains the ways of being present (of the clarity) nakedly without dissolving. This clarity is free from the defilements of delusions, uncreated by new conditions, present from primordial time and (now) awakened through the inspirations of air of the clarity itself. As the ultimate cognition which sees clearly the presence of the ultimate sphere and intrinsic wisdom, the realization of clarity radiates and shines like millions of suns.

SUBDIVISIONS OF THE THREE INNER *TANTRAS*

Each of the three inner *tantras* could again be subdivided into three categories according to their particular characteristics of view and meditation. Jigmed Lingpa explains briefly:[PZ 5b/1]

> Within each of the three (Inner) *Yoga*s,
> By dividing them subtly,
> There are nine (subdivisions):
> The development of the *maṇḍala* gradually
> Is called the *Mahā(yoga)* of *Mahā(yoga)*.
> The accomplishment of the *maṇḍala* spontaneously
> Is called the *Anu* of *Mahā*.
> The unborn ultimate sphere

Is known as the *Ati* of *Mahā(yoga)*.
Instant completion of the *maṇḍala*
Is named the *Mahā* of *Anu*.
In the *maṇḍala* of the relative deity,
Perfection of the ultimate sphere
Is called *Anu* of *Anu*.
Indivisibility of the deity and self-awareness
Is the *Ati* of *Anu*.
Realization of *saṃsāra* and *nirvāṇa* as the *maṇḍala* from primordial time
Is the *Mahā* of *Ati*.
Spontaneous accomplishment of one's mind as the body of the deity
Is the *Anu* of *Ati*.
Mind is the ultimate sphere with no entity:
Freedom from all elaboration
Is the *Ati* of *Ati*.
By the aspects of the development and perfection stages
Of the basis, path, and result,
I have explained the nine subdivisions.

SOURCES OF THE MAJOR *TANTRIC* SCRIPTURES

According to the history of the *tantric* scriptures, most of the *tantras* of the New Translation School of Tibet—such as *Guhyasamāja* and *Kalacakra* and the *tantras* belonging to the division of Outer Tantras—were expounded by Śākyamuni Buddha. But the *tantras* of the three Inner *Tantras* of the Old Translation School did not originate with Śākyamuni Buddha.

The original *tantras* of *Mahāyoga* and *Anuyoga* first appeared in the human realm when they were received by a group of five Buddhist adepts called the Five Excellent Beings (*Dam-Pa'i Rigs-Chan Dra-Ma lNga*) from Vajrapāṇī Buddha in a pure vision on Mt. Malaya [Śrīpāda, Śrīlaṅka?] twenty-five years after the *Mahāparinirvāṇa*, the passing away of Śākyamuni Buddha. They were then transmitted to King Jha (*Dza*) of the Oḍḍiyāna kingdom by Trimed Tragpa (*Dri-Med Grags-Pa, Vimalakīrti*) of the Licchavi tribe, who was one of the Five

Excellent Beings.

In *Mahāyoga*, in addition to the *tantras* there is another category of scriptures known as the *sādhanas* [propitiations]. The following eight categories of scriptures of the *sādhana* section of *Mahāyoga* were received in two ways, in canonical (*bKa'-Ma*) form and discovered Dharma treasure (*gTer-Ma*) form.

(a) The following scriptures were received by different masters by means of canonical transmission, which means transmission from person to person: *Vajraheruka* (or *Yang-Dag*) scriptures received by Hūṁkāra, *Yamāntaka* by Mañjuśrīmitra, *Hyagriva* by Nāgārjuna, *Vajramṛta* (*bDud-rTsi 'Khyil-Ba*) by Vimalamitra, and *Vajrakīla* by Prabhahasti and Padmasambhava.

(b) Discovered Treasure *Sādhanas*: The following scriptures were concealed and entrusted by *Ḍākinī* Lekyi Wangmo (*Las-Kyi dBang-Mo*) to the following masters, and those scriptures are known as the discovered treasure *Sādhanas*: *Śrīheruka* (*Ch'e-mCh'og*) scriptures entrusted to Vimalamitra, *Vajraheruka* to Hūṁkāra, *Yamarāja* to Mañjuśrīmitra, *Hyagriva* to Nāgārjuna, *Vajrakīla* to Padmasambhava, *Mamo* (*Ma-Mo*) to *Dhanasaṃskṛta*, *Chod-tod* (*mCh'od-bsTod*) to Rombhuguhya, and *Trag-ngag* (*Drag-sNgags*) to Śāntigarbha. She also entrusted the *Desheg Dupa* (*bDe-gShegs 'Dus-Pa*) to Padmasambhava. Those masters transmitted the teachings to their disciples and most of them are in practice today.

The original *tantras* of *Atiyoga* were received in pure vision by Garab Dorje (*dGa'-Rab rDo-rJe, S. Prahevajra*), the first human master of *Atiyoga*, directly from *Vajrasattva*, a Buddha in *Saṃbhogakāya* form. He transmitted them to *Mañjuśrīmitra*. The teachings of *Atiyoga* were brought to us through various lineages and are known in Tibetan as *Dzogpa Chenpo*, the Great Perfection, which is the subject of this book.

SOME MAJOR TANTRIC SCRIPTURES OF THE THREE INNER *TANTRAS*

The scriptures of Inner *Tantras* which have survived are preserved as the collections of *Nyingma Gyud-bum* (*rNying-*

Ma rGyud-'Bum) in twenty-six volumes. There are different ways of classifying the *tantras*, and I have indicated the sources on which I relied to make the following lists.

The *Tantras* of *Mahāyoga*

Mahāyoga scriptures were brought to Tibet by Indian scholars and Tibetan translators including Guru Padmsambhava, Vimalamitra, Śāntigarbha, Jñānagarbha, Vairocana, Namkha'i Nyingpo (*Nam-mKha'i sNying-Po*), and Sangye Yeshey (*Sang-rGyas Ye-Shes*). In *Mahāyoga* there are two major sections of scriptures, the eighteen *tantras* and the *sādhanas*. According to Gyurmed Tshewang Chogdrub, who says the list is based on the writings of Terchen Gyurmed Dorje (1646-1714), the major *tantras* of *Mahāyoga* are as follows:[LNT-11, 255b/2-69b/2]

(1) *Tantra* Section:

(A) The Root of all the *Mahāyoga Tantras*, the *tantras* of *Guhyagarbhamāyājāla-tantra* entitled: *Dorje Sempa Gyuthrul Trawa Tsawa'i Gyud Sangwa Nyingpo (rDo-rJe Sems-dPa' rGyu-'Phrul Drva-Ba rTsa-Ba'i rGyud gSang-Ba sNying-Po*).

(B) The Explanatory *Tantras*:

Five Major *Tantras*:

(a) *Tantra* of Body: *Sangye Nyamjor* (*Sang-rGyas mNyam-sByor*)
(b) *Tantra* of Speech: *Dasang Thigle* (*Zla-gSang Thig-Le*)
(c) *Tantra* of Mind: *Sangwa Dupa* (*gSang-Ba 'Dus-Pa*)
(d) *Tantra* of Virtues: *Palchog Tangpo* (*dPal-mCh'og Dang-Po*)
(e) *Tantra* of Action: *Karma Male* (*Karma* Ma-Le)

Five *Tantras* of *Sādhana*:

(a) *Heruka Rolpa* (*Heruka Rol-Ba*, missing)
(b) *Tachog Rolpa* (*rTa-mCh'og Rol-Ba*)
(c) *Nyingje Rolpa* (*sNying-rje Rol-Ba*)
(d) *Dudtsi Rolpa* (*bDud-rTsi Rol-Ba*)
(e) *Phurpa Chunyi* (*Phur-Pa bChu-gNyis*)

Five *Tantras* of Actions:
(a) *Langchen Rab-bog* (*Glang-Ch'en Rab-'Bog*)
(b) *Riwo Tsegpa* (*Ri-Bo brTsegs-Pa*)
(c) *Yeshey Ngamlog* (*Ye-Shes rNgam-Glog*)
(d) *Tamtshig Kodpa* (*Dam-Tshig bKod-Pa*)
(e) *Tingdzin Tsechig* (*Ting-'Dzin rTse-gChig*)
(The last four *tantras* are common to *Anuyoga*)
Two Supplementary *Tantras*:
(a) According to PKD bb/3: *Namnang Gyuthrul Trawa* (*rNam-sNang sGyu-'Phrul Drva-Ba*).
(b) *Thabkyi Zhagpa* (*Thabs-Kyi Zhags-Pa*).

(2) *Sādhana* [Propitiation] Section:
The scriptures of *Sādhanas* of Eight Great *Maṇḍalas* of Deities (*sGrub-Pa bKa'-brGyad*) of which there are two kinds, the Canonical (*bKa'-Ma*) and Discovered Treasure (*gTer-Ma*) scriptures. The Eight Great *Maṇḍalas* of Deities are: (a) *Yamāntaka* of Body, (b) *Hyagriva* of Speech, (c) *Vajraheruka* (*Yang-Dag*) of Mind, (d) *Dudtsi Chechog* (*bDud-rTsi Che'-mCh'og*) of Virtues, (3) *Vajrakīla* of Action, (f) *Mamo Bod-tong* (*Ma-Mo rBod-gTong*), (g) *Jigten Chod-tod* (*'Jigs-rTen mCh'od-bsTod*) and (h) *Modpa Trag-ngag* (*dMod-Pa Drag-sNgags*).

The *Tantras* of *Anuyoga*

The *Anuyoga tantras* were brought to Tibet by Vimalamitra, Vairocana and especially by Nubchen Sangye Yeshey (*gNub-Ch'en Sangs-rGyas Ye-Shes*). According to Gyurmed Tsewang Chogdrub, among the *Anuyoga tantras* are:[LNT-11, 253a/6-255b/2]

1. Four Root *Tantras*:
(a) *Kundu Rigpa'i Do* (*Kun-'Dus Rig-Pa'i mDo*)
(b) *Sangye Thamched Gongpa Dupa* (*Sangs-rGyas Tham-Chad dGongs-Pa 'Dus-Pa*)
(c) *Yeshey Ngamlog* (*Ye-Shes rNgam-Glog*)
(d) *Turthrod Khuchug Rolpa* (*Dur-Khrod Khu-Byug Rol-Ba*).
2. Six Branch *Tantras*:
(a) *Kunto Zangpo Chewa Rangla Nepa'i Gyud* (*Kun-Tu

bZang-Po Ch'e-Ba Rang-La gNas-Pa'i rGyud)
- (b) *Wangkur Gyalpo* (*dBang-bsKur rGyal-Po*)
- (c) *Tingdzin Chog* (*Ting-'DZin mCh'og*)
- (d) *Kabjor Dunpa* (*sKabs-sByor bDun-Pa*)
- (e) *Tsonpa Donden* (*brTson-Pa Don-lDan*)
- (f) *Tamshig Kodpa* (*Dam-Tshig bKod-Pa*)

3. Twelve Rare *Tantras*:
- (a) *Zhiwa Lhagyud* (*Zhi-Ba Lha-rGyud*)
- (b) *Chonyid Zhiwa'i Lhagyud* (*Ch'os-Nyid Zhi-Ba'i Lha-rGyud*)
- (c) *Throwo'i Lhagyud Chenmo* (*Khro-Bo'i Lha-rGyud Ch'en-Mo*)
- (d) *Throwo'i Lhagyud Kyi Togpa Chenpo* (*Khro-Bo'i Lha-rGyud Kyi rTogs-Pa Ch'en-Po*)
- (e) *Thugje Chenpo'i Torgyud* (*Thugs-rJe Ch'en-Po'i gTor-rGyud*)
- (f) *Naljor Nangpa'i Tshog-gyud Chenpo* (*rNal-'Byor Nang-Pa'i Tshogs-rGyud Ch'en-Po*)
- (g) *Palbar Khroma* (*dPal-'Bar Khros-Ma*)
- (h) *Rakta Markyi Gyud* (*Rakta dMar-Gyi rGyud*)
- (i) *Melha Zhiwar Kyurpa Barwa'i Gyud* (*Me-Lha Zhi-Bar Kyur-Pa 'Bar-Ba'i rGyud*)
- (j) *Throwo'i Jinseg* (*Khro-Ba'i sByin-bSreg*)
- (k) *Hungdzed Chenpo* (*Hung-mDzad Ch'en-Po*)
- (l) *Dasang Chenpo* (*Zla-gSang Ch'en-Po*)

The *Tantras* of *Atiyoga*

Atiyoga has three divisions of *tantras*: They are *Semde*, *Longde*, and *Mengagde*.

(1) In *Semde* (*Sems-sDe*) there are Twenty-one Major *Tantras* which were brought to Tibet by Vimalamitra and Vairocana. According to Longchen Rabjam they are:[GD 179a/4]

(A) The Five Earlier Translated *Tantras*, translated by Vairocana:
- (a) *Rigpa'i Khuchug* (*Rig-Pa'i Khu-Byug*)
- (b) *Tsalchen Trugpa* (*rTsal-Ch'en Drug-pa*)
- (c) *Khyungchen Dingwa* (*Khyung-Ch'en lDing-Ba*)

(d) *Dola Serzhun (rDo-La gSer-Zhun)*
(e) *Minubpa'i Gyaltshen Namkhache (Mi-Nub-Pa'i rGyal-mTshan Nam-mKha'-Ch'e)*

(B) The Thirteen Later Translated *Tantras*, translated by Vimalamitra, Nyag Jñānakumāra and Yudra Nyingpo (*gYu-sGra sNying-Po*):
(a) *Tsemo Chung-gyal (rTse-Mo Byung-rGyal)*
(b) *Namkha'i Gyalpo (Nam-mKha'i rGyal-Po)*
(c) *Dewa Thrulkod (bDe-Ba 'Phrul-bKod)*
(d) *Dzogpa Chiching (rDzogs-Pa sPyi-Ch'ings)*
(e) *Changchub Semtig (Byang-Ch'ub Sems-Tig)*
(f) *Dewa Rabjam (bDe-Ba Rab-'Byams)*
(g) *Sog-gi Khorlo (Srog-Gi 'Khor-Lo)*
(h) *Thigle Trugpa (Thig-Le Drug-Pa)*
(i) *Dzogpa Chichod (rDzogs-Pa sPhi-sPyod)*
(j) *Yidzhin Norbu (Yid-bZhin Nor-Bu)*
(k) *Kundu Rigpa (Kun-'Dus Rig-Pa)*
(l) *Jetsun Tampa (rJe-bTsun Dam-Pa)*
(m) *Gompa Tontrub (sGom-Pa Don-Grub)*

(C) Three Other Major *Tantras*:
(a) *The cycle of Kunched Gyalpo (Kun-Byed rGyal-Po)*
(b) *The Medchung (rMad-Byung)*
(c) *The Thirteen Sūtras of Semde*

(2) The *tantras* of *Longde (Klong-sDe)* were brought to Tibet by Vimalamitra and Vairocana. According to Gyurmed Tswewang Chogdrub, some of the major *tantras* of *Longde* are:[LNT 11, 248/5]

(a) *Longchen Rabjam Gyalpo (Klong-Ch'en Rab-'Byams rGyal-Po)*
(b) *Kunto Zangpo Namkhache (Kun-Tu bZang-Po Nam-mKha'-Ch'e)*
(c) *Rigpa Rangtsal Sharwa (Rig-Pa Rang-rTsal Shar-Ba)*
(d) *Dam-ngag Natshog Khorlo (gDams-Ngag sNa-Tshogs 'Khor-Lo)*
(e) *Phaglam Kodpa ('Phags-Lam bKod-Pa)*
(f) *Dorje Sempa Namkha'i Thatang Nyampa (rDo-rJe*

Sems-dPa Nam-mKha'i mTha'-Dang mNyam-Pa)

(g) *Yeshey Sangwa Dronma* (*Ye-Shes gSang-Ba sGron-Ma*)

(h) *Rinpoche Khorlo* (*Rin-Po-Ch'e 'Khor-Lo*)

(i) *Yeshey Sangwa* (*Ye-Shes gSang-Ba*)

(j) *Yeshey Dzogpa* (*Ye-Shes rDzogs-Pa*)

(k) *Changchub Kyi Sems Kunla Jugpa Namtag Tonpa* (*Byang-Ch'ub Kyi Sems Kun-La 'Jug-Pa rNam-Dag sTon-Pa*)

(l) *Changchub Kyi Sem Dorje Odthro* (*Byang-Ch'ub Kyi Sems rDo-rJe A'od-'Thro*)

(3) The *tantras* of *Mengagde* (*Man-Ngag-sDe*) were brought to Tibet mainly by Paṇḍita Vimalamitra and Guru Padmasambhava. Some of the major *tantras* of *Mengagde,* which belong to the *Yangsang* (*Yang-gSang*) or *Nyingthig* (*sNying-Thig*) subdivision, according to Gyurmed Tshewang Chotrub[LNT-11 245b/5] and Pema Ledreltsal are:[NN 8a/b]

(A) The Seventeen *Tantras* (*rGyud-bChu-bDun*):

(a) *Dzogpa Rangchung* (*rDzogs-Pa Rang-Byung*)

(b) *Yige Medpa* (*Yi-Ge Med-Pa*)

(c) *Rigpa Rangshar* (*Rig-Pa Rang-Shar*)

(d) *Rigpa Rangtrol* (*Rig-Pa Rang-Grol*)

(e) *Rinpoche Pungwa/Pudpa* (*Rin-Po-Che' sPung Ba/sPud-Pai*)

(f) *Kudung Barwa* (*sKu-gDung 'Bar-Ba*)

(g) *Dra Thalgyur* (*sGra Thal-'Gyur*)

(h) *Trashey Dzeyden* (*bKra-Shis mDzes-lDan*)

(i) *Dorje Sempa Nying-gi Melong* (*rDo-rJe Sems-dPa' sNying-Gi Me-Long*)

(j) *Kuntu Zangpo Thugkyi Melong* (*Kun-Tu bZang-Po Thugs-Kyi Me-Long*)

(k) *Ngotrod Trepa* (*Ngo-sProd sTras-Pa*)

(l) *Mutig Rinpoche'i Threngwa* (*Mu-Tig Rin-Po-Ch'e'i Phreng-Ba*)

(m) *Kuntu Zangpo Longtrub* (*Kun-Tu bZang-Po Klong-Drug*)

(n) *Dronma Barwa* (*sGron-Ma 'Bar-Ba*)

(o) *Nyida Khajor (Nyi-Zla Kha-sByor)*
(p) *Seng-ge Tsaldzog (Seng-Ge rTsal-rDzogs)*
(q) *Norbu Thrakod (Nor-Bu Phra-bKod)*

(B) Two Other Major *Tantras:*
(a) *Ekatsati Nagmo Throma (Ekajati Nag-Mo Khros-Ma)*
(b) *Longsal Barma (Klong-gSal 'Bar-Ma)*

There are two other important categories of scriptures in the *Yangsang* sub-section of *Mengagde,* known as the Instructional *(Man-Ngag)* category of teachings. They are as follows. According to Pema Ledrel Tsal[NCC 8b/5] the first is the *Nyingthig* teachings which contain the essential instructions of the *Seventeen Tantras* and *Throma Tantra.* It was brought to Tibet by Vimalamitra and became known as *Vima Nyingthig.* The second is the *Nyingthig* teachings which mainly contain the essential instructions of *Longsal Barwa Tantra.* It was brought to Tibet by Guru Padmasambhava and became known as *Khadro (mKha'-'Gro) Nyingthig.*

Longchen Rabjam wrote a volume of commentarial and supplemental texts on *Vima Nyingthig* known as *Vima Yangtig (Vima Yang-Tig)* and one volume on *Khadro Nyingthig* known as *Khadro Yangtig (mKha'-'Gro Yang-Tig).* He also wrote a volume on both *Nyingthigs* known as *Lama Yangtig (Bla-Ma Yang Tig)* or *Yangtig Yidzhin Norbu (Yang-Tig Yid-bZhin Nor-Bu).* These two root scriptures and two commentarial texts are known as *Nyingthig Yazhi (sNying-Thig Yab-Zhi),* the Four Volumes of *Nyingthig.* They are some of the most important texts and writings on *Nyingthig.*

The Three Inner Tantras

(A) *MAHĀ*YOGA (*rNal-'Byor Ch'en-Po*)

In *Guhyagarbha Tantra* in the discourses upon *saṃsāra* and *nirvāṇa* as the natural or self-appearances of the mind and primordial wisdom (*Sems-Dang Ye-Shes Kyi Rang-sNang*) it is said:[SDN 7a/1]

> (Delusory appearances:) Faults, the root of *saṃsāra*, arise from the concept of self.
> The birth and cessation of the six (mind-) streams [or realms] and
> The delusion of their bodies, wealth, land, sufferings and so on
> Are non-existent but (appear) as wrong concepts [delusions].
> (Buddha-fields:) The self-awareness mind, which is emptiness, selflessness and primordial wisdom,
> Transforms (phenomenal appearances) through the recollection free from conception.
> (In it phenomena) are non-existent but are as the wonders of (Buddha-) bodies, speech, virtues and pure lands.
> They are the appearances of (the primordial wisdom) itself.

View, the Basis

It is "the indivisibility or the union of two superior truths" (*Lhag-Pa'i bDen-Pa dByer-Med*). Mipham summarizes it as follows:[YDGD 36b/1]

> It ascertains the indivisibility of the "two superior truths," which is the presence of *Dharmakāya*, through the scriptural and reasoning forms of knowledge with fourfold understanding, etc., as clarity and freedom from objective aims, transcending mental conceptualizations. According to this view, the appearances (*sNang-Ba*) of phenomena, existence of relative truth, present primordially as the nature of the three cycles, *vajra* body, *vajra* speech and *vajra* mind (of the Buddha), while they are emptiness, are the "superior relative truth" (*Lhag-Pa'i Kun-rDzob*). The indivisibility of emptiness (*sTong-Pa-Nyid*), the non-existing nature, from the Buddha-bodies and primordial wisdoms is the "superior absolute truth" (*Lhag-Pa'i Don-Dam bDen-Pa*).

Lochen Dharmaśrī writes:[ZL 35b/3]

> *Mahāyoga* is predominantly based on the development stage, and by means of realization and progress of experience of the indivisibility of the "two superior truths," one attains liberation.

Meditation, the Path

The following is a summary drawn from the writings of Lochen Dharmaśrī,[LZ 37a/6] Gyurmed Tshewang Chog-trub,[LNT-I,105a] and Tenpa'i Nyima:[MK 21a]

> In *Mahāyoga* one meditates all the phenomenal existences as the *maṇḍalas* of the deities. According to the scriptures of *tantras* and *sādhanas* one trains on two *yogas*: the *yoga* with characteristics (*mTshan-bChas*) and the *yoga* without characteristics (*mTshan-Med*).
>
> (a) In the *yoga* with characteristics, one trains on two stages, the Development Stage (*bsKyed-Rim*) and Perfection

Stage (*rDzogs-Rim*):

(i) In the Development Stage one meditates on the union of one's three doors, the body, speech and mind, with the three *vajras* of the deities by emphasizing mainly the development stage with the visualization of the *maṇḍala* through the threefold contemplations (*Ting-'Dzin gSum*). The three contemplations are the contemplation on the great emptiness, the suchness, on illusory compassion, the all-pervasiveness, and on the cause, the clear, stable syllables.

(ii) In the Perfection Stage one contemplates on the primordial wisdom of great bliss through the training with the upper entrances and the lower entrances, according to the path of skillful means (*Thabs-Lam*).

(b) In meditation without characteristics, one contemplates on suchness, the ultimate nature.

Practice, the Actions

Lochen Dharmaśrī writes:[ZL 37b/3]

> Through confidence in skill-in-means one enjoys everything without attachment to any phenomena.

Result, the Attainments

The following is a summary from the writings of Mipham[YDGD 36b/5] and Lochen Dharmaśrī:[ZL 37b/4]

> Having purified all the impurities of delusions through the power of the profound path, one attains the state of fourfold knowledge-holders and achieves the five Buddha-bodies in this life or in the intermediate state.

(B) *ANUYOGA* (*rJes-Su rNal-'Byor*)

In *Kundu Rigpa'i Do Tantra* it is said:[KRD 54b/1]

> The container [world] is the ultimate sphere of the mother (-Buddha).
> The contained [beings] is the space (*mKha'*) of the father-victor [Buddha].

> The withdrawals and entries are the enjoyment by the intrinsic awareness.
> This is the *Vajra-samaya*.

View, the Basis

It is the indivisibility of the ultimate sphere and the primordial wisdom (*dByings-Ye dByer-Med*). Mipham summarizes in the following words:[YDGD 36b/6]

> *Anuyoga* ascertains that all the appearances of phenomenal existence are *Samantabhadra* (the father), the spontaneously accomplished *maṇḍala* of the deities. The emptiness nature (of phenomenal existence), free from all the extremes, is *Samantabhadrī* (the mother), the *maṇḍala* of primordial suchness. The essence both (of appearances and nature) is indivisibly present as equalness nature, and that is the great blissful son, the *maṇḍala* of enlightened mind.

Lochen Dharmaśrī writes:[ZL 38b/5]

> (All the phenomenal existents) are (the creation of) one's mind and they are pure in the womb (or ultimate sphere) of the mother *Samantabhadrī* (the emptiness mother), the nature that is unborn and free from elaborations. It is also called the *maṇḍala* of primordial suchness.... That unborn nature which shines forth ceaselessly as the intrinsic awareness, the *maṇḍala* of self-arisen light, is the primordial wisdom (the father) *Samantabhadra*. It is also called the spontaneously accomplished *maṇḍala*.... The shining forth of both (emptiness and appearances) as the inseparable essence is the great blissful son, the union of the ultimate sphere and primordial wisdom (*dBying-Ye gNyis-Med*), and it is the *maṇḍala* of root-enlightened Mind.

Meditation, the Path

The following is a summary of writings of Mipham[YDGD 37a/2] and Tenpa'i Nyima:[MK 21a & b]

> One meditates that all the deities are completed within

one's own *vajra*-body. Although the three *maṇḍalas* of father, mother, and son have never been separated from one's own mind, and all the phenomenal existents are gathered in the mind, that mind has been obscured because of the thoughts of the apprehended and apprehender, caused by the habits generated through the three perceptions.[1] Things appear in various forms of good and evil, acceptance and rejection, and one becomes attached to them. To dispel those obscurations one trains in the method of actualizing the great blissful wisdom by penetrating the channels, air and essence of the body, and one progresses through the five paths gradually.

The following is a summary from the writings of Lochen Dharmaśrī[ZL 39b/5] and Gyurmed Tshewang Chogtrub:[LNT-I, 110b/2]

In *Anuyoga* there are two major paths of training:

(a) The path of skillful means (*Thabs-Lam*) is the training which generates innate wisdom, the changeless great bliss, by means either of the upper entrance (*sTeng-sGo*), the training with the four *cakras*[2] or six *cakras*[3] of one's body, which brings innate wisdom gradually, or by means of the lower entrances (*A'og-sGo*), the union with consort, which brings innate wisdom instantly.

(b) In the path of liberation (*Grol-Lam*), there are two aspects. Meditation on the meaning (*Don*) is the contemplation on suchness, the ultimate nature without mental fabrications and freedom from conceptualizations. The meditation on the signs or characteristics (*rTags*) is the elaborate contemplation on the deities. By mere utterance of the *mantra* one visualizes instantly the world and beings as the *maṇḍala* of the deities clearly without confusion, like a fish jumping out of water.

---

[1](*sNang-gSum*): Impure, pure, and neutral perceptions.

[2]*Cakras* at the crown of the head, throat, heart and navel.

[3]Four *cakras* plus *cakras* at the secret organ and at the *uṣṇīṣa*, or four *cakras* plus *cakras* of fire at the joint (*Sum-mDo*) and air at the juncture (*sGrom-mDo*).

In *Anuyoga*, less emphasis is put on the development stage and more on the perfection stage, the *yoga* of channels, air, and essence, and on the primordial wisdom of bliss, clarity and no-thought.

Practice, the Actions

According to Dharmaśrī:[ZL 40a/6]

One mainly enjoys everything in equalness.

Result, the Attainments

According to Dharmaśrī[ZL 40b/2] and Gyurmed Tshewang Chogtrub:[LNT-II, 112a/4]

One attains the Great Blissful Body with the four Buddha-bodies and five Primordial Wisdoms.

(C) ATIYOGA (*Shin-Tu rNal-'Byor*)

Essence (*Ngo-Bo*)

Dharmaśrī summarizes:[ZL 40b/5]

Atiyoga is a means to liberate the meaning of primordial Buddhahood into its own state, and it is the nature of freedom from abandonments and acceptances and expectations and fears.

Definition

Gyurmed Tshewang Chogtrub writes:[LNT-I, 127b/1]

The definition of *Dzogpa Chenpo* (*Mahāsandhi*): In the nature of the self-arisen primordial wisdom, which is free from falling into any extremes of partiality and of dimensions, the entire content of the *yānas* is perfected and is present.

He continues:[LNT-I, 128a/5]

The definition of *Atiyoga*: *Ati* means very, excellent, best, supreme, summit, peak and innermost essence. *Yoga* is training. So it is the very training, the absolute training of all trainings.

View, the Basis

Mipham summarizes it as follows:[YDGD 37a/6]

> *Atiyoga* ascertains that all phenomenal existents are present from primordial time in the equalness nature of the Single Essence (*Thig-Le Nyag-gChig*), the self-arisen intrinsic wisdom. Although phenomena just appear before one's mind, the nature of appearances exists nowhere and they are false. The Mind dwells primordially in the nature of three Buddha-bodies: the emptiness is the Ultimate Body (*Dharmakāya*), the clarity-nature is the Enjoyment Body(*Saṃbhogakāya*), and the all-pervading compassion is the Manifested Body (*Nirmāṇakāya*). In the state of indivisibility (or union) of original or primordial purity (*Ka-Dag*) and spontaneous accomplishment (*Lhun-Grub*), *Atiyoga* ascertains that all the phenomena of *saṃsāra* and *nirvāṇa* are equal, without discriminations, in the spontaneously accomplished great *maṇḍala*.

Longchen Rabjam summarizes the special characteristics of *Dzogpa Chenpo*:[GD 163a/1]

> *Atiyoga* asserts that the clarity-Mind (*Sems-Nyid*), the sphere of natural purity, dwells primordially as the great self-dwelling spontaneous accomplishment. This changeless self-arisen intrinsic wisdom is the basis. In lower *yānas* one discriminates phenomena with contaminating efforts, and thereby the self-arisen intrinsic wisdom is obscured by expectations and doubts.

He also writes:[SYD 69a/4]

> Mind (*Sems-Nyid*) is the Buddha-essence, the intrinsic wisdom of clarity. This is the Mind, the clarity and discriminating intrinsic wisdom (at the point) when there is no mind (*Sems*), as it has ceased. In the *Aṣṭasāhasrikā(prajñāpāramitā-sūtra)* it is said:
>
> > "In mind there is no mind, as the nature of the mind is clarity."

Gyurmed Tshewang Chogtrub summarizes:[LNT-I, 115a/5]

> The Natural Great Perfection (*Rang-bZhin rDzogs-Pa Ch'en-Po*) is the Mind (*Sems-Nyid*) which is free from mind (*Sems*). It is the self-arisen intrinsic awareness and it is the internal clarity. In this all the virtues of nature are present spontaneously. It does not rely on any cause and effect of creator and creation or on any other conditions, as it is naturally liberated.

Dzogpa Chenpo is the supreme path. Jigmed Lingpa writes:[NS 332b/6]

> In *Dzogpa Chenpo*, having realized the way of presence of the changeless ultimate nature and by not moving from that state, the stains of both emotional and intellectual defilements are naturally purified without being abandoned. So this is the supremely swift path among the paths.

Division

The six million four hundred verses (*S. Śloka*) of *Atiyoga* scriptures are divided into three divisions (*sDe gSum*) by Jampal Shenyen (*'Jam-dPal bShes-gNyen, S. Mañjuśrīmitra*). These divisions are *Semde*, *Longde* and *Mengagde*.

In *Kodpa Chenpo* (*bKod-Pa Ch'en-Po*) *tantra*, quoted in (GD 166b/6), it is said:

> For people who are (inclined to) mind, the *Semde* teachings (will appear),
> For those who are (inclined) to space, the *Longde* (will appear)
> And for those who are free from gradual efforts,* *Mengagde* teachings (will appear).

Longchen Rabjam summarizes:[TCD-I, 73b/6]

> (*Semde* asserts) that as (the phenomenal existents) are nothing other than one's mind, all are the aspects of mind.

**Rim-rTsol Bral-La*, although NS 30b/2 reads: *Rim-rTsol Chan-La.*

> This view is for preventing the mind from being distracted from the self-arisen intrinsic wisdom. *Longde* proclaims that there is nowhere else to go but into the expanse of *Samantabhadrī*, the ultimate nature (*Ch'os-Nyid*). This view is just for preventing (the deviation of the mind) to other objects of expression than the vast expanse of the ultimate nature. Ascertaining the crucial point of the nature of what it is is *Mengagde*.

Jigmed Lingpa writes on this:[NS 304a/5]

> (The *Dzogpa Chenpo* teachings are) divided into three theories because of the mental degrees of trainees in the way of perceiving mental objects:
>
> Because of mental degrees there are three levels of perceiving:
>
> In *Semde*, phenomena have arisen as the play of the power (*Rol-Pa'i rTsal*) (of the Mind).
>
> In *Longde* they are attributes (or ornaments, *rGyan*) of the self-appearing array.
>
> In *Mengagde* they are the emptiness-form (*sTong-Pa'i gZugs*) of non-existent appearances.

Lochen Dharmaśrī writes:[ZL 41a/5]

> Contemplation on the state of *Dharmakāya*, the (union of) intrinsic awareness and emptiness, is *Semde*. Contemplation on the state of freedom from actions and efforts, the ultimate nature, is *Longde*. Contemplation in the state of ultimate nature (which has been) free since the primordially liberated state, without abandonments and acceptances, is *Mengagde*.

Gyurmed Tshewang Chogtrub explains:[LNT-I, 134a/6]

> Liberation from the extremes of things to be abandoned, as all phenomenal existents are nothing else but the Mind, is *Semde*. Freedom from the extremes of antidotes, as all phenomenal existents are perfected (*A'ub-Ch'ub*) in the expanse of ultimate nature, *Samantabhadrī*, is the actionless

Longde. Liberation from both the things to be abandoned and the antidotes by ascertaining the character of the meaning itself, as it is, is the profound *Mengagde*.

Pema Ledrel Tsal distinguishes the three levels of *Atiyoga*:[NCC 6b/1]

In *Semde*, the appearances are introduced as the mind, the mind as the emptiness, emptiness as the intrinsic awareness, and the intrinsic awareness and emptiness as the union. In the case of introduction of appearances as the mind, the appearances are introduced as the mind through power (*rTsal*), play (*Rol-Ba*), and attributes (*rGyan*). First, the meaning of power is the self-power of primordial wisdom, which is the aspect of mere awareness and mere moving. Having the power as the basis, and relying on it, it becomes the basis or the origin of the delusions. The defiled mind and the five entrances, etc., which arise from the power, are the play. The display of the internal and external body and places such as mountains, rocks, and houses, etc., are the ornaments. In brief, both attributes and play arise from the power, the mere awareness and flow, and the power arises from the Mind, the king, creator of all (*Sems-Nyid Kun-Byed rGyal-Po*). This is the way of introducing the appearances as the mind. Here, the crucial point is that this primordial wisdom, the king, the creator of all, is the mere clarity and awareness aspect of the mind and not the spontaneously arisen intrinsic awareness of the Great Perfection. But it is called such because the mind possesses the aspect of both clarity and emptiness, and they are indivisible.... *Longde* ascertains that mind of clarity and awareness as emptiness. But still, there is a great apprehension of emptiness....

In brief, *Semde*, by realizing that apart from the mind there is nothing to be abandoned, liberates from the extremes of things to be abandoned, but it does not liberate from the antidotes of apprehending the clarity and awareness (of the mind). *Longde* liberates from both the things to be abandoned and the antidotes by ascertaining the mind of clarity and awareness as emptiness; but the clinging to emptiness has still not been able to be reversed, and it lacks the crucial point of primordial wisdom, which transcends the mind. The Innermost Secret (*Mengagde*), in addition to transcending both things to be abandoned and the antidotes, ascertains the ultimate nature, (with the three characteristics of) essence (*Ngo-Bo*), nature (*Rang-bZhin*) and compassion (*Thugs-rJe*). The three characteristics are in union from primordial time, like water and moisture or fire and heat, and there are neither new associations nor fabrications by mind. As *Mengagde* ascertains the primordial nature as it is, it is not only superior to the theories of lower (*yānas*) but also to these two levels (of *Atiyoga*).

Three Divisions of Atiyoga

(A) *SEMDE*

In *Kunched Gyalpo Tantra* it is said:[KBG 31b/7]

> The Buddhas and beings and the phenomenal existents of the world and beings
> Have arisen from the nature of the mind [enlightened mind], the universal creator.
> Whoever conceptualizes them otherwise,
> Does not have the opportunity to meet me, the universal creator.

In *Longchen Rabjam Gyalpo Tantra* it is said:[KRG 128b/3]

> All the phenomenal existents and varieties of imputations
> Are the same in the vast expanse, the non-existing basis of designation from the primordial (time and space).
> In the single great expanse, *saṃsāra* and *nirvāṇa*
> Appear variously due to conditions. So they are adventitious,
> Like the sky and clouds and rainbow colors in the sky.
> As they arise as the very intrinsic awareness, they are (in) the state of the ultimate sphere.

Semde (*Sems-sDe, S. Cittavarga*), the Division on Mind, asserts that all phenomenal existents, the mental objects, are the power of the play of the mind. Sogpo Tentar writes:[ST 258b/5]

> *Semde* asserts that all the phenomenal existents of *saṃsāra* and *nirvāṇa* and of the path (*'Khor-'Das Lam gSum*) have arisen as the displaying power (*Rol-Pa'i rTsal*) of the mind. In *Kunched Gyalpo* (*Kun-Byed rGyal-Po*) *tantra** it is said:
>
> > "The phenomenal existents of the world and beings and the Buddhas and beings
> > Are created by mind, and they are the same in the nature of the mind."

Longchen Rabjam defines:[GD 167a/6]

> In *Semde* it is asserted that although various entities appear, they are not beyond the play of the mere Mind, like the arising of various shades of white and red in the single face of a mirror. The various appearances do not exist in reality as they are percepts (appearances) of the mind and are non-dual (in relation to the mind). The essence (*Ngo-Bo*) of the mind is Mind, which is clarity, and it is self-arisen primordial wisdom. Nowadays, foolish people say: "*Dzogpa Chenpo* asserts that the appearances are mind." That is totally wrong. (If it is so, then) mind should have color, be cognizable and have dimensions, because the appearances appear as such. So one should know that the appearances are the mysteries of the appearances [percepts] of the mind and they are non-existent in reality like reflections in a mirror. They appear in the mind in the manner of delusions due to habituations (of the mind). One should understand that the Mind is the basis of arising (of appearances) and it is free from dimensions and partialities like the surface of a mirror, and it is the essence of discriminative intrinsic awareness, which tran-

---

*I couldn't find the actual lines in the *tantra*. Is it due to differences of editions?

> scends all the extremes of elaboration of postulations of plural and singular.

Gyurmed Tshewang Chogtrub explains:[LNT-I, 134b/2]

> The theory of *Semde* transcends all the various levels of *yānas*, two truths, six perfections and two stages, all the composed and contaminated aspects of the "truth of path" which are bound with the rigid concept of apprehending. (These are transcended by) the great ultimate sphere which is the nature of innate enlightened mind, the primordial wisdom of the great equalness purity, the ultimate sphere free from elaborations, the nature of absolute truth. It is the total liberation from causes and results, virtues and unvirtues and acceptances and rejections. In brief, it is the transcendence of all the phenomena of dual perceptions of apprehended and apprehender.

(B) LONGDE

Longde (*Klong-sDe, S. Abhyantaravarga*), the Division on Vast Expanse [the Ultimate Sphere], asserts that self-arisen primordial wisdom and phenomenal existents are self-arisen attributes (*rGyan*) of the vast expanse, the ultimate nature (*Ch'os-Nyid*). Longchen Rabjam gives the following explanations:[GD 170a/2]

> The essence (*Ngo-Bo*) of *Longde*: It asserts that self-arisen primordial wisdom and phenomenal existents which have arisen from it (the primordial wisdom) are the great purity from their origin and are primordially liberated. The phenomenal existents are present as various self-appearing modes, but they do not exist since they are originally liberated and are naturally pure result. So even the aspect of mind and the play, the appearances of the mind, do not exist. In the great intrinsic awareness, which is free from the partialities of existing or not existing, *Longde* lets the phenomena appear, lets them arise or lets them not arise (naturally). Whatever imputations one makes (about the

> appearances), whether as pure or impure, at the very point of their appearance, their self-essence transcends (the extremes of) existing or non-existing. All are the great original liberation and infinite expanse.

Sogpo Tentar writes:[ST 259b/5]

> *Longde* asserts that whatever appears, like the stars and planets in the sky, is the display of the self-appearing attributes of the intrinsic awareness in the vast expanse of ultimate nature, *Samantabhadrī*. *Longde* does not assert that phenomena are the arising of the power and play (of the mind) as *Semde* does.

Gyurmed Tshewang Chogtrub describes *Longde* as follows:[LNT-I, 139a/5]

> *Longde* ascertains that all the phenomenal existents of whatever is appearing are merely self-arisen attributes of the self-arisen primordial wisdom, the vast expanse of *Samantabhadrī*, the ultimate nature. (The phenomenal appearances) do not exist as either bondage or liberation or as things to make arise or to let arise. So *Longde* does not assert that the phenomenal existents are the power or play (of the mind) as *Semde* does. *Longde* does not characterize phenomenal existents either as "interdependently co-existent," "existent or non-existent," "they are or they are not" or "pure or impure," but it asserts that all are the great primordial liberation and infinite expanse.'

(C) MENGAGDE

In *Mutig Threngwa Tantra* it is said:[MT 273a/3]

> In the ceaseless intrinsic awareness
> There is no returning (to delusion), as there is no cause of delusion. It is extraordinary as it is the "liberation-from-primordial (time and space)."
> The objective conditions are exhausted as they are "self-liberation."

The appearances are pure as they are "liberation-at-bare-attention."
The four alternatives have ceased as it is "liberation-from-(four)-extremes."
It is the emptiness of many as it is the "single liberation."

Mengagde (*Man-Ngag sDe, S. Upadeśavarga*), the Division of Esoteric Instructions, spontaneously and directly realizes the primordial pure nature, which is free from mind, expressions, and discriminations.

SUPERIORITY OF MENGAGDE TO THE TWO PREVIOUS DIVISIONS

Longchen Rabjam writes:[GD 174b/4]

> Since *Semde* (asserts that phenomenal appearances) are mind, it involves mental analysis. Since *Longde* apprehends (phenomenal existents as) ultimate nature, it (also) has mental analysis. So *Mengagde* is superior because it enlightens naturally (*Rang-gSal*) the ultimate nature (itself).

Jigmed Lingpa writes:[NS 311b/1]

> *Mengagde* is superior to the two lower divisions. *Semde* (holds that all phenomena) are Mind. Although *Semde* trains more on profundity (emptiness) than on clarity, since it does not perfect the power (*rTsal*) of clarity as the ultimate nature, it has the danger of apprehending the attributes (*rGyan*) and play (*Rol-Pa*) (of Mind) with mental analysis. Although *Longde* trains equally on profundity [emptiness] and clarity, it possesses the danger of falling into the partiality of emptiness because of apprehending the ultimate nature with mental analysis.... In *Mengagde*, as the glow (*gDangs*) of originally pure essence (*Ngo-Bo*), the great freedom from concepts and expressions, arises naturally through the doors of spontaneously accomplished self-appearances, there are no deviations and obscurations in the appearances of power (*rTsal-sNang*); and the appearances of phenomena are perfected in the ultimate nature

of phenomena, free from elaborations. So it is superior.

Pema Ledrel Tsal writes:[KT 5a/4]

> *Semde* and *Longde* perceive the mere emptiness and clarity aspect of the mind with the concept of "it is it" by analysis. They do not have the clear realization of the naked and unhindered intrinsic awareness of *Thregchod (Khregs-Ch'od*, the Cutting Through).

VIEW OF MENGAGDE

Jigmed Lingpa summarizes the view in the Prayer of Basis, Path, and Result of *Dzogpa Chenpo*:[ZM 1a/3]

> As its essence is emptiness, it is free from the extreme of eternalism.
> As its nature is clarity, it is free from the aspect of nihilism.
> As its compassion is ceaseless, it is the basis of various manifestations.
> These are divided as three but in meaning they are indivisible.
> May I realize the state of the basis of *Dzogpa Chenpo.*

Basis (gZhi)

In the view of *Dzogpa Chenpo*, the "basis" is primordially pure. As the essence (*Ngo-Bo*) of the basis is emptiness and non-existent, there is no projection of lights or forms as the outer clarity (*Phyi-gSal*). But as its nature (*Rang-bZhin*) is spontaneously accomplished, it is the presence of the primordial glow (*gDangs*), the utmost subtle appearances of light, forms, rays, and *Thigle* as the inner clarity (*Nang-gSal*), the primordial wisdom in the ultimate nature. As its essence is emptiness, it is non-existent. As its nature is clarity, it is ceaselessly self-appearing. As its compassion (power) is the unobstructed sphere, it causes the "appearances of the basis."

Appearances of the Basis (gZhi-sNang)

From the basis, the glow of five energies of primordial wisdom arises outwardly. At that time, from the nature of spontaneous accomplishment arise outwardly the appearances of five lights and the glow of compassion [power] as the cognition that analyzes the appearances. At that point, the aspect of not recognizing the self-essence of the cognition and the appearances, as it is, is unenlightenment in relation to enlightenment. Then from the basis, the primordial purity, arise the self-appearances of the "eight modes of arising of spontaneous accomplishments."

Longchen Rabjam explains the "Eight Modes of Arising of Spontaneous Accomplishment" (*Lhun-Grub Kyi 'Ch'ar-Tshul brGyad or Lhun-Grub sGo-brGyad Kyi sNang-Ba*):[TCD-I, 203a/2]

> (1) As (in the basis, the original purity) the space (or sphere, *Go*) for the arising (of the appearances of the basis) as compassion (*Thugs-rJe*) does not cease, there arises compassion towards living beings. (2) As the space for arising as the light(*A'od*) does not cease, there arises the self-lights of the primordial wisdom like rainbow colors, and they pervade (all) the appearances. (3) As the space for arising as the primordial wisdom does not cease, it remains in the state of no thoughts. (4) As the space for arising as the Buddha-bodies does not cease, the Buddha-bodies of luminous absorption (in the form of) peaceful and wrathful (Buddhas) fill the space. (5) As the space for arising as non-duality(*gNyis-Med*) does not cease, there is no analysis (of things) as plural or singular. (6) As the space for arising as the liberated from extremes (*mTha'-Grol*) does not cease, the spontaneous accomplishments are clear as the self-essence. (7) As the space for arising as the door of pure primordial wisdom (*Dag-Pa Ye-Shes*) (i.e., *Nirvāṇa*) does not cease, the appearances of originally pure essence, the cloudless sky-like appearances, appear above. (8) As the space for arising as the door of impure *saṃsāra* (*Ma-Dag 'Khor-Ba*) does not cease, the appearances of the six classes of beings appear below.

The Way of Liberation of the Primordial Buddha

At the time of arising of the "appearances of the basis," by recognizing the self-essence of the cognition and realizing the spontaneously accomplished appearances as self-appearances and as free from inherent existents, one attains liberation instantly. It is called the way of attainment of enlightenment as the Primordial Buddha, the Universal Goodness (*Samantabhadra*).

Delusion into Saṃsāra

At the time of arising of the appearances, by not realizing the true nature of the self-essence of the cognition and self-appearances of phenomena, one becomes deluded by means of three unenlightenments (*Ma-Rig-Pa gSum*) and four conditions (*rKyen-bZhi*), and one wanders into the cycle of *saṃsāra* though the "chain of twelve links of interdependent causation" (*rTen-'Brel Yan-Lag bChu-gNyis*) endlessly until one attains enlightenment through the power of merits and realization of enlightenment.

(i) *The Three Unenlightenments.* Relying on Thegchog Dzod,[TCD-I, 218a] Pema Ledrel Tsal explains the three unenlightenments:[KTT 12a/3]

> (1) The aspect of the cognition, not recognizing the self-essence of the primordially pure intrinsic awareness itself (as it is), is the unenlightenment of the single self-cause (*rGyu bDag-Nyid gChig-Pa'i Ma-Rig-Pa*). (2) While observing the outwardly (arisen) spontaneously accomplished appearances, not realizing them as self-appearances and as free from inherent existence is the innate unenlightenment (*Lhan-sKyes Kyi Ma-Rig-Pa*). The Universal Goodness (*Kun-Tu bZang-Po*) possessed these two (unenlightenments), but then the wisdom (*Shes-Rab*) arose (and it led him to the liberated state without straying into *saṃsāra*). (3) Beings, by not realizing the power (*rTsal*), the analyzer, as non-inherent existence, self-essence, and self-power, become deluded into apprehender and apprehended (dualistic

> concepts). Then through the imaginings (*Kun-bTags*) about the two selves, one thinks, "I have arisen from that" or "that has arisen from me." This is the unenlightenment of imaginings (*Kun-brTags Kyi Ma-Rig-Pa*). Due to these three unenlightenments, the grossness of the mind increases and apprehendeds the self-glow of the five primordial wisdoms (as objects) and they result in the five elements (i.e. earth, water, fire, air, and space). For example, apprehending the white light, the glow of the mirror-like primordial wisdom, results in the element of water.... As the result of apprehending the five lights as objects, there arise the gross appearances of the container [world] of the *saṃsāra* of the three realms of the five elements. As the result of apprehending the peaceful and wrathful (enlightened) Buddha-bodies, the gross bodies of the three realms arise. As the result of apprehending the self-sound of ultimate nature, speech arises. (As the result of apprehending) the power of the intrinsic awareness as "this is my mind," the mind arises.

(ii) *The Four Conditions.* Pema Ledrel Tsal also summarizes the four conditions:[KTT 11b/6]

> (1) The innate unenlightenment, which is the (aspect of) not realizing the self-essence, is the "causal condition" (*rGyu'i rKyen*). (2) The (outward) arising of the appearances as the five lights is the "objective condition" (*dMigs-rKyen*). (3) The arising of the power of compassion as the analyzer is the "subjective condition" (*bDag-Po'i rKyen*). (4) ("The immediate preceding condition," De-Ma Thag-rKyen). This is (the condition which), once the three immediate preceding conditions have gathered (*'Dus*) became the analyzer; and thereby one becomes deluded into the apprehended and apprehender (dualities). Then one goes off course from the sphere of light and gets trapped in habituations [traces] of effectuations (*rNam-sMin Bag-Ch'ags*).

(iii) *The Twelvefold Chain of Interdependent Causation of Saṃsāra*. Beings are wandering in the delusory *saṃsāra* through the chain of the twelve links of interdependent causation. Longchen Rabjam summarizes:[TCD-I, 219a/1]

> (One wanders in *saṃsāra*) through the successive (*Lugs-'Byung*) process of twelvefold interdependent causation (*rTen-'Brel*): (1) Unenlightenment: It is the arising of the three unenlightenments, which are the non-realization of the self-essence of the power (*rTsal*) of compassion. (2) Formation: It is the four conditions that formulate *saṃsāra*. (3) Consciousness: From the formation arises the gross cognition which enjoys (*sPyod-Pa*) the modes of the objects. (4) Name and Form: From consciousness arise the name (i.e., feeling, discrimination, formation, and consciousness of the five aggregates) and form due to various *karmas*. (5) Six Sense Organs: From the name and form arise various specific elements and colors of (the six sense organs: eye, ear, nose, tongue, body, and mind). (6) Contact: From the sense organs arise enjoyment of the objects. (7) Feeling: From contact arise happiness, suffering and neutral experiences. (8) Craving: From feeling arise the cognition of attachment to happiness and dislike of suffering. (9) Grasping: From craving arise the apprehension (*Dang-Du Len-Pa*) of the objects. (10) Becoming: *Karmas* and emotional defilements having developed from grasping, the actions which bring about the birth of the next life are accomplished. (11) Birth: From becoming arises birth in one of various migrations. (12) From birth arise youth, old age, and death. Beings are deluded (into *saṃsāra* and are wandering) through the twelvefold chain of (interdependent causation) from the beginning. (For example), regarding one life, the first instant of not realizing the self-essence, when the clarity (*A'od-gSal*, luminous absorption) is dissolved and the "intermediate state of existence" (*Srid-Pa Bar-Do*) is ready to arise, is unenlightenment. (The process of life) until the cessation of the outer breathing (*Phyi-*

> *dBugs*), which is death, is the turning of the cycle of (twelvefold) interdependent causation in succession. The processes of gross and subtle dissolutions which take place following (the cessation of the outer breathing until death) are the turning in reverse (of the cycle of twelvefold interdependent causation). Then the appearances of delusions will be emptied and *saṃsāra* will collapse. At that time, first there arises the vision of original purity, the spontaneously arisen ultimate nature, *nirvāṇa*. Then there arise the appearances of the "intermediate state of ultimate nature" (*Ch'os-Nyid Bar-Do*) which are the appearances of the interdependent causation of *nirvāṇa* [cessation]. At that point, if one does not realize (that absolute nature), one will be deluded into *saṃsāra*; and if one realizes it, one becomes liberated into *nirvāṇa*. (These alternatives) are called (straying into) *saṃsāra* and liberation into *nirvāṇa*. In both the "basis" and the "appearances of the basis" there is no unenlightenment; but because of adventitious arisings like clouds (in the clear sky), and particularly because of the arising of the impure (perceptions) as *saṃsāra*, beings start to wander in the six migrations.

Based on the *Dzogpa Chenpo tantras* of the *Nyingma Gyudbum* (*rNying-Ma rGyud-'Bum*) such as *Dra Thalgyur*, *Rigpa Rang-Shar*, *Rinpoche Pungpa*, and *Trashi Dzeyden*, Longchen Rabjam elucidates the view of the Innermost Secret division of *Dzogpa Chenpo* in his *Thegchog Dzod* and other works. Based on *Thegchog Dzod*, Pema Ledrel Tsal writes:[KTT 5b/1]

> All four categories: Outer, Inner, Secret, (and Innermost Secret) category (of *Mengagde*) agree that delusion takes place by not realizing the primordial wisdom, which is present at the basis with its essence, nature and compassion. But according to the *tantras*, the unique view of the "innermost secret category" is as follows: Although it is said that there are three different ways of delusion, namely that some beings are deluded from the essence (*Ngo-Bo*), some from the experiences (*Nyams*), and some from power

(*rTsal*), actually beings are deluded by being based on not realizing the true essence (*Ngo-Bo*), and by apprehending the experiences (*Nyams*) or the modes-of-arising of the "intrinsic awareness of the ways of arising" (*'Ch'ar-Tshul Gyi Rig-Pa*) with the mind, the power (*rTsal*).

The so-called Great Primordial Basis, the common ground of the Buddha and beings or the "Youthful Vase Body" is presented (in terms of): essence as the Buddha-body, nature as the speech, and compassion as the mind. (This basis is the state) which previously neither became enlightened (or became Buddha) through realization (of the self-essence) nor strayed into mind by not realizing it. The basis was present as the un-neutralized (*Dug-'Don Ma-Byas-Pa*) quicksilver or as a crystal with its rays remaining unprojected. Then, by projecting outwardly, the glow (*gDangs*) of the essence of five energies or air (*Rlung-Nga*), the life-energy (*Srog-Rlung*, S. *Prāṇa*, life-force) with its four aspects, which is present in the intrinsic awareness, breaks the shell of the "youthful vase body" (*gZhon-Nu Bum-sKu*). Then from the power (*rTsal*) or glow (*gDangs*) of the spontaneous accomplishment (*Lhun-Grub*) arise the appearances of five lights (*A'od-lNga*), and simultaneously the glow of compassion, the intrinsic awareness, arises in the mode of analytical cognition. (At that point), the aspect of merely not realizing the self-nature (of the cognition and the arising as it is) constitutes the so-called unenlightenment in relation to enlightenment. At that time the basis is not changed, but it seems to be changed because of the "appearances of the basis" and it is called the changes in the intrinsic awareness (that occurred due to the) changes of appearances in the intrinsic awareness (*sNang-Ba-La Rig-Pa 'Gyur-Ba*). At that time, from the cloudless sky-like appearances (*sNgang-Ba*) of the primordial purity, arise the "eight modes of arising of spontaneous accomplishments" as the self-appearances. (These appearances are called) the appearance in the nature of the precious casket (*Rin-Po-Ch'e'i Gau*). It is like a dream,

> the appearances having arisen in their own state, but they have neither realized their self-essence (*Rang-Ngo*), which is non-inherent existence (*Rang-bZhin Med-Pa*), nor have there (yet) arisen any gross mental concepts of extremes of apprehender and apprehended. (The process of arising of appearances) up to this point is called the mode of "appearances of the basis" from the "basis."

Longchen Rabjam explains the five energies or air (*Rlung*)★:[ZYD 3b/5]

> In the state of intrinsic awareness the life-energy (*Srog-Rlung*, Skt., *Prāṇa*, life-force) with its four aspects is present in the nature of primordial wisdom: (1) The root life-energy is the presence of the primordial wisdom (*Ye-Shes*) of the intrinsic awareness (*Rig-Pa*) as wisdom (*Shes-Rab*). This is the presence of the potential for arising of both: the arising of concepts and analysis, which are the foundation of delusion, and of self-awareness, the foundation of liberation, while nothing (yet) has arisen (as anything). At that point, it (the root life-energy) is present as the primordial wisdom which sees the objects (*Yul Rig-Pa'i Ye-Shes*). So it is the basis of arising of all the primordial wisdoms. The four secondary aspects (*Yan-Lag*) are the self-arisen power or glow which developed from the root energy. (2) The upward moving energy (*Gyen-rGyu*) which is the conveyance of primordial wisdom. (3) The downward clearing energy (*Thur-Sel*) is the radiant glow of wis-

★According to common medical texts given in *Tibetan Buddhist Medicine and Psychiatry*, by Terry Clifford, Samuel Weiser, New York, page 92:

1. Srog-dzin	-"life-accompanying wind"	-assists breathing	-seat in heart center
2. Gyen-rgyu	-"upward moving wind"	-assists speech	-seat in chest, but travels to nose and gullet.
3. Khyab-byed	-"pervasive wind"	-assists muscular motions	-seat in head but travels to all parts of body.
4. Me-mnyam	-"fire-accompanying wind"	-assists digestion and assimilation	-seat in abdomen but travels to all parts of intestines and stomach.
5. Thur-sel	-"downward clearing wind"	-assists secretion	-seat in "secret" genital center but travels to intestines, bladder, sexual organs, and thighs.)

dom. (4) The heat-assimilated energy (*Me-Dang mNyam-Pa*) has the power of causing assimilation or nurturing. (5) Pervasive energy (*Khyab-Byed*) has the power of causing completion.

The View of the Innermost Secret Category

(a) *Basis*

The following are statements by Longchen Rabjam on the view of the Innermost Secret cycle of *Mengagde*:[TCD-I, 195b/3]

> The Primordial Basis (*Thog-Ma'i gZhi*): Its essence (*Ngo-Bo*) is primordially pure like an immaculate crystal. It does not exist either as things or (as a) characteristic. Its nature (*Rang-bZhin*) is spontaneous accomplishment, and although in the whiteness (of the crystal-like nature) the subtle self-light is present as the profound (or inner) clarity (*gTing-gSal Du*), it does not appear outwardly (*Phyi-gSal*) as there are no conditions. So the basis is present in the mode of "the youthful vase body" since its outer covering (*rGya*) is not (yet) broken. The essence (of the primordial basis) is emptiness as it is primordially pure and there are no things in it. But the subtle (*Phra-Mo*) intrinsic awareness, the self-light of the profound glow, is naturally accomplished without hindrances. So it presents itself as the "basis of arising" of all the appearances. Yet its essence does not appear outwardly in the characteristics of lights, forms, or colors. In the vast expanse of essence, the primordial purity, is present the spontaneously accomplished primordial glow (*Ye-gDangs*), the self-light (*Rang-A'od*) of the subtle and profound clarity (*gTing-gSal*) and intrinsic wisdom. They are not in the modes of either one, different or separate, but are present as the supreme clarity, as the sphere of the precious spontaneous accomplishment (*Lhun-Grub Rin-Po-Ch'e'i sBubs*), as the field of the "youthful vase body" and as the nature of essence, nature and compassion. As its essence is emptiness, it does not exist as things or characteristics. As its nature is clar-

> ity, it has never abandoned the self-nature of appearances of primordial glow. Since its compassion [power] is intrinsic awareness, it is present as the ceaseless basis of the arising of knowledge (*mKhyen-Pa*) as the primordial wisdom.

Longchen Rabjam continues:[TCD-I, 197a/5]

> If you see from the standpoint of the essence (of the basis), which is the primordially pure, nothing exists, and the lights, forms, and colors of the outer clarity (*Phyi-gSal*) are not distinguishable. But (if you see from the standpoint of) the nature (of the basis), which is the spontaneously accomplished ultimate sphere, there is the primordial glow, which is the utmost subtle appearances of the five lights, forms, rays, and *Thigles* in the ultimate sphere. So (the nature) dwells as the utmost subtle intrinsic wisdom, the inner clarity (*Nang-gSal*).

He continues:[TCD-I, 197b/2]

> The nature of primordial purity is spontaneously accomplished. Its ultimate sphere, the utmost subtle primordial wisdom, the inner (dwelling) presents itself as the subtle appearances of the luminous clarity, the primordial glow. (The ultimate sphere) is free from the extreme of eternalism as there is no assertion that it is gross outer clarity (which is projecting). It is free from nihilism as it is asserted as a subtle inner clarity. Thus, the spontaneously arisen primordial wisdom, free from extremes, is nonexistent as it is emptiness in its essence, and it is ceaseless appearances as it is clarity in its nature. It is the basis of all the arisings as it is ceaseless in its compassion (power). This is the mode of the true nature of the basis.

(b) *Arisings of the Appearance from the Basis*

Longchen Rabjam explains:[TCD-I, 202b/5]

> In the primordial ultimate sphere, the "youthful vase body" is present in its essence as the Buddha-body, in na-

> ture as the speech and in compassion as the mind. By the outward emerging of the glow of the five energies, the life-energy with its four branches, which dwell as the heart (*sNying-Po*) within the intrinsic awareness, breaks the shell of the "youthful vase body." Then from the glow of spontaneous accomplishment arise the appearances of five lights. Simultaneously, the glow of compassion, the intrinsic awareness, arises as the cognition which analyzes the modes (of appearances). At that point, the aspect of just not realizing the self-essence (of the cognition and appearances) functions as the so-called unenlightenment (*Ma-Rig-Pa*) (which is established) in relation to enlightenment. At that time, although the basis is not changed, it seems to be changed because of appearances of the intrinsic awareness (*Rig-Pa-La sNang-Ba 'Gyur-Ba*). At that time, from the state of cloudless sky-like appearances of original purity, arise the "eight modes of arising of spontaneous accomplishment" as self-appearances.

(c) *The Way of Liberation of Universal Goodness (Kuntu Zangpo)*
Longchen Rabjam writes:[TCD-I, 213a/5]

> When the inner glow arises outwardly from the primordial ultimate sphere and the compassion [power] arises simply as the aspect of not (yet) realizing the (self-essence of the) intrinsic awareness itself (as it is), at that point, by watching outwardly the "appearances of the basis" one realizes them inwardly as the self-appearances. At that very instant of realization, the unenlightenments will be purified and the mode of "(eight) spontaneous accomplishments" of the basis will dissolve into the state of primordial purity and will remain in it.

The liberation as, or of, the Universal Goodness is taking place all the time, and it is not a matter of one person's or some people's having achieved such liberation in the past. Pema Ledrel Tsal writes:[KTT 10a/6]

> One shouldn't think that the mode of liberation of Universal Goodness (*Kun-Tu bZang-Po*, the Primordial Buddha) is a matter of a liberation that was attained in an ancient time. Because at the very time of our speaking now, there are many beings who are being deluded from the basis, who are liberated, and who are confused on the border between liberation and delusion.

In *Dzogpa Chenpo* the attainment of Buddhahood is not seeking something from other sources but is liberation of the intrinsic awareness in its own nature. Jigmed Lingpa writes:[NS 344a/4]

> *Dzogpa Chenpo* just gives the designation of attainment of Buddhahood to the liberation of the intrinsic awareness in its own natural state. But it does not have aspiration or seeking for Buddhahood from any other source. So the Buddhas of the three times are perfected in the state of natural intrinsic awareness free from apprehended and apprehender (the dualistic concepts).

(d) *Delusion of Beings Due to Unenlightenment*

Longchen Rabjam writes:[TCD-I, 216b/6]

> In the "primordial basis" there is no delusion. But when the "appearances of the basis" arise, (there arises) the cognition (*Shes-Pa*) which does not realize the self-essence, and that is a neutral cognition rooted in unenlightenment, which takes the "appearances of the basis" as separate (entities), and thereby one becomes deluded as a being.

Pema Ledrel Tsal writes:[NN 35a/5]

> Both the objects and the subjects of the delusions are nonexistent in their true meaning. But they appear in delusion and formulate the emotional defilements and the virtuous, unvirtuous, and neutral *karmas*. First, having the five lights becomes the ground of delusion for the objects, having the intrinsic awareness becomes the ground of de-

> lusion for the mind, and having the peaceful and wrathful forms (of the deities) becomes the ground of delusion for the body—then there occurs the building up of the habits of objects, subjects, and of various delusions. And (beings) wander around (in *saṃsāra*) experiencing happiness and suffering endlessly like the revolving of an irrigation wheel.

DIVISIONS OF *MENGAGDE*

The *Dzogpa Chenpo* master Śrīsiṅha classified the *Mengagde* teachings into Four Categories (*sKor-bZhi*). Jigmed Lingpa writes:[NS 313a/4]

> In *Mengagde* (there are four categories): The Outer Category, which is like the body, the Inner Category, which is like the eyes, the Secret Category, which is like the heart, and the Innermost Secret Category, which is like the complete body.

Longchen Rabjam explains:[GD 178a/4]

> (a) Outer Category (*Phyi-sKor*): In essence (*Ngo-Bo*), as there are no emotions to be abandoned, the five poisons are present as the path (of training). In nature (*Rang-bZhin*), as there are no efforts, whatever arises appears as the attributes of the ultimate nature. In character (*mTshan-Nyid*), as there are no partialities, the emptiness is not inclined to any (aspect).
> (b) Inner Category (*Nang-sKor*): In essence, as it doesn't exist as real form, it is the ultimate nature free from characteristics. In nature, as it is free from comings and goings, it is the primordial wisdom of the eternal continuum. In character, as it penetrates into (both *saṃsāra* and *nirvāṇa*), it is like the root (of a tree), as it is the direct realization (of the nature), it is like the trunk, as it is the development (of the power of appearances in various forms), it is like the branches, as it is the (ceaseless) clarity, it is like

flowers, and as it is the ripened (fruition) it is like fruit (of a tree).
(c) Secret Category (*gSang-sKor*): In essence, as the introduction (to the intrinsic awareness) and realizations of it are simultaneous, it doesn't rely on (the three wisdoms of) study, thinking and meditation. In nature, as the enlightenment and the cessation of breathing [death] are simultaneous, it doesn't rely on diligence and strength of experiences (*Goms-sTobs*). In character, as the development of compassion [power] and enlightenment are simultaneous, it doesn't rely on completion of the two accumulations.
(d) Innermost Secret Category(*gSang-Ba Bla-Med*): In essence, as it doesn't depend on words, it doesn't rely on the wisdom of analysis. In nature, as it is the direct realization, it doesn't remain in views of mental analysis. In character, as it is the perfection of the four visions, it doesn't have expectations (for the attainment of) three Buddha-bodies and five primordial wisdoms. Because, in this practice, one actualizes the primordially and spontaneously accomplished (result) in this very lifetime.

Pema Ledrel Tsal explains the distinctions of the four categories while explicating a four-line quotation from *Ati Kodpa Chenpo (A-Ti bKod-Pa Ch'en-Po) tantra*:[NCC 8a/2]

Generally, none of the four categories differ as to the ascertaining of the ultimate nature of primordial purity (of *Threg-chod*) either directly or indirectly. In any case, the first line, on (a) the outer category, explains the ultimate nature of the primordial basis in detail, but there are no explanations how the signs (*brDa*), meaning (*Don*) and characteristics (*rTags*) signify (the nature), how the path of fourfold visions arise, how the lights (*sGron-Ma*) arise in the intermediate state (*Bar-Do*), or how one attains liberation into the sphere (*sBubs*) of spontaneously accomplished result. (b) The second line (on the inner category), explains how the signs, meaning, and characteristics of the path signify the meaning but not other aspects (the basis

> and results). (c) The secret category, which is called "like the heart," explains the way of meditation of "four natural contemplations" (*Chog-bZhag bZhi*) of yogis, but not more (of the basis and results). (d) The innermost secret category is like a person who possesses a complete body and faculties. It explains the ultimate nature of the primordial basis, the way of signifying (the nature) by signs, meaning and characteristics, the way of arising of the path of the four categories, the way of arising of the lights in the intermediate state, and the way of liberation into the sphere of spontaneously accomplished result. Besides that, in this (innermost secret category) are explained the entire teachings of the path as the complete body, a path that is (complete) for the practice of every individual.

Longchen Rabjam characterizes the Innermost Secret Category as follows:[TCD-I, 83a/5]

> As it does not rely on words, it does not depend on (intellectual) wisdoms. As it realizes the nature directly, it does not dwell in the view of mental analysis. As the characteristics of the four visions are perfected, it does not depend on the results of three Buddha-bodies and five primordial wisdoms. So this is the innermost secret category. In the (*yānas*) lower than this, practitioners trust to mental analysis for (the realization of) the ultimate nature. But here (the ultimate nature) is perceived as the object of the direct sense (*mNgon-Sum Dang-Po*) through the power of the Lama. So it is supreme.

MEDITATION OF *MENGAGDE*

Jigmed Lingpa explains:[YL 15b/3]

> In this *yāna* the realization of the essence of the mind itself, which from primordial time is present as the great liberation, is called the intrinsic awareness (*Rig-Pa*). By maintaining the continuity of (that realized intrinsic awareness), one attains enlightenment by force.

He continues:[YL 16b/4]

> For a person who is (still) on the ordinary path (of training), when he sees a mountain, in the first moment it is unavoidable not to have the thought, "this is a mountain," but in the second moment, because of the perfection (*rDzogs-Pa*) of the power (*rTsal*) of the mind and mental events which analyze the nature of the mountain, the concept of mountain disappears without any trace. At that time, although the appearance of the mountain (in the mind) has not ceased, one will gain experience in dwelling in the ultimate nature, in which there is no apprehension of (the appearance of the mountain). Having purified (all the phenomenal existents) as the simultaneous liberation-at-arising (*Shar-Grol*), to unify(*'Dres-Pa*) the appearances and mind (indivisibly) is the unerring *Dzogpa Chenpo.*

DIVISIONS OF MEDITATION OF *MENGAGDE*

In general there are two major categories of training in *Mengagde.* They are *Thregchod* (*Khregs-Ch'od*, Cutting Through) and *Thodgal* (*Thod-rGal*, the Direct Approach). In *Mutig Threngwa* (*Mu-Tig 'Phreng-Ba*) *tantra* it is said:[MT 289a/3] "*Thregchod* and *Thodgal* are the trainings." Pema Ledrel Tsal describes them:[KT 208a/3]

> *Thregchod* is the path through which one trains on the naked intrinsic awareness, without relying on the appearances [visions] of clarity (of *Thodgal*) and which liberates without efforts. It is the crucial path for people who are intellectually sharp but lazy about (practicing for) attaining enlightenment. *Thodgal* is (the path through which one attains) liberation with efforts. Relying on appearances [visions] of clarity (*A'od-gSal Gyi sNang-Ba*), diligent people purify their gross bodies in this very lifetime and attain enlightenment.

However, *Thregchod* is the essence of the training of *Dzogpa*

Chenpo and *Thodgal* is specifically related to the Innermost Secret Division of *Mengagde*. Natshog Rangtrol explains that the entire *Dzogpa Chenpo* meditations are included in the training of *Thregchod* and *Thodgal:*[DM 7b/2]

> Generally, there are inconceivable divisions of practice in *Dzogpa Chenpo*, such as Outer *Semde*, Inner *Longde*, Secret *Mengagde* and the Innermost Secret, as well as *Ati*, *Chiti* (*sPyi-Ti*) and *Yangti*. But in brief they are all included in *Thregchod*, the training on the (union of) intrinsic awareness and emptiness, and *Thodgal*, the training on (union of) appearances and emptiness.

The root of both *Thregchod* and *Thodgal* is naked realization of the intrinsic awareness. Jigmed Lingpa writes:[NS 349b/5]

> If one could not nakedly bring out (or realize) the intrinsic awareness, the root of both "original purity" and "spontaneous acomplishment," then just gaining experiences in the phenomena of emptiness-form of *Thodgal* will not produce any benefits, except to make one take birth in the form realms.

In *Dzogpa Chenpo* practices the trainings on channels, energy [air] and essence of the *tantras* are also included. Natshog Rangtrol writes:[MCC 38b/2]

> We try to emphasize the practice as explained in the cycles of *Dzogpa Chenpo* teachings, which unite all the channels as the channels of primordial wisdom, the ultimate sphere of freedom from elaborations, all the energy [air] as the energy of primordial wisdom, the self-clarity of intrinsic awareness, and all the essences (*Thig-Le*) as the essence of great blissful primordial wisdom, unfabricated and all-pervading essence.

On the particularity of the luminous absorption of *Atiyoga*, Jigmed Tenpa'i Nyima says:[DC 27a/2]

> The luminous absorption of bliss, clarity and no-thoughts

(*bDe-gSal Mi-rTog-Pa'i A'od-gSal*) is expounded clearly in all the *anuttaratantras*. But to emphasize the naked bringing out of the aspect of knowledge, which is the aspect of the intrinsic awareness or the compassion [power] (of the intrinsic awareness), and then through that to train on the path of luminous absorption, is the special skill of the *Vajra*-summit [*Dzogpa Chenpo*].

(a) *Thregchod* (*Khregs-Ch'od, Cutting Through*)
Jigmed Lingpa writes:[NS 332b/4]

> By relying on the primordial purity, the emptiness, to bring forth the intrinsic awareness nakedly, free from elaboration, and to dissolve (the phenomenal existents into the) ultimate nature, the emptiness, (is *Thregchod*).

Lochen Dharmaśrī explains:[ZL 41b/1]

> (*Thregchod*) is the contemplation in the view (*lTa-Ba*) of primordial purity without waverings.... The master Garab Dorje (*Prahevajra*) said in *Ati Zabdon Nyingpo* (*Ati Zab-Don sNying-Po*):
>
> "The nature of the mind is Buddha from the beginning.
> Mind is like space, it has neither birth nor cessation.
> Having realized the pure and equalness meaning of phenomena,
> To remain in it without seeking is the meditation."
>
> There are four stages of realizations through meditation. As it is said,
>
> "They are dwelling, unmoving, equalness and spontaneity."
>
> In *Rigpa Khuchug* it is said:[RK 209a/3]
> Remaining naturally is the contemplation.

Mipham summarizes the *Dzogpa Chenpo* meditation in the following lines:[YDGD 37b/3]

> Having realized the view, and having contemplated effort-

> lessly on the self-present essence of primordial wisdom without negations or defendings and dispellings or maintainings, one realizes the meaning of the ultimate nature directly as it is. Although (both categories of *Dzogpa Chenpo* meditation) are the same in using the effortless self-arisen intrinsic awareness as the path in the formless "primordial purity" (*rNam-Med Ka-Dag of Khregchod*) the practice is, among others, on the fourfold "natural contemplations" (*Chog-bZhag*). In the "spontaneous accomplishment" (*Lhun-Grub* = *Thodgal*) with form, having reversed (*bZlog*) the delusions into the basis through such training as the "threefold glance" (*gZigs-sTang*), one (meditates) on perfecting the "four visions" (*sNang-bZhi*).

Jigmed Lingpa explains the four "natural contemplations":YL 17a/6

> On the method of entering into the four natural contemplations (*Chog-bZhag bZhi*) it is said in *Dronma Nangched* (*sGron-Ma sNang-Byed*):
>
> > Mountain (-like) natural contemplation is the perfection of view.
> > Ocean (-like) natural contemplation is the perfection of meditation. Contemplation naturally on appearances [percepts] is the perfection of actions.
> > Contemplation on intrinsic awareness naturally is the perfection of result.
> > A *Yogi* who has attained the four perfections
> > Has united with the absolute meaning.
>
> (a) By the view of mountain-like natural contemplation (*lTa-Ba Ri-Bo Chog-bZhag*), having been introduced to the freedom from concepts (*bSam-Ngo*) as it is, one contemplates in the great self-clarity, the intrinsic awareness freely and changelessly, without having been influenced by the antidote of meditation of mental efforts and apprehensions. (b) In the meditation of ocean-like natural contemplation (*sGom-Pa rGya-mTsho Chog-bZhag*), having

placed the body in the cross-legged posture with the eyes staring widely into space, one clears the mind (*Shes-Pa*), like the ocean unmoved by waves, through the state of not expanding the apprehension of the (objective) appearances of the six senses. (c) By the actions of instructional natural contemplation(*sPyod-Pa Man-Ngag Chog-bZhag*), having relaxed the three doors naturally, one brings forth nakedly the self-clear intrinsic awareness from the coverings of view and meditation and maintains it naturally. (d) By the result of unmodified natural contemplation (*'Bras-Bu Ma-bChos Chog-bZhag*), having contemplated on the five (external) objects naturally as they are, inwardly there arises the naked self-clarity vividly. Also thereby having maintained the five airs [energies] in the ultimate sphere, externally the clarity of self-pure perceptions arises (in the form of) smoke, mirage, rainbow rays, and so on as the common secrets.

Jigmed Lingpa writes:[NS 333a/2]

According to this, the king of the *yānas*, the essence (*Ngo-Bo*) of the intrinsic awareness is primordially free from elaborations. Therefore, there is nothing to be liberated which wasn't free. So it is the primordially pure intrinsic awareness or the natural state of original purity, as it is, without modifications. (It possesses the signs of the "three doors of liberation" (*rNam-Thar sGo-gSum*):

(a) In the basis (view), (the intrinsic awareness) is present without falling into any dimensions (*rGya*). As its nature is free from inherent existence, it is free from falling into any extremes. It is free from the intellect of conceptualizations of self and it is the naked and unhindered intrinsic awareness which is inconceivable and inexpressible. Thus it dwells in the "emptiness (*sTong-Pa Nyid or Ngo-Bo Nyid Med-Pa*) door of liberation."

(b) In the path (meditation), (the intrinsic awareness) transcends (being an object) of characterization by words and letters and it is not reachable by the mind which appre-

> hends subject and object as dual. So it is the natural entering into the "characterless (*mTshan-Ma Med-Pa*) door of liberation."
> (c) In the result, as there is neither fear nor expectation concerning achievements, it is the attainment of the ultimate sphere "(the door of liberation of) freedom from aspirations" (*sMon-Pa Med-Pa*).
>
> In any case, as (the intrinsic awareness) is the remaining in the secret link (*Dam-Tshig*), the lineage of the vajra-essence clarity, which is the full perfection of the virtues of intrinsic awareness, from it all the virtues of the three Buddha-bodies arise without any efforts.

Sogpo Tentar interprets:[ST 264a/6]

> As the intrinsic awareness is not present as a knowable object, it transcends both selves, the self of person and the self of phenomena, which apprehend (things) as "I" and "my." There is nothing else that is the meditator or to be meditated upon. If one remains in the true nature without modifications, the intrinsic awareness wisdom emerges nakedly from the womb of the eight consciousnesses, and one will see it nakedly. When (the realization of) such ultimate nature is established permanently, no ignorant apprehensions will be able to drag one into the cycle of existences. Like space, it does not change according to the clouds.... When one realizes such meaning, since the attachment to objects and to self are not created by a creator but are established by the strength of mental concepts, although for a while it appears that they have arisen from the basis and root which is (actually) non-existent even (to the size of) an atom, they will be liberated by being perfected as unborn at the very moment of their arising. Then there is no need of realization of any other wisdom. At that time, all the conventional methods created by mind, such as recitation, memorization, meditation, composition and pondering dissolve like a drawing on water. And then, as one dissolves the phenomenal appearances, all the three

aggregates (*Tshogs-Pa*), the external appearances, the internal body and the secret mind become free from their gross aspects, and one realizes them as (the union of) emptiness and clarity, like the reflection of the moon on water. For such a person there is no hindrance to passing through mountains and rocks. As his mind dwells in the noble truth, he possesses (the virtues) such as (divine) eyes and foreknowledge. He is free from rebirth.... If he attains liberation in the state of emptiness, the equalness and primordial purity (*sTong-Pa Dag-mNyam Ka-Dag Gi Sa*), he purifies even the four elements of his (mortal) body with the fire of primordial wisdom, and he disappears into space with miracles like the evaporation of mist, and his intrinsic awareness remains in the ultimate sphere. Then it is called the Buddhahood free from aspirations (for further attainments)... In some cases, when it is beneficial for others, the (*yogi*) blesses the dissolved atoms to remain in the form of *Ringsels* (*Ring-bSrel, relics*)

(b) *Thogdal* (*Thod-rGal, the Direct Approach*)
Jigmed Lingpa summarizes:[NS 332b/5]

> Relying on appearances (or visions), the spontaneous accomplishment of purifying (*Dangs*) the gross aspects into the clarity [luminous absorption] and dissolving the (phenomena into the) ultimate nature of appearances (is *Thodgal*).

Lochen Dharmaśrī also summarizes:[ZL 41b/4]

> Relying on six crucial means (of training), the four visions arise gradually. (The four visions are:) the Direct (Realization of) Ultimate Nature (*Ch'os-Nyid mNgon-gSum*), Development of Experiences (*Nyams Gong-'Phel*), Perfection of Intrinsic Awareness (*Rig-Pa Tshad-Phebs*) and Dissolution of (phenomena into) the Ultimate Nature (*Ch'os-Nyid Zad-Pa*).

In *Dra Thalgyur* (*sGra Thal-'Gyur*) *tantra* it is said:[GT 224a]

> The vision of Direct (Realization) of the Ultimate Nature
> Transcends (even) the word "apprehender," the mental analysis.
> The vision of Development of Experience
> Dissolves the delusory appearances
> And attains the primordial wisdom of the intermediate state.
> The vision of Perfection of Intrinsic Awareness
> Transcends the conceptual appearances of the path of the three *kāyas*.
> The vision of Exhaustion into the Ultimate Nature
> Ends the continuation of the chain of *saṃsāra*.

Jigmed Lingpa explains that although the attainments of the four visions correspond to the paths of the common *yānas*, the attainments of the paths of this *yāna* are greatly superior and swifter.[YL 37b/1]

> In terms of the things to be purified and the results of purification, these four stages partially correspond (*Phyogs-mTshungs*) to the five paths of common *pāramitāyāna* (of the *sūtric* path), but there are great differences in the speed of the paths, like the difference between the speed of a horse-drawn chariot and the sun and moon.

The following is a summary of the "six crucial means" (*gNad-Drug*) given in *Yeshey Lama*:[YL 22b/6]

> The "six crucial means" of training are the three crucial means of the three doors (*sGo-gSum*) and the three crucial means with which one concentrates on the clarity or luminous absorption (*A'od-gSal*). The three crucial means of the three doors are: (a) the three postures of the body: the posture of a lion for the *Dharmakāya*, of an elephant for the *Sambhogakāya* and of a sage for the *Nirmāṇakāya*, (b) the crucial means of speech is to maintain silence from expression, and (c) the crucial means of mind is to concentrate on external space. The three crucial means by which to concentrate on the luminous absorption are: (a)

> the crucial means of the door of arising, the eyes with the three ways of glancing of the three *Kāyas,* (b) the crucial means of the basis of arising, the cloudless sky (or sun or lamp), and (c) the crucial means of breathing, breathing naturally from the mouth and concentration of the intrinsic awareness on the sky, as the outer ultimate sphere brings the arising of the inner ultimate sphere as the outer ultimate sphere.

Gyurmed Tshewang Chogtrub explains the superiority of *Thodgal:*[LNT-I,147b/4]

> Thregchod liberates the delusory appearances, the objects of the apprehensions, into their true nature, without leaving any basis and root. In this (*Thodgal*), all the aspects of appearances of the three realms (*Khams-gSum*) are liberated as the clarity of the *Thigles* of five lights, the natural profundity (*Rang-gDangs*) of the intrinsic awareness. So this is superior to the lower trainings.

At the time of death an accomplished *yogi* of *Thodgal*, if he wishes, will transform his body into an intrinsic light body visible only to those who possess pure eyes, and will serve living beings until this world is emptied or until there is no further reason for him to remain. Guru Padmasambhava and Vimalamitra both came to Tibet in this body. Jigmed Lingpa explains the two attainments:[YL 46a/4]

> There are two attainments, the power [control] over birth and over entering (*sKye-'Jug*). (a) The attainment of power over birth: One transforms into the body of Great Transformation (*'Pho-Ba Ch'en-Po*) and fulfills the needs of living beings... One shines forth in (the body of) lights after having dissolved the atoms (of the mortal body). The attainment of power over birth and entering is the speciality of *Thodgal*. Because in *Thregchod* there is nothing else but that after dissolving the body into atoms (*Lus rDul-Phran-Du Dengs*, total dissolution) and the mind into ultimate nature, one attains liberation in original purity.... (b) The

> attainment of power over entering: If there is no way to serve beings with that (particular) form of body, . . . he dissolves his (light) body (of Great Transformation), like mist dissolving into the sky and enters into the inner ultimate sphere. Thereby until *saṃsāra* has ceased, he acts for others through enlightened activities of the inseparability of (four) Buddha-bodies and (five) primordial wisdoms.

ATTAINMENT OF THE PATHS AND STAGES OF *DZOGPA CHENPO*

In *Dzogpa Chenpo* one attains and perfects the paths and stages as the result of the meditative training. Longchen Rabjam's interpretation of this matter is quoted briefly in section eleven, part II, of this book.

The five paths of Buddhist training and attainments are completed in the instant realization of the intrinsic awareness of *Dzogpa Chenpo*. Paltul Jigmed Chokyi Wangpo writes:[BGT 33b/2]

> Generally in the causal and characteristic (*sūtric*) *yānas*, having developed the mind of enlightenment, one trains on the accumulations of merits and wisdom for countless eons. It is the Path of Accumulation. By developing the wisdom produced by meditation, one is joined to the wisdom of the Path of Seeing (the truth). It is the Path of Application. Seeing directly the (true) nature of phenomena and the absolute nature (of all phenomena) of the Four Truths is the Path of Seeing. The (means that) causes one to gain experiences of the (realization which) has been seen is the Path of Meditation. Having completed the trainings, when there is no more training, it is the Path of No More Training (Buddhahood). In *Dzogpa Chenpo* these Five Paths are perfected instantly.

He continues:[BGT 35a/5]

> (In *Dzogpa Chenpo*) by the aspect of realizing the meditative primordial wisdom—thorough and free from elabora-

> tions—one spontaneously completes the aspects of skillful means, such as generosity, without concepts and attachments. Also one develops the appearances of the power of discriminative wisdom and the illusion-like unreal compassion from the subsequent cognition (of the off-meditative state, *rJes-Shes*). So, in *Dzogpa Chenpo* one perfects the vast accumulation of merits and primordial wisdom instantly. That is why the great Rongzom (*Rong-Zom*, 11th century) defines *Dzogpa Chenpo*, saying: 'it is (called) the Great Perfection (*Dzogpa Chenpo*) as it perfects the vast dual accumulations.' Accordingly, the realizing of the essence of intrinsic awareness (of *Dzogpa Chenpo*)—the instant perfection of the great accumulations—is the Path of Accumulations. Some people (who claim to be *Dzogpa Chenpo* teachers) deprecate (the dual accumulations), saying: "A *yogi* who has realized *Dzogpa Chenpo* concentrates only on the intrinsic awareness, and all the other (trainings) in skillful means are errors." Some others (who claim to be scholars) assert that for a *yogi* who has realized the view (of *Dzogpa Chenpo*) there won't be any virtues, such as compassion and renunciation. Upon hearing such evil assertions, some people who boast of being scholars (of Buddhism), without examining (the true meaning of *Dzogpa Chenpo*), slander and commit grave *karmas* of "renunciation of Dharma" (*Ch'os-sPang*) saying: "*Dzogpa Chenpo* is not pure doctrine as it despises the aspect of (virtuous) activities." None of them have understood the slightest meaning of *Dzogpa Chenpo*, and they haven't even witnessed the lives of the accomplished masters of *Dzogpa Chenpo*.

All the canonical and commentarial texts of *Dzogpa Chenpo* state the following:[BGT 36b/3]

> When one realizes the meaning of *Dzogpa Chenpo* directly, all the subsequent cognitions (of the off-meditative state) will arise as free from concepts and attachments. Thereby, one will naturally become free from the attachment to ma-

> terial things, etc., and all the anger, animosity and attachment, and hatred towards self and others becomes purified as self-liberation. Naturally, the harmful activities will be uprooted and will remain in the "four disciplines of the ascetic" (*dGe-sByong Gi Ch'os-bZhi*). The four disciplines of ascetics are: Do not curse (*gShe-Ba*) others even though you are cursed by them, do not get angry (*Khro-Ba*) with others even though they are angry with you, do not insult (*mTshang Bru*) others even though you have been insulted, and do not beat (*rDeg-Pa*) others even though you have been beaten by them. One remains in the "stream-like natural continuum training" (*Ch'u-Bo'i rGyun-Gyi rNal-'Byor*) with effortless efforts. When one has aroused the power of the light of "spontaneously arisen wisdom" (*Shes-Rab Rang-Byung-Gi sGron-Ma*) as the meditative wisdom, and it has burst (*Klong-rDol*) into the depth of knowledge of words and meanings, all the virtues of the six perfections arise in one naturally without efforts.

These results will be understood even by reading the lives of Longchen Rabjam, Jigmed Lingpa and others.[BGT 39a/3]

> Owing to completion of the dual accumulations, the power of the subsequent cognition (of the off-meditative state), the obscurations of the path become thinner, and one joins the meditative wisdom, the insight of the meaning of exhaustion of phenomena—this is the Path of Application. At that time, seeing all the phenomenal existents which are comprehended in the fourfold truth as the play of inconceivable primordial wisdom, free from elaborations, is the Path of Seeing. Training on the meaning of what one has seen with stream-like meditationless training is the Path of Meditation. Having no further path to pursue since all the paths and stages are completed as one, the effortless state (of *Dzogpa Chenpo*), is the Path of No More Training (Buddhahood).

Rigpa Rangshar Chenpo tantra of *Mengagde* explains sixteen stages of attainment. They are not stages of attainment of different virtues or phenomena, however, but are phases of the realization and perfection of the same visions and intrinsic awareness, the attainments of liberation in this lifetime and in the intermediate state. As Kongtul Yonten Gyatsho interprets these phases,[SKG IV, 167b] they constitute the uniqueness of the *Dzogpa Chenpo* path. The first ten or eleven stages are identical in structure to the stages enumerated in *Mahāyāna sūtras* and the last ones are unique to the esoteric path. The *tantra* says:[RR 139a/2]

> The stages (of attainment) are not something other (than the realization of the intrinsic awareness itself). All the stages are perfected by a person who has realized the (ultimate) truth. For the person who has been introduced (to or has realized the intrinsic awareness): (the aspect of) having joy at the realization of the truth is the attainment of the first stage, "the Joyous." Recognizing it (the realization) as the self-perception of the intrinsic awareness is the second stage, "the Pure." Gaining experience of it is the third stage, "the Light-maker." Gaining experience of it by seeing the vison of lights is the fourth stage, "the Radiant." Seeing the primordial wisdom by having purified the emotional defilements naturally and by gaining experience in the insight of the vision of primordial wisdom is the fifth stage, "the Invincible." (Seeing) the light-body is the sixth stage, "the Actualization." Moving far away from the emotional defilements by perfecting the experiences is the seventh stage, "the Far-ranging." Not moving from that state is the eighth stage, "the Unshakable." The perfection of the virtues is the ninth stage, "the Excellent Wisdom." Having maintained (*Zin*) one's senses (*Shes-Pa*) in the vision of the primordial wisdom, the visions arise naturally, then seeing all the phenomenal existents as clouds (in the one sky) is the tenth stage, "the Cloud of Dharma." These (stages) are attained (in this way) by a person who has not abandoned this realm (*sBubs*; i.e.,

> life). A person who has abandoned this realm (*sBubs*; i.e., life or world and is in the intermediate state) does not attain the stages in this manner. (For him) upon the cessation of the delusory appearances, the arising of the visions of assemblages is the eleventh stage, "the Total Light." Having no attachment even to that vision (of assemblages) and being unstained by any internal and external phenomena is the twelfth stage, "the Unstained Lotus." The arising of chains of rays of the primordial wisdom from one's heart and their being present as the five assemblages of lights in the sky is the thirteenth stage, "the Great Assembly of the Wheel of Letters." Remaining in the vision of primordial wisdom is the fourteenth stage, "the Great Bliss." Attainment of certainty (*Nges-Pa*) in the spontaneously accomplished state is the fifteenth stage, "the *Vajradhara*." The arising of the primordial wisdom spontaneously in the state of primordial purity is the sixteenth stage, "the Supreme Primordial Wisdom," for there is no stage that surpasses it. . . . Although there are an inconceivable number of beings, there is only one essence of primordial wisdom. There is no other so-called path or stage. There is no need of training and attainment in (any other) path or stage.

As a result of the realization and perfection of *Dzogpa Chenpo*, one becomes free from emotions such as anger and pride and enriched with virtues such as compassion and insight. Mipham Namgyal writes:[NM 77a/2]

> Even the virtues of realization progress (limitlessly) to (the extent of) the sky.
> That there is no pride in one's mind is the extraordinary sign of this path.
> Even if one doesn't meditate intentionally, the power of compassion
> Arises naturally without efforts.
> Even if one doesn't work hard on intellectual expositions,
> One gains the insight-wisdom of ocean-like *sūtras* and

tantras.
If one possess such (perfections), that is the infallible sign
That one has perfected the essence of the excellent path of *Dzogpa Chenpo.*
Otherwise, upon the mere arising of vague experiences
Of bliss, clarity and no-thought, less learned people
Boast about them as the high stage (of attainment) and become inflated with pride, and
They judge others without any sense of their own state.
They cannot tolerate even the sharpness of a harsh word. And if that is so,
I swear that they won't be able to bear the flames of the most tormenting hell.
Not knowing that the cause of wandering in *saṃsāra* is present in themselves—
"I have no fear of falling into *saṃsāra*,"
They articulate loudly and carelessly,
While they are afraid of even tiny harm from others—how strange it is.

ATTAINMENTS OF FRUITION AT DEATH

As death is the most important aspect of life, I would like to provide some other considerations of death from the scriptures. Generally, life is a chain of births and deaths since every moment of life is the birth of a new moment and the death of a preceding moment. But conventionally, birth relates to the beginning of a life and death is its end. As we have already taken birth in this life, the important thing for us to deal with is death. According to Buddhism, even for an unrealized person, if one can deal properly with the circumstances of the time of death, one's next rebirth results in a pleasant life since everything functions through interdependent causation. A person who is an accomplished *Dzogpa Chenpo* trainee may attain the accomplishments at the time of death, in the intermediate state, or in the next rebirth. Accomplished *Dzogpa Chenpo* meditators are the most amazing adepts of Tibet, for they die displaying the wondrous signs of achievement of enlightenment described in the scriptures. They display numerous signs of attainments as a result of the training they have been pursuing.

Kunkhyen Jigmed Lingpa summarizes the significance of the signs divided into two categories:[NS 385a/2]

> As a result of the speed of attaining liberation, there are two types of (attainment at death). (a) In (*Dzogpa Chenpo*), in order to attain the cessation of sorrow, the primordial nature, and the city of sacred peace, one exhausts the contaminated (elements of the mortal) body. The result is called the Fully Enlightened One (*S. Samyaksambuddha*). (b) Death with display of five signs: the lights, sounds, images,* gDung** and earth tremblings. It is called the attainment of Manifesting Enlightenment (*mNgon-Par Sangs-rGyas-Pa, S. abhibuddha*).

Jigmed Tenpa'i Nyima explains the distinctions between the basis and the result:[DL 1b/1]

> If one does not recognize the single luminous innate mind, that is the basis of delusion. If one realizes and stablizes it, that is the state of liberation.The first case is the basis and the second is the result. The Omniscient One [Longchen Rabjam] has rejected the interpretation that they are the same. For the basis, a complete luminous absorption arises at each time of death, but by not realizing it one returns to the delusory movements (*Yo-Lang*) of apprehended and apprehender. When one reaches the result, as one attains one's own (true) essence, one will not return (to delusion). So that is the difference between the basis and the result.

The most exceptional sign of *Dzogpa Chenpo* at death is the dissolving or transforming of the mortal body. As stated before, there are two main forms of dissolution of the mortal body:

*TD 184b/2: of peaceful and wrathful deities in the bones.

**TD 184b/6: *gDung* are of various colors and are indestructible. The white ones are the size of a pea, and the colored ones vary in size from a pea to a mustard seed. *Ring-bSrel* are white, destructible, and vary in size from a sesamum seed to an atom.

the attainment of the dissolution of the atoms or the most subtle particles [total dissolution] of the mortal body, popularly known as the attainment of Rainbow Body (*'Ja-Lus*), through training in *Thregchod* (Cutting Through), and the attainment of the Light Body (*A'od-Lus*) or the Great Transformation (*'Pho-Ba Ch'en-Po*) through training in *Thodgal* (Direct Approach). Longchen Rabjam distinguishes these two attainments:[NDG 85b/2]

> The cessation (or dissolution) of the elements at the time of perfection of (the attainment of) the meaning of the primordial purity (*Ka-Dag*) (through the training of) *Thregchod*, and the exhaustion of the elements by perfecting the spontaneous accomplishment (through the training of) *Thodgal* are similar in just having purified the internal and external gross elements. But in *Thregchod*, at the very instant of dissolving the partless particles, one attains liberation in the primordial purity, and there is no manifestation of Light Body. In *Thodgal*, with (the attainment of) Light Body one accomplishes the (Body of) Great Transformation. So their difference lies in whether or not they have the Light Body and not in (the attainment of) liberation in the state of primordial purity.

Some *Dzogpa Chenpo tantras*, however, distinguish four forms of dissolution. The *Nyida Khajor* (*Nyi-Zla Kha-sByor*) *tantra* says:[NK 213a/2]

> (a) The way of death of the *Ḍākinīs*,
> (b) The way of death of the knowledge-holders,
> (c) Self-consuming like a fire, and
> (d) Invisible like space;
> In all of them, they exhaust their mortal elements (of the body) and (become) invisible and do not take (any other elemental form). This is what the supreme yogis enjoy.

Kunkhyen Jigmed Lingpa elaborates on the four ways of dissolution:[NS 385a/5]

In the supreme way (of death), one dissolves one's mortal body (in two ways): In *Thregchod,* one dissolves (the body as it is called) like space and like the way of death of the *Ḍākinīs.* In the *Thodgal,* one dissolves (the body as it is called) like fire and like the way of death of a knowledge-holder. These are the four ways of dying of an accomplished (*Dzogpa Chenpo yogi*).

> First: Having purified (down to) the subtlest defilements of air/energy and mind which obscure the ultimate sphere, one attains the exhaustion of (phenomena into) the inner ultimate sphere (*Nang-dByings*), and thereby the external body dissolves into atoms [total dissolution]. At that very moment, the suchness of (one's) intrinsic awareness, which was based in the (mortal) body, unites with the natural ultimate sphere (*Rang-bZhin Ch'os-Kyi dByings*), as the space in a vase merges with the outer space when the vase is broken. Then, having united the ultimate sphere and the intrinsic awareness in the (state of) equalness purity without separation, one becomes enlightened....
>
> Second: It is the union of the body, the basis, and the intrinsic awareness, the based. The atoms of the body (of *Dzogpa Chenpo* adepts) are present (in one moment) but (in the next moment) they dissolve into the invisible (nature). At that very moment the intrinsic awareness dissolves into the ultimate sphere without return, like an arrow shot by a skilled archer. It is similar to the way that *Ḍākinīs* or beings who have been born by miraculous birth die, their bodies (suddenly) becoming invisible. As stated before, it is the same as the manner in which Pang Sangye Gonpo (*sPang Sangs-rGyas mGon-Po*), a direct disciple of Vairocana, died at Tragmar Gon (*Brag-dMar dGon*) of Tod Khung-rong (*sTod Khung-Rong*) and in which three followers of their lineage died in a single snake year, one after another, at Wa Senge Trag (*Wa Seng-Ge Brag*).

Third: The way of dissolving the intrinsic awareness after purifying the defilments of the air/energy and mind, as well as the ultimate sphere, the place where one attains liberation, are the same (as in the two previous cases). But (in this case), as the inner elements are exhausted, the physical mortal body dissolves into a a light body (*A'od-Phung*). It is as when the fuel of a fire is burned, there is no more fuel for the fire to continue. For example, two disciples of Kyergom Zhigpo (*dGyer-sGom Zhig-Po*) attained light bodies and disappeared into the sky in the cave of Dotshen (*rDo-mTshan*).

Fourth: One dissolves his mortal body—created by the maturation (of *karma* and habituations)—into the light body and becomes visible to other beings in order to lead them to the doctrine. It is as when the knowledge-holders progress from one stage to another, they travel through the sky to other Buddha-fields with sounds and lights and serve the needs of others. And it is like Chetsun Senge Wangchug (*lChe-bTshun Seng-Ge dBang-Phyug*, 11th-12th cent.), the lord of *yogis*, whose mortal body dissolved into the light body with lights and sounds in the sky at Oyug Chikong (*A'o-Yug Phyi-Gong*).

The bodies of *Dzogpa Chenpo* meditators who still have residues of *karmic* maturations do not dissolve at death, and there are some whose accomplishments are fully perfected, but who, instead of dissolving their mortal bodies, leave them with *gDung* and *Ringsel* (relics) as objects of devotion for devotees. Also some *Dzogpa Chenpo* adepts leave their bodies with or without any signs because of various circumstances or purposes. Sogpo Tentar says:[ST 270a/2]

> Even if (a *Dzogpa Chenpo* adept) possesses the capacity to dissolve (the mortal body) through (his realization of the) view and meditation, he does not exhaust his *karmic* energies (of remaining in the mortal form) but accepts (the responsibility of) the wheel of activities for the sake of the doctrine and beings. Even in order to help beings with (the remains of their) *gDung* and *Ring-sel*, they (attain the accomplishment) in the manner of the state of "Knowledge-holder with Residues" (*rNam-sMin Rig-*

> *'Dzin*). This is like Jigmed Thrinle Odzer Palbar (*'Jigs-Med Phrin-Las A'od-Zer dPal-'Bar*, 1745-1821, the first Dodrup Chen), our supreme refuge, the lord of the sages and the master of the hundred (Buddha-) families, and the illusory manifestation of the primordial Buddha Samantabhadra for the perception of the disciples.

A less extraordinary way for a *Dzogpa Chenpo* meditator to attain death is described by Sogpo Tentar as having four signs:[ST 270a/4]

> Even if (some realized *Dzogpa Chenpo* meditators) couldn't reach the exhaustion of the four elements, if they have realized the meaning of suchness and have purified their attachments to objects, they will not be oppressed by worldly means (*'Jig-rTen mThun-'Jug*). They will not rely on physicians, divinations or prayers if they are sick, and they will not rely on the weekly death ceremonies etc. at (the time of their) death. They possess four signs: Like a deer, they enjoy solitude where men do not move around, like a lion which does not fear anyone, they do not fear death, like a beggar, even if they die in the street they do not feel sad and, like a baby, they have no worry about death or life.

Practice

Lochen Dharmaśrī summarizes:[ZL 41b/5]

> In this (the trainees) enjoy all phenomena without discriminations of abandonments or acceptances since whatever arises has arisen as the play (*Rol-Ba*) of the ultimate nature.

Result

Lochen Dharmaśrī summarizes:[ZL 42a/1]

> It is the perfection of being in the state of spontaneously perfected Universal Goodness (*Kun-Tu bZang-Po*), from this very present time. Through the perfection of fourfold confidence in it, one attains the liberation of *saṃsāra* into

nirvāṇa.

The following is a summary from Yeshey Lama on the fourfold confidence:[YL 51b/3]

> The fourfold confidence is (a) the confidence of having no fear of hell (by knowing all as delusions), (b) having no expectations of *karmic* results as *saṃsāra* is non-existent, (c) having no hope of attainments as there is no true existence of *nirvāṇa*, and (b) having no joy, but rather equanimity concerning the virtues of Buddhahood, as one has reached the natural state.

Mipham Namgyal writes:[YDGD 37b/5]

> It is the presence (in oneself of the nature) of the self-intrinsic awareness, the essence of the enlightened mind, which is inseparable from the all-pervading lord, the Universal Goodness (*Kun-Tu bZang-Po*), the stage of sublime primordial wisdom. Having purified all the adventitious obscurations, this (attainment) is the perfection of purification and realization, and is free from (changes of) decreasing or increasing.

Jigmed Lingpa writes:[YTD 45a/1]

> Thus, having realized the characteristics of the basis and path,
> One (perfects) the result, the (five) Buddha-bodies[1] and the (fivefold) primordial wisdom.
> (These results) do not come from other (sources, but) are the purification of the defilements of the universal ground, and
> The pacification of the mind and mental events into the ultimate sphere.
> In this, the sun-like primordial wisdom, totally pure from
> The cloud-like substantial cause (*Nyer-Len*) of the eight consciousnesses,
> The apprehensions of knowable phenomena of the habituations of grasping at self,

Are the "appearances of the basis" arisen from the "basis," and
They shine forth as the natural clarity, free from coverings.

[1]Changeless *Vajra*-body (*Mi-'Gyur rDo-rJe*), Fully Enlightened Body (*mNgon-Par Byang-Ch'ub*), Peaceful Ultimate Body (*Zhi-Ba Ch'os-sKu*), Enjoyment Body (*Longs-sPyod rDzogs-sKu*) and the Variously Manifested Body (*Chir-Yang sPrul-Pa'i sKu*).

Dzogpa Chenpo and Other Yānas and Traditions

According to *Dzogpa Chenpo* scriptures, *Dzogpa Chenpo* is the summit of all the *yānas*. It embodies all the merits of other *yānas*. Other *yānas* are the steps to the realization of the meaning of *Dzogpa Chenpo*. The fruition of *Dzogpa Chenpo* is the realization of the Intrinsic Awareness, the Buddha-essence. Buddha-essence is discoursed on by the Buddha in both the "Second and Third Turnings of the Wheel." To realize the naked Intrinsic Awareness, the Buddha-essence, the profound and pure meaning of the *Dzogpa Chenpo* view by the swiftest and most direct way for highly intelligent trainees is the unique distinction of *Dzogpa Chenpo*. However, some scholars of other Tibetan Buddhist schools question *Dzogpa Chenpo*'s authenticity as a pure esoteric Buddhist view and meditation. Some allege its ties with the Bon religion or Ha-shang Mahāyāna's philosophy. The following are quotations of and comments on studies of authentic sources which illustrate the distinction of *Dzogpa Chenpo* and the relationship between *Dzogpa Chenpo* and other *yānas* and traditions.

There are some scholars who negate *Dzogpa Chenpo*, alleging that it recommends remaining in just no-thought and no-meditation. But most of the great masters of all the schools see *Dzogpa Chenpo* as one of the most profound teachings. The first Panchen Lama, Lobzang Chokyi Gyaltshen (*Blo-bZang Ch'os-Kyi rGyal-mTshan*, 1570-1662) writes in his *Instructional Commentary on Mahāmudrā*:[LN 378b/5]

> *Dzogchen*, *Mahāmudrā*, *Madhyamaka*,
> *Lamdre*, *Chod* and *Zhiched*, etc.
> Are various designations.
> But if examined by an experienced yogi,
> They lead to the same realization.

Milarepa (1040-1123) sings his realization to Pha Dampa Sangye (*Pha Dam-Pa Sangs-rGyas*), illustrating it in terms of pain and death:[GB 291a/2]

> From behind I am in pain through *Mahāmudrā*.
> From the front I am in pain through *Dzogpa Chenpo*.
> I am caught by the chronic disease of vase-like breathing.
> From the top, I am tormented by the fever of primordial wisdom.
> From the bottom, I am sick with the cold of absorption.
> In the middle the fever and cold of bliss and emptiness are in conflict.
> My mouth vomits the blood of instructions.
> My chest is stretched by the bliss of ultimate nature.
> I am not only ill but dying.....
> Bury me in the cemetery of *Vajradhara*.

To a scholar of the Sakya school Jigmed Lingpa answers:[GCD 54a/3]

> In *Mahāmudrā*, *Dzogpa Chenpo*, *Madhyamaka*, *Zhiched*, *Chod*, *Lamdre*, and so forth, there is no difference as to the result, the liberated state. But regarding the immediate approach(*'Jug-sGo*), there are differences in (degree of) profundity of the path due to their slow and swift (process of fruition) as a result of whether they teach the paths (of training) directly, through the means of relative or ab-

solute truth, and in definitive or interpretable ways.

ALL THE YANAS AND TRAININGS ARE STEPS TO DZOGPA CHENPO

According to *Mahāyāna* Buddhism, the essence of the whole doctrine of the Buddha is the perfection of wisdom. *Dzogpa Chenpo* realizes and perfects the primordial wisdom directly and nakedly. By perfecting the primordial wisdom one perfects all the other perfections, as all of them are attributes of the primordial wisdom. Śāntideva says:[BC105a/5]

> All these branches (the perfections) were taught
> By the Subduer (Buddha) for the sake of wisdom.

Jigmed Lingpa specifically writes that all the trainings of the common *yānas* are steps to *Dzogpa Chenpo*:[YTD 40b/1]

> The entire meanings of the vast, excellent path,
> Are for cleaning the (defilements of the) mind.
> So the three precepts, six perfections, development stage, perfection stage, and so on
> Are the steps to the path of *Dzogpa Chenpo*.

Mipham Namgyal writes:[NMT 122b/1]

> This (*Dzogpa Chenpo*) is the only resultant *yāna* and it is the summit of all the *yānas*.
> Except for this one, other *yānas* are accompanied by accepting and rejecting, defending and negating,
> And are created by mind.
> They are the stairs (leading) to this *yāna*.
> All the different tenets, divisions of *yānas*
> And the paths and stages—
> By accomplishing the great confidence in this realization—
> Will be perfected in the equalness state without efforts.

DISTINCTIONS OF THE TEACHINGS OF THE TWO TURNINGS OF THE WHEEL

Sogpo Tentar explains the differences between the views of the

Second and Third Turnings of the Wheel:ST 244b/3

> In the Second Turning of the Wheel, Buddha elucidated all the phenomenal existents through the "three doors of liberation" (emptiness, freedom from characteristics, and freedom from aspirations) in order to liberate from apprehension of the antidotes (to the defilements).... (The Buddha-essence) is discoursed on (in the Third Turning of the Wheel) but (the Second Turning of the Wheel) is more appropriate, in conventional terms, as the antidote to the elaborated theories.... The Last (Third) Turning of the Wheel is extensively vast in discoursing upon the inconceivable primordial wisdom, the source of (ten) strengths, etc., the ocean of virtues. But it is not the case that the Second Turning of the Wheel doesn't discourse on it. As, for example, in *Sañcaya sūtra* (*mDo sDud-Pa*) it is said:
>
> "If there is no Primordial Wisdom, there is no development and enlightenment.
> The ocean-like virtues of the Buddhas will also not be there.

THE GOAL OF *DZOGPA CHENPO* IS THE ATTAINMENT OF BUDDHA-ESSENCE.

The meditation in *Dzogpa Chenpo* is to realize the Intrinsic Awareness, the Buddha-essence, and perfection of the realization is the result, attainment of Buddhahood. Buddha-essence is taught in both the Second and, especially, in the Third Turning of the Wheel. Some scholars interpret that the Buddha-essence taught in *Dzogpa Chenpo* is in accord with the Second Turning of the Wheel, and according to others it is the essence of both Turnings of the Wheel. *Dzogpa Chenpo* provides more profound, swift, and esoteric means of training to realize the Buddha-essence, however, than do the common *Yānas*.

DZOGPA CHENPO IS BASED ON THE SECOND TURNING OF THE WHEEL

According to Jigmed Lingpa, *Dzogpa Chenpo* is based on the Second Turning of the Wheel as it emphasizes elimination of elaborations through the means of the "three doors of liberation":[NS 264b/3]

> The discriminating Intrinsic Self-awareness
> Which is the essence of the "three (doors of) liberation"
> Taught by the Victorious One (Buddha) in the Second Turning of the Wheel,
> Is naturally present as the Buddha-essence in the nature (*Khams*) of living beings, and it is called *Dzogpa Chenpo.*

According to Gyurmed Tshewang Chogtrub, *Dzogpa Chenpo* is the essence of both the Second and the Third Turnings of the Wheel:[LNT-1, 118a/5]

> In the Second Turning of the Wheel the Buddha elaborately taught the inconceivable nature through the ways of non-conceptualization of the characteristics of elaborations. But in it he did not disclose the presence of the (Buddha-)essence. In the Third Turning of the Wheel he disclosed the presence of the (Buddha-)essence, but he didn't disclose the definite (*mTshan-Nyid-Pa*) path which realizes that essence. *Dzogpa Chenpo*, without contradicting them, embodies the ultimate vision of both Great Chariots; (a) the vision of the Second Turning of the Wheel elucidated by Nāgārjuna in his (*Six*) *Collections of Reasonings* (*Rigs-Tshogs*) and *Praise of the Ultimate Sphere* (*Ch'os-dByings bsTod-Pa, S. Dharmadhātu-stava*) and so on and (b) the vision of the Third Turning of the Wheel elucidated by Maitreya, the Great Regent, and the Noble Asanga and his brother (Vasubandhu).

BUDDHA-ESSENCE AS TAUGHT IN *SŪTRIC YĀNAS*

According to *Mahāyāna sūtras*, the Buddha-essence is present as the essence of all knowable phenomena. In *Candradīpasūtra*

(*Zla-Ba sGron-Me'i mDo*) it is said:[ST 245b/2]

> The Buddha-essence pervades all living beings.

Jigmed Lingpa writes:[NS 267b/1]

> The presence of the (Buddha-essence) in living beings is discoursed on in the Third Turning of the Wheel, how it is present as the nature of (all) knowable phenomena, for beings of sharp intellect. The *Mahāparinirvāṇa-sūtra* explains it clearly:
>
> > "The secret Buddha-essence, naturally and totally pure,
> > I proclaim that it does not change and does not transfer."
>
> In *Dharmadhātu-stava* by Noble (*Nāgārjuna*) it is said:
>
> > "The water that is present in the earth
> > Remains unpolluted. Likewise,
> > In the emotional defilements, the primordial wisdom is also
> > Present without stains."

In *Uttaratantra* by Asaṅga it is said:[GDC 8b/3]

> (In beings) the Buddha bodies are emanating,
> (Beings) are inseparable from suchness and
> (They) possess the lineage (*Rigs*); therefore, all the embodied ones
> Are always with the Buddha-essence.

Prajñā-nāma-mūla(madhyamakakārikā) by Nāgārjuna says:[TSC 47b/4]

> That which is the nature (*Rang-bZhin*) of the Thus-gones (Buddha)
> Is the nature of beings.
> As Thus-gones have no inherent existence,
> Beings also have no inherent existence.

SUPERIORITY OF THE BUDDHA-ESSENCE AS TAUGHT IN *DZOGPA CHENPO*

If the Buddha-essence is taught in the lower *yānas*, what distinguishes *Dzogpa Chenpo*? The unique distinction of *Dzogpa Chenpo* is not the Buddha-essence but the profundity of its view of the Buddha-essence and the swiftness of its path of training in it.

The following is a quotation from *Kunched Gyalpo tantra*. Comparing the views of the lower *yānas* with that of *Atiyoga*, it illuminates the special and essential core of *Dzogpa Chenpo*:[KBG 55b/6]

> In the *sūtras* of *Bodhisattvayāna*,
> With the intention (of attaining) "the Total Light" (11th) stage
> Through the concepts and analysis of the two truths,
> It is asserted that the ultimate nature is emptiness like space.
> (Whereas) the great bliss of *Atiyoga*
> Is the enlightened mind, free from concepts and analysis.
> The *sūtras* obscure the (state of) freedom from concepts and analysis.
> The (view with) concepts and analysis in *Dzogpa Chenpo*
> Is a diversion to the *sūtras*.
> In *Kriyāyoga*, intending to attain the *Vajradhara* state,
> One enters through the doors of three purities and
> Dwells in the purity free from (the duality of) apprehended and apprehender.
> (Whereas) the great bliss of *Atiyoga*
> Is the enlightened mind (which) transcends (the duality of) apprehended and apprehender.
> *Kriyā(yoga)* obscures the (state of) transcending the apprehended and apprehender.
> (The view with) apprehended and apprehender in *Ati(yoga)*
> Is a diversion to *Kriyā(yoga)*.
> In *Upa(yoga)*, in its view and action,
> As it follows the view of *Yoga(tantra)* and the action of

Kriyā(yoga),
There is no union of view and action in it.
It doesn't realize the meaning of non-duality.
(Whereas) the great bliss of *Atiyoga*
Is the enlightened mind of non-duality.
Upa(yoga) obscures the (state of) non-duality.
(The view with) duality in *Dzogpa Chenpo*
Is a diversion to *Upa(yoga)*.
In *Yoga(tantra)*, intending to actualize the Beautifully Arrayed (pure land),
One enters into (the trainings) with and without characteristics
And emphasizes the fourfold seal.
(But *Yogatantra*) is incapable of entering into (the state) of freedom from (discriminations of) acceptance and rejection.
(Whereas) the great bliss of *Atiyoga*
Is the enlightened mind, free from acceptance and rejection.
Yoga(tantra) obscures the (state of) freedom from acceptance and rejection.
(The view with) acceptance and rejection in *Dzogpa Chenpo*
Is a diversion to *Yoga(tantra)*.
In *Mahāyoga*, intending to attain the *Vajradhara* state and
Having entered the door of skillful means and wisdom,
In the pure *maṇḍala* of one's own mind-stream,
One trains in the fourfold "recitation-and-*sādhana*."
(Whereas) the great bliss of *Atiyoga*
Is the enlightened mind, free from efforts and acquirements.
(The view with) efforts and acquirements in *Dzogpa Chenpo*
Is a diversion to *Mahāyoga*.
In *Anu(yoga)*, intending to attain the state of indivisibility (of the ultimate sphere and primordial wisdom) and
Having entered the door of the ultimate sphere and primordial wisdom,
One sees the appearing phenomenal existents—

The pure ultimate sphere—as the cause
And the *maṇḍala* of primordial wisdom as the result.
(Whereas) in the great bliss of *Atiyoga*
Is the enlightened mind, free from cause and results.
Anu(yoga) obscures the (state of) freedom from cause and result.
If one views (things) as cause and result in *Dzogpa Chenpo*,
It is a diversion to *Anuyoga*.

Garab Dorje (*Prahevajra*) says:[ST 245b/5]

Dzogpa Chenpo is the fortress of view,
Its Paths and stages are completed instantly.
It is not comparable to the lower *yānas*.

Identifying the Intrinsic Awareness, the Buddha-essence, in accordance with *Dzogpa Chenpo*, Jigmed Lingpa explains:[NS 270a/3]

In *Dzogpa Chenpo*, by contemplating and remaining without modification in the state of the continuum of primordial wisdom, which is free from elaborations, spontaneously arisen, transcending the mind, free from actions and pacification of mind and mental events, the sudden defilements of the manifestative power (of the Intrinsic Awareness) disappear naturally. In *Changchub Kyi Sem Kunched Gyalpo* (*Byang-Ch'ub Kyi Sems Kun-Byed rGyal-Po*) it is said:

"As it is remaining in the state of (nature), it is unmoving and spontaneous accomplishment.
As it is remaining in the nature, it is unchangeable by anything.
Remaining in that unmodified suchness
Is the actionless supreme action.

Longchen Rabjam describes the nature of Enlightened Mind, the Intrinsic Awareness of *Dzogpa Chenpo*, in the following words:[CD 6b/6]

The nature of the enlightened mind, the embodiment of all is:
Not clarity, as it transcends all the phenomena of clarity,
Not emptiness, as it transcends all the phenomena of emptiness,
Not existence, as there are no things and characteristics,
Not non-existence, as it pervades all of *saṃsāra* and *nirvāṇa*,
Not (both or neither) existent or non-existent, as it is the primordial ultimate sphere, spontaneous equalness;
Not partiality, bias, foundation, root, or things,
And no discontinuity. So it is the expanse of enlightened Intrinsic Awareness.

Longchen Rabjam writes that *Vajra*-essence, *Atiyoga*, is the summit of all the *Yānas:*[CD. 11a1]

The vajra-essence, *Ati(yoga)* is:
The utmost summit of the *yānas*, and it realizes all the meanings
clearly,
And the lower *yānas* do not realize the meaning of this (*yāna*).
Therefore, this is the pinnacle, the spontaneously accomplished summit.

The different *yānas* are discoursed on for the benefit of beings of different intellectual capacities and to suit their abilities:[CD 8a/5]

For people who need the gradual (path) and efforts
To lead them (finally) to the ultimate nature and the primordial ultimate sphere,
The *yānas* of *Śrāvaka*, *Pratyekabuddha*, and *Bodhisattva*
Are expounded to those of lesser (intellect).
The *Kriyā*, *Upa*, and *Yoga* (*tantras*) are
For the three mediocre (intellects).
Mahā, *Anu* and *Ati* (*yogas*)
Appear primordially for the great (intellects).

For the attainment of Full Enlightenment, Buddhahood, one has to enter into the realization of this *yāna*. The lower *yānas* are the entrance to this *yāna*:[CD 8b/1]

> All the *Yānas* finally have to enter
> Into the great secret and marvelous meaning of *Vajra-essence.*
> So this (*yāna*) is called the summit of all the (*yānas*), the supreme and changeless clarity [luminous absorption],
> Full Enlightenment and the essence of the *yānas.*

Longchen Rabjam explains how the essential virtues of the lower *yānas* are embodied in the Intrinsic Awareness, the Enlightened Mind of *Dzogpa Chenpo*:[LT 62a/4]

> In the Enlightened Mind, the Intrinsic Awareness, all the *yānas* are included.... The view of *Śrāvakayāna* asserts that all the internal and external phenomena are "selflessness of person," like space. The *Pratyekabuddhayāna* asserts, besides (the selflessness of person), the selflessness of half of phenomena, the apprehended (objects). The *Bodhisattvayāna* asserts the selflessness of the person and phenomena, the apprehender and apprehended, like space.... These realizations are included in the vision of (Intrinsic Awareness of *Dzogpa Chenpo*), (which is) the nature of self-arisen primordial wisdom, the (union of) emptiness and clarity, like the nature of space. So the self-arisen primordial wisdom of *Dzogpa Chenpo* embodies the suchness of all phenomenal existents, and those (*yānas*) are united in (Intrinsic Awareness)....
>
> *Kriyātantra* asserts that by viewing the deities and oneself as the lords and servant, and by making offerings and praise (to the deities), one receives the accomplishments. *Yogatantra* asserts that by submerging the wisdom deities into the *maṇḍala* of visualized deities and by making offerings and praise, etc., to them, one receives the accomplishments. They are all the same in purifying the defilements of the three doors and the achievement of the accomplish-

> ments. So their views are included in this (Intrinsic Awareness of *Dzogpa Chenpo*), which is the realization of the Enlightened Mind, the total purity achieved by means of the awakening of all phenomenal existents as the *maṇḍala* (of spontaneously arisen Enlightened essence). . . .
>
> *Mahāyoga*, the father *tantra*, and *Anuyoga*, the mother *tantra*, assert that the *maṇḍala* of the basis is the Intrinsic Awareness (*Rig-Pa*). The *maṇḍala* of the path is the visualization of the world and beings as the mansions and deities, and the trainings on the indivisibility of the ultimate sphere and the Intrinsic Awareness, the skillful means and wisdom. The *maṇḍala* of the result is the attainment of the supreme enlightenment.
>
> *Atiyoga*, too, asserts that by realizing that all are primordially enlightened and by not wavering from the ultimate nature, which is the vision free from abandonments, acceptances, and modifications, one's Intrinsic Awareness reaches the (primordial) basis. So in this (Intrinsic Awareness), the essence of the meanings (of all the *yānas*) is condensed, and this is the great absolute secret *yāna*.

Jigmed Lingpa writes on the superiority of the Instruction Division (*Man-Ngag-sDe*) over the other *yānas* and the lower Divisions of *Dzogpa Chenpo* itself:[NS 323b/5]

> In the *Vajra*-essence of the clarity [luminous absorption] of *Dzogpa Chenpo*, which is the path of liberation of thoughts and emotional defilements, one realizes the nonexistence of the nature (*Rang-bZhin*) of emotional defilements in the nature (*gShis*) of Intrinsic Awareness. So this division doesn't abandon (defilements) as *Śrāvakas* and *Pratyekabuddhas* do. It doesn't subdue (the defilements) as do *Bodhisattvas*, since here, the antidotes and the things to be abandoned are of the same substance (*rDzas*). It doesn't apply (the defilements) as the path as the general *tantras* do, since here, all are in equalness of time in the continuum of the mind. It doesn't liberate (the mind) into the nature (*gShis*) (of the mind) as *Semde* does, since mind

does not see mind. It doesn't apprehend (the mind) as an ornament (*rGyan*) as *Longde* does, since primordial wisdom doesn't see mind. (According to the Instruction Division,) in the ultimate nature of the Intrinsic Awareness, suchness, all the assertions and mental theories (such as) the emptiness of self and the emptiness of others do not stand, and they dissolve spontaneously without traces. Alala! the objective appearances do not cease in the Intrinsic Awareness, but the Intrinsic Awareness doesn't mix with (or stray to) the objects. So, the apprehended and apprehender, the nature of *saṃsāra*, become the "naturally liberated antidote and the things to be abandoned," like a drawing on water. Saraha will smile (with joy at this). In the essence of Intrinsic Awareness, which is not distracted to the objects, there are no manifestations of any attachment, rejecting and achieving. So it is the state of liberation from the bonds of *saṃsāra* and *nirvāṇa*. At this (view) Dampa (Sangye) of India will rejoice. In the Intrinsic Awareness, which is perfected as the ultimate body (*Ch'os-sKu*), there is no subject of reasoning. So, it is unhinderedness as the nature of primordial wisdom, the great freedom from extremes. As the thoughts are liberated as the Intrinsic Awareness, the falsehood of view, meditation, and result is broken and there is no yearning for rituals and Dharma activities, yet one never dissociates oneself from the enlightened mind, the ultimate nature, free from elaborations. It is the perfection of Dharma (training).

Gyurmed Tshewang Chogdrub points out the imperfections of the lower *yānas* compared to *Dzogpa Chenpo*:[LNT-I, 112b/6]

In the realization of selflessness, *Śrāvakayāna* and *Pratyekabuddhayāna* assert that (the most subtle) cognition and atom are absolute truth. *Yogācārya* asserts that the consciousness of self-awareness and self-clarity is the thoroughly established absolute truth. (All of them) do not transcend mind and mental events. *Madhyamaka* apprehends space like emptiness, the truth of cessation and freedom from extremes and elaboration, etc., by analysis of the two truths, through examination of four reasonings, such as non-arising, non-ceasing, non-existing, and not non-existing. Among the lower *tantras*, *Kriyāyoga* posits achieving accomplishments by pleasing the deities of the three purities, the austerity of cleanness. *Upayoga* [*Caryāyoga*] apprehends the characteristic as it is, in accordance with the higher (*Yogatantra*) and lower (*Kriyāyoga*) *tantras*. *Yogatantra* reflects on the *yoga* of the fourfold sign (*Phyag-rGya*) by relying on the blessing of the deities for the (attainment of) ultimate truth. *Mahāyoga* proposes the development of primordial wisdom by recommending (training in) the development stage and the channels, energy and essence of the perfection stage. *Anuyoga* perceives the ultimate sphere and primordial wisdom as the *maṇḍala* of the divine creator and the creator. In brief, all these levels (of *yānas*) up to *Anuyoga* are mere theories perceived by the mind. In the mental attitude of all of them is the claim that the object and subject are the ultimate nature, arrived at by thoughts, mental creation and analysis, thinking "this is non-existent," "it is emptiness" and "it is truth." So they do not realize the ultimate nature as it is.

He continues:[LNT-I, 115a/4]

(The views of these *Yānas*) are created and modified by the mind, the mind of eight consciousnesses, which are the defilements to be abandoned. In the Natural Great Perfection (*Dzogpa Chenpo*), all the virtues of the nature are present spontaneously as uncompounded clarity [luminous absorption] in the Mind, which transcends the mind and is the Intrinsic Awareness and spontaneously arisen wisdom. So it is naturally free and does not depend on causations of creator and created or other conditions, like the character of space. It is present without any changes. So the primordial lord [Buddha], *Samantabhadra* (All Good) himself, also is enlightened by realizing this spontaneously arisen primordial wisdom itself without creation and not by other conditions such as compounding accumulations, studying, and pondering.

DISTINCTION BETWEEN THE BUDDHA-ESSENCE OF *DZOGPA CHENPO* AND OF *YOGĀCĀRYA*

In *Dzogpa Chenpo* the Intrinsic Awareness is designated as self-awareness and self-clarity. But it is free from elaborations and non-existence. So it is superior to the thoroughly established self-awareness and self-clarity of consciousness of the *Yogācārya* school. Longchen Rabjam explains:[LT 76a/1]

> In it (*Dzogpa Chenpo*) the essence (*Ngo-Bo*) of Intrinsic Awareness, the realization of the non-existence of the apprehended and apprehender, is called the spontaneously arisen primordial wisdom. But *Dzogpa Chenpo* doesn't assert it as self-awareness and self-clarity (*Rang-Rig Rang-gSal*) as *Yogācārya*, the Mind Only school, does. Because (according to *Dzogpa Chenpo*), as there is no existence of internal and external, it (Intrinsic Awareness) is not established as internal mind. As there is no self and others, it isn't established as self-awareness. As the apprehended and apprehender have never existed, freedom from the two is not established. As it is not an object of experiences and awareness, the experience is not established as non-dual.
>
> As there is no mind and mental events, it does not exist as self-mind. As it does not exist as clarity or non-clarity, it is not established as self-clarity. As it transcends awareness and non-awareness, there are not even the imputations of awareness. This is called the *Dzogpa Chenpo*, free from extremes. Although it is designated as self-arisen primordial wisdom, enlightened mind, ultimate body, the great spontaneously accomplished ultimate sphere, and the naked self-clarity Intrinsic Awareness, these ascriptions are merely in order to signify it. It should be realized that the self-essence (of *Dzogpa Chenpo*) is inexpressible. Otherwise, if you take the meaning of the words literally, you

will never find (in *Dzogpa Chenpo*) any difference from the cognition of self-awareness, self-clarity, and non-duality of apprehender and apprehended of the Mind Only school.

DIFFERENCES BETWEEN *DZOGPA CHENPO* AND *MADHYAMAKA*

Madhyamaka, having distinguished the appearances and emptiness separately, emphasizes the concept of emptiness. *Dzogpa Chenpo*, having distinguished the Intrinsic Awareness, the pure and natural state of mind, from mind, realizes and perfects the Intrinsic Awareness directly and nakedly. Thereby it realizes the truth of the whole universe free from discrimination and extremes. Longchen Rabjam explains:LT 76b/1

Most of the methods of comprehending (analyzing) the freedom from extremes (*mTha'-Bral*), and so on, of Natural Great Perfection are similar to *Prāsaṅgika Madhyamaka*. However, *Madhyamaka* regards the emptiness as the important thing. (*Dzogpa Chenpo*), relying on the primordially pure and naked Intrinsic Awareness which is just non-existent and unceasing, comprehends it (the Intrinsic Awareness) and all the phenomena arisen from it as free from extremes like space.

Jigmed Tenpa'i Nyima summarizes in the following lines:DC 7b/2

In Choying Dzod (*Ch'os-dBying mDzod*), etc., there is praise for the (view of) *Prāsaṅgika Madhyamaka* philosophy. Thus (*Dzogpa Chenpo*) follows *Prāsaṅgika* in regard to (defining) the limits of the object-of-negation (*dGag-Bya'i mTshams-'Dzin*). However, (*Prāsaṅgika*), having distinguished the appearances and emptiness separately, apprehends the emptiness of non-affirming (*Med-dGag*) negation, calling it the distinction of the appearances and emptiness or the exclusion of emptiness. It is a method of maintaining (meditation and view) by concepts. It also asserts that if one first distinguishes (the view) by con-

> cepts and gains experience (of it) through meditation, then it will become as it is said: "with the fruition of bliss, clarity and no-concept mind." In any case, *Dzogpa Chenpo* tradition uses the Intrinsic Awareness as the path, or it maintains only the Intrinsic Awareness. It does not employ concepts since concepts are mind, and it meditates (on Intrinsic Awareness after) distinguishing the mind and Intrinsic Awareness separately.

Although in pure *Dzogpa Chenpo* one doesn't train on admitting the energy into the central channel, the training is more effective and direct than the trainings given in the *tantras*. Dorje Wangchog Gyepa Tsal explains:[BN 24a/5]

> Those who have attachment to the path of skillful means (*Thabs-Lam*) think, "No matter how good the path of *Dzogpa Chenpo* is, since it doesn't rely on the method of admitting the energy into the central channel, its (realization) is not higher than an experience of (the meaning taught in) *Madhyamaka*." This kind of wrong judgment arises (due to) lack of understanding of the essential points. The (sole) purpose of admitting the energy into the central channel is (as a means) to arouse the primordial wisdom (which is realized directly in *Dzogpa Chenpo*).

UNIQUE DISTINCTION OF *DZOGPA CHENPO*

Jigmed Tenpa'i Nyima writes:[DCT 8b/1]

> Generally in the instructions of *Dzogpa Chenpo* there are endless profound, unique aspects. But the main point is the reliance on distinguishing the Intrinsic Awareness, as it is stated in *Yonten Rinpoche'i Dzod*:[YTD 42b/4]
>
> > The Intrinsic Awareness which transcends mind
> > Is the specialty of the Natural Great Perfection.

He writes:[DCT 9a/5]

> All the aspects of the mind arise as the self-power of the Intrinsic Awareness, and this is not the actual Intrinsic

> Awareness. Otherwise, the distinction of mind and Intrinsic Awareness becomes a matter of saying the distinction of Intrinsic Awareness and Intrinsic Awareness.

It transcends the eight consciousnesses:[NS 265b/6]

> The ultimate nature of the Intrinsic Awareness, which transcends the eight consciousnesses with their conceptions, expressions, and causations, is the presence of the primordial wisdom of Natural Great Perfection.

It transcends the mind and mental events:[NS 270a/3]

> In *Dzogpa Chenpo* one remains in the natural state of the continuity of the spontaneously arisen primordial wisdom, the pacification of mind and mental events into the ultimate sphere, which is the great transcending of mind and detachment from actions. There are no efforts and modifications. So the sudden defilements of the appearances of power disappear spontaneously.

NYINGMA AND *BON*

There are scholars who assert that the teachings of *Nyingma* are mixed with *Bon* because there are many texts and teachings which are common to both. The following is a brief study of this matter based mainly on the writings of Buddhist historians. *Bon* is the indigenous pre-Buddhist religion of Tibet founded by the prophet Shenrab Miboche (*gShen-Rab Mi-Bo-Ch'e*). Different sources have different views about his date. Some *Bon* sources place him many centuries before Śākyamuni Buddha, some as contemporary to the Buddha, and some after the Buddha. He was born in Olmo Lungring (*A'ol-Mo Lung-Ring*) in the Zhangzhung (*Zhang-Zhung*) country, and he visited Tibet and gave *Bon* teachings. Mt. Tise [Kailas] and Lake Manasarowar are situated in Zhangzhung. In the seventh century Zhangzhung became part of Ngari (*mNga'-Ris*), the western province of Tibet, and became known as Guge (*Gu-Ge*).

In the beginning, Tibetan *Bon* seems to have been solely

based on worshipping nature or the spirits of nature, but later it incorporated mainly Buddhist teachings, as well some others. The following is a summary of the main points of the history of *Bon* by Lobzang Chokyi Nyima (1737-1802),[LSM-9, 2b/6] who says that he based it on the Gongchig (*dGongs-gChig*) of Drikung Kyobpa (*'Bri-Gung sKyob-Pa, 1143-1217*). In this text, the early *Bon* history of Tibet is classified into three stages:

(a) Naturally Developed *Bon* (*rDol-Bon*): At the beginning, *Bon* in Tibet consisted of three aspects—methods of subduing harmful spirits (*'Dre-Srin gNon-Pa*), worshipping the divinities(*Lha mCh'od-Pa*), and performances of the home hearth (*Khyim-Gyi Thab 'Don-Pa*). Apart from those elements, *Bon* had no philosophical and religious tenets. This *Bon* tradition is called the Black *Bon* Tradition (*Ch'ab-Nag*).

(b) Stray *Bon* (*'Khyar-Bon*): At the time of the death of King Trigum Tsenpo (*Gri-'Gum bTsan-Po*), the eighth of the forty-one rulers of the Chogyal dynasty (127 B.C.-901 A.D.) of Tibet, other *Bon* practices such as displaying miracles, predicting the future, and performances of death ceremonies were brought by *Bon* masters from neighboring countries: Kashmir, Zhang-zhung and Brusha (*'Bru-Sha*).

(c) Translated *Bon* (*bsGyur-Bon*): around the reign of King Thrisong Deutsen (790-858 A.D.) of Tibet, the tradition of translated *Bon* originated. When Gyalwa'i Changchub (*rGyal-Ba'i Byang-Ch'ub*) was ordered by the king to receive teachings from Rinchen Chog (*Rin-Ch'en mCh'og*), the great Buddhist teacher, instead of obeying, in protest he translated many Buddhist texts into *Bon* terminology. After the destruction of Buddhism by King Lang Darma (d. 901?), Shergur Luga (*gSher-rGur Klu-dGa'*) of Tsang Nyangtod (*gTsang Nyang-sTod*) translated many Buddhist texts into *Bon* terminology. Later, Khyungpo Bonzhig (*Khyung-Po Bon-Zhig*) and others also translated many Buddhist texts into *Bon* terminology. The Translated *Bon* is called the White *Bon* Tradition (*Bon Ch'ab dKar*).

Thus, in *Bon* scriptures many translated Buddhist texts and teachings are transposed as *Bon* scriptures. Lobzang Chokyi

Nyima writes:LSM-9, 3b/6

> In *Bon* teachings there are substitutes for (the different sections of) *Kagyur* (or *Kajur: bKa'-'Gyur*, which is the collection of 110 volumes of Buddha's teachings in Tibetan).... In the (*Bon*) scriptures there are scattered teachings on impermanence, *karma*, loving-kindness, compassion, development of the mind of enlightenment, and the six perfections. They also contain the system of five paths, ten stages, and three bodies. They also have the (*tantric* teachings) parallel (to Buddhism) such as empowerment, development stage, perfection stage, sacred obligations (*samaya*), ceremonies of consecration and fire offerings (*homa*), propitiations of *maṇḍalas*, and death rituals. (In *Bon*) there are many teachings that are quite similar to Buddhism and many that are different. They say Yeshen (*Ye-gShen*) for Buddha, Bonku (*Bon-sKu*) for *Dharmakāya*, *Satri Esang* (*Sa-Dri E-Sang*) for the Great Mother (*prajñāpāramitā*), *Kuntu Zangpo* (*Kun-Tu bZang-Po*) for *Saṃbhogakāya*, *Sidpa Sedpo* (*Srid-Pa Sad-Po*) for *Nirmāṇakāya*, *Shense* (*gShen-Sras*) for *Arhant*, *Yungtrung Sempa* (*gYung-Drung Sems-dPa'*) for *Bodhisattva*, *Wonse* (*dBon-Sras*) for *Guru*, *Amonyid* (*A'-Mo-Nyid*) for emptiness.

According to Buddhist scriptures, Buddhist teachings appeared or are taught in various forms to benefit the followers. The sole purpose of any true teaching is to benefit beings. So there is no logical reason why Buddhism should not appear as *Bon* teachings. Pema Namgyal (19th-20th cent.) quotes scriptures to this effect:PKD 268a/1

> In the *Avataṃsaka* (*sūtra*) it is said:
>
>> "O sons of good families! The manifestations of the Thus-Gones [Buddhas] are immeasurable. They serve beings in every form, color, and name, whatever is appropriate in disciplining them."
>
> In the *Subāhu* (*sūtra*) it is said:

"Although his (Buddha's) nature is free from hatred and attachments,
He appears, for the beings-with-desire, in a form with desire;
For wrathful beings, in wrathful form to subdue their harmful (nature).
The leader (Buddha) with skillful means: to you, I pay homage."

In *Dorje Trawa (rDo-rJe Drva-Ba) tantra* it is said:

Whatever form is
Able to tame the embodied ones,
In that very form he (Buddha) manifests,
Like the wish-fulfilling gems.
Whatever means of discipline is
Able to discipline beings,
With that very means
(He) expounds the teachings."

Some *Nyingma* Ter texts specifically state how the teachings and masters of Buddhism appeared as *Bon* and *Bon* masters. Pema Namgyal again quotes:[PKD 270a/2]

In (a *Terma* text entitled) Katsi (*bKa'-rTsis*) discovered by Guru Chowang (*Ch'os-dBang*, 1212-1270) from Namke Chen (*gNam-sKas Chan*) it is said:

"When he [Guru Padmasambhava?] was in absorption at Vajrāsana
Inspired by Avalokiteśvara, he traveled to Tibet.
But it was controlled by *Bon* and it was hard to spread Dharma.
So he manifested in the form of Shenlha Odkar (*gShen-Lha A'od-dKar*) (of *Bon*),
Gave the secret signs to the (first) Dharma king Thothori,
And turned the king's mind towards Dharma so that he was able to distinguish the virtuous and unvirtu-

ous deeds."

Especially in the *Kayi Thang-yig* (*bKa'-Yi Thang-Yig*), discovered by the great Terton Longsal Nyingpo (*Klong-gSal sNying-Po*, 1625-1692), it is said:

> "Then, intending to go to Zhangzhung, he [Guru Padmasambhava?] surveyed it and saw that Zhangzhung would only be tamed by *Bon*. He went there with the retinues of self-lights and spoke thus:
> 'O sons of good families! Be aware. My father is Trenpa Yeshekyi Namkha (*Dran-Pa Ye-Shes Kyi Nam-mKha*). My mother is Oden Barma (*A'od-lDan 'Bar-Ma*). My elder brother is Tshewang Rigdzin (*Tshe-dBang Rig-'Dzin*). I am born spontaneously from the ultimate *Bon*, the changeless sphere.' Then he opened the door of numerous teachings which are free from falling into the extremes of eternalism or nihilism. A mass of eighteen hundred thousand beings attained liberation."

From the point of view of reasoning (the appearance of Dharma as *Bon* teachings) is establishable by three points: (a) Avalokiteśvara did generate the mind and he made the aspirations for taming all the trainable beings of Tibet. (b) The *Bon* followers also possess the Buddha-essence, the ultimate-body (*Dharmakāya*) and are the same in the lineage of the nature of ultimate purity. (c) If the teachings were not given that way (as *Bon*), those beings would have been difficult to discipline and the (Buddha) actions wouldn't have been completed. (Buddhist teachings which were discovered as) *Bon Ter(s)* were concealed for the future disciples (by Guru Padmasambhava) and later, when the time came, authentic (Buddhist) *Terton(s)* such as Rigdzin Godkyi Demthruchen (*Rig-'Dzin rGod-Kyi lDem-'Phru-Chan*, 1337-1408) of the Northern Ter tradition discovered them and made them available to *Bon* followers. In Katsi (*bK'a-rTsis*) it is said:

> "With *Dharma Ter(s)*, *Bon Ter(s)*, medicine, astronomy,

and art, etc.,
Whatever is appropriate for the minds (of beings)
(Buddhas) filled the mountains, rocks, temples, *stūpas*,
Landmarks, giant trees, boulders, palaces
And caves.

Dudjom Rinpoche, Jigtral Yeshe Dorje (*bDud-'Joms Rin-Po-Ch'e, 'Jigs-Bral Ye-Shes rDo-rJe*, 1903-1987) answers the accusations made against *Nyingma*:[LN 386a/3]

> Some say: "Bon and *Dzogchen* seem to have close connections as there are similarities between *Nyingma* and *Bon* teachings." Yes, there are many similarities in technical terms and so on. But since the writings of *Bon* are based on Buddhism (of the *Nyingma* translation period), why would there not be similarities? For example,... in Tibet the *Bonpos* have parallels to the (scriptures and deities of) Buddhism. They have texts on scriptures such as *Madhyamaka, Prajñāpāramitā, Vinaya, Abhidharma* and *tantras*. They have deities such as *Cakrasaṁbhara, Vajrabhairaha* and *Vajrakīla* and (teachings on) heat-*yoga*, *Mahāmudrā* and *Dzogpa Chenpo*.... In any case, (in traditional *Bon*) there are (exclusive) teachings such as *Chashen* (*Phya-gShen*), and *mantras* that provide temporary benefits for the followers. It is possible that these (also) have been taught by Buddhas and Bodhisattvas.

Dudjom Rinpoche also explains that Guru Padmasambhava kept some of the exclusively *Bon* practices for the Buddhists in Tibet:[LN 387b/4]

> Guru (Padmasambhava) saying, "The gods and demons (of the spirit world) of Tibet are happy with *Bon*," maintained divinations and astronomy (*Mo-rTsis*), offerings to the divine spirits(*Lha-gSol*), and the gathering of luck (*gYang-'Gug*) of *Bon* as they are, (for the Buddhists).

From this and other sources it is clear that the aspect of White *Bon* Tradition is very similar to Buddhism and that the

Black *Bon* tradition is the original *Bon*. Generally, because of human nature, in any religious history we find many negative events. So neither *Bon* nor Buddhism in Tibet is exclusive. Buddhist teachings were translated into *Bon* for revenge and to compete with Buddhists. In Buddhism, traditional *Bon* practices are introduced for worldly benefits. But from the positive point of view, in the White *Bon* Tradition there are many Buddhist scriptures and practices translated into *Bon* terminology and dedicated to *Bon* masters of various ages. Since the Translation period of *Bon* took place during the development of the *Nyingma* school, it is logical to find that those *Bon* teachings are more similar to the teachings of *Nyingma* than to those of other schools. Further, many masters of *Nyingma* and *Bon* of the White Tradition taught and discovered many of their common teachings and transmitted them to each other at various junctures. Further, not only in *Nyingma* teachings, but in other schools of Tibetan Buddhism as well, we find that aspects of traditional *Bon* culture, such as worship of spirits, are incorporated as worship of the *Dharmapālas*. But here it is important to know that the true Tibetan Buddhists do not practice the worship of spirits in an ordinary way but transform it into Buddhist *tantric* training with compassionate attitude, pure perception, and realized mind for dual benefit.

So the finding of *Dzogpa Chenpo* and other *Nyingma* texts and teachings in *Bon* has no other significance than that common Buddhist teachings were translated into *Bon* terminology.

DZOGPA CHENPO AND HA-SHANG MAHĀYĀNA

Some Tibetan Buddhist scholars who refute *Dzogpa Chenpo*, make allegations that *Dzogpa Chenpo* is close to or mixed with Ha-shang Mahāyāna's view, because *Dzogpa Chenpo* also propagates instant enlightenment and remaining in no-thought. The following is a study of Ha-shang Mahāyāna's view (but not on *Ch'an* Buddhism) based on Tibetan Buddhist sources.

Ha-shang Mahāyāna (Chinese: *Ho-shang Mo-ho-yen*) was a master of the *Ch'an* (Japanese: *Zen*) school of China founded by Bodhidharma in the sixth century A.D. According to Lobzang Chokyi Nyima (1737-1802),[LSM-11, 11b/6] Bodhidharma (or Bodhidharmottara) was the twenty-eighth in the line of Transmission of the Ultimate Essence (*sNying-Po Don-Gyi brGyud-Pa*) from Kasyapa, the chief disciple of the Buddha. Nub Sangye Yeshey (*gNubs Sangs-rGyas Ye-Shes*, 9th century) gives the following brief sketch of Bodhidharma's life. The spellings of most of the Chinese names are hard to figure out, so I have just spelled them as they appear in the Tibetan text:[SM 12a/5]

> The Instantanealist (*Chig-Ch'ar-Ba*) tradition came through the lineage of Kāśyapa and Dharmottara. Bodhidharmottara[1] came (to China) from eastern (India) by sea. When he reached Ledkug (*Led-Kug*)[2] in China, where he was met by Emperor Seu-yan-ang,[3] Bodhidharmottara realized that the Emperor didn't understand the ultimate (teaching). He went to Khar Lag-ch'u (*mKhar Lag-Ch'u*).[4] There the monks Kha-shi, Liu-chi, and Kvan-hong etc. became jealous of him. Li-chi (*Liu-chi?*) poisoned him six times but it didn't harm him. Finally he found a disciple[5] to whom he was able to transmit his teachings. Then he died in China and the funeral ceremonies were completed. Then a trader called Un went to Tong (sTong),[7] and at Ramatingilaka he met master Bodhidharmottara, who was holding in his hands one sandal of a pair. He had a detailed conversation (with the master). On his return, Un told of his encounters in detail in China. People opened his tomb and in it they found only one sandal of the pair. . . . All agreed that he was a Noble One.

According to Nub Sangye Yeshey,[SM 8a/2] Ha-shang was the

[1]LSM 11, 12a/4: Bodhidharmottara (*Byang-Ch'ub Ch'os-mCh'og*) was the twenty-eighth lineage-holder after Kāśyapa. He transmitted his lineage to the later or second Viśvamitra (in India) and went to China.
[2]LSM 11, 12a/5: Kiang-nan
[3]LSM-11, 12a/5: Liang U-dhi, HZB 68: Wu-ti (502-550) of Liang dynasty.
[4]LSM-11, 12b/1 Yu-gur?
[5]LSM-1112b/3: Hu-khe, HZB 69, Hui-k'o
[6]HZB: a monk, Sung-yun
[7]LSM 11, 13a/1: India

seventh[1] in the line of transmission from Bodhidharma. Also Nub's text quotes P'u-chi (651-739) first and then Ha-shang with the footnotes listing them as the tenth and eleventh. It is hard to tell how authentic these footnotes are. So Ha-shang might be a follower of P'u-chi of the northern school of *Ch'an* Buddhism. But he might not be a direct student of P'u-chi, since he was supposed to be in Tibet in the ninth century. There is not much information about Ha-shang's life. He was a highly noted Chinese teacher of Buddhism in Tibet during the reign of king Thrisong Deu-tsan (790-858 A.D.). As Ha-shang Mahāyāna was a follower of the Instantanealist teachings (Chinese: *Tun-men*, Tibetanized Chinese: *sTon-Men/Mun*) or Sudden Enlightenment, in Tibet, he faced opposition from the followers of Indian masters, who are Gradualist (Chinese: *Chien-men*, Tibetanized Chinese: *Tsen-Men/Mun*) or who teach Gradual Enlightenment. In the end Ha-shang was defeated by the great Indian master Kamalaśīla in a debate, which is called the Samye Debate by modern Western scholars. Ha-shang and his followers had to leave Tibet, and it was forbidden to practice his teachings in Tibet any more. Since then all the teachings of Ha-shang have disappeared from Tibet, except for a few passages here and there refuting him. There is not much basis for learning what his teachings were or whether they were true Ch'an Buddhism. Two recent discoveries, a text entitled *Samten Migdron* (*SM*) by Nub Sangye Yeshey, and some Tun-huan documents, shed some light on Ha-shang's teachings. They will be discussed briefly later.

It is also worth noting that some sources say that many *Mahāyāna* Buddhist scriptures were translated into Tibetan from the memory of a Ha-shang Mahāyāna. Who knows whether it is the same Ha-shang or another? Longchen Rabjam says:[GD 140a/1]

> Many *sūtras* such as the *Avataṁsaka*, *Mahāparinirvāṇa* (*sūtra*), and *Vinayāgama* (*'Dul-Ba Lung*), which were translated into Chinese before they were burned (at Nālandā

[1]But according to the footnotes to the text, SM 61b/3: he is the eleventh.

> monastery in India) by Nyima Ngodrub (*Nyi-Ma dNgos-Grub*), were translated into Tibetan by Vairocana and Ba Sangshi (*'Ba' Sang-Shis*) from the memory of Ha-shang Mahāyāna.

Traditional Tibetan scholars generally believe that Ha-shang rejects all the virtuous deeds and teaches the remaining in mere absence of thoughts. They all give an identical outline of Ha-shang's thesis. It seems to be based mainly on the thesis which it is believed that he presented at the debate with Kamalaśīla. The following lines are from Khepa'i Gaton (*mKhas-Pa'i dGa'-sTon*) by Tshuglag Threngwa (*Tshug-Lag 'Phreng-Ba, 1454-1566*). Other sources including the Tibetan Chronicle known as *Bazhed* (*sBa-bZhed*) and the *History of Buddhism* by Buton Rinchentrub (*Bu-sTon Rin-Ch'en Grub, 1290-1364*) are very similar but for some differences in wording:[KGT I, 386/17]

> (Starting the debate with Kamalaśīla) Ha-shang said: "As all are created by the concepts of the mind, through the *karmas* [the process of causation] of virtuous and unvirtuous deeds, one experiences the fruits (of rebirths) in the higher and inferior realms and one wanders around in *saṃsāra*. Whoever does not think of anything in his mind and does not do anything will be totally liberated from *saṃsāra*. Therefore, do not think anything. The ten virtuous deeds such as generosity (copying scriptures, making offerings, listening to Dharma teachings, memorizing scriptures, reading scriptures, teaching Dharma, reciting scriptures, pondering upon the meanings of Dharma, and meditating upon the meanings of Dharma) are taught for those people who do not possess a stream of virtuous *karma* and have lesser intellects and dull faculties. For those who have previously refined their minds and possess sharp intellect, the virtuous and unvirtuous deeds are (the same as) obscurations, since either white or black clouds cover the sun. So, not thinking, not conceptualizing, and not analyzing anything is the freedom from conceptualizations. It is the instantanealization (or sudden enlightenment),

equal to the tenth stage (of the path)."

Jigmed Tenpa'i Nyima (1865-1926) summarizes Ha-shang's meditation in one line:[DC 2a/5]

> He [Ha-shang] asserts that not thinking anything in the mind alone is the profound path (of enlightenment).

Natshog Rangtrol (1608-?) argues that Ha-shang's meditation is the reverse of the method of *Dzogpa Chenpo* and *Mahāmudrā* meditations:[MC 43b/5]

> The meditation of Ha-shang, which asserts (that remaining in the state of) recollectionlessness and blankness is the actual meditation, is the reverse of taking the union of clarity, awareness, and emptiness as the path by (both) *Mahāmudrā* and *Dzogpa Chenpo*.

Both Lobzang Chokyi Nyima and Khyentse'i Wangpo (*mKhyen-brTse'i dBang-Po, 1820-1892*)[TT 19b/6] write on it in one voice:[LSM 11, 13b/2]

> Ha-shang Mahāyāna, who visited Tibet, seems to have been a follower of *Tsung-men*.[1] However, Ha-shang's teachings and the view of general *Tsung-men* are not, it seems, the same. *Tsung-men* followers say:
>
> > "The virtuous *karmas*, which are not influenced by (the attitude of) emergence (from *saṃsāra*) and the mind of enlightenment, and the unvirtuous *karmas* do produce the happy and unhappy results (respectively). Yet there is no difference between them, since neither cause liberation and omniscience. For example, the black and white colors of clouds appear differently, but there is no difference in their covering the sky. But Ha-shang Mahāyāna, without distinguishing them (properly), said that all the virtuous and unvirtuous thoughts are bandages. Also in the instructions on meditation and the view of *Tsung-*

[1]Although they say that Ha-shang was a follower of Tsung-men (i.e., *Tsen-men*, usually a term for a Gradualist), they refute him as an Instantanealist, as all do. It seems that they are using the term Tsung-men for *Ch'an* Buddhism.

> *men* the terms "doing nothing" and "not thinking" are used, but that is (speaking) for those who have (already) realized the ultimate nature directly. Whereas Ha-shang Mahāyāna said that one attains liberation by not thinking anything in the mind from the beginning stage (of meditation). So a misinterpretation of one Ha-shang should not lead to the conclusion that all the Ha-shangs (of *Tsen-men* or *Chan* Buddhism are wrong)."

Jigmed Lingpa distinguishes the so-called view of Ha-shang Mahāyāna and the view of *Dzogpa Chenpo* in the following lines. (In a footnote to these lines, however, Jigmed Lingpa expresses doubt whether the popular allegations about the nature of Ha-shang's view are fair):[KZD 4b/5]

> According to your assumptions (about Ha-shang's view, the teaching of) Ha-shang doesn't have the means of distinguishing the objective mental concepts (*Yul Sems rTog*) and the objectless thoroughness (*Yul-Med Zang-Ka-Ma*). (If so,) it falls into the cognition of a mental state which doesn't distinguish between the mind and the intrinsic awareness. It is a state of extreme ignorance like an unconsciousness or deep sleep in which all the recollections, thoughts, and feelings have ceased. In *Dzogpa Chenpo* the objectless primordial wisdom doesn't analyze objective mental concepts (*Yul Sems rTog*). All the concepts have subsided (*Bag-La Zha*) into the state of immaculate crystal-like recollection of self-awareness. In its essence there are no changes, decrease, or increase. It is the dwelling in the vision (*dGongs-Pa*) of great vastness, free from extremes. So there is no way that there can be any similarities between the two (the views of Ha-shang and *Dzogpa Chenpo*).

There is an interesting story which involves Vimalamitra, one of the greatest of the Mahāyāna scholars from India who visited Tibet, Tingdzin Zangpo of the Nyang family, who was the chief recipient of *Nyingthig* teachings from Vimalamitra, and a Chinese master identified just as a Ha-shang. This Ha-shang may or may not be the Ha-shang Mahāyāna, but it is quite possible that he belonged to the *Tsen-men* tradition. The story illustrates the differences between *Dzogpa Chenpo* and this kind of meditation and shows that if one doesn't have the right meditation and perfect realization, then even if someone has attained a very stable absorption and achieved some wondrous experiences, it brings no enlightenment but delusions. Natshog Rangtrol repeats the story:[KZG 38b/5]

> In histories of *Dzogpa Chenpo* (the following) incident is related: Tingdzin Zangpo (*Ting-'Dzin bZang-Po, 9th century*), a monk from the Nyang family and a former attendant of King Thrisong Deutsen, received meditation instructions from one Ha-shang. He diligently meditated on them and became able to remain in absorption continuously for many days and nights without food and drink, and he acquired clairvoyance. While he was proud of having a good meditation, he met the great scholar Vimalamitra. He presented his meditation (to Vimalamitra for evaluation). Vimala(mitra) said: "Oh, your kind of meditation will bring birth in the *Nāga* realms and you will remain (there) asleep for eons without waking up. It won't become the cause of enlightenment." This caused the monk from Nyang to awaken his past (*karmic*) traces (in *Dzogpa Chenpo*), and then he received the teachings on *Dzogpa Chenpo* from the scholar [Vimalamitra]. Later he attained rainbow body.

New sources: In this century, two important documents have been discovered which shed some light on Ha-shang's views. The first is *Samten Migdron* (SM) or *Naljor Miggi Samten* (*rNal-'Byor Mig-Gi bSam-gTan*) by Nub Sangye Yeshey (9th century), one of the twenty-five chief disciples of Guru Padmasambhava and a contemporary of Ha-shang Mahāyāna. He lived for well over a hundred years.[LN 151a/3] This text became unavailable to scholars for centuries owing to lack of copies. The author gives a fair, respectful and unbiased account of different Buddhist schools, including the Instantanealist school of his time in

Tibet. The second is the documents discovered at Tun-huan, China at the end of the nineteenth century by some European scholars. The Tun-huan discoveries included many valuable texts and fragments of writings in Tibetan, Chinese, and other central Asian languages and are now preserved in various libraries. They are considered to be documents of the twelth century A.D. or earlier. Among the Tun-huang documents, it is said, are some fragments of writings of Ha-shang Mahāyāna, possibly a text entitled *Samten Chichar Jugpa'i Go* (*bSam-gTan Chig-Ch'ar 'Jug-Pa'i sGo*). This text is quoted in *Samten Migdron*,[SM 12b/6] but unfortunately I am not equipped to use or make any comments on it.

Samten Migdron (SM): This text is a very valuable piece of writing which provides great information about different views, meditation, and history of its time. Unfortunately, in many places the text is not very clear because of language, style, the scribe's writing, and the compact nature of the material. In many places it needs interpretation, and there is no commentary on it available. Today it is rare to find a scholar who possesses insight and knowledge of such a text. Those who render interpretations or translations might merely represent their own mental reflections and boasting echoes. Instead of trying to interpret it, it is important here to try to present a general view of its structure so that readers may reach their own conclusions.

The text has eight chapters. The fourth is on the Gradualist school (*Tsen-Men*) propogated in Tibet by Indian scholars such as Kamalaśīla,[SM 12a/5] and it is distinguished as interpretable teaching (*Drang-Don*). The fifth chapter is on the Instantanealist (*sTon-Mun*) school propogated in China by Bodhidharma and in Tibet notably by Ha-shang Mahāyāna. The sixth chapter is on *tantra* (esoteric teachings). The seventh chapter is on *Dzogpa Chenpo* (the Great Perfection), which is characterized as the summit of the *yānas*. *Samten Migdron* makes it clear that the succession of these chapters on schools is ordered according to the superiorities of the teachings and that the later teachings are superior to the earlier ones. The following are some quotations from *Samten Migdron* to illustrate the essence and the distinction of the four schools in terms of their entering into the path of contemplation:[SM 28a/6]

(a) In the Gradualist school (*Tsen-Men*), they abandon the four concepts of characteristics, such as the concept of nature (*Rang-bZhin*) (concept of antidotes, concept of suchness, and concept of attainments) gradually and enter into freedom from conceptualizations. . . .
(b) In the Instantanealist school(*sTon-Mun*), from the beginning, without any alternatives, they train on the unborn ultimate nature instantly. . . . Abbot (*Ha-shang*) Mahāyāna says: "Contemplate in the inconceivable ultimate nature (*Ch'os-Nyid, S. Dharmatā*) without any concepts."

Nub writes:[SM 85b/3]

> Here, there is no gradual training as the *Tsen-men* do. It enters into omnisicience (Buddhahood) instantly from the beginning. It is called trainingless training. . . . Here, there is nothing to abandon as the *Tsen-men* practitioners do. The intrinsic awareness of contemplation on emptiness completes the dual accumulations (merits and wisdom). There is no need of purification as there are no apprehensions and attachments.

Nub explains:[SM 31a/3]

> According to the Instantanealists, all the phenomenal existents of self and others are unborn from primordial time, and seeking (something) that is unborn is deluding the mind. Through that (seeking) one will never see the great meaning. It is like the ocean—it will not be stirred by the power of a rooster. It asserts that one enters into the ultimate nature (*Ch'os-Nyid*) if one doesn't think at all. . . . The Gradual way is taught for people of lesser intellect.

Nub writes:[SM 30a/3]

(c) According to *Mahāyoga* (*Tantra*) scriptures, all the phenomenal existents are self-clear as the intrinsic awareness. It is the indivisibility of the (two) truths, uncreated by a creator, total clarity and indivisibility of primordial wisdom and the ultimate sphere....

(d) *Atiyoga* (*Dzogpa Chenpo*), the extraordinary *yoga*: In the spontaneously accomplished suchness, all the phenomenal existents are radiantly clear primordially in the vast expanse of the totally pure and spontaneously arisen primordial wisdom. Cause and result are spontaneously perfected without seeking them separately (or without any gross efforts; *Ril Ma-bTsal-Bar Lhun-Gyis rDzogs-Pa*).

The following are some quotations from the *Platform Sūtra* of the Sixth Patriarch of *Ch'an* Buddhism:[PS 137/15]

> In the Dharma there is no sudden or gradual, but among people some are keen and others dull. The deluded recommended the gradual method, the enlightened the sudden teachings.

Platform Sūtra continues:[PS 141/6]

> See for yourselves the purity of your own natures, practice and accomplish for yourselves. Your own nature is the Dharmakāya and self-practice is the practice of Buddha; by self-accomplishment you may achieve the Buddha Way for yourselves.

The *Sūtra* says:[PS 160/4]

> Although in the teaching there is no sudden and gradual,
> In delusion and awakening there is slowness and speed.
> In studying the teaching of the sudden doctrine,
> Ignorant persons cannot understand completely.

The *Sūtra* continues:[PS 164/17]

> The master (*Hue-neng*) said: "The mind-ground, not in error, is the precept (*śīla*) of self-nature; the mind-ground,

> undisturbed, is the meditation (*dhyāna*) of self-nature; the mind-ground, not ignorant, is the wisdom (*prajñā*) of self-nature."

After going through these sources, one may find some clue to what was Ha-shang's views and whether it was similar to *Ch'an* or *Dzogpa Chenpo*. If Ha-shang Mahāyāna was teaching the remaining in mere absence of thoughts, then it is not what *Mahāyāna* or *Dzogpa Chenpo* scriptures teach. If he was saying that after having realized the meaning of the ultimate nature (*Ch'os-Nyid*), one should remain in it without any thoughts, as any kind of thoughts will only obstruct one from remaining in contemplation in the realized state, then there is no conflict with the teachings of *Dzogpa Chenpo*. But this approach is only for those who have realized such attainment and not for people who have ordinary mind, life, view, and emotions, as many of us do.

In *Mahāyāna* and especially in the *tantras* and *Dzogpa Chenpo*, there is instant realization. But it is only for those people who have already matured their minds, sharpened their intellects, and strengthened their virtuous *karmas*, the positive energies, by means of common trainings in advance in this life or in past lives.

So, according to the interpretations of traditional Tibetan scholars such as Ba, Buton, and Tsuglag Threngwa, Ha-shang's instant realization is merely remaining in absence of thoughts. *Samten Migdron* makes clear that it is remaining in the ultimate nature (*Ch'os-Nyid*) without thoughts. But here, it is necessary to do more research about this so-called ultimate nature, as to what kind of meditative or realized state it is. Also, according to *Samten Migdron*, Ha-shang states that the gradual way is for people of lesser intellect, but what distinguishes people of higher and lesser intellect for him? He seems to have given his teachings publicly without any discrimination; so did he consider most people to be beings of higher intellect?

Excerpts from the Lives of Dzogpa Chenpo Masters to Illustrate the Ways of Training in Dzogpa Chenpo

The masters who reach the highest attainment of *Dzogpa Chenpo* and display wonders as the sign of their attainment all undergo a vigorous process of training for years. It is true of the great masters of *Dzogpa Chenpo* of the past, such as Prahevajra, Mañjuśrīmitra, Vimalamitra, Padmasambhava, Longchen Rabjam, and Jigmed Lingpa, and it remains true for many recent masters including some of our own teachers. The meditative state, realization, and the perfection of the result of *Dzogpa Chenpo* are instant, effortless, spontaneous, and natural. But to reach that realization and to perfect it, almost all the trainees are bound to go through various studies and trainings step by step, according to their ability and nature, with intense dedication. It is unknown in the history of *Dzogpa Chenpo* that an ordinary follower has attained realization without essential preparations or has perfected the realization with no need of improving and refining it through meditation on it. Yet the actual realization is instant and its perfection is spontaneous. Among those great *Dzogpa Chenpo* masters, many were manifestations of the Buddhas and Bodhisattvas, but they became reincarnated as ordinary beings and went through the hardship of training to demonstrate a model of training on the path for others. Many other great masters were ordinary beings who became realized and accomplished adepts through their long and earnest training.

SOME ANCIENT *DZOGPA CHENPO* MASTERS

The following is a summary of the lives of some of the early masters from *Logyu Chenmo*[LC 49a/6] and *Dzamling Thatru Khyabpa'i Gyen*:[DTG 60b/7]

> Master Prahevajra was a great Buddhist teacher and he was the first human master of *Dzogpa Chenpo*. He remained in absorption for thirty-two years in a grass hut (*'Jag-Ma'i sPyil-Bo*). He received the empowerments and the 6,400,000 verses of the *tantras* of *Dzogpa Chenpo* from Vajrasattva in a pure vision. At the end, he dissolved his gross body into a "Light body" (*A'od-Phung*). Mañjuśrīmitra received the *Dzogpa Chenpo* teachings from Prahevajra over a period of seventy-five years and then attained "Light-body." Śrīsiṁha of China, after studying and training in various disciplines of Buddhism for decades, received *Dzogpa Chenpo* teachings from Mañjuśrīmitra and practiced them for twenty-five years. Jñanasūtra, after passing through study and training in various disciplines of Buddhism, spent decades receiving teachings and empowerments of various stages of *Dzogpa Chenpo* from Śrīsiṁha, and then he trained on them. Vimalamitra was one of the most learned monks among the five hundred scholars who lived near Vajrāsana, where the Buddha attained enlightenment. In fulfillment of a prophesy which he received from Vajrasattva in a pure vision, he went to China and for twenty years received the teachings of the First Three Categories, the Outer, Inner, and Secret Categories of *Dzogpa Chenpo*, from Śrisiṁha and then returned to India. Then, in fulfillment of a prophecy given by a *Ḍākinī*, Vimalamitra went to Jñānasūtra, who was also a

disciple of Śrīsiṅha. He received the transmission of different levels of teachings and empowerments of the Innermost Secret Category of *Dzogpa Chenpo*, the Elaborate, Non-elaborate, Simple, and Utmost Simple empowerments, gradually over an expanse of years from Jñānasūtra. Then he perfected the respective realizations of the instructions and empowerments. Like Guru Padmasambhava, Vimalamitra attained the body of "Great Transformation" (*'Pho-Ba Ch'en-Po*). In that "light body," it is believed, he is still living at Wu-tai-shan in China and is visible to fortunate beings. Longchen Rabjam, after becoming a great scholar and adept of common Buddhist disciplines, received the *Dzogpa Chenpo* teachings and transmissions from the great master Kumaradza. He then underwent intensive meditative training for six years on those teachings and became the most venerated teacher and writer of Tibet on *Dzogpa Chenpo* scriptures and instructions.

DEVOTION CAUSED REALIZATION IN GYALWA'I NYUKU

The virtuous trainings including devotion are most important in the training of *Dzogpa Chenpo* meditation. They are indispensable means to bring forth the realization and to perfect it. In his autobiography, Pema Ledrel Tsal (1879-1941) describes how his master Nyoshul Lungtog taught him in the following way:[NGR 61a/1]

> In this lineage, through devotion to the master one attains the realization. The way of having a teacher is not politeness, but devotion. *Guru yoga* is not prayers, but devotion. Once, Jigmed Gyalwa'i Nyuku was practicing meditation for many years at Tsa-ri with intensive asceticism and hardship. One day he went out of the cave into the sunlight. He looked in the direction of Lhasa, and a strong recollection of his root master (Jigmed Lingpa) and of the lineal teachers arose in his mind. He prayed to them with strong devotion. For a while it was as if he had become

unconscious. When he regained consciousness, he found that there was nothing to view or meditate upon, as all the apprehensions of attending to meditation had dissolved into the ultimate sphere. He had (actually) reached the ultimate presence of intrinsic awareness, free from waverings and delusions. But he (wasn't aware of its nature and he) wasn't satisfied (with what he was experiencing). He thought, "Alas! if I hadn't gone into the sunlight I would have a meditation, but now there is nothing. I have to leave to see the Lama because now he is old and I must get clarifications concerning my meditation. . . . He went to see (his teacher), Rigdzin Jigmed Lingpa, and he presented (his meditative) realization to him. (Jigmed Lingpa) was pleased and said: Son, that is it! You have reached the stage of "Exhaustion of Phenomenal Existents into the Ultimate Nature. . . ." Then (Gyalwa'i Nyugu) went to Thrama (*Khra-Ma*) in Dza (*rDza*) valley (in Kham) and meditated there for more than twenty years, and he became known as Thrama Lama. So, mere realization is not sufficient, but one has then got to meditate on it. The experiences (developed through meditation) should be perfected (*Klong-Du Gyur*), and the perfection should be completed. Until the perfection is completed, one should train on it in meditative periods. When for oneself the meaning of exhaustion of phenomena of *Dzogpa Chenpo* is actualized, the wisdom of discriminating all phenomena, the power of intrinsic awareness, bursts forth, and the *yānas* and tenets can be discriminated without confusion. And for others, if one has spontaneously generated great compassion free from concepts, the time for one to teach, discuss, and write has arrived.

VIRTUES DEVELOP IN THOSE WHO HAVE *DZOGPA CHENPO* EXPERIENCES

To the extent that one progresses through *Dzogpa Chenpo* training, all the virtues such as compassion will be developed and strengthened. In his autobiography Pema Ledrel Tsal says:[NGR 59a/4]

> (Nyoshul Lungtog) asked me: "Do you have pride?" I told (him): "No, I don't. During the off-meditation periods, I do not have any experiences except loneliness (*sKyo Lhang-Lhang*), since all the appearances are unreal and unimportant." (Nyoshul Lungtog) said: "It should be like that. One should have the experiences (of the virtuous thoughts), as the Omniscient One (Longchen Rabjam) said:
>
> > By gaining experiences in (*Dzogpa Chenpo*), these virtuous experiences arise:
> > The (realization) of impermanance and of reducing the range of the mind, from the depth of the heart,
> > Loving-kindness and compassion without cessation and
> > Pure perception and devotion without partiality.

REALIZATION ATTAINED INSTANTLY BY NYOSHUL LUNGTOG

Although one has to go through intensive preparations of study and meditation to get the introduction to the realization and to perfect it, the actual realization is instant when the meditator has ripened, and there is no need of intellectual and mental concepts. When the disciple is ready, through various means the teacher introduces the disciple to the realized state. Nowadays, generally the teachers bestow the transmission of *Dzogpa Chenpo* realization through meditative concentration, devotional chant, and ceremonial performances. If the disciple is ready he will attain realization, otherwise it may only act as a special blessing from the master. But if the disciple is ready and the master is a realized adept, then even the simplest indication could bring forth the highest realization. The following is a piece of teaching that Nyoshul Lungtog gave to Pema Ledrel Tsal about how Paltul Rinpoche (1808-1897) introduced Nyoshul Lungtog to the *Dzogpa Chenpo* realization. Nyoshul Lungtog had already become a great scholar and had spent years in preliminary and actual practices of *tantra* and *Dzogpa Chenpo*, and when he received the following transmission from his teacher, because he was ready, his realization took place in a very simple way. Nyoshul Lungtog narrates the story to Pema Ledrel Tsal:[NGR 59b/5]

> If there is no crucial means of teaching by (individually given) oral instructions, the (intellectual) words, supposed to be of high realization from a Lama, will get nowhere. Nowadays teachers (just) dance to the tunes of the texts. That is not sufficient. Once, Abu (Elder Brother = Paltul Rinpoche) was living with us disciples in a field on this side of Nagchungma (hermitage). . . . Every day at dusk, Abu would do a meditation session on the training of Namkha Sumthrug (*Nam-mKha' Sum-Phrug*), stretched out on his back on a new woolen carpet on a piece of grass the size of himself. One evening, while he was lying there as usual, he said to me: "Lungchey (*Lung-gChes* = dear Lung-tog)! Did you say that you do not know the essence of the mind?" (I answered,) "Yes, sir, I don't." (Abu said:) "Oh, there is nothing not to know. Come here." So, I went to him. (He said:) "Lie down, as I am lying, and look at the sky." As I did so, (the conversation went on as follows:)
>
> > "Do you see the stars in the sky?"
> > "Yes."
> > "Do you hear the dogs barking in Dzogchen monastery?"
> > "Yes."
> > "Well, that is the meditation!"
>
> At that moment, I arrived at a certainty (of realization) from within. I had been liberated from the fetters of "it is" and "it is not." I had realized the primordial wisdom, the naked (union of) emptiness and intrinsic awareness. I was introduced to this realization by his blessing, as Saraha said:
>
> > "He in whose heart the words of the master have entered
> > Sees (the truth) like a treasure in his own palm."

> Afterwards, when the words (of Paltul Rinpoche) were (intellectually) examined, there was nothing much, but just his having said that the eye-consciousness and ear-consciousness are the intrinsic awareness. However, it should be understood that the introduction (to *Dzogpa Chenpo*) took place (through these words) because of the transmission of blessing, the absolute transmission of the realization of the meaning of the Heart Essence (*sNying-Thig*).

PALTUL ATTAINED REALIZATION THROUGH THE TEACHER'S *YOGIC* POWER

Sometimes great *yogis* give the high transmissions such as that of the realization of *Dzogpa Chenpo* through various means and indications, and the disciple who is ready receives the introduction miraculously. There are no logical and intellectual reasonings or ceremonial performances, but just a skillful display of whatever is appropriate. Dodrup Chen Jigmed Tenpa'i Nyima writes about how Paltul Rinpoche was introduced to *Dzogpa Chenpo* realization by Khyentse Yeshey Dorje (1800-?):[DZ 4a/5]

> When Jigmed Yeshey Dorje (*'Jigs-Med Ye-Shes rDo-rJe*), the Precious Excellent Incarnation of the Omniscient One (Jigmed Lingpa), was wandering to perform ascetic disciplines (*sPyod-Pa*), he arrived one day where the Lord Paltul Rinpoche was staying and shouted: "O Palge (*dPal-dGe*—Paltul Rinpoche's lineage name)! Are you brave? If you are, come here!" When Paltul Rinpoche went to him, he held Paltul by the hair, threw him on the ground and dragged him around. After a while, an odor of alcohol was suddenly emitted and Paltul Rinpoche thought: "Oh, he is drunk. Even a great adept like him is capable of this kind of behavior because of his drinking. This is the fault of alcohol as discoursed upon by the Blessed One (Buddha)." At that very moment, Khyentse Yeshey Dorje freed Paltul from his grip and shouted: "Alas! you who

are called intellectuals (*rTog-Ge-Ba*), how could such an evil thought arise (in you)? You old dog." He spat on Paltul's face and showed him his little finger (sign of the worst insult) and then he left. Immediately Paltul realized, "Oh! I have been deluded." It was an introduction. And he resumed the (meditative) posture. (At that moment) Paltul realized the unhindered intrinsic awareness, (clear) like the cloudless sky. The dawn-like (clear) introduction (to the realization) given by Jigmed Gyalwa'i Nyugu had become (bright) like the rising of the sun. Later on, Paltul Rinpoche would say jokingly, " 'Old Dog' is my esoteric name given by Kushog Khyentse."

IMPORTANCE OF EARNEST TRAINING

It is very important to study and practice intensively. Otherwise, merely having the best teacher, the most profound path, or being a wise disciple won't work and may only create pride in oneself and contempt for others. The great yogi Milarepa, before he met the great translator Marpa, received *Dzogpa Chenpo* teachings, but he didn't make any progress on his meditative path because he did not practice them. The biography of Milarepa relates:[MN 39/20]

(Milarepa goes to Rongton Lhaga (*Rong-sTon Lha-dGa'*), a *Dzogpa Chenpo* master and says:) "I am a man from Latod. I have committed grave evil deeds. Please give me a teaching which leads me to liberation in this very lifetime." The Lama said: "My sacred teaching, the *Dzogpa Chenpo,* is a triumph at the root, triumph at the summit, and triumph at the fruition. If you meditate on it by day, you will become a Buddha that day. If you meditate on it by night, you will become a Buddha that night. For fortunate people who have (ripened their) *karmic* connections, there is not even the need of meditation, for by hearing this (teaching) one attains liberation. It is the share of Dharma for the most intellectually gifted people. I shall give you this teaching." He gave me the empowerments and instructions. Then I thought: "In the past when I was practising spells, I produced the great signs in fourteen days. Seven days were sufficient for a hailstorm. Now I have met a Dharma which is even easier than the spells and hailstorm, such that if I meditate on it by day, I will become a Buddha that day, and if I meditate on it by night, I will become a Buddha that night. For fortunate people who have (ripened their) *karmic* connections, there is no need of meditation. So I must be a person who has (ripened his) *karmic* connections." With this pride, I spent the time sleeping without doing any meditation, and dharma and the person (myself) went two separate ways.

IMPORTANCE OF RELYING ON AUTHENTIC SCRIPTURES

It is very important to rely on authentic scriptures such as the *tantras* and the writings of Longchen Rabjam as the basis and to have the teacher's instructions as the keys. But some people rely on oral instructions from a teacher and don't know anything about the scriptures, the sources of the teachings. In addition to conveying the blessings of the lineal Buddhas, Vidyādharas and masters, these scriptures contain various levels and means of practice in both detailed and condensed forms. Nyoshul Lungtog teaches Pema Ledrel Tsal:[NGR 62b/1]

> From now on refine (the realizations of) your own mind by (comparing them with) the meaning of the great (scriptures:) the *Seven Treasures* (*mDzod-bDun*) of the Omniscient One (Longchen Rabjam) as well as the *Mother and Son Heart Essences* (*sNying-Thig Ma-Bu*). There are people who just listen to the words of an old Lama and put the *Seven Treasures* and *Four Volumes* (*Ya-bZhi*) aside and say: "These books are textual expositions. The unexcelled oral transmission is given to me by so and so Lama," and they give new designations (to the meditations such as:), "dwelling, moving and aware (*gNas 'Gyu Rig*)," to the tranquillity (*Zhi-gNas*) with or without characteristics.

> These (tendencies) which deceive trainees (of *Dzogpa Chenpo*) of both higher and lesser (intellect) are perverted teachings influenced by demonic forces [*māra*].

REFRAIN FROM BEING TAKEN OVER BY CERTAIN MYSTICAL EXPERIENCES

While one is doing the meditative training of *Dzogpa Chenpo*, it is important not to be taken over by any kind of experience, even if it seems to be a wonderful and important sign, but to remain on the path of meditation without wandering, for those experiences might not be the true *Dzogpa Chenpo* realization and its virtues. Nyoshul Lungtog tells Pema Ledrel Tsal:[NGR 15b/1]

> Once (Paltul Rinpoche) was giving us teachings on *The Three Cycles on Relaxation* (*Ngal-gSo sKor-gSum*) and experiential instructions of *Dzogpa Chenpo*, and we were doing meditations on them, while making "three-body tea" in Ari forest in Do valley (near Dodrup Chen monastery). At that time, all the false caves of my apprehensions (of self and phenomena) as real collapsed. All the phenomena arose (for me) as the phases of illusion. I (Pema Ledrel Tsal) asked him: "Is this a realization?" He [Lungtog] answered: "No, it is a good experience."

SINCERE MIND IS BETTER THAN MANY SO-CALLED HIGH REALIZATIONS

There are many so-called great meditators, who ignorantly believe, cleverly pretend, or arrogantly boast that they have achieved high realizations. But in truth only their ego and emotional defilements have increased. This is proof that those people were not even doing any practice on *Dzogpa Chenpo* as it is taught but were misusing it to fool themselves and others. Pema Ledrel Tsal asks Nyoshul Lungtog:[NGR 29a/1]

> "Nowadays there are many people who say that they have realized emptiness, but their emotions have not decreased. What is that, Sir?" He [Lungtog] answered: "These are

empty claims. In this dark age, there are people who say, 'I have realized emptiness or the nature of the mind and my (realization of) the view is high.' But (in actual fact) they have increased their confidence (only) in indulging in the unvirtuous deeds, and their emotions have become rougher. They only focus on verbal tradition. When they face the crucial junctions of birth, death, and the intermediate state, (their confidence in so-called high realization) turns out to be lower than that of someone who (just) has a good mind."

DODRUP CHEN'S TESTAMENT AND TRANSMISSION AT THE TIME OF HIS DEATH

In ancient times, when an accomplished *Dzogpa Chenpo* meditator, at the time of his death or the dissolution of the mortal body, would leave his or her testament to his chief disciple, the disciple became inseparable with the master in realization and he became the main lineage-holder. Mañjuśrīmitra received Prahevajra's testament, *The Three Words that Penetrate the Essence*, Śrīsiṅha received Mañjuśrīmitra's testament, *The Six Meditative Experiences*, Jñānasūtra received Śrīsiṅha's testament, *The Seven Crucial Points*, and Vimalamitra received Jñānasūtra's testament, *The Four Methods of Contemplation*. But even in recent centuries many masters left their testaments to their chief disciples, sometimes directly and sometimes in pure visions. At the time of the death of the first Dodrup Chen Rinpoche, one of his chief disciples, Do Khyentse Yeshey Dorje, was away from his teacher at a distance of a few weeks' travel by horse and wasn't directly informed, maybe for months. But on the very day that Dodrup Chen died, Do Khyentse received the following pure vision and the testament:[KZ 107a/4]

> At dawn on the thirteenth day of the first month of the iron-snake year (1821), I saw the peerless lord, the king of Dharma, the triply gracious one in the form of a light-body attired in a five-colored silken costume blazing with

radiance in a chariot of brocades carried by four *Ḍākinīs* in the midst of rainbow lights in the sky. In an enchanting voice he said:

"I am going to the vast expanse of Primordial Wisdom of the Ultimate Sphere,
The primordial wisdom of the ultimate sphere is inexpressible and inconceivable.
I am going to the state of Mirror-like Primordial Wisdom,
It is a vivid and unceasing glow of clarity.
I am going to the sphere of the Primordial Wisdom of Equanimity,
It is the dissolution of the concepts of apprehension of *saṃsāra* and *nirvāṇa* into the ultimate sphere.
I am going to the state of the Discriminative Primordial Wisdom,
It is the means of clear arising of the six foreknowledges (*mNgon-Shes*).
I am going to the state of the Primordial Wisdom of Accomplishment,
It displays various manifestations appropriate to the wishes of trainable beings.
I am going to Glorious Copper Colored Mountain, the Buddha-field of knowledge-holders;
When I attain equal realization with the *Heruka*,
Three incarnations will appear for your assistance.
The testament, which appears clearly in the symbolic script of *Ḍākinīs*,
Until the time arrives,
Keep secret and closed, like a tomb,
The symbolic sign will not disappear. May it be stable!
Son, for a while stay healthy.
Now you are victorious over the obstructions in your life.
Until the phenomenal existents are liberated in accordance with the indications and texts (of teachings),
See *saṃsāra* and *nirvāṇa* as dreams and illusions.

Devote yourself to taking (all) into the path of freedom from objective thoughts.
This is the empowerment of complete aspiration and transmission.
This is the commanding empowerment among empowerments."

Then from the white 'Āḥ' syllable, clear like a water-crystal at his heart, a five-colored light was emitted and merged into me. Again a second 'Āḥ' syllable shot (from the Āḥ syllable at his heart) and merged into my heart. Instantly I became unconcious and remained in the great *Vajra*-waves. Then the Lama had disappeared with no trace of where he had gone. At sunrise I came out of the unconscious state, but all the gross and subtle concepts had been liberated as "no apprehension at arising." I saw the spontaneously arisen intrinsic awareness nakedly and vividly. For three days I remained in the unmodified and thoroughness state, unpolluted by either doubts or confidence. I was free from the views of analysis of "it is" and "it is not." Then, in my mind, I realized that the mind of the lord, the triple gracious one, the second Buddha, had dissolved into the ultimate sphere, and I remained for a while in the darkness of sorrow, since the orphans, I myself and other disciples, had been (left behind), wandering in the field (of *saṃsāra*).

WONDROUS SIGNS AT THE TIME OF DEATH OF KONME KHENPO

Many accomplished *Dzogpa Chenpo* meditators display various signs of their accomplishments at the time of death. Some have pure visions of Buddhas, Bodhisattvas, and adepts and receive inspirations, empowerments, and introductions. Many remain in the meditative state, for hours or days, even after the energies of the elements are dissolved, breathing has ceased, and mind is submerged into the inner clarity [luminous absorption], yet one's mind is not separated from the body. As an external sign of the meditator's being still in the meditative state, the body will be warm at the heart and the head will still be held up. Many leave various signs in the ashes from their cremation. They include images, relics in the form of pellet-shaped white particles called *Ringsel* (*Ring-bSrel*), and special larger, hard relics which are *Ringsel* of various colors and are called *Dung* (*gDung*). At the time of death and of cremation, many wondrous signs such as rainbow rays, sounds, sweet odors, and earth tremors take place. The following is a brief account of the events at the time of the death of Khenpo Konchog Dronme (*dKon-mCh'og sGron-Me*), alias Lobzang Kunkhyab (*Blo-bZang Kun-Khyab*), popularly known as Konme (*dKon-Me*) Khenpo (1859-1936), of Dodrup Chen monastery. Just before his death, Khenpo received from a *Ḍākinī* a special introduction to the inner clarity [luminous absorption] as the five primordial wisdoms. A one-page note prepared by the disciples who were present says:

> Just before his death early on the night of the 28th day of the 12th month of the wood-pig year (1936), he told his disciples who were present before him:
>
> > "I had a dream (although his disciples were sure that he didn't sleep). A woman told me: 'Sokhe Chomo (*Sog-Khe Jo-Mo*) says: 'This present luminous absorption is the realization of emptiness. Because if this is not the emptiness which is the nature of primordial knowledge, then the Primordial Wisdom of the Ultimate Sphere of final Buddhahood and the present luminous absorption will not be able to be established as indistinguishable.This (present luminous absorption) is the Precious Majestic Virtue (*Yon-Tan Rin-Ch'en rGyal-Po*). Because, if all the virtues of the result are not spontaneously present (in it) without (need of) seeking, then the primordial wisdom of the Buddhas and present luminous absorption will not be able to be established as undifferentiable.' I told the woman: 'Yes, that is a perfect understanding. In any case, if one extends it fur-

> ther by meditating on it through the path of Unmodified Natural Contemplation (*Ma-bChos Chog-bZhag*) and if one realizes the total perfection of the intrinsic awareness, then this (luminous absorption) becomes as the Five Primordial Wisdoms. The clarity and no-concept which has not arisen as either of the two obscurations is the Mirror-like Primordial Wisdom. The freedom from falling into partialities and dimensions is the Primordial Wisdom of Equanimity. Knowing all the phenomenal existents without confusion is the Discriminative Primordial Wisdom.' "

Then Khenpo sat in the posture of Relaxing in the Natural State of the Mind (*Sems-Nyid Ngal-gSo*) and passed away.

He remained in the meditative absorption without leaving the body for a couple of days. According to the tradition, after a couple of weeks, with a huge ritual ceremony his body was cremated in a specially constructed temporary *stupa*, in the midst of signs of rainbow rays in the sky, and then the *stupa* was sealed. After a couple of days, when the *stupa* was opened to collect the ashes, his disciples found hundreds of relics in white, red, yellow and blue which had emerged or were emerging from the burned bones. Later, they built a golden *stupa* and preserved almost all the relics in it. I had a set of four of these relics in four different colors in my locket, but at about the same time that the golden *stupa* in the Dodrup Chen monastery in Tibet was destroyed, I lost my locket in India. It seems that when the time comes, everything that is supposed to go goes, in one way or another, wherever it is.

RAINBOW BODY ATTAINED BY SODNAM NAMGYAL

As referred to before, there are two supreme physical attainments of the most highly accomplished *Dzogpa Chenpo* masters. The first is the attainment of the Great Transformation (*'Pho-Ba Ch'en-Po*) achieved by very few known adepts such as Vimalamitra, Padmasambhava, and Chetsun Senge

Wangchug (*lChe-bTsun Seng-Ge dBang-Phyug*), who transformed their mortal bodies into subtle light bodies and live without death, appearing whenever it is appropriate. The second is the attainment of Rainbow Body (*'Ja'-Lus*) achieved by many *Dzogpa Chenpo* meditators throughout the age of *Dzogpa Chenpo* in India, and in Tibet till the middle of the twentieth century. At the time of death these meditators, having attained the ultimate nature through the practice of *Dzogpa Chenpo*, dissolve their mortal bodies with a display of lights and leave behind only the nails and hair. The last *Dzogpa Chenpo* meditator who attained Rainbow Body in well witnessed circumstances attracting much attention occurred in 1952. He is Sodnam Namgyal (*bSod-Nams rNam-rGyal*, 1874?-1952) of the Tag-rong (*sTag-Rong*) clan in Yidlhung (*Yid-Lhung*) valley in Kham, Eastern Tibet. He was the father of the late Lama Gyurtrag (*'Gyur-Grags, d.1975*), a close Dharma friend of mine. The following is the narrative of the event given to me by Lama Gyurtrag, and also some information drawn from prayers to his father written by Lama Gyurtrag:

> My father was a hunter in his youth. But later he became very devoutly religious and practiced a lot. But we didn't know that he was such an accomplished *Dzogpa Chenpo* meditator. He was very secretive about his meditation. He had completed the Fivefold 100,000 Preliminaries thirteen times. He had received *Dzogpa Chenpo* meditation instructions from the meditator Jinpa Zangpo (*sByin-Pa bZang-Po*), a disciple of Khyentse Yeshey Dorje (*mKhyen-brTse Ye-Shes rDo-rJe*, 1800-?). For most of his life my father spent his time carving images, *mantras*, and scriptures in stones in many places, mainly at Mani Kedgo in Yidlhung valley. He was very humble and no one ever expected him to be such a special person, which is as it should be for a true *yogi*. Once I was in retreat. My brother came to me and said: "Father is slightly sick. I don't see anything serious, but he says he is going to die." Then after a couple of days, on the evening of the seventh day of the fourth

month of the Water-dragon year (1952), Father died at the age of 79. A lama had advised my brother that they should take special care of their father's body when he died, but my relatives didn't understand what that meant. So, soon after his death they arranged the body in the same way as for an ordinary lay person. But they began noticing rainbow lights and rainbow tents around their place, and the body started to reduce in size. Then they realized that their father had attained enlightenment in the ultimate nature through *Dzogpa Chenpo* meditation and that his gross body was dissolving in what is popularly known as "Dissolution into Rainbow Body." After a couple of days (I can't remember how many days he told me), his whole mortal body was dissolved. I hurriedly concluded my retreat and went home. Then everything had gone and only the twenty nails of the fingers and toes and the hair of the body was left behind on the spot where his body was being kept. We collected these remains and except for a few little pieces that we kept for ourselves, we offered all the nails and hair to Jamyang Khyenste Chokyi Lotro (*'Jam-dByangs mKhyen-brTse Ch'os-Kyi Blo-Gros*, 1893-1959), as he wished to have them. Everybody in the valley was talking about my father's death. If a famous Lama died in this manner, it wouldn't be a suprise, but when a humble lay person displayed such a great accomplishment, it amazed us all. In truth, ofcourse, a humble life is a great support for meditation and accomplishment. Name, fame, and wealth could easily become obstructions. Humbleness is a great priviledge for a *Dzogpa Chenpo* meditator, but ordinary people don't see things in that way. They are only attracted to and believe in empty names, deceitful material riches, and arrogant intellectual reasonings.

Lama Gyurtrag had a small piece of a nail of his father with him as a relic and he gave me a very small piece of it.

YUKHOG CHATRALWA, A GREAT *DZOGPA CHENPO* TEACHER

Most people generally overestimate their own capacity, intelligence, and nature because they are enveloped in the ignorant darkness of their own egoistic shadows. Their ambitions and expectations exceed what their actual capacity could provide for them. It is important to realize the extent of one's own ability and to pursue the goals accordingly. The following is the account of our visit to a most famous *Dzogpa Chenpo* master, Yukhog Chatralwa (*gYu-Khog Bya-Bral-Ba*), the Hermit or ascetic from Yu valley named Choying Rangtrol (*Ch'os-dByings Rang-Grol*, d.1953?). My tutor Kyala Khenpo, Chochog (*Kya-La mKhan-Po, Ch'os-mCh'og, 1893-1957*) and I went to see Chatralwa accompanied by Khenpo's brother, Kyali Loli, and a few others.

In 1951 we went to the hermitage called Yagegar (*Yag-Ge sGar*), the Beautiful Camp, to see Chatralwa, the ascetic. He had about two hundred disciples, mostly monks. Almost all the disciples lived in small huts and caves outfitted with a small bed-cum-seat on which they could sleep, sit, and meditate. Near their beds they had small stoves for making tea, and little altars with some books. Many could hardly stand up in their cells. Many of his disciples were doing *Dzogpa Chenpo* meditation, but the majority of them were still doing common *sūtric* and *tantric* studies and practices and the preliminaries of *Dzogpa Chenpo*, and they were being taught by the Chatralwa's senior disciples. For the most part Chatralwa only gave teachings and clarifications on the meditation and philosophy of *Dzogpa Chenpo* and only saw disciples individually, giving meditation instruction according to the experiences (*Nyam-Khrid*) of the disciples. He didn't give public talks or teachings to groups since disciples have different meditative needs. The most impressive thing about that hermitage was that while almost all the disciples lived on mere life-sustaining means, yet their peace, cheerfulness, calmness, compassion, contentment, and energy, and the smiles on their faces told the whole story of their lives and achievements. Generally, unless you were committed to staying for a long time, Chatralwa wouldn't see you. But, he was fond of children, and they could go to his house at any time when he was free. He played with them and told stories. He was very old, perhaps in his 80's or even around 90, but no one knew his actual age. Usually people had to help him stand up or walk because of his bad knees; but there were incidents such as his once running after pages of his books when they had blown away in the wind, and no one had shown up in response to his call. People believe that he could read others' minds and everyone was always fearful about their own thoughts when they were with him. After the first day interview, which my tutor Kyala Khenpo and I had, Khenpo told his brother Kyali Loli some of the clarifications on *Dzogpa Chenpo* meditation he received from the Chatralwa. The next day, before we took our leave at the end of the second interview, Chatralwa told Khenpo out of the blue: "Don't immediately try to find someone with whom you can sharpen your lips [chatter]." It enforced our belief and fear that he possessed clairvoyance. And of course Khenpo felt compelled to stop passing on the clarifications to his brother.

Chatralwa lived as a celibate yogi. He had thin gray hair; his hair was long and a little clotted. I remember his saying: "My teacher, Adzom Drugpa (*A-Dzom 'Brug-Pa, 1842-1924*), told me that I should lead a *tantric* life, and he prophesied that I would become a *Terton* (*gTer-sTon*), a Dharma Treasure Discoverer. But neither do I want to be married, as it could lead to a life of struggle, nor to discover any new *Terchos*, Discovered Dharma Treasure Teachings, as there are so many authentic golden *Terchos* which are available. So, as a symbol of observance of my teacher's words, I kept this long hair as a *tantric* costume."

As it was very hard for anybody to see the Third Dodrup Chen Rinpoche and because Chatralwa, too, had never any chance to see him, he had received clarifications from the Rinpoche through Terton Sogyal (*gTer-sTon bSod-rGyal*, 1856-1926), with whom Chatralwa stayed for a long period of time. Chatralwa told us: "Of course I never had the good fortune to see Rinpoche, but I received so many wonderful clarifications from him. When I was staying at Terton Sogyal's Latrang (residence), whenever Terton returned from seeing Rinpoche, he would always call me and would pass on to me all the instructions on doctrinal and meditational points that he received from Rinpoche, or whatever they had discussed on crucial points." Raising his voice he would continue: "Abe (elder brother's)! How could I forget those golden teachings? I am not mad!"

Chatralwa had rather a big comfortable house with lots of books and religious objects and a few attendants. If you gave him any presents or offerings, sometimes he would accept them or send them for religious services, but sometimes he would show rage and throw them away. But if you brought him a nice meal, especially *Zhemog* (*bZhes-Mog*), he would always take it with great pleasure and would say his famous line: "Oh, it is worthy of hundreds of horses and cows (*mDzo*)."

There is a funny story about Chatralwa's big house. One day a well-known Lama named Rinchen Targye (*Rin-Ch'en Dar-rGyas*), who was prophesied by the first Dodrup Chen as a great adept, had an interview with Chatralwa. This Lama entered Chatralwa's room and kept looking around instead of sitting down and talking to the Chatralwa. Chatralwa asked him sharply: "What did you lose?" The Lama answered: "I heard you are a Chatralwa, an ascetic. But you have enough to be called a rich man. How can one call you a Chatralwa?" Chatralwa answered: "Chatralwa means someone who has cut off his emotional attachments to worldly materials or to life. It does not mean being poor and hankering for them as many do." Chatralwa always enjoyed people who are direct and bold.

We spent eighteen days at Yagegar. Kyala Khenpo and I saw Chatralwa many times. Chatralwa gave the answers to Khenpo's questions in very great detail, and after each answer he told an interesting story of the past before going on to the next question. I didn't understand much of the main teachings but enjoyed the stories. Looking at him gave one a feeling of his being so ancient, ageless, wise, natural, and vast. I kept thinking again and again: "Oh, Kunkhyen Jigmed Lingpa must have been like this Lama." At that time I didn't think much about its unusual significance, but later, and still now whenever I try to understand, I don't find any answer to the question of why he let me be in on those very esoteric interviews. Is it because I had been recognized as a Tulku of a great Lama for whom Chatralwa had great respect, or because I was just a child of twelve years old? I don't think either of these is the reason. Whenever I think about him and his presence, it still brings a great peace within me. That must have been the true reason that this great Lama who had clairvoyance permitted me to be present.

A couple of days before we left, Khenpo arranged for his brother, Kyali Loli, to have an interview with the Chatralwa. Loli was neither a scholar nor an accomplished meditator. Anyhow, he had already received *Dzogpa Chenpo* teachings and had practiced them after completion of his common practices and preliminaries. But when he met Chatralwa it was disappointing for him. It is not because he wasn't doing well with his *Dzogpa Chenpo* meditation, but that he wasn't even ready to start it.

On that day, one of the most important days of his life, Kyali Loli went to see Chatralwa. Loli was a very courageous person and nothing would intimidate him. So Loli explained his practice, especially concerning his *Dzogpa Chenpo* experiences, and he requested instructions and clarifications. Chatralwa, without making any remarks about Loli's presentation, said:

> You should first try to say with devotion the "name prayer" of Amitābha Buddha 100 times a day, then increase it to 200, and so on. One day there might be a time when whatever you are doing, you will always be united with the expression of the "name" of the Buddha and the feeling of the presence of the Buddha. If that happens, when you die, you will die with the expression and feelings of the

> presence of the Buddha. Then, because of your merits and the blessings of the Buddha, perceptions will manifest as the Buddha-field, and your future will be in peace and happiness. Then you will be equipped to serve others.

Then he wrote down a few lines, a quotation from a *sūtra* which reveals the merits and benefits of the "recitation of the name of Amitābha Buddha."

Kyali Loli was disappointed because he didn't get any *Dzogpa Chenpo* teachings, and it broke his proud heart. But, now thinking back, I can understand how these teachings were perfect for him, and how it will be beneficial if he or anybody uses those instructions. It is important for the teacher to be fair, frank, certain, and clear, and for the disciple to be realistic, careful, tolorant, and open, as a line says:

> "Having the *Dzogpa Chenpo* as teachings is not enough,
> The person needs to become *Dzogpa Chenpo*."

LIFE OF KUNKHYEN LONGCHEN RABJAM

Among masters of *Dzogpa Chenpo* since the time of Guru Padmasambhava and Vimalamitra (9th century), Kunkhyen Longchen Rabjam (*Kun-mKhyen Klong-Chen Rab-'Byams*, 1308-1363) has been the greatest adept, meditator, philosopher, and writer. He was born in a village called Todtrong (*sTod-Grong*), in the Tra (*Grva*) valley of the Yoru (*gYo-Ru*) region—one of the two regions of central Tibet (*dBus*), Yoru and Wuru (*dBu-Ru*)—on the tenth day of the eleventh month (TTD 3a/4: 8th of 2nd month) of the earth monkey year of the fifth Rabchung (*Rab Byung*, a sexagenary cycle). His father, Master Tensung (*Slob-dPon bsTan-Srung*) was the son of a *Nyingmapa* sage called Lhasung (*Lha-Srung*) of the Rog clan. Lhasung, who lived to the age of one hundred and five, was the twenty-fifth descendant of the nephew of Gyalwa Chog-yang (*rGyal-Ba mChog-dByangs*), one of the twenty-five chief disciples of Guru Padmsambhava. Longchen Rabjam's mother was Sodnamgyen (*bSod-Nams-rGyan*) of the clan of Drom (*'Brom*).

Miracles accompanied his birth. When he was conceived,

The *Life of Kunkhyen Longchen Rabjam* is based on: TRL, TRT, ZDO, ZDS, LGY, KNRT, NLC, TTD, DTG, LNTT, PKD and LG unless otherwise indicated.

his mother dreamed of two suns on the head of a huge lion illuminating the whole world and dissolving into her. At his birth the Dharma protectress Namtru Remati (*Nam-Gru Re-Ma-Ti*) appeared before his mother in the form of a black woman brandishing a sword. Holding the baby in her arms the protectress said: "I will protect him." She handed him to his mother and disappeared. One day while his mother was working in the fields, a hailstorm occurred and she ran home, forgetting the baby in the field. When she remembered him, she went in search of him, but the baby had disappeared. She began to cry and the black woman appeared again, this time with the baby in her arms, and gave him back to his mother.

According to many prophecies, one of Longchen Rabjam's previous incarnations was Princess Pemasal (*Padma gSal*), the daughter of King Thrisong Deutsen, (790-858). When she was dying, Guru Padmasambhava had entrusted her with the transmission of *Nyingthig*, the Innermost Essence teachings of *Dzogchen*.

In the series of lives of Princess Pemasal, the incarnation directly preceding Longchen Rabjam was Pema Ledreltsal (*Padma Las-'Brel-rTsal*, 1291?-1315?), who discovered the *Nyingthig* teachings. They were entrusted to Princess Pemasal by Guru Padmasambhava as a Terma (*gTer-Ma*, Discovered Dharma Treasure) and became known as *Khadro Nyingthig* (*mKha'-'Gro sNying-Thig*).

From childhood he possessed the noble qualities of a Bodhisattva, such as faith, compassion, and extraordinary intelligence. When he was five, he perfected the skills of reading and writing. When he was seven his father gave him empowerments, instructions, and training in the rituals and meditations of *Nyingma tantras* and *Termas*, such as *Kagyed Desheg Dupa* (*bKa'-brGyad bDe-gShegs 'Dus-Pa*). He was also taught medicine and astrology. When he was nine his mother died.

He memorized both the "*Eight Thousand*" and "*Twenty (or twenty-five) Thousand-Verse Prajñāpāramitā (Transcendental Wisdom)*" texts after having read them one hundred times. When he was eleven his father died. At twelve he took the ordination of renunciation (*Rab-Byung*) from Khenpo Samdrub Rinchen (*mKhan-Po bSam-'Grub Rin-Chen*) and Lobpon Lha Kunga (*Slob-dPon Lha Kun-dGa'*) of Samye (*bSam-Yas*) monastery, and was given the name Tshulthrim Lodro (*Tshul-Khrims Blo-Gros*). He gained mastery of *Vinaya*, the teachings on monastic discipline, and taught them at fourteen. At sixteen he received many teachings of New *Tantra* (*sNgags gSar-Ma*) from Trashi Rinchen (*bKra-Shis Rin-Chen*) and others. From the age of nineteen he studied scholarly texts including the seven treatises on logic by Dharmakīrti, the five texts of Maitrinatha/Asaṅgha, and many Madhyamaka and Prajñāpāramitā texts at Sangphu Neuthog (*gSang-Phu sNeu-Thog*) monastic university for six[LY 127b/3] years with many great teachers including Lobpon Tsengonpa (*Slob-dPon bTsan-dGon-Pa*), the fifteenth throne-holder, and Latrangpa Chopal Gyaltshen (*Bla-Brang-Pa Chos-dPal rGyal-mTshan*), the sixteenth throne-holder of the Lingtod (*Gling-sTod*) school of Sangphu. After the 7th throne-holder[UNTG 22a/3] of Sangphu, Tsangpa Jampal Senge (*gTsang-Pa 'Jam-dPal Seng-Ge*), the monastery divided into two seats; Lingtod (*Gling-sTod*) and Lingmed (*Gling-sMad*).

Sangphu was founded in 1073 by Ngog Legpa'i Sherab (*rNgog-Legs-Pa'i Shes-Rab*), one of the three chief disciples of Atīśa. It was the seat of Ngog Loden Sherab (*rNgog Blo-lDan Shes-Rab*, 1059-1109), the celebrated translator of the period of "Later Spread of Dharma." For centuries it was one of the most important institutions of learning in Tibet, but in recent times the studies for which it was famous have been discontinued except at the summer camp of Gelugpa scholars and students. When Khyentse Wangpo (*mKhyen-brTse'i dBang-Po*, 1820-1892) visited Sangphu around 1840, he found that it had become a village of lay people possessing some objects of religious value. Sangphu and Samye are the two monastic institutions, in addition to the hermitage of Master Kumaradza (*S. Kumārarāja*), at which Longchen Rabjam mainly obtained his education and training. With the translator Panglo Lodro Tenpa (*dPang-Lo Blo-Gros brTan-Pa (1276-?*), he studied Sanskrit, poetics, composition, drama, five major *sūtras,* and Abhidharma. He beheld the pure visions of many deities, such as Mañjuśrī, Sārasvati, Vajravārāhī, and Tārā, as a result of his meditation on their *sādhanas.* He made an academic tour (*Grva-sKor*) of different learning institutions, and because of his scholarship he came to be renowned by the honorific names, Samye Lungmangpa (*bSam-Yas Lung-Mang-Pa*), the One from Samye Who Has Enhanced Many Scriptures, and Longchen Rabjam, the Profound and Infinite, or the Doctor of Profound Metaphysics.

He wandered in different places and studied with many celebrated scholars. He received the teachings of the *Sūtras* (*mDo*), *Māyājāla* (*sGyu-'Phrul Drva-Ba*) and *Cittavarga* (*Sems-sDe*), and the three major divisions of the Old *Tantras* (*sNgags rNying-Ma*) from master Zhonu Dondrub (*gZhon-Nu Don-Grub*) of Danphag (*Dan-Phag*) (monastery?), Nyonthingmawa Sangye Trag-od (*Myon-mThing-Ma-Ba Sangs-rGyas Grags-Pa*), and others. From about twenty teachers, including Sangye Tragpa (*Sangs-rGyas Grags-Pa*) of Nyothing (*Myos-mThing*), Zhonu Gyalpo (*gZhon-Nu rGyal-Po*), Zhonu Dorje (*gZon-Nu rDo-rJe*), Karmapa Rangchung Dorje (*Rang-Byung rDo-rJe,* 1284-1334), Sonam Gyaltshen (*bSod-Nams rGyal-mTshan,* 1312-1375) of Sakya (*Sa-sKya*) and others, he received all the teachings and transmissions of both old and new *tantras* of various lineages which were taught in Tibet at that time.

He felt distaste for the rough and jealous nature of some monks from Kham (*Khams*) province at Sangphu, his main monastic college, and he chose to leave. In the fifth month of an eight month dark-retreat at a cave at Gyama'i Chogla (*rGya-Ma'i lCog-La*), he had a vision at dawn. He was standing on the sandy bank of a river, from which he could see some hills. He heard the sound of singing accompanied by music. Looking in the direction of the sound, he saw a beautiful sixteen year old woman attired in brocade, ornamented with gold and turquoise and wearing a golden veil over her face. She was riding a horse with leather saddle and bells. He held on to the end of her dress and prayed: "O, Noble Lady (i. e. *Tārā*), please accept me with your kindness." She put her crown of precious jewels on his head and said: "From now on, I shall always bestow my blessings upon you and grant you powers."

At that point his body and mind became absorbed in a contemplative state of bliss, clarity, and freedom from conceptions. "I did not wake up for a long time!" as he put it. Although he awakened at sunrise, for three days[1] he remained in the same experiential state. It established the interdependent causation of his encountering the *Nyingthig* teachings. After the retreat he gave the empowerment (*dBang*) of Vairocana to about thirty men and women. It may have been the first empowerment he had given. From there he went to Samye monastery.

At twenty-seven[2] as prophesied by his tutelary deities, he went to meet Rigdzin Kumaradza (*Rig-'Dzin Kumārarāja*, 1266-1343), the great transmission-holder of *Nyingthig* in general, and especially of the *Nyingthig* teachings transmitted in Tibet by Vimalamitra, known as *Sangwa Nyingthig* (*gSang-Ba sNying-Thig*) or *Vima Nyingthig*.

The master was staying in Yartod Kyam (*Yar-sTod sKyam*) with his disciples in a camp of about seventy wind-breaking shelters. The master received Longchen Rabjam with joy and inspired him with the prophecy that he would become the transmission-holder of *Nyingthig*. The master said: "Last night I dreamed of a wonderful bird, said to be the divine bird, with a flock of a thousand birds. They came and carried away my texts in all directions. It is a sign that you will become a transmission-holder of my teachings. I shall give you the complete teachings."

Longchen Rabjam was highly pleased with the master's acceptance and his inspiring words. But he had no material possessions with which to make a Dharma-contribution to the community, and this was a requirement for admission. He was so sad, and he thought, "I shall be the only person who has to leave the Lama for lack of a Dharma-contribution. I ought

[1]TTD 9b/1: a month

[2]Twenty-seven, according to PKD 108a/3 & TTD 9b/6, and twenty-nine according to DTG 120a/3 & LG, 122b/6.

to get out of this valley during the night before dawn, for it will be shameful to leave after daybreak in front of everyone's eyes." The master read Longchen Rabjam's thoughts by means of foreknowledge.

At dawn when Longchen Rabjam was getting up, two messengers arrived from the master saying, "The Lord of Dharma (*Chos-rJe*) wants you to come to see him." The master gave him tea and said to the caretakers of the community: "I am paying the Dharma-contributions to the community on Geshe Samyepa's (*dGe-bShes bSam-Yas-Pa,* i.e., Longchen Rabjam's) behalf. He will be the best among all my students." In that year he received the empowerments (*dBang*) and instructions (*Khrid*) of *Nyingthig* teachings of the Vimalamitra lineage. The next year, in addition to other empowerments and instructions, he received the transmissions of all the other *tantras* and instructions of the three categories of *Dzogpa Chenpo.*

While he was studying with Rigdzin Kumaradza, Longchen Rabjam lived under circumstances of severe deprivation. During the extremely cold winter, he had only one ragged bag to use as a mattress and blanket, and to protect himself from the snow and cold. For two months he had to live on only three "Tre" (*Bre*, quarts) of flour and twenty-one pills of Ngulchu (*dNgul-Chu*), the size of a pea. To combat the development of attachment, it was the Lama's teaching to move the camp from one no-man's-land to another. During one spring alone they moved camp nine times, and that caused great hardship to Longchen Rabjam. Just as he got settled, the time would come to move again. It was under these circumstances that he received, among others, the complete innermost teachings of *Nyingthig* from the master, like water poured from one vessel into another. And by practicing day and night he realized the same attainment as that of his master. He was empowered as the Dharma-heir of the master and the lineage-holder of the transmission for future disciples.

As he promised his Lama, he practiced the teachings of the master in different sacred places for seven (or six) years in retreat (including a three-year retreat?) at Chimphu (*mChims-*

Phu) of Samye. He beheld the pure visions of Peaceful and Wrathful manifestations of Guru Padmasambhava, Vajrasattva, Tārā, and the Root Deities. Dharma protectors vowed to serve him and fulfill his wishes. With the deities of the Eight Great Maṇḍalas (*bKa'-brGyad*), he became able to communicate as person to person.

Form time to time he visited Rigdzin Kumaradza and received clarifications of the teachings and his training. He pleased his teacher with his offerings of practice of Dharma: realization of view, progress of meditation, and wisdom of knowing all the knowable subjects. He also made the offering of all his material possessions seven times. Longchen Rabjam himself describes his attainments in *The History of Lama Yangtig* (*Bla-Ma Yang-Tig*):[LRT 29a/6]

> There is no more attachment to *Saṃsāra* in me. I am liberated from the chain of hopes and fears. I always remain in the view and contemplation of Absolute *Dzogpa Chenpo*."

While he was praying and making offerings to the Chowo (*Jo-Bo*) image in Lhasa, he saw a light emerge from the forehead of the image and dissolve into his forehead. It caused him to recollect his previous lives as a scholar at Vulture Peak in India and also in the Li country, and his knowledge of scriptures from those times was awakened. It broadened his scholarship further. At thirty-one he gave empowerments (*sMin*) and instructions (*Grol*) of *Nyingthig* to some disciples, for the first time, at Nyiphu Shugseb (*sNyi-Phu'i Shug-gSeb*).

Then his disciple Yogi Odzer Gocha (*A'od-Zer Go-Cha*) offered him the texts of *Khadro Nyingthig* (*mKha'-'Gro sNying-Thig*), which he had found after a very hard search. At the same time, Shenpa Sogdrubma (*Shan-Pa Srog-sGrub-Ma*), the Dharma protectress, also presented him with a copy of the same text, which had important significance. *Khadro Nyingthig* is the teachings of *Nyingthig* transmitted in Tibet by Guru Padmasambhava to Lhacham Pemasal (9th century) and then concealed as a Terma and discovered from a rock at Danglung

Thramo (*Dangs-Lung Khra-Mo*) of Dagpo (*Dvags-Po*) valley by Pema Ledreltsal, the immediate previous incarnation of Longchen Rabjam.

The next year, at thirty-two, he gave the empowerments and teachings of *Vima Nyingthig* to eight fortunate male and female disciples in the midst of wondrous manifestations, visions, and experiences at Chimphu Rimochen (*mChims-Phu Ri-Mo-Chan*). The Dharma protectress Ekadzati gave prophecies through a female disciple whom she possessed. Dancing, Longchen Rabjam sang the *vajra*-song:[TRT 114b/6]

O yogis, how joyous and happy it is!
Tonight, in the unexcelled Buddha-field,
In one's own body, the palace of the Peaceful and Wrathful deities,
The *maṇḍala* of the Buddhas, clarity and emptiness, has developed.
The Buddha does not exist externally, but within (oneself). . . .
This is because of the kindness of the Lama.
The Lama does not dwell outside but within (oneself),
The Lama of primordial purity and spontaneous presence
Dwells in the state of clarity and emptiness, free from apprehensions. . . .
O meditators! Whose mind dwells alone?
Do not hold your thoughts in yourself, but let them go wherever they are at ease.
As the mind is emptiness, whether it goes or dwells,
Whatever arises is the play of wisdom. . . .
By knowing the process of the inner five lights,
The external lights of sun and moon have arisen continuously,
By ending inner thoughts at their roots,
Good and bad external circumstances have arisen as the great bliss.
By increasing the inner essence-drops,
The clouds of external *Ḍākinīs* have always gathered.

By liberating the inner knots of the light-channels,
The external knots of apprehender and apprehended are liberated.
I go to the state of clarity of great bliss.
O *vajra* brothers and sisters, it is happy and joyful."

In visions Guru Padmasambhava gave the transmission of *Khadro Nyingthig*. He gave Longchen Rabjam the name Trimed Odzer (*Dri-Med A'od-Zer*) and Yeshe Tshogyal gave him the name Dorje Zijid (*rDo-rJe gZi-brJid*).

At Chugpotrag (*Phyug-Po-Brag*) near the Do'i Choten (*rDo'i mChod-rTen*) of Zurkhardo (*Zur-mKhar-mDo*), after performing a Tshog (*Tshogs*) offering, he opened the *Khadro Nyingthig* teachings. That night, he experienced the state of meditative clarity of remaining in the state of original purity, the *Dharmakāya*, manifesting its power, the *Saṃbhogakāya*, and projecting its clarity externally, the *Nirmāṇakāya*. Then he discovered and transcribed the *Khadro Yangtig* (*mKha'-'Gro Yang-Tig*) as Mind Dharma Treasure (*dGongs-gTer*), the esoteric supplementary texts for *Khadro Nyingthig*.

While he was writing *Khadro Yangtig*, he had visions of Guru Padmasambhava, Yeshe Tshogyal (*Ye-Shes mTsho-rGyal*), and Yudronma (*gYu-sGron-Ma*). In particular, Yeshe Tshogyal, the consort of Guru Padmsambhava, was present for seven days, giving introductions and mind-mandate (*gTad-rGya*) transmission of the signs, meaning, and examples (*brDa, Don and dPe*) of *Khadro Nyingthig*. Although he discovered the seed of this text at Chimphu, he actually transcribed it at Kangri Thodkar (*Gangs-Ri Thod-dKar*),[LG.129a/5] and so the colophon says that he wrote it at Kangri Thodkar. Although Longchen Rabjam was the incarnation of Pema Ledreltsal, the discoverer of *Khadro Nyingthig*, and he also received the transmissions from Guru Padmasambhava and Yeshe Tshogyal in his very lifetime, he received the transmission from Sho'i Gyalse Legpa (*Sho'i rGyal-Sras Legs-Pa*, 1290-1366/7), the direct disciple of Pema Ledreltsal, in order to set an example for future followers of the importance of receiving proper transmissions. There were

Earth Dharma Treasures (*Sa-gTer*) for him to discover but he declined saying, "I am opening the door of Dharma Treasures of the inner clarity, there is no need of Dharma Treasure from the cracks of rocks."

Then he went to Ogyen Dzong Odzer Trinkyi Kyedmo'i Tshal at Kangri Thodkar (the Fortress of *Oḍḍiyāna* in the Grove of Radiant Clouds at the White-Peaked Snow Mountain), and this hermitage became his main residence. Here he discovered and composed most of his famous Termas and writings, consisting of about two hundred and seventy treatises.[TTD 41b/4] But unfortunately, many of his writings are lost. Longchen Rabjam describes Kangri Thodkar in the following words:[SC-II, 187a/5]

> It is situated north-east of the Trashi Gephel (*bKra-Shis dGe-'Phel*) temple of Onkyangdo (*A'on-Kyang-rDo*). It seems that this mountain was adorned by a mane of ice and dressed in moon(-like) whiteness in the past. But with the passage of time, its peak is now decorated with rocky toppings and its faces are (covered with) medicinal herbs and clean running creeks. The sweet scent of flowers and medicinal herbs is diffused about it. On the south of this mountain, in the midst of a forest of junipers, is the Ogyen Dzong (*O-rGyan rDzong*, the Fortress of Oḍḍiyāna, i.e., Guru Padmasambhava), the pleasure grove of sages blessed by Padma (sambhava), stretching out like the neck of a peacock.

At the request of Yogi Odzer Gocha, he transcribed the fifty-five treatises of *Khadro Yangtig* (*mKha'-'Gro Yang-Tig*), the supplementary texts for *Khadro Nyingthig*, as Mind Dharma Treasures (*dGongs-gTer*). While the texts were being transcribed, the sky was constantly filled with rainbow lights, and wondrous magical displays of *Ḍākinīs* could be seen by all who were present. Longchen Rabjam saw Vimalamitra in pure visions and received blessings, transmissions, and prophecies. Inspired by Vimalamitra, he wrote *Lama Yangtig* (*Bla-Ma Yang-Tig*) in thirty-five treatises, as a support text for *Vima Nyingthig*. He also wrote *Zabmo Yangtig* (*Zab-Mo Yang-Tig*), a commentary on both *Nyingthigs*. Various Buddhas, deities, teachers, and Dharma protectors, such as the Peaceful and Wrathful Deities, the Deities of the Eight Great *Maṇḍalas*, Guru Padmasambhava, and Vimalamitra periodically appeared before him, bestowed their blessings, and inspired him to write those most esoteric texts. In many instances, his disciples saw Dharma protectors in his room. Ekajati, Vajrasādhu and Rāhula used to prepare paper and ink for his writing.

Some of Longchen Rabjam's major scholarly and sacred works are:

A. *Dzodchen Dun* (*mDzod-Chen bDun*), *the Seven Great Treasures:*

1. *Yidzhin Rinpoche'i Dzod* (*Yid-bZhin Rin-Po-Che'i mDzod*) in twenty-two chapters, and its auto-commentary, *Pema Karpo* (*Padma dKar-Po*), with associated treatises. A survey of the whole range of *Mahāyāna* Buddhist doctrine, elucidating the ways of study, analysis and training in *Mahāyāna* and *Vajrayāna*.
2. *Mengag Rinpoche'i Dzod* (*Man-Ngag Rin-Po-Che'i mDzod*). A treatise using various series of six constituents to summarize the Buddhist *sūtras* and *tantras*, particularly the essence of the path and result of *Dzogpa Chenpo* in their entirety in the form of ethical, philosophical, and meditative instructions.
3. *Choying Rinpoche'i Dzod* (*Chos-dByings Rin-Po-Che'i mDzod*), in thirteen chapters with auto-commentary, *Lungki Terdzod* (*Lung-Gi gTer-mDzod*). An exposition of the profound and vast teachings of basis, path, and result of the three main categories of *Dzogpa Chenpo*, namely *Semde*, *Longde*, and *Mengagde*, and in particular *Longde*.
4. *Trubtha Dzod* (*Grub-mTha' mDzod*) in eight chapters. An exposition of the various philosophical standpoints of all the *yānas* of *sūtric* and *tantric* Buddhism.
5. *Thegchog Dzod* (*Thegs-mChog mDzod*) in twenty-five chapters. The meaning commentary of the *Seventeen Tantras*

(*rGyud bChu-bDun*) and *One Hundred and Nineteen Instructional Treatises* (*Man-Ngag Gi Yi-Ge brGya bChu-dGu*) of *Mengagde* (*Man-Ngag-sDe*). It expounds a wide range of Buddhist doctrine, from the manifestation of the absolute teacher, the *Trikāya*, to the achievement of the spontaneously accomplished final result of the practice of the path of *Dzogpa Chenpo*, including *Thodgal* (*Thod-rGal*, Direct Approach). This text is said to have been written to fulfill the aspirations of Rigdzin Kumaradza at the time of his death.

6. *Tshigton Dzod* (*Tshig-Don mDzod*) in eleven chapters. A summary of *Thegchog Dzod* explaining the crucial points of practice. It begins with a description of the basis and concludes with the result, the state of ultimate liberation.
7. *Nelug Dzod* (*gNas-Lugs mDzod*) in five chapters with its auto-commentary. It explains the ultimate meaning of all three divisions of *Dzogpa Chenpo*.

B. *Ngalso Korsum* (*Ngal-gSo sKor-gSum*), *Three Cycles on Relaxation*. *Ngalso Korsum* consists of three root (*rTsa-Ba*) texts, three summaries, called "garlands" (*Phreng-Ba*), three auto-commentaries, called "chariots" (*Shing-rTa*), and three "meaning commentaries" (*Don-Khrid*) or *Instructions on Practice*, totaling fifteen treatises:

1. *Semnyid Ngalso* (*Sems-Nyid Ngal-gSo*), the root text in thirteen chapters; its summary, *Kunda'i Threngwa* (*Kunda'i Phreng-Ba*) (lost); an auto-commentary on the root text, *Ngeton Shingta Chenmo* (*Nges-Don Shing-rTa Chen-Mo*), a summary of the auto-commentary, *Pema Karpo'i Threngwa* (*Padma dKar-Po'i Phreng-Ba*), and the instruction on practice, *Changchub Lamzang* (*Byang-Ch'ub Lam-bZang*). The *Semnyid Ngalso* explains all the stages of the path, the beginning, middle, and end of the *sūtric* and *tantric* teachings.
2. *Gyuma Ngalso* (*sGyu-Ma Ngal-gSo*), the root text in eight chapters; its summary, *Mandara'i Phrengwa* (*Mandara'i Phreng-Ba*); the auto-commentary, *Shingta Zangpo* (*Shing-

rTa bZang-Po); and the instruction on practice, *Yidzhin Norbu* (*Yid-bZhin Nor-Bu*). This text is an instruction on cutting the ties of attachment to phenomenal existents through the teachings on eight illusory examples.

3. *Samten Ngalso* (*bSam-gTan Ngal-gSo*), the root text in three chapters; its summary, *Pundarik'i Threngwa* (*Pundarika'i Phreng-Ba*), its auto-commentary, *Shingta Namdag* (*Shing-rTa rNam-Dag*); and the instruction on practice, *Nyingpo Chuddu* (*sNying-Po bCud-'Dus*). The text is an instruction on the profound path of absorption, the self-existent natural wisdom. There are two additional texts, a summary of *Ngalso Korsum* entitled *Legshed Gyatsho* (*Legs-bShad rGya-mTsho*) and a table of contents (*dKar-Chags*) called *Pema Tongden* (*Padma sTong-lDan*). The three auto-commentaries of *Ngalso Korsum* are also known as the *Shingta Namsum* (*Shing-rTa rNam-gSum*), *The Three Chariots*.

C. *Rangtrol Korsum* (*Rang-Grol sKor-gSum*), *Three Cycles for Natural Liberation*. They are the "meaning commentaries" on the instructions of the *Semde* division of *Dzogpa Chenpo*.

1. *Semnyid Rangtrol* (*Sems-Nyid Rang-Grol*), *Naturally Liberated Mind* in three chapters and a meaning commentary or instruction on practice entitled *Lamrim Nyingpo*. (Translations of both of these texts are included in this book.)
2. *Chonyid Rangtrol* (*Chos-Nyid Rang-Grol*) in three chapters, and an instruction on practice entitled *Rinchen Nyingpo*.
3. *Nyamnyid Rangtrol* (*mNyam-Nyid Rang-Grol*) in three chapters, and an instruction on practice entitled *Yidzhin Nyingpo* (*Yid-bZhin sNying-Po*).

D. *Yangtig Namsum* (*Yang-Tig rNam-gSum*), *The Three Inner Essences*. It contains the crucial points of the esoteric teachings of *Mengagde*, the highest of the three divisions of *Dzogpa Chenpo*. In these texts special emphasis is placed on *Thodgal* training.

1. *Lama Yangtig* or *Yangzab Yidzhin Norbu* (*Bla-Ma Yang-*

Tig or Yang-Zab Yid-bZhin Nor-Bu) consists of thirty-five treatises. It condenses and interprets the vast material of the *Four Volumes of Esoteric Teachings* (*Zab-Pa Pod-bZhi*) of *Vima Nyingthig* and *One Hundred and Nineteen Treatises of Instruction* (*Man-Ngag Gi Yi-Ge brGya bCu-dGu*) of *Mengagde* of *Dzogpa Chenpo*. The Four Volumes of Esoteric Teachings are: *Seryig Chen* (*gSer-Yig Chan*), *Yuyig Chen* (*gYu-Yig Chan*), *Dungyig Chen* (*Dung-Yig Chan*) and *Zang-yig Chen* (*Zangs-Yig Chan*) with *Phrayig Chen* (*Phra-Yig Chan*).

2. *Khadro Yangtig* (*mKha'-'Gro Yang-Tig*) consisting of fifty-five treatises. In Longchen Rabjam's previous life as Pema Ledreltsal, he had authority over the texts of *Khadro Nyingthig*. In his present life he received the transmissions and gained realization of the *Khadro Nyingthig* teachings, and wrote the texts entitled *Khadro Yangtig* on *Khadro Nyingthig*.
3. *Zabmo Yangtig* (*Zab-Mo Yang-Tig*) is the most detailed and profound commentary on both *Vima Nyingthig* and *Khadro Nyingthig*.

E. *Munsel Korsum* (*Mun-Sel sKor-gSum*), *Three Cycles on Dispelling the Darkness*. These three texts are commentaries on the *Guhyamāyājāla-tantra* according to *Nyingthig* views:

1. *Chidon Yidkyi Munsel* (*sPyi-Don Yid-Kyi Mun-Sel*),
2. *Dudon Marig Munsel* (*bsDus-Don Ma-Rig Mun-Sel*),
3. *Drelwa Chogchu Munsel* (*'Grel-Ba Phyogs-bChu Mun-Sel*).

He attained the Perfection of Intrinsic Awareness (*Rig-Pa Tshad-Phebs*) through the secret path of Direct Approach (*Thod-rGal*), the spontaneously perfected state of clarity of *Dzogpa Chenpo*.

At forty-two, in accordance with a prophesy given by Vimalamitra in a pure vision, he repaired the Zha Pema Wangchen (*Zhva Padma dBang-Chen*) temple at Drada (*sBral-mDa'*) in the Wuru (*dBu-Ru*) region. This temple was built in the ninth century by Nyang Tingdzin Zangpo (*Nyang Ting-'Dzin bZang-Po*) on the order of King Thrisong Deutsen for protection from invasions by foreign "heretics." Longchen Rabjam also recognized this temple as the one which was prophesied in the Langri Lungten (*Glang-Ri Lung-bsTan*) text in the Kajur (*bKa'-'Gyur*) as "the sacred presence of the Zhva country." He discovered enough gold to fill one Gutse (*'Gu-Tse*, a vessel for ritual performances) at Samye, and with it he financed the construction. Every day a young boy with a turquoise earring helped the construction crew, but at mealtime he was not present. The crew became suspicious and kept an eye on him. When they stopped work they saw him disappearing into the walls, and they told this story to Longchen Rabjam. He said that it was Vajrasādhu (*rDo-rJe Legs-Pa*) who was helping them. While they were digging, many buried effigies of evil and negative forces were unearthed and flew around with a strong rain of earth and stone. People ran for their lives. With his contemplative power Longchen Rabjam danced with wrathful gestures, uttering mantras in *Sanskrit*. He summoned them back and miraculously buried them again before the eyes of all who were present. At that time many saw him in the form of Wrathful Guru Padmasambhava. Once when the workers could not erect two fallen stone pillars, he waved his robes and uttered the words-of-truth (benediction), and instantly they were able to erect them. At the time of consecration many saw him displaying himself in various forms such as Samantabhadra, and many Buddhas and Bodhisattvas appeared in the sky and sent down a rain of blessing flowers. Maitreya Buddha, pointing at Longchen Rabjam, gave the prophecy: "After two lives, you will become the Buddha renowned as Rirab Marme'i Gyaltshen (*Ri-Rab Mar-Me'i rGyal-mTshan*) in the Buddha-field named Pema Tsegpa (*Padma brTsegs-Pa*)."

Longchen Rabjam was a hermit, and he declined to have any bureaucratic organization. But because of his scholarship and saintly nature, thousands of devotees including scholars, meditators, and lay people continually flocked to him. The greatest scholars and highest political authorities of the time were inspired by him. Because of their pure spiritual interest, they paid respect to what he was naturally and spiritually and never because of the power of his bureaucratic organization or for any political or social gain.

Gompa Kunrig (*sGom-Pa Kun-Rig*) of Drigung (*'Bri-Gung*) became his disciple and Longchen Rabjam, fulfilling a prophecy of Guru Padmasambhava, diverted him from the path of warfare. In the prophecy Guru Padmasambhava had said:

> In the place known as Dri (*'Bri*)
> Will (come a) son of the demons called Kunga (*Kun-dGa'*).
> On his body there will be the mark of a sword.
> After death he will go to hell.
> Yet, if an emanation of Mañjuśrī from the south (of Tibet)
> Can subdue him,
> He may be freed from taking rebirth in hell.

Kunrig recognized himself as the subject of the prophecy as he had the mark of a sword on his back and was planning to make war in Wu (*dBus*) and Tsang (*gTsang*) provinces of Tibet. He assigned a Lama called Palchogpa (*dPal-mCh'og-Pa*) to search for the emanation of Mañjuśrī. At that time there was no one in Central Tibet who was more learned than Longchen Rabjam. So, after searching, the Lama became convinced that Longchen Rabjam was the emanation of Mañjuśrī. Kunrig received many teachings from Longchen Rabjam, and he offered him a monastery called Trog Ogyen (*Grogs O-rGyan*). Drikung Kunrig was the most powerful rival to Tai Situ of Phagtru (*Phag-Gru*), the ruler of Tibet, so Longchen Rabjam actually averted a serious war in Tibet.

At Tidro (*Ti-sGro*) he made Tshog (*Tshogs*) offerings for a long time. He hoisted a victory-banner on a rock which no man could reach, and the minds of many people were awakened to the Dharma. On the way to Lhasa, he was surrounded by a force of hostile people from Yarlung (*Yar-Klungs*) who were planning to kill him, thinking that he was the teacher of Drigung Kunrig. But by his enlightened power he became invisible to them. In the Jokhang (*Jo-Khang*) before the Jowo, he had various visions of Buddhas and received blessings. When he reached Shugseb (*Shugs-gSeb*), through his foreknowledge he became aware of the coming war of the earth-pig year (1359). So he went to Mon (Bhutan). He gave teachings in Bumthang (*Bum-Thang*) and Ngalong (*rNga-Long*), thereby lighting the light of Dharma there, and he put restrictions on hunting and fishing.

At Bumthang he built a monastic hermitage, naming it Tharpaling (*Thar-Pa Gling*), the Land of Liberation, since approximately one hundred thousand people gathered for his teaching, having the wish for liberation. In Bhutan, he had a daughter and then, after five years, in the fire-monkey year (1356), a son to Kyidpala (*sKyid-Pa Lags*). In Zhulen Serthreng[ZDS 16b/5 and TRL 43b/6] his son Tulku Tragpa Odzer (*sPrul-sKu Grags-Pa A'od-Zer*) or Dawa Tragpa (*Zla-Ba Grags-Pa, 1356-1409?*), was prophesied as a manifestation of Tadrin (*rTa-mGrin, S. Hyagriva*). Tragpa Odzer later became a great scholar and a holder of the Nyinthig lineage. Longchen Rabjam lived as a celibate for the rest of his life.

Longchen Rabjam was invited to Lhotrag (*Lho-Brag*). At Layag Lhalung (*La-Yag Lha-Lung*) and Manthang (*Man-Thang*) he gave teachings of *Nyingthig* to approximately a thousand disciples who were mainly monks. He was venerated by Lama Dampa Sodnam Gyaltshen (*Bla-Ma Dam-Pa bSod-Nams rGyal-mTshan*, 1312-1375) of Sakya and Tragzang (*Grags-bZang*) of Nyephu for his scholarly responses to their questions, which dispelled their doubts on many crucial points of philosophical views and meditation training. Tai Situ Changchub Gyaltshen (Ta'i Situ Byang-Chub rGyal-mTshan) of Phagtru, who became the ruler of Tibet in 1349, at first disliked Longchen Rabjam because he was the teacher of Drigung Kunrig, his chief enemy. Later, when he realized the greatness of Longchen Rabjam's scholarship and his Bodhisattva nature, he took the lotus feet of Longchen Rabjam as a jewel in his crown. At the Tai Situ's request, Longchen Rabjam gave him and some two thousand devotees the teachings of Innermost Essence (*Yang-gSang Bla-Med*). Many noble chieftains (*Khri-dPon*) of that time such as Dorje Gyaltshen (*rDo-rJe rGyal-mTshan*) of Yardrog (*Yar-'Brog*) and Situ Shakya Zangpo (*Shakya bZang-*

Po) of Wurtod (*dBur-Stod*), became his devotees.

In Lhasa he was received by a procession of many monks. From a throne placed between Lhasa and Ramoche (*Ra-Mo-Che*), he gave Bodhicitta ordination and other teachings to the public. He tamed many proud scholars through dialectical reasoning and introduced them to true faith in Dharma. Thereby he became publicly known as Kunkhyen Choje (*Kun-mKhyen Chos-rJe*), the Omniscient Lord of Dharma.

At Nyephu Shugseb he gave teachings of *Dzogpa Chenpo* to an assembly of more than one thousand devotees. In the rocky hills near Trog Ogyen (*Grog O-rGyan*) monastery, he gave the empowerments and teachings of the Clarity of *Vajra*-essence (*A'od-gSal rDo-rJe'i sNying-Po*) to approximately three thousand people, including some forty teachers of Dharma. At the end of the teachings they held a Feast (*Tshogs*, S. *Gaṇa-cakra*) Offering ceremony and he addressed them, saying:

> This Feast Offering is going to be the last one we shall do together. You should renounce your worldly activities and get the ultimate essence (of life) though the profound path of training (in Dharma).

Then he went to Zha temple, and at the time of public teachings, wonders occurred such as a rain of flowers from the sky.

At fifty-six, in the water-hare year of the sixth Rabjung (1363) in the midst of giving teachings, he asked Gyalse Zodpa (*rGyal-Sras bZod-Pa*) for paper and ink. To the utmost sorrow of his disciples, he wrote his spiritual testament, entitled *Trima Med-pa'i Od* (*Dri-Ma Med-Pa'i A'od*), The Immaculate Radiance. Here are some lines from his testament:ZDO 132b/5

> As we have known the nature of *saṃsāra* long ago,
> Mundane possessions have no essence;
> So now I am leaving this impermanent illusory body, and
> I will tell you what alone is good for you. Listen to me....
> Today, as I am inspired by
> The Face of compassionate lord Pema,
> My delight at death is much greater than

The delight of traders at making their fortune at sea,
Of the lords of the gods who have proclaimed their victory in war;
And of those (sages) who have accomplished absorption.
As when the time comes, travelers go on their way,
Now Pema Ledreltsal will not remain here any longer,
But will go to dwell in the secure, blissful, and deathless state....
Now we will not have any more connection in this life.
I am a begger who is going to die as he likes,
Do not feel sad but pray always.

Then he traveled to the forest of Chimphu by way of Gyama (*rGya-Ma*) and Samye. He said: "(The spiritual power of) Chimphu is equal to the Sitavan cemetery in India. Death in this place is better than a birth in other places. I am going to leave my worn-out body here."

Then he displayed sickness of the body. But he kept giving teachings to the huge gathering of people who were assembled there to receive them from him. When the disciples requested him to take rest, he said: "I would like to finish the teachings."

On the sixteenth of the twelfth month of the same year, he performed elaborate offerings to the *Ḍakas* and *Ḍākinīs*. He then gave his last public teaching, saying: "You should devote yourself solely to Dharma practice. There is no essence in compounded phenomena. Especially you should emphasize the practices of *Thregchod* and *Thodgal*. If you face any difficulties in understanding the practices, read *Yangtig Yidzhin Norbu* (or *Bla-Ma Yang-Tig*); it will be like a wish-fulfilling jewel. You will attain *nirvāṇa* in the state of Dissolution of all Phenomena into the Ultimate Nature (*Chos-Nyid Zad-Pa*)."

On the eighteenth, he said to a few disciples: "Arrange an offering and then all of you leave the room." When the disciples expressed their wish to stay near him, he said: "Then, I am going to leave my worn-out illusory body. Do not make any noise, but remain in contemplation."

Then his mind dissolved into the primordial state and left his body sitting in the posture of *Dharmakāya*. Those present witnessed the trembling of the earth and roaring sounds, which the scriptures identify as signs of high attainments. They kept his body for twenty-five days. During that period tents of rainbow lights constantly arched across the sky. Even in the twelfth and first months (around February), the coldest months in Tibet, the earth became warm, the ice melted, and roses bloomed. At the time of his cremation, the earth trembled three times and a loud sound was heard seven times. The remains, his heart, tongue, and eyes, were found unburnt. Five kinds of gDung (*gDungs*) and numerous *Ringsel* (*Ring-bSrel*) emerged from the bones as an indication of his attainment of the five bodies and five wisdoms of Buddhahood.[LG 136b/6] It is well known that the big *Ringsels* increased to hundreds and thousands. One of Longchen Rabjam's main incarnations was the great *Terton* (*gTer-sTon*) Pema Lingpa (1450-?), who was born in Bhutan.

Longchen Rabjam was one of the highest and greatest scholars and adepts of Tibet. But his daily conduct of life was simple, human, and precise. He was the reincarnation of realized beings, yet he demonstrated the life of a humble individual devoted to the activities of studies, training, and discipline in order to fulfill the goal of his manifestation, which was to be an example of a trainee and teacher of the Dharma. Here are some of the many inspiring and interesting passages from his biographies:

Anything offered to him out of faith would be used only for the service of Dharma and never for himself or for any mundane purpose. He never allowed any material dedicated to the Dharma to be diverted to another purpose. He never showed respect to a layman, however great or powerful, and said: "Respect should be paid to the Three Jewels but not to an unvirtuous person." He never offered a seat or paid respect to people who were proud because of power and riches. When he distributed offerings to monks, he started from the end of the row saying "We should be careful not to miss people at the end of the row; people who are at the top of the row will get the offerings anyway.'' According to scriptures, if an ordinary person receives and accepts respect from a high spiritual person, much of his merit is thereby consumed. However great the offerings made to him, he said dedication prayers but never expressed gratitude, and he said, ''Patrons should have the opportunity to make merits.'' So the patrons would receive merits instead of expressions of gratitude for their offerings. As he was detached from hopes and fears of worldly achievement, he spent his life in hermitages and refused to establish or live in any residences, saying, ''If I tried, I would be able to establish a monastery, but to do so causes distractions. So it is better to concentrate on disciplining the minds (of people).''

He observed the offering ceremonies of both tenths (of the waxing and waning of the moon, that is, the 10th and 25th of the Tibetan lunar calendar) and the 8th of every month. He was immensely kind to poor and unfortunate people, and he used to enjoy with great pleasure the food offerred by poor people, even if it was of terrible quality, and then would say lots of prayers for them.

This brings one to a very interesting observation. From the social point of view, a common person may think that if Longchen Rabjam was immensly kind to poor people, his effort must have been to give all the material things he had to the poor. In many cases he must have done so. But in the biographies there is no mention of such conduct. In any case, there is a spiritual point behind this. Most of the material things Longchen Rabjam could have had, which he never kept but passed on for religious purposes, were the ''offerings-of-faith'' made by his devotees, and these were dedicated to religious purpose. A material-of-faith must be spent for a religious purpose, for the service of *Buddha*, *Dharma*, or *Saṅgha*, and not for mundane purposes or to be enjoyed by lay persons. If a material-of-faith is enjoyed by an ordinary person instead of being used for religious purposes, the lay person will be creating demeritorious *karma*, which will create more hardship in future. From the Dharma point of view, by accepting their offerings, he gave an opportunity for the poor people to make merits, which is the cause of future happiness. So he was indeed doing a favor to the poor by providing himself as a means for them to make merits, although he could get the best meals in the richest families. That is why the biographers speak in particular about Longchen Rabjam's enjoying the food offered by the poor to illustrate his kindness to them.

In the *History of Lama Yangtig* Longchen Rabjam advises his followers in simple words:[LRT 30a/1]

> My future followers! Leave your mundane activities of this life behind. Begin the preparations for the next lives. Rely on a perfect virtuous teacher. Receive instructions on the essence of clarity. Practice the secret teachings of *Nyingthig* in solitude. (Attain the result of) transcending (the differentiations of) *saṃsāra* and *nirvāṇa* in this very lifetime. If you receive any prophecy, devote yourself to the service of others (by teaching, and so forth) as much as you can. Propagate the teachings while tolerating ingratitude and hardship.

One of the most outstanding characteristics of Longchen Rabjam's teachings is his stress on harmony with nature: the peaceful vastness and beauty of external nature as the support and the peaceful vastness and awareness of the inner nature of enlightened mind as the goal. By seeing the undisturbed peacefulness, unpolluted clearness, and uncomplicated simplicity of outer nature as it is and by relying on them, one gets inspiration that brings forth the realization of the inner natural state. He appreciates the nature of external phenomena and sees their virtues. He emphasizes that for a beginner, positive external phenomena are an important basis for generating meditative progress. The following are quotations from his writings to illustrate his views on outer and inner nature.[SC-I, 20a/2]

> Enchanting caves and fields in peaceful forests
> Adorned with flowers moving in dance and streams sounding Lhung,

In them, may we without wavering contemplate our tired minds,
And remain there to fulfill the purposes of precious human life.
In that place, not having encountered any wild beings,
Having pacified emotional defilements, and having achieved the seven noble qualities,
At the time of leaving the living body,
May we attain the king of the mind, the primordial state.

External nature is beneficial for inner spiritual training:[STN 2a/1]

At the top of a hill, in a forest, on an island
Which is enchanting and harmonious during the four seasons,
Contemplate one-pointedly without distractions
On the clarity free from conceptualizations....
As the outer and inner (phenomena and mind) are interdependent,
One should live in an enchanting, solitary, and pleasant place.
Mountaintops, as they broaden and clear the mind,
Are good places for dispelling dullness and auspicious for (training on) the development stage.
Snow-mountains, as they clean the mind and clear contemplation,
Are good places for (training on) insight, and there will be fewer obstructions.
Forests, as they stabilize the mind and develop the abiding of contemplation,
Are good places for (training on) tranquillity and the growth of bliss.
Rocky mountains, as they generate the feeling of remorse and impermanence,
And are clear and powerful, are good places to achieve the union of insight and tranquillity.
Riverbanks, as they shorten (mundane) thoughts,

Generate the development of emergence (from *saṃsāra*) swiftly.
Charnel grounds, as they are powerful and cause the attainments to come swiftly,
Are good places for (training in) both the development and perfection stages.

The choice of places for meditation depends on the strength and need of individual meditators:[STN 3a/3]

Places such as towns, fairs, empty houses, single trees,
Where human and non-human beings move about,
Distract beginners and become obstructions.
But they are supreme supports for well stablized meditators.

The beauty and peace of solitude generate inspiration, joy, and tranquillity in one's mind and life. Longchen Rabjam conveys the virtues of solitude by describing the tranquillity of forests in his *Narrative of Joyfulness in the Forest*:[NKT 68b/6]

In a forest, naturally there are few distractions and entertainments,
One is far from all the suffering of danger and violence.
The joy is much greater than that of the celestial cities.
Enjoy today the tranquil nature of forests.
O, mind, listen to the virtues of the forests.
The precious trees, worthy objects to offer to the Buddhas,
Bend under the load of fruit that is growing splendidly.
Blossoming flowers and leaves emit sweet odors.
Fragrant scents fill the air.
Mountain streams sound the enchanting music of drums.
The coolness of the moon touches everything. The middle (of the trees)
Are covered with dresses of dense rain-clouds.
(The sky is) decorated with stars and planets.
Flocks of swans fly around the sweet-smelling lakes.
Birds and deer move about in peace.

Wishing-trees, lotuses, and blue lilies
Are filled with honey-bees singing "dar" and "dir."
Trees are moving with dancing gestures.
The hands of hanging creepers
Bend down, conveying "welcome" to the visitors.
The cool and clean ponds covered with lotuses
Radiate like smiling faces.
The blue meadows are as if covered by the sky (descending to earth).
Pleasure groves beautified by chains of flowering trees
Are like the rising of stars and planets in a clear sky.
As if the gods are playing in a pleasure garden,
Cuckoos emit sweet sounds, intoxicated (with joy).
Seasonal breezes (blow) as they distribute flowers.
The clouds resound with joyous thunder.
The excellent showers arrive as if they are cooling (the heat).
The food of roots, leaves, and fruit
Are uncontaminated by unvirtuous deeds and are provided in all four seasons.
In forests emotions decline naturally.
There no one speaks unharmonious words.
As it is far from the distractions of entertainment in towns,
In forests the peace of absoption grows naturally.
(Life in forests) is in accordance with the holy Dharma, and it tames the mind
And achieves the happiness of ultimate peace.

For a beginner, it is important to see the virtues including the beauty of solitary places such as forests to inspire the mind to solitude. If one does not develop a habit of seeing the ordinary but positive aspects of solitude, such as its beauty, one may never dare to leave mundane entertainments. The purpose of seeing the beauty of nature is not to create an emotional relationship with it. Longchen Rabjam illustrates the beauty of nature for ordinary eyes as follows:[LNTT 3a/5]

On the banks of rivers ornamented by garlands of bubbles with breezes
In flower gardens, the six-legged ones (honey-bees) are intoxicated (with joy).
Hand-like branches of trees bend down as if upon seeing the (bees),
They are alerting the fairies of the forest.
As soon as the flower garden has provided the honey-bees,
The trees of the forest, as if intolerant with rage,
Wave the attractive twigs of their branches
As if to avenge the flowers.

He explains the way of seeing and interpreting ordinary scenes as an illustration of and inspiration to Dharma:[LNTT 3b/1]

In the garden of exquisite flowers at the bank of a river
The Bliss-gone honey-bees are sitting on the flowers,
Totally beautifying the garden and emitting the sound of the Dharma drum,
And the whole garden manifests as if listening to the holy Dharma with respect. . . .
The forest, as if it were the clear sky shining with stars and planets,
Is peaceful and rich with the ornament of garlands of virtues.
It is beautified with the glories of ascetic (nature).
Such prosperity never exists even in the heaven of *Brahmā*.
Trees carry loads of fruits and leaves.
Gardens provide different pleasures in the four seasons.
Rivers emit various music sweet to hear.
Forests are ornamented by ascetics in contemplation.
From the sounds of trees touched by winds,
Birds, bees, and deer
Hear the pacifying holy Dharma in Brahmā voice.
These sights make blossom the thousand-petalled flower of faith.
It seems that all the virtuous *karma* perfected in the past,

And the blessings of the kindness of the holy ones
Have entered the beings of this land,
And that the *saṃsāric* ocean is going to end.

Longchen Rabjam explains how, after entering the peaceful solitude of the forest, to proceed on the path of meditation in it:[NKT 69b/5]

After going to the forest, settle in a cave at the foot of a hill,
At the foot of a tree in a meadow with medicinal herbs and flowers,
Or in a hut of straw or leaves.
With water, wood, and fruit,
In simple living sustain the body
And devote day and night to virtuous Dharma.
In the forest, by the example of dead leaves
Come to realize that the body, youth, and senses
Change gradually and do not possess any true essence,
And that all types of prosperity are certain to decline.
By the example of the separation of leaves and trees
Come to realize that friends, enemies, as well as one's own body,
Who are gathered (at present), are subject to dissociation
And are bound to separate.
By the example of empty lotus ponds
Come to realize that various objects of desire, wealth, and prosperity
Are finally going to change, that there is no true essence in them,
And that what is accumulated will be exhausted.
By the example of the change of days, months, and the four seasons,
Come to realize that the blossoming spring flower-like body
Is subject to change as time passes, its youth fades away,
And the arrival of the lord of death is certain.
By the example of the fall of ripened fruit
Come to realize that all, young, adult, or old,
Are subject to die, that the time of death is uncertain,

And it is certain that what is born will die.
By the example of the arising of reflections in ponds
Come to realize that various phenomena appear but have no true (existence).
They are like illusions, a mirage and a water-moon,
And are certain to be empty of true existence.
Having realized phenomena in that way,
On a wide seat sit straight and comfortably.
With the attitude of benefiting living beings, meditate on the mind of enlightenment.
Do not follow after the thoughts of the past and do not bring forth future thoughts,
And release the present sense from thinking.
Comtemplate in the unwavering state, without projections and withdrawals. . . .
Remain in freedom, clarity, directness, and vividness (*Sa-Le*),
(The union of) emptiness and clarity, free from apprehensions.
It is the realization of the Buddhas of the three times.
Except for contemplating naturally with ease
In the innate meaning, the intrinsic nature of the mind as it is,
Think nothing, release all the thoughts.
Freedom from thoughts, analysis, and conceptualizations
Is the vision of the Buddhas.
So, pacifying the forest of thoughts,
Watch the ultimate peace, the intrinsic nature of the mind.
At the end (of a meditative session) dedicate the merits by the means known as "pure from three aspects."

Most of the Tibetan writers express their humility in their writings, such as describing themselves as ignorant and illiterate although they are great scholars, wild and deluded although they are realized persons, and as the most insignificant and inferior members of the community although they are the most respected ones. It is a way of training themselves to avoid creating pride and arrogance in their scholarship and to be humble, humane, and equal with all and also to teach others humility. But Longchen Rabjam, as some other great realized scholars do, discloses his true self and proclaims his fearless and limitless roar of scholarship and insight to inspire and generate confidence in the teachings in the minds of the followers.

Till the middle of this century, in their writings most of the great scholars of Tibet have relied on scriptures and the teachings of sages who have realized the truth as it is, or on their own realization of the truth as it is. Today many modern scholars write their judgments and criticism of scriptures without having a clue, even intellectually, of what the actual meaning is.

Longchen Rabjam writes as he learned from his realized masters and from authentic scriptures and as he has realized the truth directly by himself through vigorous training on the path to which he was properly introduced. He presents nothing based on his mere intellectual view. Longchen Rabjam himself writes:[LT 210b/1]

Because of training for lives after lives,
And having been introduced into this path by holy teachers,
I have realized the meaning of the utmost profound essence
And have perfected the (insight of) the ocean-like utmost supreme *yānas*.
Therefore, in my sky-like vast wisdom,
From the great clouds of learning and analysis with lightning of benefits and happiness,
Acompanied by thunder of realizations and contemplations,
This great rain of teaching has been showered.
Because of the vastness of my intellectual learning and analysis,
I have absorbed the meaning of all the *yānas*
And am learned in this excellent path of the *Vajra*-essence.
So I have written this commentary on the profound and vast ultimate sphere.

In *Shingta Chenpo* he writes:[SC-II, 188b/6]

The glorious Padma(sambhava), born from the great ocean of compassion and wisdom,
Whose follower, endowed with a thousand Immaculate Rays (Longchen Rabjam),
Is the sun of beings, who dispels the darkness of minds and
Remains in the unobscured primordial sphere.

In *Gyuma Ngalso* he writes:[GN 1b/4]

The Victorious One (Buddha) said that all phenomena are of the character of two (perverted and pure) illusions.
For the purpose of realizing that,
By condensing the essence of all the *sūtras* and *tantras*,
I shall explain what I have realized.

In *Semnyid Rangtrol* he writes:[SR 1b/3]

Phenomenal existents are unborn and are equalness,
In which the orginally liberated perceptions (percept and mind)
prevail evenly without apprehensions;
Concerning that marvelous sovereign, Naturally Liberated Mind,
Listen while I tell you what I have realized.

Sometimes the purpose of writing is for the writer's own learning. The best of three ways of studying is to write. The other two are hearing (studying) the teachings and discussion or debate. So the main purpose of writing is to dispel the darkness, the ignorance of one's own and others' minds. Longchen Rabjam explains why he has written *Semnyid Rangtrol:*[SR 17a/6]

This teaching, the essence of the sun,
Is illuminated by the rising of Immaculate Rays (i.e., Longchen Rabjam).
Today we are in the struggling age, covered by the darkness of wrong views;

In order to dispel them, I wrote this text of definitive meaning.

Longchen Rabjam concludes the commentary of *Nelug Dzod* saying:[NDG 90b/6]

From the vast sky of knowable subjects,
By wisdom, the thousand Rays of the Sun (i.e., Longchen Rabjam),
Condensing the essence of the heart of *tantras*, scriptures, and instructions,
Composed (this teaching) at the neck of Mt. Kangri Thodkar.

Longchen Rabjam, unlike many other Buddhist writers, is very direct and honest in pointing out others' wrong views, as a Tibetan proverb says: "Pointing out the faults of disciples directly is the characteristic of a teacher." It is not out of hatred or harshness but because of his pitying mind and unpretentious, honest, and open nature. In *Choying Dzod* he writes:[CD 8b/5]

Now, elephant (-like arrogant people), who are boasting that they are Ati (followers),
Are claiming that the hosts of flickering thoughts are the enlightened mind.
Oh! these fools (have fallen into the) pit of darkness,
They are far away from the meaning of *Dzogpa Chenpo.*
If you do not know the (differences between) the power of arisings and the power (of intrinsic awareness),
How can you understand the essence of the enlightened mind?

As the Buddha said in the scriptures, Longchen Rabjam also explains that he can only teach the Dharma, the way of reaching enlightenment, if people follow it, for he has no power to bring enlightenment to the minds of living beings just by living among people. So he makes aspirations that he may live in solitude and by practising may attain Buddhahood and serve beings more effectively:[RG 88a/5]

For living beings I am here,
Giving some (teachings) out of compassion,
But I do not possess the power to bring realization of suchness to them.
So I live alone in forests.
In a (forest which is) rich with pure water, abundance of fruits, flowers, and leaves,
Enclosed with a fence of. . . bamboo and vines,
With cool, pleasant, and attractive dwellings of bamboo,
May my mind attain tranquil absorption.
There, seen neither by people nor demons,
Living on pure water and only ascetic substances,
And meditating on the meanings of nectar-instructions of the Lama,
May I leave my living body.
At that time, by realizing the clarity-at-death,
Liberating the clarity of the intermediate state into the primordial state,
And having become inseparable from the bodies and primordial wisdoms,
May I perfect the dual benefits spontaneously.

By reading Longchen Rabjam's warm, enchanting, and penetrating writings, one can feel the touch of his compassionate mind. The following lines are some of the frequent expressions of his spontaneous and natural feelings in the form of aspirations in his scholarly treatises:[LT 211a/3]

Whoever towards me
Generates anger or faith, or whoever hurts,
Praises, or follows me,
May I lead them all swiftly (to enlightenment).

He concludes *Shingta Chenpo* with the following aspirations:[SC-II 190a/2]

May my happiness be experienced by all living beings,
May the sufferings of living beings be transferred to me.

Until *saṃsāra* is emptied
May I lead living beings (to happiness and enlightenment).

Like other Buddhist masters, Longchen Rabjam uses the suffering and impermanent nature of *saṃsāra* as the tool to inspire disciples to Dharma training. In *Terjung Rinpoche'i Logyu* he writes:[TRL 50b/3]

Life is impermanent like the clouds of autumn,
Youth is impermanent like the flowers of spring,
The body is impermanent like borrowed property,
Wealth is impermanent like dew on the grass,
Friends and relatives are impermanent as a visitor in a shop;
Although they are associated, they will become dissociated like traveling companions; and
The lord of death, like the shadow of the western mountain,will not delay....
Birth is more fearful than death,
Wherever one takes rebirth in *saṃsāra*, there is no place of happiness,
The Buddha has said; it is like a pit of fire....
By studying one will not attain liberation from suffering:
Can a patient be cured from sickness by hearing the prescription?
First, by determining through unerring studies,
Dispel all doubts and fabrications by pondering.
And then by meditating on it, one gets liberation (from sufferings).
So, having learned the unerring profound meaning,
It is important to practice it alone in forests....
This life ornamented with freedom and endowments (of human life),
It is not known when it will decay; it is like a clay vase.
The perception of tomorrow or of the next life,
Which one will appear first is unknown.
So please practice Dharma this very day.
The works of this life will never finish until death.

When you stop them, it is their nature that they are finished.
Faith in Dharma is hard to develop,
So whenever you remember (*Dharma*), practice it.

The following are some of the series of six constituents given by Longchen Rabjam in *Mengag Dzod* (*MD*) to summarize and illustrate various ethical, philosophical, religious, and meditational points of Dharma.The important factors for entering the Dharma:[MD 1b/4]

The six important things for entering the Dharma are
Observing discipline, the basis of the path,
Studying various subjects without falling into bias,
Pacifying the three doors and one's own mind,
Refraining from unvirtuous deeds, and developing virtuous deeds,
Having shame, embarassment and developing faith,
And having a virtuous master and virtuous friends.
These are very important for beginners.

The characteristics of solitude:[MD 2a/4]

The six important factors for living in solitude are
A solitary place with (virtuous) signs,
Which past adepts have touched with their feet,
Where the vow-holders assemble because it is unpolluted by defilements,
Where there are no distractions and entertainments,
Where the provisions of living are easy to obtain,
And where there is no danger from either human or non-human beings.

Longchen Rabjam stresses that the condensing of all the different *Yānas* into one is the means of reaching Buddhahood, and he rejects the view that they are contradictory bodies of teachings. He concludes *Semnyid Ngalso* with the following words:[SN 55b/4]

Now, ordinary people whose minds' eyes are not pure,

Take the different paths of the continuum (*tantra*) and of perfection (*pāramitā*)
To be contradictory. They are unaware of the way to unite them as one.
Therefore, they have the eyes of partiality.
Here (in this text), the supremely profound meanings of (all) the *yānas*, of causation and result,
(I) have condensed as one, as the means of training.
This was written in the fortress of Ogyen at White-topped Snow Mountain
By the raising of Immaculate Rays (i.e., Longchen Rabjam).

According to Longchen Rabjam's view, all the virtues of the nine *yānas* are condensed in the awareness, the enlightened mind (*Byang-Chub Sems*) of *Dzogpa Chenpo*:[CD 10a/5]

The scriptures of the *'Srāvakas*, *Pratyeka-buddhas*, and *Bodhisattvas*
Agree in (the view of) determining non-existence of "self (of person)" and "self of (phenomena)"
And in the freedom from conceptualizations, like space.
In the scriptures of the supremely secret and great *yoga* of *Ati*,
In the space-like freedom from distinctions of self and others,
The self-arisen primordial wisdom, one remains.
So all the meaning (of the previous *yānas*) is condensed in this supreme essence (awareness).
The classes of (outer *tantras*), *Kriyā*, *Upa(yoga)* and *Yoga(tantra)*,
Agree that by the means of offering-clouds of self, deity, and contemplations
One attains the accomplishment of the purification of the three doors.
In the secret vajra-summit, the king of the teachings,
One actualizes the perceptions, sounds, and thoughts as the deities from the primordial state
And accomplishes the purification of the three doors.

So the realization of those (three *yānas*) is completed in this supreme essence (awareness).
The three (inner *tantras*), *Mahā*, *Anu*, and *Ati* agree:
The world and beings, phenomenal existents, are the male and female deities and their pure lands,
The ultimate sphere and primordial wisdom are perfect in union,
And the ultimate nature is changeless and self-arisen primordial wisdom.
In this most supreme secret (awareness), since all are (primordially) perfected,
And, except for (the appearances of) uncreated mansions in the pure land of blissful primordial expanse,
Which has no outer or inner dimensions, are omnipresent,
There are no characteristic phenomena of efforts, acceptances, or rejections.
All are liberated in the infinite expanse of *Dharmakāya*.
So all the realizations of the (nine *yānas*) are completed in this great secret essence (awareness).

Longchen Rabjam describes the realization of *Dzogpa Chenpo* in simple, vivid, but profound words:[NDG 92a/3]

If one realizes *saṃsāra* without basis, it is (the attainment of) *nirvāṇa*.
If one realizes *nirvāṇa* as merely nominal, it is the (attainment of the) primordial sphere.
If you are free from efforts and transcend mind, it is the (attainment of) *Dharmakāya*.
If you are in contemplation without thoughts, it is the (attainment of) transcending the thoughts and expressions.
If there are no concepts and attachments, it is the (attainment of the) natural state.
If you transcend the mind and dissolve phenomena, it is (the attainment of) the ultimate meaning.
If you are free from "is" or "is not," it is (the attainment of) freedom from extremes.
If you cut off the root of fears and doubts, it is the (at-

tainment of) enlightenment.
(*Dzogpa Chenpo* teaching) is the ultimate and true essence;
I taught it for the future fortunate followers.
You and other fortunate followers,
Secure the eternal attainment in the state of dissolution.

The following are some quotations from Longchen Rabjam's poetic writings to illustrate his vision of human life and mundane phenomena, and his presentation of the view, meditation, and results of *Mahāyāna* training:[MD 22a/3]

Six aspects on which one should rely until the final attainment:
Leave relatives and rely on excellent spiritual friends,
Leave unvirtuous friends and rely on learned and disciplined teachers,
Leave agreements and rely on ultimate concord in Dharma,
Adopt study and pondering and apply them to the mind,
Leave towns and stay in solitude in mountains,
And seek teachings and practice them with diligence.
If one can follow thus, one will achieve the attainments swiftly.

MD 7b/1:

For (pacifying the) apprehension of truth of self of objects, look at their changes during the four seasons,
For grasping at the permanence of life, look at the dew on the grass,
For ignorance of cause and effect, look at the seeds and their fruits,
For the ignorance of percept and mind, look at dreams in sleep,
For ignorance of one taste, look at molasses and its reflections,
And for the ignorance of non-duality, look at water and ice.
These sights are the great antidotes.

MD 43a/3:

The abandonment of six mixed virtuous and unvirtuous deeds are:
Do not rely on a teacher who has no spiritual essence but causes hatred and attachments to increase,
Do not accept a disciple who is an improper vessel (of Dharma) and who thinks about the faults (of others),
Do not practice (so-called) virtues which are (actually) the accumulating of unvirtuous deeds,
Do not give charity with expectation of respect and response in return,
Do not make offerings which are for serving one's relatives and wealth,
And do not give teachings which are for deceiving (people) to earn (personal) gain.
By following these recommendations, one will be in accord with Dharma.

MD 9a/5:

Attainment of Buddhahood depends on six aspects:
The excellent tool for Dharma training depends on having a precious human life,
(Attainment of liberation) depends on training since without training one does not attain liberation,
Training depends on knowing perfectly,
Knowing depends on study,
Perfection of study depends on pondering,
And all depends on having a virtuous master.

MD 13a/4:

The six excellent supports of the practice of Dharma:
Respect the excellent Three Jewels as the supreme object of worship,
Sacrifice the activities of this life as the supreme sacrifice,
Have faith, learning, and pondering as the supreme wealth,
Recognize the self-nature of Mind as the supreme friend,
Abandon clinging to selfish desires as the supreme attitude,
And see the Lama as Buddha, which is the supreme ac-

complishment.
If one acts in these ways, one will accomplish the dual purposes.

MD 64b/4:

The six important virtues are:
Compassion for beings is important for realization of no-self,
Belief in *karma* is important for devotion (*Mos-Pa*) to emptiness,
Not remaining in *saṃsāra* is important for dwelling in peace,
Not expecting results is important for giving charity,
To abandon boasting is important for observance of discipline,
And modesty of needs is important for living in solitude.
If one possesses these six he will accomplish Dharma training.

MD 46a/1:

The necessities of six equalities:
It is necessary to (feel) that one's son and enemy are equal by knowing that the beings of the six realms are mothers,
It is necessary to see the equality of gold and pebbles (*Bong*) by realizing that material wealth is delusion,
It is necessary to see the equality of virtuous and unvirtuous deeds as there is no cause and effect in their true nature,
It is necessary to see the sameness of meditation and off-meditation periods by realizing the true nature of the six consciousnesses,
It is necessary to see nondiscrimination by eliminating the emotions as wisdoms,
And it is necessary to see the equality of *saṃsāra* and *nirvāṇa* as their nature is primordially pure.
Seeing those equalities is the great *yoga*.

MD 48a/5:

> Training on six perfections without separation is:
> Not letting generosity be stolen by the enemy of miserliness,
> Not letting the robbers, immoral conduct, destroy moral discipline,
> Not letting tolerance be pierced by the weapon of anger,
> Not letting effort be bound by the chain of laziness,
> Not letting contemplation be polluted by the poison of waverings,
> And not letting primordial wisdom be obscured by the darkness of ignorance.

MD 50a/4:

> Training on six excellent natures is:
> Renouncing the activities of the deluded body,
> Renouncing the expressions of meaningless speech,
> Renouncing the projections of thoughts of the mind,
> Renouncing the attachments of desire for enjoyments,
> Renouncing engagement in distractions and entertainments,
> And renouncing flattery as a means of guarding others' minds.

MD 59b/4:

> The six condensed ways of training in the *Yānas* are:
> Training on pure perception by identifying the world and beings as delusory perceptions,
> Training on compassion by identifying *saṃsāra* as misery,
> Training on loving-kindness by identifying the beings of the six realms as mothers,
> Training in the three vows by identifying *karma* as interdependent causation,
> Training in the development and perfection stages by identifying the four empowerments with the three doors,
> And training on the ultimate nature by identifying the ap-

pearances, sounds, and thoughts as the ultimate nature.
If one perfects these trainings there will no obscurations and errors.

MD 33b/6:

The six *vajra*-words of *Dzogpa Chenpo*:
The *Dzogchen* of the basis is the ascertainment of the Mind,
The *Dzogchen* of the path is the penetration of the crucial point for liberation,
The *Dzogchen* of result is the attainment of the cessation of hopes and fears,
The *Dzogchen* of objects is the freedom of the percepts without apprehensions,
The *Dzogchen* of mind is the arising of the thoughts as supports,
And the *Dzogchen* of meaning is the natural dissolution of movements.
Whoever realizes those is the king of *yogins*.

MD 74a/3:

The six confidences of realization of the profound vision are:
Realization of phenomena as the middle free from extremes,
Realization of phenomena as the great clarity, the union,
Realization of phenomena as equality, the great bliss,
Realization of phenomena as non-dual, the single essence,
Realization of phenomena as spontaneous accomplishment, free from partialities,
And realization of phenomena as primordially pure, natural. Although one perfects them,
(In their true nature) there is no one who wishes to realize,
Nor does the realization itself have any mentality of boasting about realization.
So, this *māyā yoga* is free from examples.

MD 74a/5:

Having realized thus, there are six ways of liberation:
The external objects, at the very moment of their appearance,
Are liberated at the appearances (themselves), as ice melting into water.
The inner cognition, at the very moment of its cognizing,
Is liberated at the cognition (itself), as bubbles merging in water.
The middle two thoughts, at the very time of their movements
Are liberated at the movements (themselves), as lightning into the sky.
Sounds, designations, and names, at the very moment of their sounding
Are liberated at the naming (itself), as the sounds of an echo.
The theories of apprehension, at the very point of assertion,
Are liberated at the assertions (themselves), as rainbows disappearing in the sky.
The results of accomplishment, at the very moment of attainment,
Are liberated at the attainments (themselves), as wishes granted by wishing-jewels.
The nature is self-liberated and the antidotes are self-disappearing.
It is free from designations and objects, and it is the spontaneous accomplishment of the realization.

TRL 52b/2:

See the spontaneously arisen wisdom, the king of views,
Meditate on the spontaneously arisen clarity, the king of meditations,
Train on the phenomenal existents as illusions, the king of actions,
Attain the dissolution in the primordial state, the king of results.
One will become *Samantabhadra*, in the spontaneously ac-

complished state.

YD 42a/6:

The perfect result of meditation is:
The attainment of bodies and wisdoms by perfecting abandonings and realizations.
As the sun and moon uncovered by clouds,
When the nature is freed from obscurations,
It is called enlightenment, and then the spontaneously present virtues appear,
And the appearances of body, consciousnesses, and percepts,
The habituations of three obscurations, will be liberated.
(Like) a lamp in a broken vase, an image in a flower that has opened,
The spontaneously present virtues show forth.
When the habituations of three obscurations have been liberated,
They appear as the Buddha-fields, wisdoms, and Buddha-bodies.

In Longchen Rabjam's writings he occasionally attributes a quotation to the wrong text. He also sometimes changes words in a quotation, but there is no error in the meaning. According to the celebrated scholar Mipham Namgyal (1846-1887), Longchen Rabjam had memorized vast numbers of scriptures. He also composed many of his writings in solitude where he did not have texts to refer to. So he didn't rely on copying the texts when he quoted them but wrote them from memory. When Mipham edited *Pema Karpo* (PK) and its commentary for publication, he didn't correct them, as there were no differences in meaning, and he saw the changes as a sign of the author's greatness. Mipham says in his *Explanation of Some Difficult Points of Yidzhin Rinpoche'i Dzod:*[KS 35a/3]

There are many errors in the titles of source-texts. It is well known that the Great Omniscient One memorized all the *sūtras*, *tantras*, and their commentaries, and he became popularly known as the "One who is from Samye with Many Scriptures" (*bSam-Yas Lung-Mang-Ba*). It is said that later when he composed his writings in solitude, without looking at the texts he quoted them from memory, and this is true. There are errors in the (titles) of the quotations and also there are some differences in the words in the quotations, but there are no differences in meaning (from the original) texts.They are not mistakes of later calligraphers. Since they belong to his original writings, I kept them, because if they are maintained without changes they preserve his great blessings. In those errors, there are not the slightest differences in the important points of meaning. If one can see this, then these events possess the capacity to generate wonder. So it will be better for them not to be changed (or corrected) by anyone in future also.

NAMES OF LONGCHEN RABJAM AND THEIR SIGNIFICANCE

Longchen Rabjam uses his various names in the colophons of his writings to distinguish the subjects of the texts:[LT 209b/2]

> In the writings which are mainly on interpretable subjects, the mundane sciences such as poetry, metre, and the science of words (language) it is said: "by Samyepa Tshulthrim Lodro (*bSam-Yas-Pa Tshul-Khrims Blo-Gros*)." In the writings which are common to both outer and inner *tantras* it is said: "by Dorje Zijid (*rDo-rJe gZi-brJid*)." In the writings which are mainly on profound subjects explained through the stages of the *yānas*, and on the words and meaning which explain the divisions of contemplations (*Ting-Nge-'Dzin*) it is said: "by Drimed Odzer (*Dri-Med A'od-Zer*)." In the writings which teach the expanse of inconceivable nature in greatest detail it is said: "by Longchen Rabjam." In the writings in which the *yānas*, theories, suchness, and so forth, are explained in detail it is said: "by Kunkhyen Ngagi Wangpo (*Kun-mKhyen Ngag-Gi dBang-Po*)."

PART II

ANTHOLOGY OF LONGCHEN RABJAM'S WRITINGS

ON

DZOGPA CHENPO

Summary of the Sections

VIEW (BASIS):

1. HOW *SAṂSĀRA* AND *NIRVĀṆA* ORIGINATE FROM THE "BASIS" AS "THE APPEARANCES OF THE BASIS"

The first chapter is on the arising of the "appearances of the basis" (*gZhi-sNang*), *saṃsāra* and *nirvāṇa*, from the "basis" (*gZhi*). This philosophical view is unique to *Dzogpa Chenpo*. The chapter is composed of excerpts from the first four chapters of *Tshigdon Dzod* (*TD 1-63*), which is based on the *Dzogpa Chenpo tantras* including *Thal-'Gyur, Klong-Drug-Pa, Rig-Pa Rang-Shar, Mu-Tig Phreng-Ba, Seng-Ge rTsal-rDzogs* and *rDo-rJe sNying-Gi Me-Long*.

The "basis" is the primordial purity, free from expressions and concepts. It has the threefold nature of primordially pure essence (*Ngo-Bo*), spontaneously accomplished nature (*Rang bZhin*), and omnipresent compassion (power) (*Thugs-rJe*). Compassion, the "spontaneous appearances of the basis," arises from the "basis" with "the eight modes of arising of spontaneous accomplishments" (*Lhun-Grub Kyi 'Ch'ar-Tshul brGyad*). If, when they arise, one does not realize them to be self-appearances, that is, the "basis" and "the appearances of the basis," but sees them as other than self-appearances, one will become associated with three unenlightenments (*Ma-Rig-Pa*). One will be distracted into the distinctions between *saṃsāra* and *nirvāṇa* and will be trapped in them. The "eight modes of arising of spontaneous accomplishments" of the "appearances of the basis" arise from the "basis." If, when they arise, one realizes them to be self-appearances, no distraction will occur, and the appearances will dissolve into the primordial purity. That is the attainment of primordial Buddhahood. The "appearances of the basis" are the basis of liberation if one realizes them as self-appearances. They are the basis of delusion if one perceives them as other than self-appearances.

The "basis" in *Dzogpa Chenpo* is totally different from the "universal ground" (*Kun-gZhi*) of the *Cittamātra* school. "Universal ground" is the basis of the distinctions between *saṃsāra* and *nirvāṇa*. The "basis" here has three aspects: essence, nature, and compassion, which are the Primordial Wisdoms(*Ye-Shes*) of the Ultimate Body (*Ch'os-sKu*). It is the space-like Intrinsic Awareness (*Rig-Pa*), unstained by *saṃsāric* phenomena.

It is also crucial to know the differences between the mind (*Sems*) and Primordial Wisdom (*Ye-Shes*). Mind is a *saṃsāric* phenomenon having the stains of *karma* and its traces. Mind's objects are the delusory appearances of *saṃsāra*, the sixfold objects. When the true nature of mind, the Intrinsic Awareness, becomes free from mind, that is the attainment of enlightenment. Primordial Wisdom is the virtues of *nirvāṇa*; it is free from *saṃsāric karma*, traces and concepts. The object of Primordial Wisdom is the space-like Ultimate Nature and Luminous Buddha-fields of Buddha-bodies and Primordial Wisdoms. For the attainment of liberation, the "appearances of the basis" are the basis of liberation; and the "basis" is the goal at which one attains liberation.

2. *KARMA* OF *SAṂSĀRIC* DEEDS, THE CAUSE OF WANDERING OF BEINGS IN DELUSORY *SAṂSĀRA*

The second chapter is on the *karma* of *saṃsāric* deeds (*Srid-Pa sGrub-Pa'i Las*). This chapter is an abridged translation of the first section of the fourth chapter of *Shingta Chenpo* (*SC I, 78b-97a*), which is based on *Mahāyāna sūtras* and texts including *Karmaśataka, Mahāyānaratnakūṭa-sūtra, Suvarṇaprabhā-sottama-sūtra, Avataṁsaka-sūtra, Uttaratantra-śāstra, Ratnāvalī, Madhyamakāvatāra, Abhidharma-koṣa* and *Abhisamāyālaṃkāra*.

In their view of *karma*—the ways of wandering in *saṃsāra* after delusion—*Dzogpa Chenpo* and other *Mahāyāna* scriptural traditions are identical. Ordinary people, after being deluded into *saṃsāra* because of their unenlightenment, begin to cling to their egoistic selves, enveloped in the darkness of ignorance and soaked in poisonous negative emotions. As a result, they are bound to the torment of *saṃsāra* by the chains of *karma*.

Buddhists believe that as long as one is not enlightened or liberated, one will wander in the world endlessly through the interdependent causations of one's own deeds and the traces created by those deeds, the basis of which is one's mental apprehensions and unenlightenment. The ten negative and ten positive deeds of body, speech, and mind with their traces produce painful and pleasant births in different migrations. The systematic functioning of cause and result is called *karma*. This chapter also illustrates the causation of external phenomena and internal phenomena as the chain of interdependent causation.

3. *KARMA* OF LIBERATIVE VIRTUES, THE MEANS OF LIBERATION FROM *SAṂSĀRA*

The second chapter is on the *karma* of *saṃsāric* deeds (*Srid-Pa sGrub-Pa'i Las*). This chapter is an abridged translation of the first section of the fourth chapter of *Shingta Chenpo* (*SC I, 78b-97a*), which is based on *Mahāyāna sūtras* and texts including *Karmaśataka, Mahāyānaratnakūṭa-sūtra, Suvarṇaprabhā-sottama-sūtra, Avataṁsaka-sūtra, Uttaratantra-śāstra, Ratnāvalī, Madhyamakāvatāra, Abhidharma-koṣa* and *Abhisamāyālaṃkāra*.

maitreyaparipṛcchā-sūtra, *'Phags-Pa gZungs-Kyi rGyal-Pos Zhus-Pa*, *dPal-'Phreng Seng-Ge'i Nga-Ro sGras Zhus-Pa*, *Bu-Mo Rin-Ch'en Gyis Zhus-Pa*, *Bu-Mo Dri-Ma Med-Pas Zhus-Pa*, *Aṣṭasāhasrikāprajñāpāramitā-sūtra*, *Prajñāpāramitā-sañcayagāthā*, *Uttaratantra-śāstra*, *Ratnāvalī*, *Guhyagarbhamāyājāla-tantra* and *Dvikalpa-tantra* of *Hevajra*.

Beings possess the Buddha-essence (*S. tathāgatagarbha*), the absolute truth, although it has been obscured by *karma* and its traces created by their apprehending a self, so that unenlightened mind and negative emotions cover the Buddha-essence like clouds before the sun. They have the potential to become Buddhas, should any one of them pursue the path of realizing and perfecting the Buddha-essence. To dispel the obstructions and to attain liberation, one must train in the dual accumulations, the accumulations of merits and primordial wisdom. By perfecting the dual accumulations, one purifies negative *karma* and its traces together with the unenlightened mind. Thereby one realizes the Buddha-essence, and by perfecting the realization by meditating on it one attains Buddhahood. This view is common to the *Dzogpa Chenpo* tradition and many other *Mahāyāna sūtric* and *tantric* traditions.

It is important to note here, as I explained in the introduction, that *Dzogpa Chenpo* asserts that all beings possess the Buddha-essence, as the *sūtras* of the "second turning of the Dharma Wheel" and their followers including the *Yogācārya* school maintain, and as the *tantras* also teach. But, instead of viewing the Buddha-essence as "thoroughly established" (*Yongs-Grub*) as *Yogācārya* does, *Dzogpa Chenpo* views the Buddha-essence as free from extremes of elaborations, expressions, designations, and conceptions as *Prāsaṅgika Madhyamaka* does. Longchen Rabjam concludes that in comprehending the freedom from extremes, *Dzogpa Chenpo* is similar to the views of *Prāsaṅgika Madhyamaka*.

4. PHILOSOPHICAL VIEW OF PHENOMENAL EXISTENTS

The fourth chapter is on the philosophical view of the realization of the "basis," the Primordial Wisdom which does not dwell in either of the two extremes, eternal or nil. The chapter is an abridged translation of the tenth chapter of *Shingta Chenpo* (SC-II, 60a-92a), which is based on *Mahāyāna sūtras, tantras, Dzogpa Chenpo tantras,* and their commentaries. They include *Ārya-ratnakara-sūtra, Ārya-samadhinirmocana-sūtra, Laṅkāvatāra-sūtra, Ārya-ratnamegha-sūtra, Avataṁsaka-sūtra, Ratnakūṭa-sūtra, Ārya-maitreyaparipṛccha-sūtra, Prajñāpāramitāhṛdaya, Ārya-samādhirāja-sūtra, Dohākoṣa, Guhyagarbha-ṃāyājāla-tantra, Padma rNam-Par Rol-Pa, sPyan-Ras-gZigs brTul-Zhugs, rMad-Byung rGyal-Po, dGongs-'Dus, Kun-Byed rGyal-Po, Mūlamadhyamakakārikā-prajñā* and *Mūlamadhyamaka-vṛtti-prasanna-padā.*

The chapter explains the essence of phenomenal existents, which is unborn (*emptiness*); the view of realization; the unenlightened mind that is to be purified; and the Awareness Wisdom, the true nature of the mind free from extremes, which purifies obscurations. It emphasizes that through theoretical or intellectual words and understanding one will neither realize the essence nor perfect the realization of the "basis." This chapter lays the foundation of the views common to *Dzogpa Chenpo* and other *Mahāyāna sūtric* and *tantric* traditions.

MEDITATION (PATH):

5. MEDITATION ON THE MEANING OF THE VIEW

The fifth chapter is on the meditation on the view. It is an abridged translation of the first section of the eleventh chapter of *Shingta Chenpo (SC-II, 92a-123b)*, which is based on *Mahāyāna sūtras, tantras* and *Dzogpa Chenpo tantras* and their commentaries. They include *Samādhirāja-sūtra*, *Ratnakūṭa-sūtra*, *Ratnamegha-sūtra*, *Prajñāpāramitā-sūtra*, *Upāliparipṛcchā-sūtra*, *Tattvaprakāśa-sūtra* (?), *Sañcayagāthā-sūtra*, *Ye-Shes Rol-Pa*, *Ye-Shes mNgon-Par 'Byung-Pa'i rGyud Phyi-Ma*, *sGyu-'Phrul rDo-rJe*, *Kun-Byed rGyal-Po*, *Abhisamāyā-laṁkāra-śāstra*, *Catuḥśataka-śāstra*, *Dohā*, *Caryāmelāpaka-pradīpa*, and *Bodhicaryāvatāra*.

After determining the view, one needs to meditate on it in order to attain the realization of its meaning. This chapter summarizes the different levels of meditations for meditators of higher, mediocre, and lesser intellect. Meditators of high intellect attain liberation at the realization of the natural state of the mind, the ultimate state. Meditators of mediocre intellect train in and realize the innate wisdom through five aspects of meditation and eight ways of contemplation. Meditators of lesser intellect train in and attain virtues of various modes of absorption through meditations in tranquillity, insight, and their union. These meditations directly or indirectly introduce to, lead to, or lay the foundation for the *tantric* and *Dzogpa Chenpo* meditations and realizations.

6. TWENTY-SEVEN COURSES OF TRAINING IN *DZOGPA CHENPO*

The sixth chapter is on *Dzogpa Chenpo* meditation. It is an abridged translation of *Changchub Lamzang* (BL 43a-52a). It is an instruction condensing the training in *Dzogpa Chenpo* meditation given in *Semnyid Ngalso* (SN), *Relaxation in the Natural State of Mind*, arranged in meditation periods. It consists of twenty-seven courses of training: four courses in determination of the view, twenty courses in meditation on maintaining the realization of the view, and three courses on the attainment of confidence in the result of the meditation. The instruction is that meditators who are ready for this training should meditate on each course for five days, three days, or at least one day.

7. NATURALLY LIBERATED MIND, THE GREAT PERFECTION (*DZOGPA CHENPO*)

The seventh chapter is the complete translation of *Naturally Liberated Mind* (*Sems-Nyid Rang-Grol*) (SR). This text is hard to understand in many places, and there is no commentary to clarify it. It elucidates the view of the Mind Division (*Sems-sDe*) of *Dzogpa Chenpo* teachings, the view that all phenomenal existents are nothing but the Mind, which is free from all defilements and elaborations. The text consists of three chapters totaling seven hundred and forty-three lines of verse. It provides instructions on the view, meditation, and result of the naturally liberated and enlightened mind, which is unborn and free from concepts, perceptions, and apprehensions. The first chapter is on the attainment of self-liberation by realizing the view of the "basis." The second chapter is on the attainment of self-liberation through the experiences of the path of meditation. The third chapter is on the attainment of self-liberation by achieving the great spontaneously accomplished result of *Dzogpa Chenpo.*

8. INSTRUCTIONS ON THE MEDITATION ON NATURALLY LIBERATED MIND, THE GREAT PERFECTION (*DZOGPA CHENPO*)

The eighth chapter is the complete translation of *Lamrim Nyingpo'i Donthrid, the Meaning Instruction of the Essence of the Stages of the Path* (NDK 17b-28a). It expounds the ways of training on the essential teachings given in *Naturally Liberated Mind* (SR). It divides the training into three categories. The first is the instructions for meditators of higher intellect on the attainment of self-liberation in this lifetime. It covers the preliminary trainings, the actual introduction and meditation, and the turning of various activities of off-meditative periods into training or support of training. The second is the instructions for meditators of mediocre intellect on the attainment of self-liberation by contemplation on the luminous absorptions, the basis for arising of the Intermediate State (*Bar-Do*). The third is instructions for meditators of lesser intellect for generating virtuous perceptions and meditations in the Intermediate State to attain self-liberation or at least a better rebirth. The final result of these trainings is the attainment of Buddhahood endowed with three Buddha-bodies and five Primordial Wisdoms.

9. TRAININGS AND ATTAINMENTS OF FIVE PATHS OF *MAHĀYĀNA*

The ninth chapter is on the stages of the five paths (*Lam-lNga*) taught in the *sūtras*. It is an abridged translation of the last section of the eleventh chapter of *Shingta Chenpo* (SC-II, 123b-136a), which is based on *Mahāyāna sūtras*, texts and commentaries. They include *Ratnakūṭa-sūtra*, *Avataṁsaka-sūtra*, *Ārya-subāhupari pṛcchā-sūtra*, *Commentary of Pañcaviṁśatisāhasrikā-prajñāpāramitā*, *Great Commentary of Ārya-aṣṭasāhasrikā-prajñāpāramitā*, *Uttaratantra-śāstra*, *Abhisamayālaṁkāra-śāstra*, *Mahāyānasūtrālaṁkāra-śāstra*, and *Madhyāntavibhaṅga-kārikā*.

It explains the trainings and perfections of the "thirty-seven aspects of enlightenment" (*Byang-Ch'ub Kyi Phyogs Ch'os Sum-Chu rTsa-bDun*) in the stages of the first four paths—the paths of accumulation, application, seeing, and meditation—and, as the result, the attainment of the path of "no more training," which is Buddhahood. It is important to note that there are great differences between the methods of training employed in the stages of the paths of *sūtras*, *tantras*, and *Dzogpa Chenpo tantras*. But they all train in and perfect the "thirty-seven aspects of enlightenment" in the stages of "the five paths." Therefore, to understand the path of training in *Dzogpa Chenpo* it is important to study the aspects, stages, and paths in this chapter and in other common scriptures.

10. TRAININGS AND ATTAINMENTS OF PATHS AND STAGES OF *TANTRA*

The tenth chapter is on the stages of the path of *tantric* training. It is an abridged translation of the twenty-first chapter of *Pema Karpo* (PK-II, 175a-183a), which presents a comparative study of *sūtric* and *tantric* paths relying on both *sūtric* and *tantric* texts including: *Samādhirāja-sūtra*, *sGyu-'Phrul Dam-Pa*, *Abhisamayā-laṁkāra-śāstra*, *Mahāyānasūtrālaṁkāra-śāstra*, and *Catuḥaśataka-śāstra*.

By perfecting the mind (*Sems*) and energies (*rLung*) in the four wheels of channels (*rTsa-'Khor bZhi*), one perfects the "thirty-seven aspects of enlightenment" in the first four levels of the path and arouses the virtues of the ten stages. As the final result, one attains the path of "no more training," Buddhahood itself, and having pacified the mind and mental events into the ultimate sphere, one remains with the Buddha-bodies and Primordial Wisdoms.

11. ATTAINMENTS OF THE PATHS, STAGES, AND VISIONS OF *DZOGPA CHENPO*

The eleventh chapter is on the attainments of the paths of *Dzogpa Chenpo.* The following are excerpts from *Choying Dzod* (CD), *Namkha Longchen* (NKC), *Namkha Longsal* (NKS) of *Lama Yangtig* (Vol-II), *Sem-nyid Rangtrol* (SR), and *Tshigdon Dzod* (TD). They explain the attainment of Enlightened Mind (*Byang-Ch'ub Sems*) and the "four visions" (*sNang-Ba bZhi*), the attainments of *Thodgal* and *Thregchod* trainings of *Dzogpa Chenpo.* By training in and perfecting the "enlightened mind" and "four visions" of *Dzogpa Chenpo* one accomplishes the paths and stages with the "thirty-seven aspects of enlightenment." The mind and mental events dissolve into the ultimate sphere and from the sphere of the Ultimate Body arise the Form Buddha-bodies with all the other Buddha-virtues. They serve the needs of beings, assuming the appearance of various manifestations with the primordial wisdom of dual Knowledge (*mKhyen-gNyis*).

This chapter is very brief. I did not include any texts of Longchen Rabjam which give detailed explanations of the "four visions." The main purpose of this chapter is just to show the principles of the path of training which are common to *Dzogpa Chenpo tantras* and other common *sūtras* and *tantras.* It is appropriate to present full details of such teaching only to those who have been matured by the common trainings.

RESULT

12. ATTAINMENT OF THE RESULT, THE BUDDHA-BODIES AND PRIMORDIAL WISDOMS OF BUDDHAHOOD IN *MAHĀYĀNA SŪTRAS* AND *TANTRAS*

The twelfth chapter is on the result of the path of training. It is an abridged translation of the twenty-second chapter of *Pema Karpo* (PK-II, 183a-192b). It is based on *Mahāyāna sūtras* and *tantras* including *Avataṁsaka-sūtra*, *Āryamañjuśrīnāmasaṁgīti-tantra*, *Cakrasaṁvara-mūla-tantra*, *Padmamukuṭa-tantra*, *Mahāguru-guhyagarbha-tantra*, *Guhyagarbhamāyājāla-tantra*, *Uttaratantra-śāstra*, *Mahāyāna-sūtrālaṁkāra-śāstra* and *Madhyamakāvatāra*.

When one completes the tenth stage (*Sa-bChu-Pa*) and the fourth path, one attains the result, the fifth path, which is Buddhahood. Buddhahood consists of Buddha-bodies (*sKu*) as the basis and the Primordial Wisdoms (*Ye-Shes*) as the essence.

This chapter, based on *Mañjuśrīnāmasaṁgīti-tantra* and *Guhyagarbhamāyājāla-tantra*, classifies the Buddha-bodies into five aspects. They are the three Buddha-bodies: the Ultimate Body (*Ch'os-sKu*), Enjoyment Body (*Longs-sKu*), and Manifested Body (*sPrul-sKu*). In addition to the three Buddha-bodies, the Great Blissful Body (or *Enlightened Body*) (*bDe-Ba Ch'en-Po'i sKu or mNgon-Par Byang-Ch'ub Pa'i sKu*) and the Changeless *Vajra*-body (*Mi-'Gyur rDo-rJe'i sKu*) constitute the Five Buddha-bodies. In many scriptures, such as *Suvarṇaprabhāsottama-sūtra*, the Buddha-bodies are classified as three Buddha-bodies. *Mahāyānottaratantra-śāstra* and *Mahāyāna-sūtralaṁkāra*, and so forth, classify them into four Buddha-bodies—the three Buddha-bodies and the Essence-body (*Ngo-Bo-Nyid sKu*). *Dvikalpa-hevajra-tantra* classifies them into four Buddha-bodies; the three Buddha-bodies with the Great Blissful Body. These classifications are made on the basis of the varieties of virtues of the Buddha-bodies, but they are all one in essence and the same in the phenomena of Buddhahood. In*Shingta Chenpo* it is said:[SC-II,157a/2]

> The (different systems of dividing Buddha-bodies) are just ways of dividing and condensing the classes and virtues (of the Buddha-body). In actual meaning they do not differ, as they are merely the different ways of classifying the *dharma* of the Buddha-stage. Their essence is one.

Primordial Wisdom, the essence of the Buddha-bodies, has five divisions. They are the Primordial Wisdom of the Ultimate Sphere, Mirror-like Primordial Wisdom, the Primordial Wisdom of Equanimity, Discriminative Primordial Wisdom, and the Primordial Wisdom of Accomplishment. This chapter concludes with the description of Buddha-actions, which fulfill the needs of beings spontaneously.

13. THE BUDDHA-BODIES AND PRIMORDIAL WISDOMS OF *DZOGPA CHENPO*

The thirteenth chapter is on the result of the path of training. It is an abridged translation of the eleventh chapter of *Tshigdon Dzod* (TD 227b-240a). This chapter is based on *Thal-'Gyur* and *Rang-Shar*, two of the ancient *tantras*. It also includes quotations from other scriptures including *Avataṁsaka-sūtra*, *Mahāyāna-sūtralaṁkāra*, *Abhisamayālaṁkāra*, *Mahāyānottaratantra*, and *Madhyamakāvatāra*.

It describes the attainment of the Buddha-bodies and Primordial Wisdoms, the results of the path of training. The Buddha-body consists of three aspects: the Ultimate Body, the Enjoyment Body, and the Manifested Body. The Ultimate Body is endowed with three Primordial Wisdoms, which are called "the Primordial Wisdoms at-the-basis" (*gZhi-gNas Kyi Ye-Shes*). They are the Primordial Wisdoms of originally pure essence, spontaneously accomplished nature, and omnipresent compassion. This classification of the Primordial Wisdom of the Ultimate Body is based exclusively on the *Dzogpa Chenpo tantras*. The Enjoyment Body is endowed with five Primordial Wisdoms, which are called the "Primordial Wisdoms Endowed with Characteristics" (*mTshan-Nyid 'Dzin-Pa'i Ye-Shes*). They are the Primordial Wisdom of the Ultimate Sphere,

Mirror-like Primordial Wisdom, the Primordial Wisdom of Equanimity, Discriminative Primordial Wisdom, and the Primordial Wisdom of Accomplishment. The Manifested Body is endowed with two Primordial Wisdoms, which are called "the Primordial Wisdom of Omnipresence" (*Kun-Khyab Kyi Ye-Shes*). They are the Primordial Wisdoms of the two kinds of Knowledge (*mKhyen-gNyis*); the Knowledge of "suchness" (*Ji-lTa-Ba*) and of the "varieties" (*Ji-sNyed-Pa*).

Dzogpa Chenpo tradition agrees with the *Mahāyāna sūtras* and *tantras* in their interpretations of general view, meditation, and result concerning relative truth and their presentation of the general meaning of absolute truth. But concerning the most definitive meaning of the innermost essence of the Absolute Truth, *Dzogpa Chenpo* has a unique interpretation of view, meditation, and result. Essentially these unique aspects of *Dzogpa Chenpo* are:

View: The "basis" is the absolute purity and the "appearances of the basis" are the source and way of arising of the delusions as *saṃsāra* and *nirvāṇa*.

Meditation: The innermost essence of the way of training is that one distinguishes the Intrinsic Awareness (*Rig-Pa*), the Buddha-essence, from the mind, and remains in it without stains and waverings; and one accomplishes the appearances as the power, play, and vision of the Intrinsic Awareness.

Result: The attainment of the Ultimate Body, the union of the primordially pure essence (emptiness), the spontaneously accomplished nature (clarity), and the omnipresent compassion (power).

VIEW (BASIS)

1. How Saṃsāra and Nirvāṇa Originated from the "Basis" as "the Appearances of the Basis" According to the Innermost Dzogpa Chenpo Teachings

In *Thegchog Dzod*, *Tshigdon Dzod*, and other works, Longchen Rabjam gives the interpretations of the "basis," the primordial purity, and the arising of the "appearances of the basis" and the delusions through the chain of twelve interdependent causations, according to the Innermost Esoteric teachings of *Dzogpa Chenpo*. He explains the distinction between the fourfold "universal ground," and the "Dharmakāya" (the ultimate body) and between "mind" and "primordial wisdom" (*Jñāna*). The following are abridged translations of selected passages from *Tshig-Don Rin-Po-Ch'e'i mDzod* (TD):

THE BASIS (*gZhi*): THE PRIMORDIALLY PURE (*Ka-Dag*) ESSENCE (*Ngo-Bo*)[TD 8a/3]

The primordial purity of the original basis transcends the extremes of existence and non-existence, and it is the great transcending of (the objects of) conception and expression. As the essence (*Ngo-Bo*) (of the basis) is primordially pure, it transcends the extreme of existence, eternalism, and it is not established as the phenomena of things or characteristics. As the nature (of the basis) is spontaneously accomplished, it transcends the extreme of non-existence, nihilism, and it is present as the purity, the ultimate nature (*Ch'os-Nyid*) of emptiness clarity, as the nature of the primordial Buddha, as the state (*dGongs-Pa*) of changeless ultimate body (*Dharmakāya*), as non-existent either as *saṃsāra* or *nirvāṇa*, and as the self-arisen great intrinsic wisdom which is present from primordial time like space.

12a/2 In Rangshar (*Rang-Shar tantra*) it is said: "The primordial purity, the basis, is present (in the mode of) essence [entity], nature [character], and compassion [power]. The essence is the ceaselessness of the changeless intrinsic wisdom, and it is called the nature of "the youthful vase body" (*gZhon-Nu Bum-sKu*). The nature is the ceaseless appearances of the five lights. The appearances of compassion are (pervasive) like the cloudless sky. These are called the nature of primordial purity as they do not fall into any (extremes) of dimensions or partialities.

HOW THE APPEARANCES OF THE BASIS (*gZhi-sNang*) ARISE

15a/2 Having broken the shell (*rGya*) of the "youthful vase body," the primordial basis of the originally pure inner ultimate sphere, by the flow (*gYos-Pas*) of the energy/air of primordial wisdom, the self-appearances of the intrinsic awareness flash out (*'Phags*) from the basis as the "eight spontaneously accomplished doors" (*Lhun-Grub Kyi sGo-bGyad*).[1]

15a/5 As everything (*nirvāṇa* and *saṃsāra*) is spontaneously arisen from the appearances of the "eight spontaneously ac-

[1]TCD-I, 203a/2 (*The Eight Spontaneously Accomplished Doors (Lhun-Grub sGo-brGyad or lHun-Grub Kyi 'Ch'ar-Tshul brGyad*) are:) (1) As (in the basis, the orginal purity) the space for the arising of (the appearances of the basis) as compassion (*Thugs-rJe*) is ceaseless, there arises compassion towards living beings.(2) As the space for arising as the light (*A'od*) is ceaseless, there arise the self-lights of the primordial wisdom like the colors of the rainbow and they pervade all the appearances. (3) As the space for arising as the primordial wisdom (*Ye-Shes*) is ceaseless, it remains in the state of no-thoughts. (4) As the space for arising as the bodies (*sKu*) is ceaseless, the bodies of clarity [luminous absorption] (in the form of) peaceful and wrathful (*Buddhas*) fill space. (5) As the space for arising as non-duality (*gNyis-Med*) is ceaseless, there is no analysis (of things) as plural or singular. (6) As the space for arising as the liberated from extremes (*mTha'-Grol*) is ceaseless, the spontaneous accomplishments are clear as the self-essence. (7) As the space for arising as the door of pure primordial wisdom (*Dag-Pa Ye-Shes*) (i.e., *nirvāṇa*) is ceaseless, the appearances of the orginally pure essence, the cloudless sky-like appearances, appear above. (8) As the space for arising as the door of impure *samsāra* (*Ma-Dag 'Khor-Ba*) is ceaseless, the appearances of the six classes of beings appear below.

complished doors," it is called the "great simultaneous arising of the appearances of *saṃsāra* and *nirvāṇa*." When they (the appearances) spontaneously arise from the inner clarity (*Nang-gSal*) as the outer clarity (*Phyi-gSal*), the appearances of (their) essence (*Ngo-Bo*) are self-clarity, which is the space of unobstructedness, the appearances of (their) nature (*Rang-bZhin*) are the original (or natural) glow(*gDangs*) as the five lights, and the appearances of compassion (*Thugs-rJe*) are the aspect of providing the cloudless sky-like space. (This is the arising of the appearances of the basis from the basis.)

16b/4 When (the appearances of the basis) arise, phenomenal existents arise as the lights and (Buddha-) bodies. It is called the appearances of everything as the spontaneously accomplished (Buddha-) field (*Lhun-Grub Kyi Zhing-sNang*). From the power of the essence of that (field) arise the appearances of *Saṃbhogakāya*, from the power of their qualities arise the appearances of *Svabhavanirmāṇakāya*, and from their power of compassion arise the door (aspects) of *saṃsāra*, like dreams.

LIBERATION AS THE PRIMORDIAL BUDDHA

18a/3 At the very movement of the arising of (the intrinsic awareness) from the basis, "the eight spontaneous appearances of the basis" arise naturally. (At that moment) by not apprehending those appearances as others and by realizing them as the natural glow (or self-radiance) (*gDangs*) with a pure mind (*gZu-Bo'i Blos*), the movements (*'Gyu-Ba*) (of the intrinsic awareness) cease in themselves. At the first movement, by realizing the self-essence of the self-appearances, the realization (of the true meaning) develops. . . . At the second movement, the delusions are dispelled and the (perfection) of primordial wisdom develops. That is the development of the basis (itself) as the result (of enlightenment). It is called the re-enlightenment (or self-liberation) through the realization of the essence, the primordial Buddhahood. Having dissolved the self-appearances into the primordial purity and become enlightened at the basis before all, it is (also) called the Lord Universal Goodness (the primordial Buddha).

ARISING OF DELUSION (*'Khrul-Tshul*)

20b/3 Through the aspect of not realizing the essence of the "appearances of the basis" themselves (as they are), one becomes distracted into the delusions.... When (phenomena) arise as the "appearances of the basis," there arises the cognition which is the power of compassion arisen naturally (in the nature of) clarity and awareness with the ability of analyzing the objects. (At that point,) owing to (*lTos-Nas*) not realizing itself (as it is), it (i.e., the essence of the "appearances of the basis") becomes associated (*mTshungs-lDan*) with three unenlightenments (*Ma-Rig-Pa*): (a) The not knowing of the arisen cognition (itself) as (the primordial purity) is the unenlightenment of single self, the cause (*rGyu bDag-Nyid gChig-Pa*). (b) The simultaneous arising of the cognition and the not knowing of the self-essence (watching the spontaneously accomplished appearances, not knowing that they are self-appearances without existence) is the "innate unenlightenment" (*lHan-Chig sKyes-Pa*). (c) The analyzing of the self-appearances as others (i.e., apprehended and apprehender) is the unenlightenment of imaginaries (*Kun-Tu brTags-Pa*). These three are one in essence (*Ngo-Bo*) and have different aspects (*lDog-Pa*). So, when one analyzes the self-appearances, because of not realizing the "basis" and the "appearances of the basis," that the "basis" (as the) essence, nature, and compassion and the mode of spontaneous accomplishments is the "appearances of the basis," and because of apprehending the (self-appearances) as others, one becomes distracted into delusions. When, through the aspect of the cause, (namely) the three unenlightenments, and because of the four conditions,[1] the impure concepts, the appearances (of the basis), one becomes deluded into the appear-

[1] TD 22a/3 Four conditions (of delusions): (1) (Because of the three unenlightenments) not knowing the "appearances of the basis" has arisen (from) itself and is the condition of cause (of the delusions). (2) The arising (of the appearances of the basis) as the objects is the condition of conceptually (observed) object. (3) Apprehending them as "I" and "my" is the empowering condition. (4) Simultaneous arising of these three (conditions) is the immediately preceding condition of the delusions.

ances (of the basis) as the (dualistic) cognitions of apprehended and apprehender; (then) six thoughts[1] (*Yid*) arise as the ceaseless apprehenders; and the six emotional defilements[2] arise in the (form of) dormancies; they bind the intrinsic awareness, and one becomes deluded into the appearances of six objects.[3]

[24a/4]The intrinsic awareness having flashed out (*'Phags*) from the "basis" and not (yet) having ripened (through realizing it as it is), one wanders in the three realms and six migrations of beings through the chain of twelve interdependent causations because of the *karmas* of individual (beings). . . . (The twelve interdependent causations are:) (1) When the "appearances of the basis" arise from the "basis," mental cognition arises from the power of the intrinsic awareness, and as this (cognition) is accompanied by not realizing its own essence, it is unenlightenment (*Ma-Rig-Pa*). (2) From which arise the delusions, and that is the compositional factor [formation of *karma*] (*'Du-Byed*). (3) From which arise the analyses of the modes of the objects, and those are the consciousnesses (*rNam-Shes*). (4) (From which arise) the distinguishing (of the objects) by designations such as "this is an object" and "this is an appearance," and then the consciousness apprehends the named objects as forms. That is the primary delusion into the existents (*saṃsāra*), and it is name-and-form (*Ming-gZugs*). (5) From which arise the senses and projections towards the six objects, and those are the six sources [sense organs] (*sKye-mCh'ed Drug*). (6) From which arises the apprehension of the objects, and that is the contact (between objects, faculties, and consciousnesses) (*Reg-Pa*). (7) From which arise attachment, hatred (or happy, unhappy) and neutral experiences, and that is feeling [sensation] (*Tshor-Ba*). (8) From which arises attachment to the objects, and that is craving [desire] (*Sred-Pa*).

---

[1]TD 21b/4 Six thoughts (*Yid*): The thought associated with unenlightenment, thought of mind-consciousness, thought of seeking, thought of ascertaining, the gross (emotional) thought, and the thought of contemplation.

[2]TD 21a/6 Six emotions: unenlightenment, desire, hatred, ignorance, pride, and jealousy. Unenlightenment prevails in all the five poisons, and ignorance is one of the five poisons. So they are counted separately.

[3]TD 21a/6 The six objects: Form, sound, smell, taste, feeling, and mental objects (*dharma*).

(9) From which arise the grasper and grasping of the objects, and that is grasping [attachment] (*Len-Pa*). (10) From which arise the (formation of) uncertain appearances and. . .experiences of numerous delusions, and that is becoming [existence] (*Srid-Pa*). (11) From which arise births in the desire, form, and formless realms, and that is birth (*sKye-Ba*). (12) From which arise old age and sickness up to death (and that is old age and death) (*rGa-Shi*). In that process, one wanders again and again (in *saṃsāra*). That is the first arising of the chain of twelvefold interdependent causation, the cause of *saṃsāra*, from the "appearances of the basis." Then the (various succeeding chains of) twelvefold interdependent causation take place, while one wanders in different existences (of *saṃsāra*).

[25a/4]Thus, the delusory appearances manifest as *saṃsāra* because of the strength of the traces (*Bag-Ch'ags*) of not knowing (the true nature of the appearances) themselves (as they are), and apprehending them as self. Thereby the appearances become established as the (five) aggregates, (eighteen) elements, and (twelve) sources [sense organs] of the body of the individual being, who wanders through successive (lives) and remains in *saṃsāra* forever.

[40a/6]The Buddha-essence is present and pervades the nature (*Khams*) of living beings. . . . In *rDo-rJe Sems-dPa' sNying-Gi Me-Long Gi rGyud* it is said: "In all living beings of the world, the Buddha-essence is present and pervades like oil in sesame seeds."

SOME CRUCIAL POINTS OF THE *DZOGPA CHENPO* VIEW:

THE DISTINCTION BETWEEN THE UNIVERSAL GROUND AND *DHARMAKĀYA*

[52a/4]As the universal ground (*Kun-gZhi*) is the root of *saṃsāra*, it is the foundation of all the traces, like a pond. As the *Dharmakāya* (ultimate body) is the root of *nirvāṇa*, it is the freedom from all traces, and it is the exhaustion of all contaminations....

In the state of clear ocean-like *Dharmakāya*, which is dwelling at the basis, the boat-like universal ground filled with a mass of passengers—mind and consciousnesses, and much cargo, *karmas* and traces—sets out on the path (of enlightenment) through the state of intrinsic awareness, *Dharmakāya*.

In some *sūtras*, and *tantras*, the aspect of the "basis" is termed the universal ground. Here, some people who did not understand the actual meaning asserted that the basis and the universal ground are the same. This is a grave mistake. If they are the same, then there are many faults: since the universal ground has traces, the *Dharmakāya* would also have traces; since the universal ground changes, the *Dharmakāya* would also change, and since the universal ground is temporary, the *Dharmakāya* would also be temporary.

UNIVERSAL GROUND

[53a/5]The entity: It is unenlightenment and a neutral state, which belongs to the (category of) mind and mental events, and it has become the foundation of all *karmas* and traces of *saṃsāra* and *nirvāṇa*....

Definition: It is called universal ground (*Kun-gZhi*), as it is the basis of masses of traces.

Divisions: There are four. (a) The aspect of (unenlightenment, the not knowing the intrinsic awareness which is) simultaneously arisen with the intrinsic awareness, like gold and its oxide from primordial time is the "ultimate primordial universal ground" (*Ye Don-Gyi Kun-gZhi*). This unenlightenment (is defined as such) in relation to (*lTos-Pa'i*) enlightenment. This is the aspect of being the primary foundation of all *saṃsāric* phenomena. (b) A neutral state which is the foundation of the aspect of action (*karma*) and the root foundation that connects (one) to *saṃsāra* and *nirvāṇa* through different deeds is the "ultimate universal ground of union" (*sByor-Ba Don-Gyi Kun-gZhi*). (c) A neutral state which is the aspect of various dormant actions of the mind and mental events that create the (births) in *saṃsāra* is the "universal ground of various traces" (*Bag-Ch'ags sNa Tshogs-Pa'i Kun-gZhi*). (d) The aspect of unenlightenment, which is the foundation of the arising of the three different aspects of appearances of bodies: the appearances in the gross body with limbs and secondary parts, formed of atoms (of the desire realm), the clear light body (of the form realm), and the body appearing as the absorption (of the formless realm) are the "universal ground of the body of traces" (*Bag-Ch'ags Lus-Kyi Kun-gZhi*).

DHARMAKĀYA (THE ULTIMATE BODY)

[55a/4]The entity: It is the space-like intrinsic awareness unstained by *saṃsāra*. . . .

Definition: In Thalgyur *(Thal-'Gyur tantra)* it is said: "By definition, the Dharma *(Ch'os)* means the perfect path. Body *(sKu)* means the accomplishment derived from it [the path]."

Division: Again it says: "It is classified into kāyas of the Dharma, Saṃbhoga, and Nirmāṇa. . . ."

According to (the *Dzogpa Chenpo* interpretation), the *Dharmakāya* is described as the ultimate body, pure in nature and dwelling at the basis with the characteristics of essence, nature, and compassion. In *Rangshar (Rang-Shar tantra)* it is said: "Essence, nature, and compassion are the characteristics of the Dharmakāya."

DISTINCTIONS BETWEEN MIND AND PRIMORDIAL WISDOM

[56a/1]Whatever is mind, that is the phenomena of *saṃsāra*. When the faults, the mode of *karma* and traces, arise as stains and are associated with its intrinsic awareness, it is called a being. Through mind beings are deluded in six migrations of beings (*'Gro-Drug*). When one's intrinsic awareness becomes free from the mind, one is called the Buddha, who has become detached from the adventitious defilements. Whatever is intrinsic awareness, that is (the phenomena) of *nirvāṇa*. It burns up the *karma* and traces like a fire. As it is detached from all conceptions, its nature is emptiness and clarity like space.

Mind According to Innermost Dzogpa Chenpo

60b/3The entity of mind (*Sems*) is a cognition (in the mode) of apprehender and apprehended and (in the form of) the mentalities of any of the three realms. Mind has three aspects: mind (*Sems*), which is the consciousness of the universal ground; thought (*Yid*), which enters into everything and enjoys the objects; consciousness (*rNam-Shes*), which is the consciousnesses of the six entrances. These three are cognitions of one entity, which is rooted in not knowing itself (and accompanied) by five poisons.

Primordial Wisdom

61b/2The entity: It is the luminous intrinsic awareness, the Buddha-essence (*Tathāgatagarbha*)....

Definition: It is primordial wisdom as it is present primordially (*Ye*) and it is the holy cognition (*Shes*)....

Division: There are three: The primordial wisdom which dwells at the basis; the primordial wisdom which is endowed with characteristics; and the primordial wisdom which pervades all phenomenal objects.... The essence, nature, and compassion are the intrinsic wisdom which dwells at the basis. The primordial wisdoms of the ultimate sphere, mirror-like, equanimity, discriminative, and accomplishment are the primordial wisdom which is endowed with characteristics. Knowing (the ultimate truth, quality) as it is (*Ji-lTa-Ba mKhyen-Pa*) and knowing all phenomena (of relative truth as they appear, quantity) (*Ji-sNyed-Pa mKhyen-Pa*) is the primordial wisdom which pervades the phenomenal objects....

The dwelling places: The dwelling place of mind is the universal ground and of primordial wisdom is the *Dharmakāya*.

2. *Karma of Samsaric Deeds, the Cause of Wandering of Beings in Delusory Samsara*

In chapter four of *Shingta Chenpo* (*SC Vol. I*), on the cause and effects of actions (*karma*), Longchen Rabjam divided *karma* into two categories, *saṃsāric* deeds and liberative virtues. To clarify *saṃsāric* deeds he terms the ultimate sphere (*dByings*) "the universal ground", which is a neutral state with respect to *saṃsāra* and *nirvāṇa*. He differs from the interpretation in the previous section and divides it into two aspects instead of four: the ultimate universal ground of union (*sByor-Ba Don-Gyi Kun-gZhi*) and the universal ground of various traces (*Bags-Ch'ags sNa-Tshogs-Pa'i Kun-gZhi*) of *saṃsāra* with its root, unenlightenment (*Ma-Rig-Pa, S. avidya*) and the eight consciousnesses. Although the universal ground itself is one entity and has no differentiations, it appears as two because of the two aspects which are based on it, just as the earth remains the same but because of day and night it appears clear and dark. He also explains the process of the cause and effect of actions in the case of the ten non-virtuous deeds with their root, unenlightenment. The *Pema Karpo* (*PK 5a4-*) and *Thegchog Dzod* (TCD-I301b/6) have different ways of classifications and different meanings for the universal grounds. For further details of the categories of *Karma*, see Appendix I.

THE NATURE (*Ngo-Bo*) OF *KARMA*

[SC-I,78b/3]What is the reason for the various occurrences of happiness and suffering to every individual while wandering in the painful cyclic existence? It is because of *karma*.... The fruit of different *karmas*, composed of different causal conditions, of each individual being ripened in the form of various migrations and resources, as well as happy and painful experiences. In *Karmaśataka* it is said:

> E-ma-ho! The world has arisen from *Karma*.
> Happiness and suffering are the drawings of *karma*.
> The formation of *karma* takes place when the conditions are completed.
> *Karma* (in turn) produces the happy and painful (results).

and

> The *karma* for hundreds of eons
> Will not be exhausted, and when the time comes
> And (circumstances) gather, by embodied beings
> It is certain that the effects will be experienced.

In *(Saddharma)puṇḍarīka (sūtra)* it is said:

> *Karma* creates all like an artist,
> *Karma* composes like a dancer.

There are two categories of *saṃsāric karma* from the point of view of their effects. The first is the *karmas* of evil or non-virtuous deeds, which create suffering. The second is the *karmas* of virtuous deeds associated with merits, which create the happiness of *saṃsāra*.

SAṂSĀRIC KARMA

79a/4 *Saṃsāra* is produced by the ten merit-making virtuous deeds and the ten non-virtuous deeds. . . . Non-virtuous deeds generate sufferings and birth in the inferior migrations and by virtuous deeds one obtains birth in high migrations and among happy beings.

In the *(Ārya-saddharma)smṛtyupasthāna* it is said: "By non-virtuous deeds one obtains (life in) inferior migrations and suffering. By virtuous deeds one obtains happiness and (birth in) high migrations."

THE GROUND OF *KARMA*, THE UNIVERSAL GROUND AND CONSCIOUSNESSES

[80a/1]Briefly: Where are the *karmas* based and being stored?... All the *karmas* both of *saṃsāra* and enlightenment are based on the universal ground as the seed. In the *'Jam-dPal Ye-Shes Dri-Ma Med-Pa'i sūtra* it is said: "The universal ground is the ground of all. It is the basis of *saṃsāra* and its cessation (*nirvāṇa*) and the basis of enlightenment."

The ultimate sphere of suchness (*dByings De-bZhin Nyid*) has been designated as the universal ground, the basis of divisions, and it is the aspect of the (mere) indivisible neutral state (in respect to *saṃsāra* and *nirvāṇa*).

The aspect of intrinsic awareness (*Rig-Pa*), the nature of which is primordially uncompounded, and spontaneously based on the state (of the ultimate sphere), is called the ultimate universal ground of union (*sByor-Ba Don-Gyi Kun-gZhi*).

Because of not realizing it (the intrinsic awareness of the ultimate sphere of suchness), the *saṃsāric* elements such as the eight consciousnesses and their habitual tendencies are (established and conjoined by) being based on it (the ultimate sphere).This aspect is called the universal ground of various traces (*Bags-Ch'ags sNa-Tshogs-Pa'i Kun-gZhi*). With all the compounded categories of virtuous and non-virtuous actions based on it (the universal ground of traces), the various experiences of happiness and suffering arise....

In Detail: All the phenomena of non-virtuous *karmas* and of the lesser virtuous *karmas*, which are the causes and effects of *saṃsāra*, are based on the neutral universal ground (*Kun-gZhi Lung-Ma bsTan*), and all the virtuous *karmas* associated with liberation, which cause the freedom of *nirvāṇa* and realizations of the path of enlightenment, are also based on it. The (aspect of) virtuous *karmas* associated with liberation and belonging to the truth of the path, which are compounded and adventitious, is based on the universal ground of traces as the cause of freedom. The result of freedom is based on the lineage (or essence—*Rigs*), as the sun's clarity because of (clouds) clearing is based on the sun itself. . . .

In the Mind, which is naturally free like space, are present primordially the pure lands and the qualities of Buddhas in the form of two lineages (which are) the beginningless virtuous nature (*Thog-Ma Med-Pa'i Ch'os-Khams dGe-Ba*, i.e., Buddha-essence). It is the basis of freedom, and it is the basis of *nirvāṇa*.

In this matter (the attainment of freedom) there are four aspects to be understood: (a) The basis of freedom is the essential nature or essence (*Khams* or *sNying-Po*). (b) The cause of freedom is the means of virtues associated with liberation and the means of purifying the defilements from it (the essential essence). (c) The result of freedom is to become the Buddha-essence (*Tathāgagarbha*) free from all the defilements and having attained the qualities (of the Buddha-essence). (d) The aspect from which to be freed is the eight consciousnesses with their habits, as they are based on the universal ground of traces.

In *tantric* scriptures these (four aspects) are known as the basis of purification (*sByang-gZhi*), the means of purification (*sByong-Byed*), the result of purification (*sByang-'Bras*), and the aspect which is to be purified (*sByang-Bya*). The terms are different but their meaning is the same. Thus, upon the unenlightened nature of the universal ground of traces, the cause of impure *saṃsāra* with the consciousnesses and the compounded virtuous aspects which lead to liberation appear to be based for a long time without (actually) being based (anywhere). From the point of view of being, it (the ultimate sphere) is the base of the qualities of *nirvāṇa*, and it is called the absolute universal ground.

The (absolute universal ground's) essence (*Ngo-Bo*) is voidness, its nature (*Rang-bZhin*) is clarity, its compassion (i.e., manifestative power) is all-pervading, and its qualities are spontaneous accomplishment like wishing-jewels. It is neither stained nor free from stains. It is the absolute meaning, luminous from the primordial state, the vision of non-fusability and inseparability (*'Du-'Bral Med-Pa*) of the bodies and wisdoms. Although from the point of view of the purity of its nature it is designated as space-like, free from characteristics, voidness, uncompounded, and so forth, it is not nothing, an extreme of voidness, because it is a spontaneously accomplished state of luminous bodies and wisdoms, and it is the liberation and voidness of all elements of *saṃsāra*.

In the *Ghanavyūha sūtra* it is said:

> The immaculate disc (*maṇḍala*) of the moon
> Always is unstained and completely full.
> But in relation to the days of the world
> It is perceived as waxing and waning.
> Likewise, the ultimate universal ground also
> Has always been with the Buddha-essence (*Tathāgatagarbha*),
> And this essence in terms of the universal ground
> Has been taught by the Thus-Gone (*Tathāgata*, i.e., Buddha).
> The fools who do not know it,
> Because of their habits, see even the universal ground
> As (having) various happiness and suffering
> And actions and emotional defilements.
> Its nature is pure and immaculate,
> Its qualities are as wishing-jewels;
> There are neither changes nor cessations.
> Whoever realizes it attains liberation. . . .

There are numerous synonyms for (the ultimate universal ground) according to its basis, source, and its being the cause of freedom, such as the absolute universal ground, virtue of beginningless ultimate nature, Buddha-essence, nature (*Khams*), luminous nature of the mind, ultimate sphere, the meaning of the suchness nature, naturally pure thatness, transcendental wisdom, and so on.

The aspect of the habits of *saṃsāra* being based on the Mind (*Sems-Nyid*, i.e., neutral state of universal ground) is called the universal ground of traces. Why? Because it is the basis of accumulation of the *karmas* (which generate the) virtues, non-virtues, liberation, and enlightenment, which do not exist in the true nature from the primordial state but arise adventitiously. It is the basis of both virtuous and non-virtuous *karmas*, its nature (*Ngo-Bo*) is ignorance (*gTi-Mug*), and it is neutral (in respect to both virtuous and non-virtuous *karmas*).

Some say that this is not ignorance because it is the basis of all the five poisons (including ignorance) as well as of enlightenment. That is just a misunderstanding. This is not the ignorance of the five poisons. (But) it is the innate unenlightenment (*Lhan-Chig sKyes-Pa'i Ma-Rig-Pa*) arisen from the time of the delusion leading into *saṃsāra*, and it has also been called ignorance. Also, it is subject to examination whether this is the basis of enlightenment. This is the basis of neither the essence nor the wisdom of the Buddha, which possess two purities, the purity from the primordial state and the purity of adventitious defilements, because the universal ground has to transform (into wisdom). In the *Suvarṇaprabhāsottama sūtra* it is said: "The transformed universal ground is the essence, the ultimate body (*Ngo-Bo Nyid-Kyi Ch'os-Kyi-sKu*)."

In *'Byung-bZhi Zad-Pa'i rGyud* it is said: "The purified universal ground is the ultimate sphere (*Ch'os-dByings*)." (The universal ground of traces) is not the basis of the nature (*Khams*), as it is (only) the basis or the cause of freedom from the defilements. So it does not act other than as the basis merely of (becoming) enlightened through the training on the compounded path of accumulation of merits and wisdom. They (the accumulations) belong to the category of the "truth of the path," and they are delusory and temporary, because of their being based on the universal ground of traces. How can it (the training) be harmful to (the universal ground of traces) while depending on it? As fire based on wax burns down the wax itself and fire based on firewood burns the firewood itself, by being based on the universal ground of traces the path of two accumulations purifies the habits of *saṃsāra* and dispels the stains from the essential nature, and causes enlightenment to be fully attained, as it is, primordially. Therefore, the (two accumulations) are known as the pure conditions (*rKyen Dag-Pa*). Then later on, the antidotes, the means of purifications (the two accumulations) themselves, will also be burnt down because they are the virtues imagined by the mind....

In *Madhyamakāvatāra it is said: "The peace (achieved)* by burning the entire fuel of knowable subjects is the ultimate body of the Buddhas....

Synonyms for the universal ground of traces are: innate unenlightenment (*Lhan-chig sKyes-Pa'i Ma-Rig-Pa*), the universal ground of traces, beginningless and endless obscuration, great darkness, originally present unknowing, and so on.

The Mind (*Sems-Nyid*), the beginningless sphere, present like space: from the point of view of liberation being based on it, it is known as the ultimate (universal ground) and from the point of view of its being the basis of *saṃsāra*, it is known as the (universal ground of) habits. And (from the beginningless sphere) the happiness and suffering of various appearances of *saṃsāra* and *nirvāṇa* and the faults and virtues arise. In the commentary of *Uttaratantra* it is said:

> The (ultimate) sphere of beginningless and endless time
> Is the abode of all the Dharmas.
> Because of the presence of this (in them), every living being
> Is able to attain *nirvāṇa*.

THE DIVISION OF THE UNIVERSAL GROUND AND THE EIGHT CONSCIOUSNESSES

[83a/5]The universal ground of various traces, the neutral state (with respect to virtues and non-virtues), is like a mirror. Of the consciousness of the universal ground (in the *'Jam-dPal Ye-Shes rGyan*)[SC Vol. I, 49a/3] it is said: "Mind (*Sems*) is the consciousness of the universal ground. Apprehending selfhood is thought (*Yid*)." It is like the aspect of clarity of a mirror. The five consciousnesses of entrances are like the arising of reflections (in a mirror). Arising first, the analysis of the preceding percept (*Don*) or raising of the (recognition of the) percept of the five sense-doors (as just) "this is this" is (thought or) mind-consciousness. Following it, the arising of hatred, attachment, or neutral emotions towards the objects is the defiled-mind-consciousness.

Some earlier masters have said that the six consciousnesses (i.e., mind and the five sense-faculties) do not accumulate *karma* if one does not analyze (the percepts) with defiled-mind-consciousness, because they are not composed of any of the three poisons. But this (observation) needs to be examined. While one is pursuing (the path of) view, meditation, and conduct, after the realization of the (ultimate) nature of phenomenal existents, there will be such a state (of not producing any *karma*), but people whose minds have not yet reached such a level have ignorance and they produce evil *karmas*.

The means of producing *karma* are the faculty of mind and the five faculties of the sense-entrances with their bases. The producers of *karma* are the defiled mind, the virtuous mind, and the mind that is neutral (in respect to virtues and non-virtues). The basis on which the *karmas* are being accumulated is the universal ground (of neutral state). The consciousness of universal ground provides the space for the developing, maintaining, decline, and so forth, of *karma*. In the great commentary on the *Mahāyānasūtrālaṃkāra* by *Ācārya Sthiramati* it is said:

> The mind and the five faculties, such as that of the eyes, are the entrance, the doors of *karma*. The virtuous, non-virtuous, and neutral minds are the producers of *karmas*. The six percepts, such as form, are the objects of *karma*. The consciousness of the universal ground provides the space for (producing *karmas*). The universal ground is the basis, like the place and the house (where and in which the *karmas* are stored).

Here, the consciousness of the universal ground is the aspect of the sense which is clear but cognizes neither object nor subject. From this the senses (consciousnesses) of the five entrances arise. The eye-consciousness is the aspect of a sense which sees (the object) as the form, but no (analytical) thoughts have arisen yet. Likewise, the senses which (just) see generally (the respective objects), sound, smell, taste, and touch as the objects by the (senses of) ear, nose, tongue, and body while no thoughts have yet arisen (are their consciousnesses).

The clear (appearances) arisen from the object of percept of the five entrances or a similar form of percept arising (before the senses) is phenomena (*Ch'os, S.dharma*), and it is also the mind-consciousness. Here, the aspect of object is phenomena and the aspect of the arising of those phenomena in the senses is called the (mind-) consciousness. . . . The consciousness which has arisen immediately at the point of cessation of the aspect of the universal ground-consciousness and six senses, the five entrance-consciousnesses of (perceiving) the previous object is called thought (*Yid*). In the *Abhidharmakoṣa* it is said: "The consciousness (arisen) immediately after the cessation of the six (consciousnesses) is the Mind."

For example, when a form is perceived, the aspect of the object seeing clearly but without apprehending is the consciousness of the universal ground, and the aspect of the arising of the form to the senses is the eye consciousness. Leaving (or moving out from) those two states is called the cessation of them, and then the arising of the momentary thought, "This is form" is thought (*Yid*) or mind (*Sems*). (In some contexts, Sems was explained as the consciousness of the universal ground.) This momentary thought moves very fast and doesn't think subtly, so it is called "no-thought" (*rTog-Med*). It is also called percept (or objective thought) (*gZung-Ba'i rTog-Pa*) as it sees the object first. After this, the subtle analysis (of the percept arises and) is called perceiver (or subjective thought)(*'Dzin-Pa'i rTog-Pa*). Even if one first sees the percepts, if one doesn't continue it by analysis (through the perceiver), it will not produce any *karma*. All the lords of the sages agree on this.

Longchen Rabjam made two statements on how consciousnesses produce *karma*. His earlier observation, quoting earlier masters, is that although there is no defiled-mind-consciousness, still the six consciousnesses (mind and the five sense-consciousnesses) produce *karma* because the mind-consciousness is complete with both its aspects, percept [objective perception] and perceiver [subjective perception] and it is based on ignorance. Here the point is made that although the percepts are appearing in the mind-consciousness, there is neither the aspect of analysis by perceivers nor any contemplations, so it does not produce any *karma*.

HOW THE CONSCIOUSNESSES PRODUCE *KARMA*

84b/5By virtuous, non-virtuous, and neutral *karma* with discriminative thoughts of gross apprehended and apprehender, one falls into (or takes birth in) the desire realm. Contemplation in the state of an absorption (*Ting-Nge 'Dzin*) which is not the essential nature (*gNas-Lugs*), and in which the percept (*sNang-Yul*) appears but no thought has yet arisen, accumulates *karmas* in the universal ground to take rebirth in the form-realm. Contemplation on no-thought by preventing percepts, sows the *karmic* seed in the universal ground to take birth in the formless realm. . . .

(One's mind) flowing one-pointedly without any thoughts toward any object is the state (*sKabs*) of the universal ground. The stage of seeing percepts clearly yet remaining without any thoughts about them is the consciousness of the universal ground. The stage of perceiving any of the various percepts which have arisen clearly (before any of the senses) is the consciousnesses of the five entrances. (When one perceives) any object, in the first stage, for a moment, they arise as a percept, then in the second stage the analyzer mixed with emotional defilements arises as the perceiver, and they are (respectively) the mind-consciousness and the defiled-mind-consciousness.

DIFFERENT STATES OF COGNITIONS

85b/5There are (different levels of) cognitions (*Shes-Pa*) which have no connection with liberation (from *saṃsāra*) and which are in the state of the universal ground. They are (a) the cognition which is in the state of contemplation, a stable one-pointed tranquillity, (b) the cognition which is in the contemplation of clarity and no-thought, stable and a partial insight (*Lhag-mThong*), and (c) the cognition which is gross cognition arisen after (the appearances) of objects with the dominant conditions (*bDag-rKyen*), the six sense faculties. The virtuous and non-virtuous *karmas* accumulated through those three kinds of cognitions delude beings (respectively) in the formless realm, form realm, and desire realm.... The reason is that they do not lead to liberation and do not transcend the apprehender and apprehended (duality). Here the state of contemplation of no-thought (itself) is the apprehended and contemplation on that one-pointedly without wavering is the apprehender. Pure contemplation is (as follows): although it is a meditation on the skillful means of compassion and on the wisdom free from extremes, it has no conceptualization of subject and object and there is no meditation designating "in this state." So it relates to the inconceivable nature. Although in this contemplation one achieves joy, bliss, miracles, and foreknowledge, there will not be attachment to the pleasure of it, nor are they apprehended in characteristic form.

WHICH CONSCIOUSNESSES HAVE MAJOR ROLES IN THE THREE DIFFERENT REALMS

[86a/5]The various consciousnesses have their various roles as principal and subordinates in their own and others' realms.... In the commentary of *Kun-gZhi Dang Ye-Shes brTag-Pa* by Ācārya Buddhaguhya it is said:

> In the realm of desire the seven consciousnesses, such as that of the eyes, are principals and the others (universal ground and the consciousness of the universal ground) are subordinates. In the form realm the consciousness of the universal ground and the consciousnesses of entrances (consciousnesses of five faculties, of mind and of defiled mind) are the principal and the other (the universal ground) is subordinate. In the formless realm the universal ground itself is the principal and the others (the eight consciousnesses) are inactive.

DISSOLUTION OF THE CONSCIOUSNESSES

[86b/5]A person of the desire realm goes to sleep, (first) the consciousnesses of five entrances and of defiled-mind dissolve into mind-consciousness. The mind-consciousness dissolves into the consciousness of the universal ground and (then a state of) clarity and no-thought arises for a while. Some masters of New *Tantra* (*gSar-Ma*) assert that those who are able to realize this state and can contemplate on it, enjoy the ultimate nature of clarity without having any dreams. The consciousness of the universal ground dissolves into the thoughtless universal ground. Then upon the dissolving of the universal ground into the ultimate sphere (*Ch'os-dByings*), the gross and subtle perceptions dissolve and the ultimate nature, (union of) emptiness and clarity, free from elaborations, arises. If one realizes this, then (all) the delusions will be repulsed.... Then they regenerate again. From the ultimate state arises the universal ground, from the universal ground arises the consciousness of the universal ground and from that the mind-consciousness arises alone. At this point, various kinds of dream (-like phenomena) arise and one apprehends the phenomena, the objects of the mind of habituations.

UNITY AND PROJECTION OF THE CONSCIOUSNESSES IN DIFFERENT STATES

[89b/1]Sleep is the time when all the consciousnesses are in union with the universal ground, and there is no outward projection (of any consciousness). While dreaming, the mind-consciousness has arisen from the consciousness of the universal ground. So it is the time when the consciousness projects outward slightly and the universal ground and the consciousnesses of the universal ground and of the mind are in one entity. When one awakens, one's consciousnesses have projected outward from the universal ground and the universal ground and the eight consciousnesses are in one entity.

CONCLUDING SUMMARY

[89b/3]The luminous Mind (*Sems-Nyid*) is the basis and source of all existents. In Mind there is no differentiation of *saṃsāra* and *nirvāṇa*, and they are inseparable and changeless. So it is the...ultimate nature of union (*sByor-Ba Don-Gyi gNas-*

Lugs), the Buddha-essence and the source of *saṃsāra* and *nirvāṇa*. In *Doha* it is said:

> Mind alone is the seed of all.
> For beings it projects *saṃsāra* and *nirvāṇa*;
> It provides the fruit of wishes:
> Wish-fulfilling gem-like Mind, to you I pay homage.

[90a/2]In the *Ghanavyūha sūtra* it is said:

> Various stages (of the path) are the universal ground.
> The *Tathāgatagarbha* (Buddha-essence) is also that.
> That essence, designated as the universal ground,
> The *Tathāgata* (Buddha) has expounded.
> He proclaimed the essence as the universal ground.
> (But) people of foolish intellect do not understand it.

As this nature (*gShis*) is the cause of perfections such as the bodies and wisdoms (of Buddhahood), it is called the stainless ultimate universal ground (*Don-Gyi Kun-gZhi*). As it is the basis of *saṃsāra*, it is called the universal ground of traces with stains. The essence (*Ngo-Bo*) of the basis, the universal ground, is one, but it is divided (into two) because of the different qualities which are based on it. . . .

In the nature of the moon there is neither increase nor decrease, but because of circumstances, in the four continents we see the differences of waxing and waning. Likewise, in the nature of the luminous Mind after becoming enlightened there is neither real happiness nor real suffering, but beings in *saṃsāra* perceive different entities, such as high and inferior migrations. If one has trained in (or attained) the absolute meaning, it is called reaching the perfection of the universal ground as the absolute meaning. . . . .

Karmas are produced by the delusions of the unenlightened mind-consciousness. In the (*Udānavarga*) *sūtra* it is said: "Mind is the chief and it is swift. Mind is the forerunner of all things."

Because of imaginaries (*Kun-bTags*) and not knowing the thoroughly established nature (*Yongs-Grub*), one becomes dependent (*gZhan-dBang*) on various impure delusory appearances. To overturn the dreamlike delusory *saṃsāra*, one has to realize the thoroughly established Mind and meditate on the infallible path of the development and perfection stages, skillful means and wisdom, to attain the essential nature in the primordial state, as it is.

THE ROOT OF *KARMA*, UNENLIGHTENMENT

91a/3 All beings are deluded in *saṃsāra* by laying the foundation of apprehended (object) and apprehender (subject) through not realizing the self-face of the Mind. In (*Prajñāpāramitā*)*sañcayagāthā* it is said: "All living beings of low, medium and excellent (type) have arisen from unenlightenment. Thus it is said by the Blessed-Gone."

The beings of the lower, the inferior migrations, medium, the human migration, and higher, the god migration are all experiencing happiness and suffering (produced) by their own different *karmas*. The root of *karma* is enlightenment accompanied by the three poisons and followed by the non-virtuous *karmas* as well as the merit-making virtues which create the happy results of *saṃsāra*.

THE PRODUCER OF *KARMA*, THE MERIT-MAKING VIRTUES AND NON-VIRTUOUS DEEDS

91a/6 Virtuous (merit-making) *karmas* produce happiness and birth in the happy migrations (in *saṃsāra*), and non-virtuous *karmas* produce suffering and births in the inferior migrations (in *saṃsāra*).

(A) THE NON-VIRTUOUS *KARMAS*

91b/1 There are ten non-virtuous deeds which cause one to fall into the inferior migrations from the higher migrations and which generate only suffering. They are:

The three non-virtuous *karmas* of the body:
Killing, taking what is not given, and sexual misconduct.
The four non-virtuous *karmas* of speech:
Lies, divisive talk, harsh words, and senseless speech.

The three non-virtuous *karmas* of mind:
Covetousness, ill-will, and wrong view.

Effects of the Non-Virtuous Karmas

93b/4 Briefly: Non-virtuous *karmas* are generated through non-virtuous object, intention, thought, and efforts. They produce three categories of effects. In the great scriptures they are classified as the effects of maturation (*rNam-Par sMin-Pa*) (which is the principal effect), compatibility (*rGyu-mThun*), and dominance (or environment) (*bDag-Po*). In the instructional teachings (commentaries) there are four effects with the addition of culmulative effect (*Byed-Pa'i 'Bras-Bu*)....

(1) The effect of maturation: In (*Ārya-saddharma*)*smṛty-upasthāna* (*sūtra*) it is said:

> The maturation of the effect of a minor *karma* (of any of the ten non-virtuous deeds) produces birth in the animal realm, of a medium deed produces birth in the hungry-ghost migration and of a grave deed develops into birth in the hell migration.

After completion of the experience of the actual effect of the evil *karmas*, as the effect of maturation in one of the three inferior migrations, even if one takes rebirth in a higher migration because of one's other virtuous deeds, one still has to experience three more after-effects:

(2) The effect of compatibility: It has two categories: the effect of campatibility of cause (*Byed-Pa rGyu-mThun*) and the effect of compatibility of experiences (*rNam-sMin rGyu-mThun*)....

(a) Concerning the effect of compatibility of cause, in *Karmaśataka* (*sūtra*) it is said:

> Since a person has been habituated to the non-virtuous *karmas* even after (he has already experienced the effect of maturation), he will take birth where he will rely on non-virtuous deeds and will perform and follow them.

(b) The effect of compatibility of experience: in this effect there are two types for each of the ten non-virtuous *karmas*....

In the *Karmaśataka* (*sūtra*) it is said:

> Even if a person takes rebirth in the god migration or human migration (because of his other, virtuous deeds), still he will experience the following after-effects: having a short life and many illnesses because of (the non-virtuous *karmas* of) killing (in the past), having few possessions and sharing them with enemies because of taking what is not given, having an unattractive spouse and sharing one's spouse with others because of adultery, being abused and deceived by others because of lying, having bad and unharmonious companions because of slandering, hearing insults and (even if one speaks gently) provocations because of harsh speech, one's words not being considered worthy of respect and oneself not inspiring confidence in others because of foolish chatter, becoming greedy and discontented because of covetousness, becoming the object not of benefits but harm because of ill will, and being around evil views and cunning because of wrong view. . . .

(3) The effect of dominance: (*In Semnyid Ngalso (SN)* it is said:)

> The effect of dominance refers to the effects on the environment.
> While one is in the impure (*saṃsāra*) controlled by external factors:
> By killing (one takes rebirth as the after-effect) in a land which is unattractive,
> Where the medicine, trees, crops, flowers, food, drink, and so on
> Will provide little nourishment, will be hard to digest and will be life-threatening.
> By taking what is not given, in a land where no crops are harvested,
> Where there are the dangers of frost, hail-stones, and famine, one will take rebirth.
> By adultery, among pits of excrement and urine,

Filth, dirt, and stench,
In a narrow, fearful, and unenjoyable land, one will take rebirth.
By lies, in a hostile and frightening land
Where wealth is insecure and one is deceived by others, one will take rebirth.
By divisive speech, in a land where travel is difficult, which is uneven,
With deep rugged chasms and narrow ravines, etc.,
Various uncomfortable conditions, one will take rebirth.
By harsh words, in non-virtuous lands (full of) logs, sharp pebbles, and thorns,
Dust, rubbish, poor crops, a rough and
Saline (environment), and so on, one will take rebirth.
By senseless speech, in lands where crops and fruit do not ripen and the seasons are inconsistent,
Where nothing is stable and durable, one will take rebirth.
By covetousness, in lands where there is little harvest but many husks,
Seeing good times turn to bad, one will take rebirth.
By ill-will, in a land where the grain and fruit will have a burning, bitter taste,
Where there are rulers, robbers, wild men, snakes and so on,
Many circumstances of a harmful nature, one will take rebirth.
By wrong view, in lands where there is no source of precious substances
And few medicinal trees, flowers, and fruit,
Where there is no refuge, protector, or supportive force, one will take rebirth....

(4) The Cumulative Effect: In the short (*Ārya-saddharma*)-*smṛttyupasthāna* it is said: "Those who are ignorant and have committed evil deeds (in the past) will further increase their evil deeds and will suffer more."

The differences between effects of compatibility and cumulative effects: In compatibility one will be involved in doing the same *karma* or deeds as an effect of that which one has committed and of which the results previously have been experienced; and in cumulative, the evil deeds and the experiences of the same *karma* increase as after-effects.

Conclusion

95b/2In the *Vinayāgama* it is said:

> Non-virtuous *karmas* are like poison, which even in small doses creates great suffering. They are like wild men who destroy the accumulated merits. Therefore, one should try to abandon non-virtuous deeds and devote oneself to virtuous *karmas*.

(B) THE VIRTUOUS *KARMAS*

95b/6The mere absence of the ten non-virtuous *karmas* does not become the ten virtuous *karmas* because the disciplining of the mind by acting according to them is lacking. The abandoning of the ten non-virtuous deeds is the ten virtuous deeds (associated with the accumulation of merits).

The Effects of Virtuous Karmas

96a/2In respect to their maturation effects, the minor virtues produce rebirth in the human realm, the medium ones among the gods of the desire realm, and the major ones, combined with contemplation, in the (two) upper realms, the form and formless realms. By the virtuous deeds one achieves (the happiness of) higher migrations and seals the doors of inferior migrations.

The after-effects of the virtuous *karmas* will be the experiences of the reverse of the results of the ten non-virtuous deeds. The ten virtuous deeds are the means of perfecting the accumulation of merits.

INTERDEPENDENT CAUSATION

According to *Mahāyāna* Buddhist philosophy, nothing is present with true existence. In relative truth, however, all things appear through the law of interdependent origination, like reflections in a mirror or appearances in a dream. An external phenomenon such as a flower is subject to arising through the interdependent causation of arising, in the process of succession of its seed, new shoots, leaves, stem, flower, and so forth, and with the coming together of the conditions of earth, water, fire, air, space, and time. The internal phenomena, the mind, mental events, and the bodies of beings in *samsāra* arise and function or cease through the interdependent causation of the successive reverse process of the twelve-linked interdependent causation. A set of twelve links of causation completes itself in two or more lives. Also, in one life and at one time there are many more sets of twelve-linked causations that are starting, are in progress, and are ceasing. The internal phenomena arise, function, or cease depending on the coming together or separation of the six interdependent conditions: earth, water, fire [heat], air, space, and time. That is broadly or roughly known as *karma* or causation, the process of cause and its effects. Through it beings wander in *samsāra* endlessly, like counting on a rosary, or they attain *nirvāna* by its cessation. Longchen Rabjam touches on the subject of interdependent origination in his *Shingta Chenpo*.

External Interdependent Causation

SC-I, 301a/3 It is the objective appearances of the mind, the appearances as the external phenomena such as the appearances in the form of mountains, walls, earth, water, fire, air, and space, which are designated as the secondary qualities of the elements (*'Byung-'Gyur*) or the forms of the elements (*'Byung-gZugs*). These develop in various types of material through their own common and specific causes and conditions, as cloth (from) thread and woolen cloth (from) woolen thread. It is called the interdependent causation of external phenomena, because they arise by depending on each other and appear as external inanimates (*Bem-Po*).

Internal Interdependent Causation

(a) Interdependent Causation

301a/6 The (process) by which from unenlightenment arise the formations (and so forth in succession) through old age and death is internal interdependent causation. . . .

The twelve (interdependent causations) are: (1) Unenlightenment: It is the (aspect of) not knowing perfectly the absolute essence, the ultimate nature, the nature which is primordially pure, and also the phenomena (*dharma*) characterized (*mTshon-Pa*) by it (unenlightenment). From this arises the formation of *karma*, since it formulates the *karma* of *saṃsāra*. (2) Formation of *karma*: The virtuous deeds which are associated with merits, the ten unvirtuous deeds, and the neutral *karmas* of body, speech, and mind, which are obscured by unenlightenment, are formation. Virtuous (*karma* formulates birth in) high migrations and non-virtuous in inferior migrations. Neutral (*karma*) contributes to both (births) and is associated with non-virtuous *karma*. . . . *(3)* Consciousness: Then, in accordance with the formulated *karma* (which has been sown in the consciousness of the universal ground), one enters into one of the (six) migrations and develops the cognition of that (particular migration). This is consciousness. . . . (4) Name and Form: Then, when consciousness enters into its (particular) migration by means of the coming together of the mind, energy (*rLung*), and the (parental) white and red essences, one establishes the (five) aggregates: "four names"—the feeling, discrimination, formation (of *karma*), and consciousness—and the "form". . . . When one enters into the womb of the mother, "name" and "form" are established. . . . (5) Sense Organs: Then the sense organs (*sKye-mCh'ed*) of eye, ear, nose, tongue, body, and mind develop. . . . (6) Contact: Then, the coming together of the objects, sense faculties (*dBang-Po*), and mental application (*Yid-La Byed-Pa*) is contact. . . . (7) Feeling: From contact arises feeling. The arising of happy, unhappy, and neutral experiences with desirable, undesirable, and neutral objects respectively is feeling. . . . (8) From feeling arises craving for it. There are three cravings: craving the feeling of (for example the taste of) the sweetness of brown sugar is the craving for happiness (or craving of desire). Having experienced unhappiness, wanting to abandon it is craving for happiness (or craving of fear). From neutral (objects) craving develops for (remaining in) neutral (feelings). . . . (9) Grasping: From craving arises grasping (of the objects directly) for which one is craving. . . . (10) Becoming: From grasping arises becoming. The arising of the five aggregates, form, feeling, discrimination, formation, and consciousness (for birth in the next life in one of the six migrations) is becoming. . . . (11) Birth: From becoming arises birth. . . . (12) From birth arises youth, old age, and cessation of life, which is death. . . .

The Mind Only school asserts that a cycle of cause and result (of the twelve-linked causation) is completed in two lives.

In the first life the six causes are completed and in the second life the six results.... The six causes are unenlightenment, formation, consciousness, craving, grasping, and becoming. The remaining six are results. According to *Śrāvakayāna*, a cycle of the entire cause and result (of the twelve-linked causation) is completed in three lives. Based on the causes, the unenlightenment and formation of the previous life, the five results arise, such as consciousness (name and form, sense organs, conduct, and feeling) in the present life, and the craving, grasping and becoming of this life generate the birth and death of the next life.

According to *rTen-sNying 'Grel-Ba* by the third Dodrup Chen (based on Nāgārjuna's *Pratītyasamudpādahṛdaya*), 2a: Unenlightenment, craving, and grasping are the three emotional defilements. Formation and becoming are the two means of *karma*. Those are the five causes. Consciousness, name and form, sense organs, contact, feeling, birth, old age, and death are the seven results.

(b) *Internal Dependent Condition*

[303b/5]Because in those (twelve-linked) causations, the preceding ones cause the succeeding ones to arise, it is called interdependent causation. Because those (interdependent originations) are developed on condition of the coming together of inner earth, fire, air, space, and consciousness, they are called origination from interdependent conditions (in the formation of the lives of beings).

3. *Karma of Liberative Virtues, The Means of Liberation from Samsāra*

The *karma* of virtuous deeds associated with liberative virtues leads the person to enlightenment. *Kunkhyen Longchen Rabjam* explains in his *Shingta Chenpo* (*SC, The Great Chariot*), autocommentary on *Semnyid Ngalso* (SN, "Relaxation in the Natural Mind") the presence of two lineages (*Rigs*) of the Buddha-essence (*Tathāgatagarbha*) in all living beings, because of which we have the potential to become Buddhas if we train ourselves in the virtuous *karmas* which lead to Buddhahood. The first of the two lineages is "the naturally present lineage" (*Rang-bZhin gNas-Rigs*), which is the aspect of the lineage or essence which is primordially present as the absolute nature of beings. The second is "the developed lineage" (*sGrub-Pa Las Byung-Ba or rGyas-'Gyur Gyi Rigs*), which is the aspect of the essence which has been developed by dispelling the coverings, which are the defilements. He explains who should awaken the lineage and by what means, or else how one strays into *samsāra* if one does not realize the lineage, and how it is important to train in the liberative virtues in order to realize the lineage.

GENERAL LIBERATIVE VIRTUOUS *KARMA*

SC-I, 97a/6 The virtuous *karmas* which transcend both merit-making virtues and evil deeds and are free from all the stains that are causes of taking rebirth in *saṃsāra* are (the *karmas*), the causes of liberation. Of these, the virtues with conception (*sNang-bChas*), such as the ten virtuous deeds and the first five of the six perfections of the accumulation of merits, are deeds of the level of relative truth. The virtues without conception, the wisdom free from the two extremes, is the accumulation of primordial wisdom (the absolute truth). The unity of these two accumulations, which is embodied in the stages of the five paths, leads one to Buddhahood. So it transcends the *saṃsāric* virtues. *Saṃsāric* beings perceive (the virtuous deeds) as substantial and as having characteristics. But in respect to the (liberative virtues), from the beginning of the training there is no perception (of them) as substantial or as having characteristics. They are free from the concepts of merits or demerits, and they have the essence of voidness and compassion....

Generosity, and so forth, the (first) five (of the six perfections) are for the accumulation of merits, and wisdom is for the accumulation of primordial wisdom. Through the combined (training) in these two (accumulations one) attains the two bodies (of the Buddhas).

THE VIRTUES, THE CAUSE OF LIBERATION

[99b/3]The actual liberative virtues belong to the "truth of the path" (of liberation), the cause of cessation (*Bral*) (from suffering). Although they are based on the universal ground of habits, the result, cessation itself, which is achieved through the cause (of cessation of suffering and *saṃsāra*), is based on the lineage (*Rigs*) or the (*Buddha*)-essence (*sNying-Po*). That is why the virtues become the cause of changeless supreme liberation. (In the root-text [SN] it is said):

> The basis of the virtues is the lineage (*Rigs*).
> That is the luminous natural (*Rang-bZhin*) state of mind,
> The immaculate nature (*Khams*), and it is "the naturally present lineage" (*Rang-bZhin gNas-Rigs*).
> The appearance aspect (*sNang-Ch'a*) of the (nature) is the two bodies,
> Which have been characterized by nine examples.
> It is the nature of compassion present primordially, and
> It is "the developing lineage" (*rGyas-'Gyur Gyi Rigs*). This was said by the Bliss-gone (*Buddha*)....

The scriptures of the third turning of the Dharma wheel

expound the definitive meaning and show the great secret (qualities) of all the Buddhas, as they are. These scriptures are:

Ārya-dhāraṇeśvarāja-paripṛcchā-sūtra.
Ārya-śrīmaladevī-siṁhanāda-paripṛcchā sūtra.
Bu-Mo Rin-Ch'en Gyis Zhus-Pa'i mDo.
Vimaladevī paripṛcchā.
Ārya-aṅgulimāla sūtra.
Ārya-mahāparinirvāṇa sūtra.
Ārya maitreya paripṛcchā sūtra.
Ārya tathāgatagarbha sūtra, and so on.

In these scriptures are given the explanations of the nature (*Khams*) or the natural state (*Rang-bZhin*) of the mind, which is present primordially in all living beings, and is the Buddha-essence (*Tathāgatagarbha*). It is present from primordial time and is changeless. In this (nature) are present primordially the spontaneous accomplishment of its appearance aspect as the source of major and minor signs of the form-bodies (*gZugs-sKu*) and its voidness aspect as the freedom of the ultimate-body (*Ch'os-sKu*) from all the elaborate extremes. This nature is explained by examples: the spontaneous accomplishment of virtues by the wish-fulfilling jewel, changelessness by space, and omnipresence in all living beings by clear water. In *Uttaratantra* it is said: "As a wish-fulfilling jewel, space and water, the (*Buddha*) nature is always free from defilements."

In its essence (*Rang-Ngo*) there is no defilement from the very moment of obscuration (of the essence) by stains, and it remains (pure) as it is. In (*Ārya*)-*aṣṭasāhasrikā (prajñāpāramitā sūtra*) it is said: "In mind there is no mind, as the nature of the mind is luminous."

It is the nature or lineage of the Buddhas and it is present in every living being. In *Uttaratantra* it is said: "Because they are indivisible from suchness, and because they possess the lineage, living beings always possess the Buddha-essence."

The (lineage) is also called "the beginningless (or omnipresent) virtuous ultimate nature" because it is Buddha from the primordial ground. In *Mañjuśrīnāmasaṁgīti* it is said: "Buddha has neither beginning nor end, the primordial has no partiality."

In *(Hevajra)dvikalpa-tantra* it is said: "Living beings are the very Buddha. No matter that they have been obscured by adventitious defilements, when the obscurations have been cleared, they are the very Buddha."

When one is a living being, in the suchness of one's mind one possesses the perfection of the virtues of the form-body (of the Buddha) in its aspect of appearances and the virtues of the ultimate body in its aspect of voidness. But (the Buddha-essence) has been obscured by defilements and the virtues have become manifestatively unclear. So it is called nature (*Khams*) or lineage (*Rigs*).

When one becomes Buddha, one will be free from all obscurations. So it is called enlightenment.The difference is just whether the power (*Nus-Pa*) of the nature of the mind is manifested completely. We do not assert that it is a development of a new virtue which did not exist when one was (an ordinary) living being, because the nature is changeless.

In *sNying-Po Rab-Tu brTan-Pa sūtra* it is said:

> The ultimate sphere (*Ch'os-dByings*) of beginningless time
> Is the abode of all phenomenal existents.
> Because of the presence of that, all living beings
> Are able to achieve *nirvāṇa*.
> The suchness (*tathatā*) is changeless.
> It was and will be as it is.

The luminous nature of the suchness (*Ch'os-Nyid*) of the mind is never defiled by emotional obscurations. In *Uttaratantra* it is said:

> The nature of the mind, which is luminous,
> Is changeless like space.
> By attachment and the rest, which came from defiled concepts,
> The adventitious obscurations do not defile it.

DIVISION OF THE LINEAGE

101a/3There are two divisions (in the lineage): (a) The naturally present lineage (*Rang-bZhin gNas-Rigs*), which exists primordially, and (b) the developed lineage (*bsGrub-Pa'i Rigs*), which is generated depending on the cleansing of the adventitious defilements.

(1) In the naturally (present lineage there are two aspects): (a) The naturally present lineage of the ultimate nature of phenomena (*Ch'os-Nyid*), which is voidness, free from all elaborations, the Mind (*Sems-Nyid*), and the cause of freedom of the essence-body (*Ngo-Bo Nyid-sKu*). (b) The naturally present lineage of phenomenal existents (*Ch'os*), which is the cause of freedom of the form-bodies (*gZugs-sKu*). They abide as phenomena and their nature from primordial time. In the *Mahāparinirvāṇa sūtra* it is said:

> O son of good family! The nature of the mind, which is naturally luminous and naturally non-existing essence, is not separate from the appearances, the radiant attributes of major and minor signs and marks (of the Buddha-bodies) of the naturally pure mind. In any case, they are classified by (the denominations) appearance and voidness.

(2) The developed lineage: through training in the development of the mind of enlightenment and so on, the skillful means and wisdom of the "path of training" and the "dual accumulation," the accumulation of merits and primordial wisdom, perfect one into the naturally present lineage. In the *Gaṇḍavyūha sūtra* it is said:

> 'O son of the victorious one! That which is known as the lineage of enlightenment is the attainment of the ultimate sphere (*Ch'os-Kyi Byings*) by realizing the space-like vastness and natural luminosity and by training in the great accumulations of merit and primordial wisdom.

In *Uttaratantra* it is said:

As a treasure and as the fruit of a tree
The two lineages should be known.
They are (a) the naturally present lineage which exists primordially and
(b) The excellent (lineage) which arises by development—
From these two lineages the three bodies
Of the Buddhas will be acquired.
From the first (lineage) one acquires the first (essence-body).
From the second (lineage) one acquires the two later (form bodies).
The beauty of the essence-body should be understood as a gem,
Because it (the essence-body) is naturally uncreated, and
Is the treasure of virtues.
Because it has the greatness of lordship of phenomena,
The enjoyment body is like the universal king.
As it is the nature of the reflection of (the enjoyment body),
The manifested body (*sPrul-sKu*) is like a golden image.

The essence-body, the naturally present lineage of the Mind (*Sems-Nyid*), has been accomplished spontaneously as a gem. From this basis (the essence-body) arises the reflection of the naturally present lineage of phenomena (*Ch'os-Chan*), the enjoyment-body, the universal lordship, and the manifestative body for living beings. But the bodies have become invisible and obscured by defilements while one remains as a living being. Thus the accumulation of merits through the development of the enlightened attitude, and so forth, cleanses the obscurations to the form bodies, and the accumulation of wisdom through meditation on voidness, and so forth, cleanses the obscurations to suchness, the essence-body. The two lineages are present primordially, relating as the basis and the based. The naturally present lineage is the basis, like clear water. The developed lineage is that which is based on it, comparable to the arising of various reflections (in the water).....

The naturally present lineage of the nature of phenomena

and (the naturally present lineage of) phenomena exist as the cause of freedom but not as the result, freedom (itself). The developed lineage, which purifies the defilements, functions as antidotes and not as the actual causes of the two bodies, as cause and result of a creator and creature. In the *Mahāyānasūtrālaṁkāra* it is said:

> One should understand that natural and developed (lineages)
> Are the basis and the based.
> (The natural lineage) exists (as cause but) not (as result).
> Through the virtues one attains liberation.

ILLUSTRATION OF THE PRESENCE OF THE BUDDHA-ESSENCE IN BEINGS BY NINE EXAMPLES

[102b/1]The Buddha-essence pervades all living beings. Nine examples show how it is present in the midst of emotional defilements.... (The following is an abridged translation):

The Buddha-essence is present in the midst of four defilements in lay people (*So-So sKye-Bo*) who have not entered the path (of enlightenment) and who have entered the path of accumulations (*Tshogs-Lam*) and the path of application (*mThong-Lam*): (a) The Buddha-essence is present in the midst of quiescent (*Bag-La Nyal*) desire (*'Dod-Ch'ags*) like a Buddha in an unattractive bud, (b) in the midst of quiescent anger like honey in the midst of honey-bees, (c) in the midst of quiescent ignorance like grain in a husk, and (d) in the midst of the arising of strong desire, anger and ignorance, the manifest emotions, like gold in a pit of filth. (e) The Buddha-essence is present in the midst of habits of ignorance of *Arhats*, *Śrāvakas*, and *Pratyeka-buddhas* like a treasure in the earth. There are two examples illustrating the presence of the Buddha-essence in the midst of (objects of) abandonment in the path of insight of *Bodhisattvas*: (f) It is like the seed of a mango (which has the potential to give fruit) and (g) like a Buddha-image made out of a gem wrapped in rags. There are two examples illustrating the presence of the Buddha-essence in the midst of (objects of) abandonment in the path of meditation of *Bodhisattvas*. (h) It is like the embryo of a royal child in the womb of a poor and unattractive woman, and (i) like a piece of gold in the mud.

QUOTATIONS FROM THE SCRIPTURES EXPOUNDING THE BUDDHA-ESSENCE

106a/2 In *Ārya-atyayajñāna sūtra* it is said:

> The water in the earth
> Remains clean.
> In the emotional defilements primordial wisdom
> Likewise abides unstained.

In *Guhyagarbha (māyājāla tantra)* it is said:

> In any of the four times and ten directions
> Enlightenment will not be found
> Except in the Mind, which is the fully enlightened state.
> Do not seek the Buddha in any other source.
> (Otherwise) even if Buddha (himself) searches, it will not be found.

In brief, . . .one should understand that in all living beings the bodies and wisdoms of the Buddhas are present without any separation, primordially, like the sun and its rays. The (*Buddha-*) nature (*Khams*) is always and naturally pure, its essence is changeless, and its defilements are changing, adventitious, and imaginary.

VIRTUES OF THE BUDDHA-ESSENCE

106b/1 The Buddha-essence is pure (*gTsang-Ba*) because there has never been any stain on it. It is self-sacred (*bDag Dam-Pa*) because it is changeless. It is eternal (*rTag-Pa*) because it is present at all the times. And it is the perfection of bliss (transcending mundane bliss) because it will not be subdued by suffering even if one falls (takes rebirth) into the totally suffering *saṃsāra*. In *Uttaratantra* it is said: "Pure, self, bliss and eternal—The perfection of these is the result."

The Buddha-essence is omnipresent. The *Mahāyānasūtra-*

lamkāra says, "People assert that space is always all-pervading. As space pervades all forms, it also pervades all beings."

Thus, although the Buddha-essence is obscured by emotional defilements, it remains unstained like the sun in clouds. This essence remains indestructible from primordial time to enlightenment.

WHO REALIZE THE BUDDHA-ESSENCE?

107a/4 Who realize (or attain) the lineage as it is? People who have not realized the natural state (*gNas-Lugs*) yet (but) are guided by a virtuous teacher,the *Śrāvakas*, and *Pratyeka-buddhas*, who have appreciation (*Mos-Pa*) for the Mahāyāna, and the *Bodhisattvas* who have attained stages can have a general understanding of it. *Bodhisattvas* who are in the tenth stage have a partial realization of it. But except for the Buddhas no one else (fully) realizes it as it is....

The (Buddha) nature or essence abides in the form of one's own Mind's (*Sems-Nyid*) wheel of prosperities [riches] of the Buddha-fields with three bodies and primordial wisdoms. If one realizes it, that is enlightenment.... People who are in the path of training (*Slob-Lam*) have a general undestanding (of the Buddha-essence) through faith. *Uttaratantra* says:

> The ultimate truth, (the object of) spontaneously arisen (wisdom),
> Is to be realized by faith alone,
> (As) the brightness of the disc of the sun
> Cannot be seen without eyes.

The *Buddhagarbha sūtra* says:

> Beings who are lay people, *Śrāvakas*, *Pratyeka-buddhas*, and *Bodhisattvas* do not realize the Buddha-essence as it is. For example, a blind person asks others, "What does the color of butter look like?" A person answers, "It looks like snow." The blind person touches snow and feels the coldness of it, and he assumes that the color of butter is cold. Another person answers, "It is like the wing of a

> swan." He hears the sound of swans' wings and assumes that the color of butter is "oor-oor." Another answers, "The color of butter is like a conch." He feels the smooth touch of the conch and assumes that the color of butter is smooth. As a blind person cannot know color as it is, the Buddha-essence is also very difficult to realize (for anyone other than the realized ones). . . .

The difficulties of ordinary people in realizing the Buddha-essence have been (further) illustrated in the same text (*Buddhagarbha*):

> A king summons many blind people and asks them to describe the shape of an elephant. The person who touches the trunk describes the elephant as a hook, the one who touches the eye describes it as a bowl, the one who touches the ear describes it as a winnowing basket, the one who touches the back describes it as a mount, and the one who touches the tail describes it as a rope. Their descriptions are not unrelated (to the elephant), but they did not have complete understanding. Likewise the Buddha-essence will not be understood by different interpretations, such as voidness, apparition-like, and luminescent.

PURPOSE OF TEACHING THE BUDDHA-ESSENCE

[108b/5]So what is the use of teaching the Buddha-essence, which is subtle and difficult to analyze, since it won't be realized by ordinary people? There are five merits in pointing out the presence of the Buddha-essence: (a) The fear (in a person's mind) will be removed and he will become eager to achieve liberation, knowing that it is not difficult (to realize), (b) contempt for other beings will be removed and he will become respectful to all, who are equal to the Buddhas, as to our teacher (*Śākyamuni Buddha*), (c) ignorance concerning the presence of the absolute meaning, the visions of the bodies and wisdoms, will be removed from our minds, and the wisdom of the realization of the ultimate sphere (*Don-Dam-Pa'i dByings*) will arise. (d) By understanding the nature in this way one removes the exaggerations and diminishments of existing and not existing and eternal or nil, and the primordial wisdom of the realization of perfect meaning (*Yang-Dag-Pa'i Don*) will arise, (e) and the sense of the importance of self and of attachment to self will be removed, one will see self and others as equal, and will develop great loving-kindness towards others.

DISTINCTION BETWEEN THE (BUDDHA-ESSENCE OF) *YOGĀCĀRYA* AND THE SELF OF SOME OTHER SCHOOLS

[109b/5]The view of the "self" in the perverted schools is not similar to (the Buddha-essence). For they impute a self without any knowledge of it. (According to them) this self does not exist in its natural state. They assign it limits of size and do not assert that it has the virtues of the (Buddha-) bodies and primordial wisdoms. Your (*Madhyamaka*) view clings to no-self and voidness as just an antidote to (the view of) self and non-voidness, but it is not the absolute meaning. Therefore, the *Mahāparinirvāṇa sūtra* says: (Abridged translation:)

> A woman's infant son who is breast-feeding gets sick and the worried mother calls a physician. The physician mixes medicine with milk and brown sugar, gives it to the infant, and instructs the mother, saying, "I have given medicine to the child. Until the medicine has been digested, do not feed the child milk." The woman applies bile to her breast so that the infant will not have milk, and she tells the infant, "You can't have milk as I have applied poison to my breast." The child tries to get milk but he can't stand the bitter taste of bile. When he has digested the medicine, the mother washes her breast and says to her son, "Come here, have some milk." The infant is suffering from thirst but he doesn't want to have milk even if he is invited, because of the previous taste of bitterness. The mother insists again, explaining the details, and only then does the child relax and come and take milk. So, son

of good family! The Buddha likewise, for the sake of liberating all living beings, emphasizes the teachings of no-self to all living beings. By his emphasizing it, the thought of self will not remain (with the trainees) and they will attain the cessation of sorrow (*Parinirvāṇa*). So in order to dispel the wrong views of *Lokāyata* (nihilism) and to teach the transformation into a perfect body through the meditation on voidness, the Buddha taught that all phenomenal existents have no self and he taught (his disciples) to meditate on voidness. The Buddha said it just as the woman applied bile to her breast for the sake of her son. As the woman washes her breast and asks her son to take milk, I, the Buddha, teach you the Buddha-essence. O *Bhikṣus!* Do not be afraid, as the mother calls her son and lets him have milk, *Bhikṣus*, you also should identify (yourself with the infant). The Buddha-essence is not non-existence. You should understand that in the past I taught all phenomena as voidness in the *Prajñāpāramitā* teachings and that it was meant merely to teach the non-existence (of phenomena) in (their true) nature (*Rang-bZhin Med-Pa*). Otherwise, by meditating on the voidness of nothing, the bodies and wisdoms of the Buddha will not be developed, since results follow causes.

The voidness is the voidness of conceptualizations (*sPros-Pa*) of perceiving phenomena from the very moment of their appearance as one or many (*gChig Du-Ma*), and it is the voidness in their own essence (*Ngo-Bos sTong-Pa*), like a reflection in a mirror. But it doesn't mean that ultimately there will be nothing and that there was and is nothing in the past and present but just illusory appearances.The *Prajñāpāramitāhṛdaya* says:

Form is voidness,
Voidness is form,
Form is not other than voidness,
Voidness is also not other than form.

> Likewise feeling, perception, compositional factors and consciousnesses are void....

Uttaratantra says:

> In this Buddha-essence there is nothing to abandon,
> There is nothing to maintain.
> If you view the perfection (nature) properly,
> And if you realize it, that is liberation.
> The (Buddha-)essence is voidness of the characteristics
> Of adventitious (defilements) with discriminations,
> But it is not voidness of the supreme attributes (of Buddhahood),
> Which have the character of differentiations....

The two bodies of the Buddhas are present primordially and the obscurations (in them) are dispelled by the two accumulations, but they (the accumulations and bodies) are not the cause and result of a creator and creation. Otherwise the ultimate body and enjoyment body become composite, and therefore they will become transitory. Concerning the changelessness of the ultimate body the *Madhyamakāvatāra* (MDA 57a) says:

> The peaceful (pacified of conceptualization) body is clear as a wish-fulfilling gem,
> As a wish-fulfilling gem it doesn't conceptualize (anything).
> It is always present until all beings are liberated.
> It appears for (*Bodhisattvas*) who are free from conceptualizations....

One should understand the meaning of no-self, voidness, and non-duality and so forth as follows: The *Āryamahāparinirvāṇa sūtra* says:

> I teach you that the totally pure nature of the Buddha, the secret essence of the Thus-gone (*Tathāgata*, i.e., the Buddha) is unchanging and inexhaustible (*Mi-'Pho-Ba*). But if I say that it does exist, it is not correct for learned and wise people to cling to it (its existence). If I say that

it does not exist, then I am not speaking the truth, and uncultivated people would propagate nihilism and would not know the secret essence of the Thus-gone (i.e., Buddha-essence). If I talk about suffering, they won't know of the existence of the blissful nature of the body. Foolish people take the body to be like an unfired clay pot, thinking, "All bodies are impermanent." Wise people make distinctions, and they do not say that all are impermanent by all means. Why? Because in one's body is present the seed, the Buddha nature. Foolish people apprehend that the attributes of the Buddha are no-self. The view of wise people is that the term no-self is purely a conventional expression and that it is "untrue." By understanding thus they won't have any doubts (about the Buddha-essence). If I say that the Buddha-essence is voidness (*sTong-Pa*), when foolish people hear it, they will develop the view of nihilism or of non-existence. Wise people will determine that the Buddha-essence is unchanging and inexhaustible. If I say that liberation is like an apparition (*Māyā*), foolish people perceive liberation as the teachings of Mara (the devil). The wise discern that among men, like a lion (among animals), the Thus-gone alone is eternal, present, changeless, and inexhaustible. If I say that because of unenlightenment (*Ma-Rig-Pa*) the compositional factors (*'Du-Byed*) arise, foolish people by hearing it distinguish a duality between enlightenment and unenlightenment. Wise and learned people realize the non-duality (*gNyis-Med*) (of enlightenment and unenlightenment); and what is non-dual, that is perfect.... If I say that phenomenal existents have no self and even the Buddha-essence has no self, foolish people perceive the duality (of self and no-self). Wise and learned people realize that they are naturally non-dual. Both self and no-self in their nature do not exist as dual. All the fully enlightened Buddhas praised the meaning of the Buddha-essence as inconceivable, inmmeasurable, and endless, and I also discoursed elaborately on its virtues in the *sūtras*.

SIGN OF AWAKENING OF THE LINEAGES

[113b/5]There are two signs of the awakening of the lineages (*Rigs Sad-Pa*): The first is the awakening of the natural lineage, the ultimate body. The *Madhyamakāvatāra*[SD14b/6] says:

> Even at the time that one is an ordinary person, by hearing of voidness
> Great joy is generated in one again and again.
> Tears of joy moisten one's eyes.
> The hairs rise from the pores of the body. That is because
> In one is the seed of wisdom of the Buddha.
> One is a potential vessel for receiving the teachings on it (voidness).
> So one should be given the (teachings on) supreme absolute truth.

The second is the awakening of the lineage of phenomenal (qualities) (*Ch'os-Chan*) (of developed lineage), the form bodies. The *Mahāyānasūtrālaṁkāra*[DGC 9b/4] says:

> (Even) before entering (into the training) for having compassion,
> Devotion, patience, and
> Devoting oneself properly to virtues
> Are said to be the definite signs of (possessing) the lineage.

THE VIRTUES OF THE AWAKENING OF THE LINEAGES

[114a/2]Concerning the virtues of the awakening of the lineage, the *Mahāyānasūtrālaṁkāra*[DGC 10a/2] says:

> After a long time, even if one has to take rebirth in an inferior migration (because of past *karmas*),
> One will be liberated quickly.
> (Even in the inferior migrations one) will experience little suffering
> And will develop revulsion and help to mature other beings.

After the lineage has been awakened, even if one has to take rebirth in inferior migrations, one will be liberated as quickly as the touch of a silken ball. There will be little suffering, in one will arise strong revulsion, and one will help to ripen other living beings (into the right path). If beings did not possess such a lineage, they would have no revulsion from suffering, and they would have no wish for renouncing *saṃsāra* and attaining *nirvāṇa*, and it would be impossible for the wish for liberation to arise in them. So developing compassion toward other suffering people without being taught by anyone, and developing revulsion by experiencing suffering, and so on, occur because of the power of possessing the "beginningless virtuous ultimate nature" (i.e., the Buddha-essence). *Uttaratantra*[GLC 11a/3] says:

> If there were no Buddha-nature,
> There would be no revulsion from suffering;
> One would not have the wish for *nirvāṇa*, and
> One would not have aspirations for it nor would one seek for it.
> To recognize suffering and happiness and the virtues and faults of *saṃsāra* and *nirvāṇa*
> Is a result of possessing the lineage.
> For if one did not have the lineage, one would not have these (faculties).

BEINGS ARE WANDERING IN *SAṂSĀRA* BECAUSE OF NOT RECOGNIZING THE LINEAGE

[115a/1]Even though everyone possesses the lineage of that nature, they wander in *saṃsāra*. Why is that so? The causes of beings wandering in *saṃsāra* are that they do not realize the presence (of the Buddha-essence in themselves) and they apprehend self without reason; and the conditions are successive emotional defilements, (influences of) of evil friends, poverty and external control. The *Mahāyānasūtralaṁkāra*[DGC 9b/6] says:

The experiences of emotional defilements, the force of evil friends,
Poverty, and external control—
In brief these are the four faults (obscuring) the lineage
Which you should understand.

Od-Rim says:

Not realizing the luminous primordial wisdom,
Perceiving mind as "I" and being attached to the selfhood (of it),
Perceiving objects as "others" and apprehending the self-hood (of them),
Because of these, beings are wandering in *saṃsāra*
And experiencing varieties of happiness and suffering.

HOW THE WANDERING IN *SAṂSĀRA* DEVELOPS

115b/1 The primordial Mind is luminosity, voidness, clarity, and self-arisen wisdom. Its essence (*Ngo-Bo*) is voidness like space, its nature (*Rang-bZhin*) is clarity like the sun and moon, its radiance (*mDangs*) of compassion is ceaseless arising like the surface of a stainless mirror. It is the Buddha-essence, the nature of the ultimate body, enjoyment body, and manifested body, and it is free from falling into the partiality of *saṃsāra* and *nirvāṇa*. (Anyhow,) in that state, the delusions develop (as follows, because of not realizing the spontaneously arisen awareness wisdom as it is and the appearances as its manifestative power:) (The aspect of) void essence (*Ngo-Bo*) opens (or provides) the door (or opportunity) of arising; from (the aspect of) clear nature appear the five spontaneously arisen lights as objects (by not realizing the lights as the power of awareness wisdom); and (the aspect of) compassionate awareness wisdom arises as the analytic cognition. The *Guhyagarbhamāyājālatantra* says: "Wonderful! From the Buddha-essence beings are deluded by concepts and *karma*."

THE TWO UNENLIGHTENMENTS

115b/4 At the time (of distraction into delusions), the aspect of one's not realizing the wisdom (which dwells in) oneself is called innate unenlightenment (*Lhan-Chig sKyes-Pa'i Ma-Rig-Pa*). The aspect of perceiving self-percepts as others is called imaginative unenlightenment (*Kun-Nas brTags-Pa'i Ma-Rig-Pa*). By not realizing that (the delusions have) arisen from the natural state, and by clinging to the apprehended selfhood (*bDag-'Dzin*) (of the percepts) as objects, beings are deluded by them as the external world and internal beings having individual bodies (created by) the maturation (of their *karma*) and habituations, and minds with the five poisons....

The root (of delusion) is unenlightenment. (*Prajñāpāramitā*)-*sañcayagāthā* says: 'All beings of lesser, middle, and excellent (intellect) arise from unenlightenment. Thus said the Buddha."

Concerning apprehending duality, the condition of delusion, (*Prajñāpāramitā-*)*aṣṭasāhasrikā* says: "By apprehending "I" and "my" beings are wandering in *saṃsāra*."

HOW BEINGS ARE WANDERING IN *SAṂSĀRA*

[116a/5]Beings are wandering in *saṃsāra* through the twelve (links in the chain of interdependent causation). From the two unenlightenments arise the formation (of one's life process) in *saṃsāra*, and from this arise successively becoming, name and form, and so on. Then, after the completion of the body, starting from the stages of "aquatic creative" (*Mer-Mer-Po*) to birth, (they experience) contact, feeling, the six sense entrances, and old age and death, and they wander in *saṃsāra*.

WHY BEINGS ARE WANDERING IN *SAMSĀRA*

[116a/6]If you think that it is not correct that the wandering (in *saṃsāra*) occurs from the Buddha-essence, the primordial state which does not exist as *saṃsāra*, it is wrong. Even clear, unpolluted, and unhindered water becomes ice, hard as stone, because of the winter wind. Likewise, because of the arising of apprehended and apprehender, from the primordial state delusory appearances appear in various forms as being solid. *Dohākoṣa-nāma-caryāgīti* says:

By being blown and stirred by the wind,
Even soft water becomes (hard) like stone.
Stirred by thoughts, the non-existent but delusory forms
Become very firm and solid.

In the Mind is present the state of ultimate body, which is primordially pure essence (*Ngo-Bo*), called the ultimate universal ground of union, with the attributes of form bodies, Buddha-fields, and wisdoms. But when one is distracted (*'Khrul*) from the Buddha-essence, those attributes (of Buddhahood) will be obscured because of the deluded unenlightenment of (seeing) them as apprehended and apprehender, thereby sowing the seed of various delusory habits from beginningless time in the universal ground of habits. Thereafter, depending on the strength (of various habits), beings will experience the happy and inferior realms, and so on. While beings are wandering in *saṃsāra* as in a dream, they apprehend (the perceptions as) "I" and "self," become involved in hatred and desire and the rest, the five poisons, and accumulate *karma* and habits. They become deluded without any reason and indulge in various types of attachment (perceiving them) as real, and they wander continuously in the round of delusory appearances, day and night without cessation. But the continuity (of wandering in *saṃsāra*) has no basis. So (although) it seems that they are distracted from liberation (the Buddha-essence), they are wandering with happiness and sufferings like the delusion of a dream. For example, when a prince wanders through the streets, suffering from the loss of his princely state, although he naturally possesses the excellent wealth inherited by birth in the royal lineage, he might be suffering temporarily.... Likewise, at the very moment when one is wandering aimlessly in *saṃsāra*, the Buddha-essence is present in living beings.

ATTAINMENT OF LIBERATION BY AWAKENING THE LINEAGE

118b/6 The Mind, the wisdom of the Buddhas, which is the naturally pure and immaculate essence (*Ngo-Bo*), is present primordially. Through the manifestative aspect of the luminous nature of the mind (the Buddha-essence), the attributes of the form-bodies of the Buddha have been spontaneously accomplished. This has been explained by nine examples (as given earlier in this section). The aspect of voidness (of the luminous mind) is the attributes of the ultimate body, which has been explained by the example of space in all the *tantras* and *sūtras*. The inseparability (of appearances and voidness) is the "virtues of the beginningless ultimate nature" of all phenomena. Although it is called the "naturally present lineage" because it is changeless, and it (the lineage) is also called the "developed lineage" because it manifests the development of virtues by the purification of defilements, its root is the luminous self-awareness wisdom itself. When, by accomplishing the two accumulations, one awakens the two lineages, the obscurations of the two lineages are dispelled and their virtues become capable of manifesting, and finally one obtains the two bodies with their virtues. The six perfections are included in the two accumulations, as are also the stages of "development" (*bsKyed-Rim*) and "perfection" (*rDzogs-Rim*).... The three empowerments (*dBang*), the vase (*Bum-Pa*), secret (*gSang-Ba*), and wisdom (*Shes-Rab*) empowerments, are for perfecting the "development stage." So they belong to the accumulation of merits, which includes the visualization of the *maṇḍalas* of deities, and so on, all the (spiritual trainings) associated with conceptualization. The precious verbal empowerment (*Tshig-dBang Rin-Po-Ch'e*) is for perfecting the "perfection stage." So it belongs to the accumulation of wisdom, which includes all the contemplations on luminescence and all the (trainings) associated with freedom from conceptualization. By undergoing training in these (two accumulations), one purifies the obscurations of the lineages, and from the womb of obscuration the Buddhahood which abide in oneself arises like the sun from the midst of clouds.

PERFECTION OF THE TWO ACCUMULATIONS COMBINED

119b/4The ten virtuous deeds and (contemplations of) absorptions (*bSam-gTan*, of the form realms) and (the contemplations of) the formless realms belong to merit-making virtues (and not liberative virtues). But if a person is able to apply the mind of enlightenment through skillful means and wisdom, then the ten virtuous deeds and the absorptions (of the form realm) and (the contemplations of) the formless realm, and so forth, will become liberative virtues. The Middle *Prajñāpāramitā* says:

> O Subhuti! When one develops the excellent mind of enlightenment, even the ten virtuous deeds, the four absorptions (of the form realm) and the four (contemplations of) the formless realm, the practices of an ordinary person, will become (the training associated with) liberative virtues. So, it will become the cause of omniscience. . . .

TRANSCENDING BOTH THE EXTREMES OF *SAṂSĀRA* AND PEACE

120a/2If you think that since the merit-making virtues cause wandering in *saṃsāra*, the liberative virtues, too, might cause *saṃsāra*, (the answer is) no. Training in understanding the non-reality of *karma* leads one to liberation, and this has been explained by examples. It is a method to attain liberation from *saṃsāra* but not to generate it. Because of great compassion, even if one remains in *saṃsāra* for the protection (of others), one will not be defiled by the faults of *saṃsāra* because of one's realization that all phenomena are unborn, and because of one's not falling into the bias of peace (or *nirvāṇa* for oneself) because of skill of great compassion. The *Abhisamayālaṁkāra* says: "Because of realization one does not remain in *saṃsāra*, because of compassion one does not remain in peace (for oneself)."

THE FOUR RESULTS OF LIBERATIVE VIRTUES

[120b/1](There are one main and three subordinate effects:) (a) Maturation Effect: (The liberative virtues) will never be exhausted, unlike the merit-making virtues. For the time being one will experience happiness in the human and gods' realms and finally one will attain enlightenment. The (*Prajñāpāmitā-*)*aṣṭasāhasrikā* says:

> O Venerable Śāriputra! Because of such root-virtues, after taking birth in realms of gods and human beings, they (those who perfected the two accumulations) attain supreme enlightenment. Why? Because the ten virtuous deeds, four absorptions, four contemplations of the formless realms and six perfections, which were generated with the supreme mind of enlightenment, will never be exhausted mid-way (until the attainment of the goal).

(b) Effect of Compatibility: The *Daśakuśalanirdeśa-sūtra* says:

> One will keep endeavoring in the ten virtuous deeds and the effects of virtues will keep increasing. They will have long lives, great prosperity, harmonious spouses, no opponents, no one slandering them, they will be pleasant for all to see, their words respectable, having charming speech for all to hear, contented minds, affection for each other, and right view.

(c) The effects of Dominance: (As the effect of) refraining from killing, one will take rebirth in an excellent and pleasant land, refraining from taking what is not given, one will take rebirth in a land with nutritious and tasty food and drink and effective medicines, refraining from adultery, one will take rebirth in a clean land with scented medicinal trees, refraining from lying, one will take rebirth in a land where there is no deception and danger from enemies, robbers and so forth, refraining from divisive speech, one will take rebirth in a land with few sharp pebbles and thorns, where people will be living harmoniously, refraining from harsh words one will take rebirth in a land where the seasons will be regular and the crops and fruit will ripen in time, refraining from senseless speech, one will take rebirh in a smooth land ornamented with lakes and ponds, refraining from covetousness, one will take rebirth in a land where one will witness the best harvests, fruit and flowers, refraining from ill will, one will take rebirth in a land with many good-tasting medicinal herbs and fruits, and refraining from wrong view, one will take rebirth in a land of great resources of crops and gems, prosperity of protection and strength. . . .

(d) The Cumulative Effect: The *Lalitavistara* says:

> One will become eager for virtues, will increase the accumulation of merits, and
> Will possess the accumulation of excellent enlightenment.

HOW KARMA AND EMOTIONAL DEFILEMENTS APPEAR

124b/5 Although *karma* and the defilements do not exist in their true nature, their appearance is ceaseless. *Karma* and the defilements are rooted in unenlightenment, they arise through the circumstantial conditions of objects, and are related to the cause, the three poisons. The *(Ārya-sadharma)smṛtyupasthāna (sūtra)* says:

> The basis of *karma* is unenlightenment because if one knows (or is enlightened), one will not be influenced by *karma*. *Karma* produces various (creations) like a painter. Its circumstantial condition is the conceptualizing of the objects. *Karma* acts in various manners like a monkey, and it remains in the *saṃsāric* ocean like a fish. It accumulates various types of habits like a householder, and appears without (even) existing like an apparition. *Karma* follows beings like a shadow. It does not alternate like suffering and happiness. *Karma* is difficult to reverse, like the flow of a river, and it dictates the (experiences) of happiness and suffering like a king. *Karma* is vast like space and (the effects) are not interchangeable as the masses of blue lo-

tus (*S. utpala*) and white water-lily (*S. kumuda*) (are not).

KARMA AS THE RESULT OF INTERDEPENDENT CAUSATION

125a/6Even if one searches for *karma* and defilements in the inner sphere (sense-faculties, etc.) and in external phenomena by thought and analysis, they can never be found. The *Bodhicaryāvatāra* says:

> The defilements exist neither in objects, sense-faculties, in between, nor
> In any other place. So where do they abide and harm all beings?
> It is like an apparition, so one should try to understand (how to) free the heart of fear (of them).

Although *karma* does not exist in its true nature, in the dream-like relative truth the virtuous and non-virtuous deeds create happiness and suffering separately.

OPPOSING CONTEMPT FOR THE CAUSE AND RESULT OF DEEDS

126a/1Some foolish and arrogant people who do not know the (various) meanings of the Dharma say, "There is no *karma* and no effects of *karma*. In suchness there is nothing. It is like space;" and they abandon virtuous deeds and indulge in evil deeds. They say, "Beings are self-appearance like a dream. They do not exist as an external factor. So even killing is not an evil deed, since they are like a piece of wood." Those are nihilists and not followers of the Dharma. The *Subāhu-sūtra* says,

> Some say, "There is no *karma* and no effect of *karma*. The (*karma* theory) is taught (by the Buddha) to lead the simple-minded people," and they live with hosts of non-virtuous deeds. You should know that they are not followers of this Dharma but are boasting. They are based on the path of atheists and are deceived by māras (devils).

DENIAL OF NIHILISM

[126a/6]Some say (from Root Text, SN):

> Cause and effect, compassion and merits
> Are the Dharma for ordinary people, and it will not lead to enlightenment.
> O great *Yogis*! You should meditate upon
> The ultimate meaning, effortless as space.

These kinds of statements are

> The views of the utmost nihilism.
> They have entered the path of the most inferior.
> It is astonishing to expect the result while abandoning the cause.

OPPOSING THE MIND OF THE SUMMIT OF THE WORLD.

[126b/4]Is (your meditation) like space? If it is, then there is no use in meditating upon it since it has already been established (as space). If it is not, then even if one meditates upon it, it is useless, since one cannot create anything that is not there as space, which is empty and changeless. So what is the use of it? If you say that it is for attaining liberation, freedom from defilements, you have represented suchness as the result of a cause. Now do not say that there is no cause and result. If you attain liberation by meditating upon non-existence (*Chi-Yang Med-Pa*), then even the existentialists (*Tshu-Rol mDzes-Pa*) will achieve liberation for the same reason. Because of that *Dohā* says: "The Archer (*Saraha*) said: for space-minded people there is no liberation at all."

THE CORRECT VIEW OF CAUSE AND RESULT OF DEEDS

[127a/5]Enlightenment is achieved through the apparition-like dual accumulations, which appear but do not exist in (their true) nature. The *Bhadramāyākāra-paripṛcchā sūtra* says:

By acquiring the apparition-like accumulation,
One attains apparition-like enlightenment.
For the sake of apparition-like beings
(One) performs apparition-like services.

4. Philosophical View of Phenomenal Existents

Longchen Rabjam explains the philosophical views of common *Mahāyāna* as well as of *Dzogpa Chenpo* and how to realize them in the tenth chapter of *Shingta Chenpo* (SC Vol-II). The view of the ultimate nature of all phenomenal existents is unborn and non-existent in its true nature from the beginning, and the innate primordial wisdom is the essential nature of all.

THE NATURE OF ALL PHENOMENA IS UNBORN

[SC-II, 60a/6]All aspects (of training), starting from the entry (into the path of training) up to its perfecting, are for the purpose of learning the nature. The nature is unborn and it transcends the four extremes.

[61a/1]Attachment to external objects will be abandoned by realizing them as (the projections of) one's mind, and so forth, or as the deities and their mansions. (Then) by realizing that the view (of phenomena being projections of the mind itself) is unborn, the antidote itself (becomes) nonexistent. So the nature of phenomena is unborn.

THE VIEW OF THE REALIZATION OF THE NATURE

Nature (gNas-Lugs)

[61b/1](The nature of) all phenomena is emptiness and selflessness. But by not realizing it, because of apprehending "I" and "my," beings are deluded in the dream-like *saṃsāra* and they are experiencing varieties of happiness and suffering. So one should realize the non-existent nature of (phenomena).

Refutation of the Assertion That the (Phenomenal) Appearances Are Mind

63a/5 Although forms appear to the mind, the (objective) appearances are not mind.... When the reflection of your face appears in a mirror, it appears as the face looks, because the clear surface of the mirror is capable of making the reflection appear and the face has the potential of appearing or of projecting the reflection. At that time, the reflection of the face is not the face, nor is there any other face than the face which imprinted it. Likewise, various kinds (of phenomena) are appearing in the deluded mind because of the interdependent origination of the causes and conditions of delusion. The various objective appearances, such as mountains, are not mind. Also there is nothing in the mind which truly exists, but (merely) appearances (created by the) delusory habituations of the mind. So they are the forms of delusory appearances. They are wrong appearances, just as a person who has "hairy vision" will see hair before his eyes....

Some (scholars) inquire: "What are the appearances of earth and stone and so on if they are neither external (objects) nor internal (senses)?" Response: I say—"You who think that all (phenomena) exist in the duality of (either) apprehender or apprehended are pigs!" Anyhow, it is said (in the scriptures) that all phenomena of *Saṃsāra* and *Nirvāṇa* are non-existent as external, internal, or in between, from the very time of their appearance, as (illustrated by) the eight examples of illusion....

From those appearances (of the objects in the mind), which are non-existent, arise the delusions of the apprehenders and the apprehended. Here, the apprehended means the thought arisen at the first instant (of encountering the appearances),through the apprehended objects. So it is the mind itself arisen as the apprehended. The apprehender is the analyzing (thought) which arises after (the thought of the apprehended) and it arises from the mind (*Sems*). In sPyan-Ras-gZigs brTul-Zhugs it is said:

> The apprehended arises from the mind which apprehends (the appearances) as the objects,
> The apprehender arises from the mind which analyzes it (the apprehended objects). . . .

Here, some foolish and arrogant people boast: "The apprehended is the appearances, such as mountains, and the apprehender is one's senses." Herdsmen! Enough of your inverted thoughts! If that is so, do the objects appear for a Noble [Realized] One, who has renounced apprehender and apprehended? If they appear, then the apprehender and the apprehended would appear (for them), as you have accepted that the object is the apprehended and the senses are the apprehender and that they (the objects) are appearing (for the Realized Ones). If the objects do not appear for him (the Realized One),then there are numerous sources (in scriptures to refute it), saying, for example: "the appearances for the Noble Ones are like *Māyā*," "the mountains seen by the *Arhats* of *Śrāvakas*" and "Appearing as the objects (the relative truth) of the knowledge of the all-knowing Buddha. . . ."

The appearing objects [percept or things that appear] (*sNang-Yul*) are not mind (*Sems*), because the objects remain, even when the person himself is not there. The objects won't move when the person moves elsewhere; and the (objects) possess various colors, and so on. If the objects are the mind itself, then they should change as he changes. They should be present if he is present and if he is not, they shouldn't be. As mind has no color and design, neither should the objects have them. The presence and absence of appearance are the projections of the mind. So the mere appearances can be classified as the mind. But boasting that the objects of appearance are the mind is a grave folly.

Phenomena Are Like Illusions

65a/2 The reflections appear in a mirror without the face passing into the mirror, nor do the reflections occur separately from the face. Likewise, it should be understood that from the very moment that all phenomena appear in the mind, they exist neither as the mind nor as anything other than the mind, as illustrated by the eight illusory examples.

Non-Inherent Existence of Mind

65b/2 All phenomena seem true while they are not analyzed. But if you investigate the external appearances, reducing them to (partless) atoms, they (will be found to be) non-existent in their nature; so the objects of the grasping are inconceivable. (If you analyze) the subject, the mind, there is no aspect of a moment of inner apprehender, so its essence is beyond apprehending, and the mind of the apprehender is inconceivable (*Mi-dMigs*). They are non-dual, free from elaborations, and beyond subject and object of expression.

Illustrations of Non-Existence (in True) Nature

66b/4 Phenomena appear while they do not exist.... They are unborn from the very moment of their birth, like the water-moon (reflection of the moon in water) and the water in a mirage.

(The Ignorance) Which Is to Be Purified

68a/1 For example, when a patient with phlegm (*Bad-Kan*) has "hairy visions," he should receive treatment. Likewise, (the eyes of) all living beings are covered, from beginningless time, with the cataract (*Ling-Tog*) of ignorance and the concepts of "self" and "of self." Hence, they are not only not seeing as it is the luminous Mind, the Buddha-essence which is present in themselves, but they see the appearances of external objects, such as mountains and rocks, and the internal passionate thoughts generated by emotional defilements like "hairy visions." They do not exist from the very moment of their appearance, but they function like tricks to fool infants....

Since the *Āryas* [the Realized Ones] see (phenomena) as non-existent in their (true) nature, they realize them perfectly in accordance with the nature of the (Buddha-) essence and the non-existence of the true nature.

(THE MEANS) OF PURIFYING (IGNORANCE)

To Learn the Middle Way, Free from Extremes

69a/1For dispelling the cataract of ignorance, the pure wisdom is the discriminative awareness wisdom. When one is observing the nature of phenomena through (discriminative wisdom), one attains liberation by means of the emptiness (openness) of seeing the *karma*, emotional defilements with their traces, appearing without truly existing in the manner of apparitions (*sPrul-Pa*) and so on....

The non-existence of separate relative and absolute truth is the indivisible truth. The suchness of the middle view is pure as the very essence of the non-existence of things (*Ngos-Po Med-Pa*) from primordial time. By learning this, one attains *Nirvāṇa*, which is free from the categories of eternalism and nihilism and of *Saṃsāra* and *Nirvāṇa*. That is called the meaning of the Natural Great Perfection (*Rang-bZhin rDzogs-Pa Ch'en-Po*), which transcends actions and efforts.

Cutting the Root of the (Apprehending) Mind

70b/2The appearances themselves do not bind (you to the delusions of *Saṃsāra*) because if you do not attach by clinging to the appearances, they will not defile you, since there is no connection. The bondage is the attachment, and it is important to abandon that attachment....

Even if you renounced attachment to the appearances of form, sound, smell, taste, and touch by investigating their non-existence and impurity in (their true) nature, the mind which becomes attached has itself not been liberated. If a stone is thrown at a dog, the dog chases the stone and does not catch the thrower of the stone. That kind of (*Dharma*) training will not bring liberation from the emotional defilements. If a stone is thrown at a lion, the lion kills the thrower. Similarly, the root of all the emotional defilements, such as anger and attachment, is the mind. So one should ponder inwardly and pacify (the mind) through the wisdom of (the realization of) non-existence in (the true) nature.

The Mind Which Is Projected at (the Objects of) the Six Consciousnesses Is Not Real

[72b/6]When your mind watches your mind, realizing that the essence of the mind is nowhere recognizable is the realization of its nature.... This nature transcends all concepts, thoughts, and elaborations.... This nature has no basis and root (of existence).

Mind Is Unfabricated

[73b/6](Mind) seems to be projecting (*'Ch'ar-Ba*), but it is not an entity since it does not develop or decline during the three times. From the very moment of its arising, the past (of the mind) has ceased and its future has not yet arisen. In its present, there are no separate aspects of rising, dwelling, and cessation, and it doesn't exist (even) if you search for it down to temporally indivisible moments. So the mind exists neither as the perceiver nor the perceived. Therefore, one should remain natural.

Mind Is Momentary

[74a/3]Whatever kind of thought arises in the mind, if you search for it, it will not be found, because (mind) itself is the searcher. The reason that when it is searched for by itself it will not be found is that they (searcher and searched) are not two. If the mind is perfectly investigated, not only (will it be seen that) the mind itself does not exist, but all the concepts will be pacified.

Mind Is Primordially Pure and Has No Birth

[74b/3]The Mind (*Sems-Nyid*) is called emptiness as it is naturally pure and doesn't have basis and root. (In the mind) the mode of the arising of a variety (of things) is ceaseless, and it is called appearance. Even if one investigates, it is free from the extremes of eternalism as it has no substance and character, and it is free from the extremes of nihilism as the aspect of just awareness does not cease. There is no third aspect of "both" or "neither." So it is beyond expression but merely can be called "the natural purity," since it transcends recognition as "this is it." It is the wisdom unstained by extremes. . . . It has aspects such as being eternal, because it is free from change, it is free from the nets of reverse concepts, and it is enlightened.

(In the Mind) There is Nothing to Be Abandoned

[75b/5]When the mind is examined with many kinds of investigation it is proven to be non-existent in its (true) nature; likewise it is non-existent while it is not being investigated. So the mind is non-existent. (In scriptures) It has been taught that one should remain in the state of non-continuity of analysis, recognition, and thoughts, as when the hungry Brahmans and elephants are satisfied with food, without renunciation or acceptance and expectations or doubts.

MIND IS UNREALIZABLE THROUGH THEORIES.

It Will Not Be Realized by a Person Who Has Pride

[76a/3]People who comprehend only the words of the theories will not understand the pure meaning of it "as it is." Those people (logicians) who are stewing the concepts of calculating "the property of the subject (*Phyogs-Ch'os*)," "forward pervasion" and "reverse pervasion" (*rJes-Su 'Gro-lDog*), and whether the reasoning has been applied to "similar classes" (*mThun-Phyogs*) or to "dissimilar classes" (*Mi-mThun Phyogs*) and so on, fan the fuel of emotional defilements with the bellows of perverted (views), ignite the huge fire of manifold suffering, and burn their minds and those of others. Their pride is equal to a mountain. . . .

(The teachings on the nature) are not like those (so-called) teachings in the form of elaborate nets of imagination (*Kun-bTags*) which have been multiplied into thousands by those people. The nature of the mind and of phenomena is primordially pure. Therefore, there is nothing to be established or rejected. . . .

All phenomena are in their nature non-dual and pure. If you realize the insight of the very essence (*Ngo-Bo-Nyid*) which is non-existent in its real nature (*Rang-bZhin Gyis Med-Pa*), then you realize the natural state of (how things are) present (*gShis-Kyi gNas-Lugs*). If you realize the mind, free from goings or comings, then there is no place where the emotional defilements are arising and ceasing. Thereby, you realize that the antidotes and the (defilements) which are to be abandoned are non-existent as two, and they will (spontaneously) be perfected in their own (natural) place. . . .

(The attainment) of liberation by realizing the essential point does not rely on recognition of the objects. (It is as) when you are having a dream, if you recognize the object and perceiver itself (as a dream), you will at once spontaneously be awakened (from the dream). Although other (*yānas*) assert that liberation will be achieved by renouncing the objects, one will not be bound by the mere appearances of the mind and the objects (*Yul Dang Ch'os-Su sNang-Ba*), but will be bound if one attaches (*Zhen-Pa*) to them. So it is taught (in scriptures) that one should renounce apprehension and attachment. Tilopā said: "Appearances do not bind but attachments do. So, Nāropa, cut off the attachments. . . ."

Mere appearance is not the entity to be rejected or accepted. So one should not apprehend and attach (to the objects). Except at the beginning, when one realizes the mind as unborn essence, one does not make intellectual investigations all the time (about its being unborn). Because even if one analyzes, there is nothing more to realize than one has already, and it will (only) distract one with conceptualization.

(Mind) Will Not Be Realized through Theoretical Distinctions

79b/3The real meaning of the nature, the Mind, is freedom from concepts and expressions. So it won't be understood by conceptual tenets and expressions. It neither exists nor is non-existent and it is neither the extremes nor middle. So, in it there is nothing to be designated as tenets. It is non-dimensional like the nature of space, and has not fallen into any biased assertion that "this is the system of it. . . ."

There are no words and letters because the (true) meaning of phenomena is beyond (the object of) mental conceptions and concepts, which cause delusions. . . . So it should be known that all phenomena are peaceful, natural, pure, and that they transcend all the characteristics of conceptualizations.

Example to Illustrate That the Basis Is Non-Existent and It Will Not Be Realized by Investigation

[80a/4]What is the purpose of arguing about the meaning of the nature which is free from (the concept of) center and extremes? It is like arguing about whether the color of the lotus in the sky is yellow.

Instructions on How Intellectually Created Meditation Vitiates (the Mind)

[81a/1]Through the elaborate (training of) the development and perfection stages, the nature which is spontaneously present from primordial time will not be realized but will be deviated from, and the nature which is beyond rejections and acceptances will not be seen. So one has to reach (*La-bZa-Ba*) the great perfection of spontaneously present equality. . . . In nature (*gShis*) there is no path in which to be trained.

FOUR PERFECTIONS

The Perfection of the Nature Which Is (Changeless) Equal to Space

[81b/6]The Mind (*Sems-Nyid*) is enlightened from the origin and there is nothing new to be purified. So there is no need of clinging to rejecting and acquiring. . . . Since there is no apprehended and apprehender of either external or internal (aspects), there is no apprehending. . . . As there is not a single aspect which can be pointed out, saying, "this is it," the attachment is uprooted.

When One Realizes, One Perfects (the Goal) Totally through Confidence

[82a/5]When one realizes (the nature), one will attain confidence and will perfect realization totally in the (changeless) nature of space.... In the state of one's changeless mind, whatever joy or distress and happiness or suffering arise, at that very moment (of arising), if one does not apprehend it, it will be liberated by itself. So there are no other antidotes. It is instant liberation, as it has no earlier and later aspects.

Perfection (of the State), Free from the Watcher and the To Be Watched

[82b/5]By watching whatever arises, the watcher loses (itself) in its own place. By searching where it has gone, not only will it be found nowhere or in any direction, but the searcher itself will dissolve into non-conceptuality. Thereby, both the senses which do the searching and the rejections and acceptances of the objects of the search disappear without a trace. Absence of any thing to be recognized is my (Longchen Rabjam's) Mind, which is like space.

The Perfection without Dwelling Place by Reaching the Basis

[83a/2]At that time, having spontaneously accomplished (for) one's Mind the vision which is indivisible from space, one has secured the state of the Ultimate Body, which is present in oneself.... Whatever arises (in one's mind, if) one has attained the realization of liberation into the basis, like clouds clearing in the sky, the Mind will be unified with the ultimate sphere (*dByings*) and the naturally liberated wisdom of whatever arises. Therefore, there is no place or dwelling to which the Mind will return from the natural state. Since it is the perfection of the dissolution of phenomena, it is freedom from the adventitious negating and accepting senses and (freedom) from the narrow path of grasping (things) as real and of characteristics. Now the perfection of the ultimate nature, freedom from goings and comings, has been achieved. Then where to go?

Nowhere. The *yogi* who has reached that kind of state has transcended the objects of delusion, and no one will return to the *saṃsāric* cities, because he has reached the space-like basis. Therefore, when my (Long Chen Pa's) Mind has attained the (ultimate) sphere, the apprehending thoughts are purified into the basis of the primordial state and my three doors are liberated without efforts. How can other people see in what state of (realization) I am? Even if I speak, those less fortunate people do not see it "as it is." This is the occasion of having confidence in the (attainment of absolute) meaning.

CONFIDENCE (IN THE NATURE) THROUGH REALIZING (IT)

[83b/6]This is the time when I have no aspirations for other (teachings), since I have total confidence in my (realized) nature. Other *yogis* who have been liberated are, because of their realizations, as I (*Longchen Rabjam*) am. Now I do not have any more doubts to clear (through other sources), as there is no one who has more to teach than I have already realized. . . . There are people who, in the past, through the levels and sequences of excellent views, meditations, and activities, and by relying on the higher and lower stages and paths like steps, have gained their intellects and the experiences of the phases of development of the higher and lower training (*yogas*), but have now lost them all because they have lost the root-basis of the mind. Now, for me (*Longchen Rabjam*) there is no objective (*gTad-So*) or goal to aim for. However things appear, like a drunk, I have no apprehension. Although things appear, like an infant, I do not identify (*Ngos-gZung*) them. For me all the activities arise as equalness, naturalness, openess, and aimlessness, and they are sameness because of transcending apprehension. It is said in the *Dohā*, "The wish-fulfilling gem-like realization of the learned ones who have dissolved the delusions is wonderful. . . ."

By the arising of whatever arises as the ultimate nature (*Ch'os-Nyid*), one attains liberation from *Karma* (actions) and the compounds, because one has cleansed the delusions into the basis and perfected the state (*dGongs-Pa*) which has no object, like space.... Whatever one does, since (now) action has been liberated as having no aim (*gTad-Med*), it is naturally absence of grasping. So there is neither liberation nor bondage.... When one reaches such a stage, that is liberation by the transference of the blessings of the *Lama's* realization (*dGongs-Pa*).... At the time (when the realization is perfected), one sings the innate absolute song of the self-arisen wisdom Mind. You should know that this (teaching, which is) the realization of the essential point, the great freedom from falling into partialities, and (from labelling) whether it is the nature or not, is illuminated (discoursed upon) by the arising of thousands of Immaculate Rays of Light (*Dri Med A'od-Zer*) for intelligent seekers of liberation, and that he (*Longchen Rabjam*) has gone to the state of great blissful *Samantabhadra*.

THE APPEARANCES AND THE MIND ARE LIBERATED FROM THEIR ORIGIN

Reaching the Great Perfection

(i) *The object of appearances is emptiness.* [85a/1]The reflections arising in a mirror are identical to the clarity of the mirror's face. Actually these are not forms distinct from the brightness of the mirror. Likewise, all phenomena do not exist separately from emptiness.

(ii) *The mind which discriminates (the appearances) is emptiness.* [85a/5]When one is enjoying the appearances which are non-existent:

> Watch the mind which distinguishes the appearances,
> The mind is like sky, free from rejecting and accepting.
> In the sky, although the clouds gather and disappear,
> The display of the sky is non-dual and pure.
> Likewise, the nature is unstained, primordial Buddha,
> Uncreated and spontaneously accomplished nature.

The watcher mind is liberated at the (arising of the) objects and the forms of the objective appearances are cleansed. It is the perfection of the three times into the nature of space as the mind has been liberated at (the arising of) the objects. For example, when the clouds in the sky disappear, they dissolve into themselves and become invisible without going anywhere but the sky. . . . Always, all phenomena first arise from the unborn sphere, then dwell in it, and finally are liberated in it. Whatever senses arise, first they arise from the state of emptiness, the Mind, at present they dwell in it, and finally they will cease in it.

(iii) *The objects and the mind are non-dual and emptiness.* [85b/6]The appearing object [percept] (*sNang-Ba'i Yul*) and the apprehending senses [perceiver] (*'Dzin-Byed Kyi Shes-Pa*) in actuality appear like a dream but do not exist as two. So they should be understood as free from abandoning and acquiring or rejecting and accepting. . . . Therefore, by realizing whatever appears as empty of true (existents), like water in a mirage, one should train in the aimless mind (*Blo gZa'-gTad Dang Bral-Ba*), perceiving all phenomena as the same as reflections.

(iv) *Uncertainty of the objects and the aimlessness of the mind.* [86a/4]As the appearances are (manifest in) various (forms) and are not certain in any (form), the mind which apprehends them is also aimless and (it attains its) liberation in the sole impartiality, the Natural Great Perfection. . . . Reason (*rGyu-mTshan*): One should understand that all phenomena have no distinction of good or bad for one to accept or reject, since they are in fivefold equality. (i) All phenomena are equal, for their past has ceased without returning. (ii) They are equal, for their future has not yet been born, so they are not present. (iii) For the present they are equal in appearing for an unexamining mind, and if they are examined, the means of recognizing their identities will not be found. . . . (iv) The time is equal in being emptiness, since the three times do not exist as times, for they are totally unrelated (*'Brel..Med*). (v) They are equal in being unborn and not existing anywhere since they have arisen from, are dwelling in, and cease in the unborn state.

(vi) *The mind is changeless.* [87a/1]Whatever appears are delusory traces, like the arising of reflections in a mirror. . . . All phenomena, the perishable container (world) and its dependent, the perishable contained (beings), are appearing like a dream, because of one's experiences of the traces of the deluded mind, and they are not established from (the very moment of) their appearing. Hence, one has to confirm that the appearances are delusions of the mind, and the mind which grasps the appearances is emptiness, like space.... Space is changeless.... The meaning of that changelessness is peace and *nirvāṇa* from primordial time, and it is the nature of *Samantabhadra*.

Completion of All in the Great Marvelous (Nature)

(i) *The appearances and emptiness are sameness from primordial time.* 88b/1All phenomena are completed in the primordial, infinite, marvelous Great Perfection.... All phenomena transcend the elaborations of single or plural and they are nonduality of emptiness and appearances. So there is no falling into partiality, as their meaning is as the nature of space.... Space is sameness in its meaning, in the same way that the appearances (of all phenomena are) the same (*mNyam-Pa*) (in being) like a reflection in a mirror. The appearances (of all are) the same (in being) like (the reflections which) do not have a real form. They are the same in (having) just the capacity to act for the deluded mind, as both a form and its reflections have the capacity to create for the eye-consciousness the sense of apprehending the forms. They are the same in their falseness as, in the nature of nothingness, the delusory appearances appear, like the visions produced by eating *datura*. They are the same in their presence like the apparition (*sPrul-Ba*) of a cow. They are the same in their non-presence as the water in a mirage. They are the same in transcending the extremes as (having a nature) like the sphere of the vastness of space. They are the same from primordial time, in the sphere (*dBy-ings*) of ultimate nature (*Ch'os-Nyid*), which transcends rejecting and dividing and is beyond examples. It is emptiness from primordial time.

(ii) *All the assertions of the intellect are empty of entity.* 88b/1The theories of aggregates and constituents (*Phung Khams*) and so on are the assertions of the intellect (*Blos-bTags*), and as those (things) are asserted by the intellect, they do not exist as things (*Ch'os*); they are emptiness of entity. All the attributions of names do not exist either externally or internally in relation to those things. So they are adventitious (*Glo-Bur*) and non-existent. The attributions of specific characteristics to things are also pictures of the mind. Although people consider that the object of attribution is like the fire (igniting) from fuel, it is the form of delusory appearance from habituation, like a fire in a dream, and it does not exist in its nature (*gShis*). So all the phenomena which appear for deluded (mind) are appearances of mere attributions. The objects (of the aspect of appearance) from their very moment of appearance, are the same in being only false, but (in their true nature) there is no duality, neither truth nor falsehood, in them. If the appearances of the objects and the senses which apprehend them are analyzed, since they do not stain each other, there is actually no relation between them.If the objects and the subjects are analyzed, they are like space; there is no object related to and subject relating, so in reality there is no relation. Not only is there no relation (between the perceiver and perceived objects), but also the things which are designated as general and specific by our intellects do not exist with their specific characteristics (*Rang-mTshan*), because they are equal in that no improvement or decline is made by designating them as general or specific. This analysis shows that the meanings (subjects) of expressions are unrelated and that there is nothing to grasp the duality of grasped and grasper. So all the apprehensions by ignorance are delusions. (For example,) in the period of infancy (in one's mind) there are no assertions of theories and divisions, but later the experience of assertions develops, and it is an obscuration which arises by learning the wrong theories.

[89a/3]The Middle Length *Prajñāpāramitā* (*Yum Bar-Ba*) says: "Subhuti ! All phenomena are mere indications and assertions. Whatever is mere indication and assertion, that is adventitious and empty of entity."

(iii) *The mind has not been transferred and the objects have not arisen.* 89a/6In a mirror, when the reflection of a face appears, it appears without the face and its reflection becoming two or the reflection being transferred (*'Phos-Pa*) from the face to the object. Likewise, various objects of the sense-faculties appear for the six individual consciousnesses. At the time (that the objects appear to the mind), the mind does not transfer to the object because it is the forms of the object that are appearing to the sense-faculties. For example, the appearance of the face in the mirror is not that the face has been transferred to the mirror, but that the reflection or its form is appearing in the mirror. So (beings) are deluded into cyclic existence (the world) because of apprehending the forms with their intellects when they appear. If (we) analyze the meaning further, it is not established that the mind has not been transferred (to the objects) but that the forms have arisen to it; because (firstly,) the mind, to which the objects have arisen, itself does not exist externally, internally, or in between, and so the apprehender of the form does not exist. (Secondly,) if (we) analyze the form itself, its entity (*Ngo-Bo*) is non-existence, so that which arises is not established. Therefore, it is correct that the appearances are established with neither object nor subject.

In the *Mūla-madhyamakākarikā*:

> Whatever arises by depending on others,
> Is temporal, neither itself
> Nor other than it.
> Therefore, it is not nothing or eternal.

(iv) *Mind and objects are naturally liberated since they do not exist naturally.* 90a/1All (the phenomena) which appear in various (forms) are the same in not existing in (their true) nature. They are like the various dreams which are the same as the state of sleep. The intellects in which the appearances seem to be arising are the same in the state of unrecognizable being. They are like the waves which are the same as the nature of water. The mind and the appearances do not exist as two and they are the same in the ultimate nature. Similarly, shadowy (visions) and the eye-sense which apprehends them are the same in being delusions. There is nothing to analyze for anything. It is like the garden in the sky, which is beyond analysis. So (the objects and subjects) are (the same) in the nature of space.

(v) *Whoever realizes the natural liberation of whatever arises is a learned one.* [90b/2]The rivers flowing in the four directions are the same in the ocean. Likewise, *saṃsāra* and *nirvāṇa* are the same in that they are the states of mind. . . . All the changes of the four elements are not (taking place) outside of (the sphere of) space. Likewise, whatever experiences of view, meditation, activities, and effects arise, they are the same in the innate nature. . . . The arisings of rejecting and accepting thoughts in the mind are the same in emptiness because they haven't moved away from the innate wisdom. The waves are the same in (being) water. Likewise, whatever arises is the same in the unborn (nature). (That is to say) that the elaborations of the mind are (the same) in the state of Mind, and that the Mind is the state which is primordially free from projecting and withdrawing. . . . The dissolving of the thoughts into the basis is like water being poured into water.

Conclusion

(i) *Instructions on the meaning of the freedom from accepting and rejecting which has no apprehending and apprehender.* [91a/3](All phenomena) arise as the play of "as-it-is" (suchness, the absolute truth), which is pure in its essence (*Ngo-Bo*). So, contemplate upon the non-dual great bliss, transcending activities, efforts, recollection, and thoughts.

(ii) *Absence of grasping is the natural great apprehension.* [91a/5]When contemplating on it, . . .on whatever (object) one negates or affirms, at that (very) time, the natural awareness arises free from grasping and the Great Perfection will spontaneously be accomplished.

MEDITATION (PATH)

5. *Meditation on the Meaning of the View*

For meditation, having realized the view free from extremes, one contemplates on it to purify the defiled emotions and to perfect the paths and stages in order to reach the ultimate goal. Longchenpa summarizes the meditation in three categories of approach to meditation for the three intellectual levels of trainees in the eleventh chapter of *Shingta Chenpo* (SC Vol-II).

MEDITATION AFTER HAVING ASCERTAINED THE VIEW

SC II, 92b/1 After having ascertained (the meditation) by (realizing the) view, it is necessary to contemplate in the meditative state. Otherwise, one will not achieve liberation from the hosts of emotional defilements and will not be able to perfect the stages and paths. So it is certain that one should practice meditation. (The meditation) is to contemplate in the natural state, which is naturally pure like space, by the means of freedom from conceptualizations, doubts, and expectations....

(First, one) should study (the path), then ponder upon it, and after that one should enter into the practice on it, as it is necessary to generate the essential meaning in oneself.

MEDITATIONS FOR DIFFERENT LEVELS OF INTELLECT

Meditation for People of High Intellect

(i) *People of most gifted intellect attain liberation upon realization.* [93a/4]Fortunate people of most gifted intellect,who have accumulated merits in the past, attain liberation merely upon realizing the natural state of the Mind, the space-like meaning, which transcends meditation and non-meditation, due to the circumstances (of the blessings) of the *Lama*. They remain naturally in the state of the *yoga* of the stream of the Mind, all the time, with no need of meditation with effort.

(ii) *For a totally realized person, there is no meditation to be praticed.* [93b/3]When a person attains the totally realized state (*Klong-Gyur*)...because he has been liberated from attachment to (the concept of) true (existence) (*bDen-Zhen*), there will be no antidotes on which to meditate. So the realized state is meditationless. Having remained in the continuity of the absence of attachment to the true (existence), it is a (meditative) play of indefinite (character) with no intervals, transcending dimensions, and it is enjoyment of the Buddha-field of self-liberated *Samantabhadra*.... (In this meditation) there are no signs and levels, as there are (in training on) materialistic and characteristic meditations.... (In it) there are no places of deviation, as it has gone nowhere. There are no obscurations of the watcher, as it has not been watched....

The occurence of obscurations and errors: when the meditator watches the Mind, which is imperceptible by watching, that becomes itself the obscuration. Proceeding to (where there is) no place to go becomes itself the error.... By first having the certainty that one's Mind is spontaneously the real Buddha from primordial time, later one realizes that there is no need of aspiration for Buddhahood from any other source. At that very time one dwells in Buddhahood.

(iii) *For people of mediocre and lower intellect it is necessary to meditate.* [94b/6]For people who are of mediocre and lower intellect, it is necessary to meditate with great diligence, because they have not been liberated from apprehension of self(*bDag-'Dzin*), the cause of *saṃsāra*. The distinction between meditation and no-meditation is made according to whether or not (the concept of) apprehender and apprehended (subject and object) in the mind has been dissolved.

(iv) *Rightness of doing meditation.* [95a/2]As long as the arisings (in one's mind) are not self-arisen and self-liberated, all thoughts are ordinary concepts.... So they lead to rebirths in the inferior realms. ... By meditating to pacify those concepts, it is certain that wisdom, the liberation of phenomena, will arise later.

(v) *Need of uniting tranquillity and insight.* [95a/6](Root, SN:) "Tranquillity subdues the emotional defilements, insight uproots the emotional defilements...."

There are two aspects of the identities, (the sameness and separate identities of tranquillity and insight). For sameness: The aspect of abiding is the tranquillity and the aspect of clarity is the insight. The union of tranquillity and insight, the realization of clarity and emptiness free from extremes, liberates one from *saṃsāra*....

For separate identity: etymologically, the mind concentrated on the meaning of what has been learned is tranquillity and the realization of the meaning is insight. According to the meaning, being able through meditation to concentrate (the mind) one-pointedly at the beginning is tranquillity, and then realizing that (contemplation) as absence of inherent existence (*Rang-bZhin Med-Pa*) is insight.

(vi) *The reason (why the meditation is necessary).* [96a/5]For people of high intellect, just as on a golden island, even if you search, you won't find earth or stone, whatever arises is liberated into the ultimate nature (*Ch'os-Nyid*). So the antidotes have been purified into the ultimate sphere (*dByings*), and there is no longer a need for contemplative periods....

For people of mediocre intellect: after having realized the view, by contemplating without moving, in the state of birthlessness and clarity which is free from torpor and elation, like an unpolluted pond, (one) unites tranquillity and insight and dissolves the concepts into the ultimate sphere, and space-like realization arises....

For people of lesser intellect, one should meditate and tame the monkey-like wild mind, which does not abide even for a while, by means of one-pointed tranquillity. When one becomes able to concentrate, then by meditating, as the antidote, upon the discriminative insight such as emptiness, the absence of inherent existence in phenomenal existence, and by meditating that all appearances are illusions, one realizes the meaning of birthlessness.

THE WAY OF CONTEMPLATION FOR PEOPLE OF MEDIOCRE INTELLECT

Method of Meditation

(i) *Advice to contemplate on no-thought.* [97a/2]When there are strong waves in water no reflections appear, although the water has the potential of having reflection. Likewise, mind spontaneously possesses the qualities such as foreknowledge, but because of the speed of the waves of discursive thought, the qualities do not manifest. So it is important to contemplate one-pointedly.... If you contemplate, then the disturbing waves of concepts will disappear and the light of the luminous Mind-lamp will naturally shine forth. So contemplate without disturbing the mind-water.

(ii) *Body postures and the way of contemplation.* [97a/6]One should contemplate in the three unmoving states free from extremes....

(a) For a motionless body there are sevenfold physical posture: legs crossed, hands in the contemplative gesture, spine straight, tongue touching the (upper) palate, breathing slowly, eyes looking at the (level of the) tip of the nose and the neck slightly bent.

(b) For motionless sense-faculties: eyes (keep fixed) without moving and do not stop the sense-faculties of ear, nose, tongue, body, and mind. Whatever forms, sounds, smells, tastes,touch, and thought are encountered, neither block the door (of their arising) nor follow after them. If those sense-faculties are blocked, then the five (enlightened) eyes, such as the divine eyes and the six foreknowledges of the mind, which are the virtues of the purified aspect of the sense-faculties, will not be attained. If the thoughts are followed, the continuous chain of thoughts will never cease and (one will) remain indistinguishable from an ordinary person. Therefore, one should contemplate in the motionless pond of the sense-faculties with ceaseless arisings of various appearing objects (*sNang-Yul*), like reflections of the stars and planets. If the various objects are not apprehended by thoughts, then not only will the (objects of appearance) not harm (one's contemplation), but their qualities will arise. It is called "the primordial wisdom with no thoughts" (*rNam-Par Mi-rTogs-Pa'i Ye-Shes*), as the (forms) appear but there are no concepts. If there is no (appearance of) forms, then there is no intellect (that sees) them, and then there is no question of being with thoughts or without thoughts, and there won't be "the primordial wisdom with no concept." Therefore, when the objects appear to the senses, by remaining in no-thought, the master (*Lama*) of discriminative awareness attains directly the cessation of goings and comings of the thoughts, and that is designated as "the cessation of breathing." Although breathing through mouth and nose continues, thoughts will not waver. The cessation of conceptualization is designated as the death of thoughts. When there is no conceptualization, there is no need of meditation as its antidote and there is no need of wisdom, the *yoginī* of freedom from conceptualizations, which is the antidote of conceptualizations. . . .

When one perfects that essential point (of cessation of breathing), it is called the (state of) the natural or unfabricated six conciousnesses. Since the objects are appearing to the senses, the senses do not conceive the objects, and although the "senses fall to the objects" or the objects become clear (in the senses), not only do the senses not affect the contemplation, the luminous vision, but they help it to progress. . . .

(c) For a motionless mind: the contemplation (of the mind) in the freedom from extremes occurs spontanously when the body and sense-faculties are motionless. It is the contemplation unmoving from the state of clear and luminous mind free from projections and withdrawals....

At that time, if you are distracted by conceptions to the substances of the external appearing objects (*sNang-Ba'i Yul*) and to the insubstantials of the internal mind, then a tie is created which obscures the Buddha-essence, the innate Mind. So one should not have the slightest apprehension and attachment to *saṃsāra* and *nirvāṇa* as bad or good, and even to the contemplation. Thus, having no concepts of either substances or insubstantials, there will be no thoughts of any other things. At that time, all the movements of thought dissolve into the Mind, the basis (*Sems-Nyid gZhi*). Then, when the mind becomes changeless and stable, one attains liberation from *saṃsāra* and will not have attachment to oneself and others and apprehension of duality. That is the attainment of the excellent Ultimate Body, transcendent to elaborations, conceptions, and expressions.

(iii) *Way of developing virtues.* [99a/2]When contemplating (in that way), all the conceptualizations will be freed.... Then as the conceptions are transcended in the ultimate nature (*Ch'os-Nyid*) and all the thoughts are dissolved into the (ultimate) sphere, there arises the Luminous Great Perfection (*A'od-gSal rDzogs-Pa Ch'en-Po*), the realization of one-tasteness as the *Dharmakāya*, which transcends the signs and significances of bliss, clarity and no-thought with their experiences (*Nyams*).

(iv) *Realization of the ultimate nature.* [99b/2]At the time of arising of the self-arisen innate primordial wisdom in the mind of the *yogi*, ...he sees completely the inseparable identity of emptiness and the appearances as the eight illusory examples, and the ultimate nature of phenomena, the unborn nature.... The Mind arises as the play of non-duality of *saṃsāra* and *nirvāṇa*, the primordial wisdom of transcending existence and non-existence, and the changelessness of clarity.... At that time, the primordial wisdom which is non-dual in respect to the objects to be known and the knower intellect arises in the equalness (state).

(v) *It is the direct cause of the primordial wisdom of the noble ones.* [100a/3]After immense progress in the experiences of the primordial wisdom of non-conceptualization, as the result of deeds, the high attainments such as the Path of Insight will be achieved spontaneously.

Method of Contemplation

(i) *Contemplation in (the state of) unwaveringness and non-conceptualization.* [100a/6]In the sky-like Mind, by letting the thoughts of the mental events remain naturally (*Rang-Sor bZhag*), they dissolve (*Dengs-Pa*) like clouds disappearing (in the sky). One should contemplate in the state of that view, the nature of the example (the sky), without wavering.

(ii) *Contemplation in clearness and clarity without pollutions.* [100b/3]Contemplate with clarity in the state which is unpolluted by concepts of apprehender and apprehended and in clarity without torpor and in calmness without elation, like a peaceful ocean, that remains where it is.

(iii) *Contemplation without partiality, like space.* [100b/6]Contemplate in the state of the Mind, which is emptiness from its origin like space, without projections and withdrawals of thoughts.

(iv) *Contemplating naturally and effortlessly.* [101a/3]Contemplate on the mind in the state of changelessness like Mt. Meru, without (any concept of) preventing or defending and expectation or doubt.

(v) *Contemplation of the objects of appearances without ceasing.* [101a/6]In the state of purity and clarity of mind, contemplate on the objects of appearances (which appear) before the senses, vividly without concepts of apprehending or wavering.

(vi) *Contemplation in the originally liberated clarity and purity.* [101b/3]Contemplate in the vivid clarity and purity without torpor or elation.... Contemplating thus, one will realize the appearances as emptiness, like rainbow lights.

(vii) *Contemplation in one-pointedness like an archer.* [101b/6]Contemplate on the mind in the state of ultimate nature, nakedly and straight, without wavering, like aiming an arrow straight.

(viii) *Contemplation in effortlessness and spontaneity.* 102a/2(First) having confidence (in the realization of) the Ultimate Body in its own place by contemplating the mind naturally, later contemplate by relaxing in the state of freedom from expectations and doubts.... There is no need of very active recollection, but of relaxing the three doors naturally and merely remaining,without wandering. Even if the (mind) is freely distracted, since it has fallen into the ordinary state (of mind), contemplate naturally in the ordinary mind (*Tha-Mal-Gyi Shes-Pa*) without wavering.

(ix) *Conclusion of the eight ways of contemplation.* 102b/4(In those contemplations) there is no apprehended and apprehender, so they are the naturally pure contemplations. They are the union of tranquillity and insight. Although it is said that the aspect of their abiding in "what it is" is tranquillity and the aspect of their clarity is insight, (actually) they are indivisible, and it is called the union. At that point, having no distinctions of either aspect, the concept of tranquillity subsides and the insight is no longer conceived as insight. It is the indivisible, the innate union.

The Progress of the Path in Seven Aspects

(i) *The way of seeing the inexpressible (state) through eight contemplations.* 103a/1Explanation of the progress of the path through four levels of primordial wisdom as the result of contemplation.... Having pacified the penetrations of the intellect into the state of Mind which transcends thoughts and expressions, the arising for the first time of the clear, bright and changeless primordial wisdom is (1) the "manifesting primordial wisdom" (*sNang-Ba'i Ye-Shes; i.e., the Path of Accumulations*). It is the perfection of the luminous primordial wisdom.

(ii) *Signs of attainment of the path of liberation.* 103a/6Having realized, (1) the luminous "manifesting primordial wisdom," one has recognized the Mind, the innate wisdom. By having entered the path of liberation, the seed of enlightenment has been sown (in oneself).... When a person recognizes the

Mind, "the luminous ground primordial wisdom" (*A'od-gSal gZhi'i Ye-Shes*), the adventitious thoughts are liberated instantly and the son and mother luminescences are unified. Because all the activities have become solely virtues, he becomes free from attachment to various phenomena, the five external objects and the internal recollecting and aware mind of negating and affirming (thoughts). Through the state of self-clarity and emptiness mind, he enjoys the virtues of developing compassion toward all living beings without distinctions of distance and dimensions. He also inspires others to virtuous (activities). He renounces distractions and entertainments and enjoys solitude in mountains and forests. Even in his dreams, there will be only pure, virtuous thoughts. Because his body, speech, and mind are highly trained, he develops the qualities of the "Path of Accumulation" and sees various luminous visions in his meditation cell.

(iii) *Primordial wisdom of progress.* [104a/5]When one has made great progress in the experiences through the previous meditation, and the obscurations to emptiness and clarity mind, "spontaneously accomplished primordial wisdom" (*Rang-Byung Gi Ye-Shes*), have been reduced, wisdom, contemplation and experiences become powerful. The external appearances will spontaneously be seen as dreams and illusions. The realization of (seeing) various phenomena as having the same taste will arise and remain in the space-like state. It is (2) the "primordial wisdom of progress" (*mCh'ed-Pa'i Ye-Shes*, i.e., Path of Application).

(iv) *The signs of attianment of heat.* [104b/3](At that time,) as the realization is extraordinarily immaculate, one attains extraordinary signs of pliancy (*Shin-sByang*) of body and mind. Remaining day and night in the united extraordinary contemplation, one cannot possibly be separated from it. Because of compassion one acts for the benefit of living beings and develops uncommon revulsion and definite emergence from *saṃsāra*. Even in dreams, one sees phenomena as dreams and illusions and so on. There will be no worm inside the body nor lice and their eggs upon it. These are the attainments of

the signs of the "Path of Application" (*sByor-Lam*), and one soon reaches the "Path of Seeing (*mThong-Lam*)."
(v) *The realized noble primordial wisdom.* [105a/2]Having first seen the Mind, the uncontaminated (*Zag-Med*) luminous primordial wisdom, one attains what is known as the (3) "realized primordial wisdom" (*Thob-Pa Zhes-Bya-Ba'i Ye-Shes*). (At that time,) the hundred-petalled (*'Dab-Ma*) air which dwells in the *cakras* of the heart will be purified. The wisdom of clear essence (*Khams Dangs-Ma*) becomes highly luminous, and by radiating other *cakras* too, 1200 virtuous (aspect of) air and mental (events) will be stabilized and 1200 emotional airs will cease. Then (as a result) according to *tantras*, the primordially present pure lands appear in (one's) internal essence (*Nang Gi Khams*). According to *Sūtras*, the external pure lands, such as the faces of hundreds of Buddhas, appear (before him). One will achieve a great many more pure and unobscured eyes and foreknowledges than the eyes and foreknowledges of ordinary beings (*So-So'i sKye-Bo*), which have obscurations and limitations of the stages. One has been liberated from the emotional defilements of imagination, the "objects of abandonment of the Path of Seeing" (*mThong-Bas sPang-Bya*), and has actualized primordial wisdom, the luminous vision.
(vi) *By training in what has been realized, the primordial wisdom arises.* [105b/3]To train in what has already been seen (in the path of insight) is the "path of meditation" (*bsGom-Pa'i Lam*). One attains lower, middle and higher (cycles of this path), and in each stage one achieves the previously mentioned virtues manyfold and acts for the benefit of living beings. From the attainment of the first through the seventh stage, there will be concepts during the off-meditation periods and differences between meditation and off-meditation. In the three pure stages (eighth-tenth), as there are no direct (*mNgon-Gyur*) thoughts, there is the unification (of meditation and off-meditation), and here everything is one taste in the very primordial wisdom.
(vii) *Full perfection, the completion of the noble path.* [106a/1]The primordial wisdom of the "meditation path" is called the "fully realized primordial wisdom" (*Nye-Bar Thob-Pa'i Ye-Shes*).

Having meditated upon the eight noble paths, one has purified the defilements of the nine stages (of the meditation path). Generally, the virtues of the path and stages appear by relying on the proper veins, air, and essence. The accumulations of merits and primordial wisdom are generated through the perfections (of veins, air, and essence) and through the efforts of training in their perfection.

(The Path for) People of Lesser Intellect

(i) *The stages of meditation.*

(a) TRANQUILLITY (*Zhi-gNas*)

(1) TAMING THE THOUGHTS

[110b/1]First (the question) is how to find tranquillity.... One should contemplate in a place where there are no thorns (disturbances) of contemplation, such as danger from people, entertainments, and noise, but where the mind will naturally be able to relax. Sit on a comfortable seat in the crossed-legged posture, cover the knees with the palms and visualize the three channels (in the body). While exhaling, think that one exhales through the white *Roma* channel on the right (side of the body) and then the right nostril, and that all the sickness, harmful effects, and unvirtuous obscurations are cleared like smoke going out a chimney. While inhaling, think that the absorptions of the Buddhas, in the form of light have entered through the left nostril, the red *Kyangma* (channel at the left side of the body) and then have emerged into the central channel. For a little while, hold the breath (directly) below the navel (by pushing the breath a bit) both downwards and upwards. Then slowly exhale as before, but hold in a little (of the remaining breath). During the three spring months, the air is earth-air, and it is the time that phlegm develops. So, as its antidote, one should visualize it as air-of-air in green. During the three summer months, to dispel the heat-of-fire, visualize it as water-air in white. During the three autumn months, to dispel the movements of the bile, visualize it as earth-air in yellow. During the three winter months, as the antidote of coldness-of-water, visualize it as fire-air in red. For the shape of the air, visualize the essence of the mind and air in the designs of a bow, triangle, circle, and square in the heart. (Visualize them) as having the same feeling. For the number (of breaths): count up to seven cycles in the mind. A beginner should visualize the air in the form of a square and so forth, and while emitting it through the nostrils, it gradually grows bigger till it becomes the size of the three thousand world system, and so on. One should contemplate on it without one's mind wavering. When the elements are congested, it should be overcome by saying a forceful Ha! without holding in any breath. When bliss and devotion, and so forth, arise, one should hold in the breath (for a while). By practicing breathing for a few days and nights, the tranquillity of clear and radiant mind without concepts will arise. At that time, as there will be no moment of gross air and there are no thoughts, the white and red moon and sun, the essence of the *Roma* and *Kyangma* channels, will become stable. In that (stability), there will not be (even a) subtle movement of air, because one remains in the state of no-thought in the central channel and thereby realizes the innate primordial wisdom.

(2) ONE-POINTED CONCENTRATION

[111a/4]After suppressing the gross thoughts, . . .one should train in the four boundless states of mind, such as loving-kindness, and in the two minds of enlightenment, which are aspirations and practice. The *Bodhicaryāvatāra* says: "Having pacified the thoughts, meditate on the Mind of Enlightenment." Or concentrate on the developing stage or on (objects such as) volumes and paintings of deities. The *Samādhirāja-sūtra* says: "On the golden color of the image beautifying the world, whoever focuses his mind is a *Bodhisattva* who is in contemplation." Briefly, a person who has not yet become experienced in the meditation of "no-thought" should contemplate on any virtuous objects without deviating to any other objects.

(3) THE ACTUAL ABSORPTION OF TRANQUILLITY

[111b/4]When there is no projection of thoughts as long as one doesn't abandon the contemplation of concentrating on the object, mind and body are at ease, speech is lessened, words become gentle and the complexion becomes rich; then one has accomplished the one-pointed tranquillity.

(b) INSIGHT (Lhag-mThong)

(1) WAY OF TRAINING IN INSIGHT

[112a/2]Meditate on (perceiving phenomena as) non-existent from their origin but appearing like the eight illusory examples.... In their true meaning, all things, the world and beings, which are the impure perceptions of the deluded mind, and the triple gem, which are the pure perceptions, are non-existent like a dream. But in the deluded mind they appear because of the accumulation of habituations. All appearances seem to be true, but they are false since they appear to the dualistic perceptions.... The Buddhas who have appeared to the deluded perceptions are false, as they have the nature of manifested bodies like reflections of the moon in water, and as they are appearances (for ordinary people), while (the Buddhas themselves) do not descend from the spheres of the Ultimate Body and the Enjoyment Body. The pure nature of the Buddhas, however, which is present in the unexcelled pure sphere, is not false. Because of deluded thoughts, it seems that one wanders in *saṃsāra* during one life after another and experiences successive suffering and happiness, and that one goes through successive lives. But at that very moment (of wandering), according to the view of the unborn state of the Mind, there is no distinction between wandering or not wandering in *saṃsāra*. The dream-like appearances of delusion are non-existent at the very time of their appearing during the sleep of delusory habituations....

Briefly, the phenomena of appearance and imputation

are non-existent but appear like the eight examples of illusion. One should contemplate upon this with clarity but no apprehensions.

(2) WAY OF ARISING OF INSIGHT

113a/2It is the meditation of (seeing all) as space without having any conceptualization even of the perception (of things) as illusions. . . . Even the (view of) "appearing but being unreal" (*sNang-La bDen-Par Med-Pa*) is itself a (mere) assertion. In meaning, it (the nature) is not an object of conceptualizations about whether it exists or not in its true nature. So one should contemplate on this meaning. By this practice, the thought of viewing external phenomena as true or as untrue like illusions will also be arrested. So, when one realizes the non-conceptualization of the objects of apprehension, since the thought of apprehended, the aspect of the attachment (to the object also) does not exist, subsequently (*Zhar-La*) one realizes the non-existence of the apprehender. Contemplate on the realization of the nature of non-existence of any entities and the nature of the transcending of concepts.

(ii) *Analysis of contemplation.*

(a) ANALYSIS OF THE MIND

113b/6In the mind, when the chain of thoughts of liking and disliking, true, and false, and happiness and unhappiness arises, one should make efforts to examine it without wavering even for a moment: where did the thoughts come from at the beginning, where do they remain now, where do they go in the end, what are their color, design, and characteristics?

(b) WAY OF SEEING THE NATURE

114a/6Perceiving the existence of the mind is a pollution by thoughts. Because in its (true) meaning it has no existence, (mind) has no cause of arising. So it is empty of the cause of arising. There is nothing which exists because nothing has been born. So the presence (of the mind) is emptiness of entity. As (the mind) is not present, there is nothing to cease. So the cessation (of the mind) is empty of characteristics. (Mind) has no color, design, and there is nothing to be shown or to find, even if one examines it and searches thoroughly outside, inside, or in between. This not finding (the mind) is a space-like state, clear, equal, free from designations and analysis, and detached from actor and acted upon. It is the vision of the nature of the Ultimate Body.

(c) CONTEMPLATION IN RELAXED STATE

114b/5 Like resting after exhaustion from carrying heavy loads, it is, by abandoning the past experiences of applying gross and subtle analyses, to be in total ease, like reaching the goal or the resting place when one has been totally exhausted. In accordance with this tradition, contemplate by remaining in total ease through relaxation, in the state in which all appearances show clearly, fully and perfectly, free from any memories or thoughts and without the ceasing of the natural glow (*mDangs*) of awareness and bliss.... Generally, it is natural that if you meditate and concentrate the mind one-pointedly, the mind projects. If you ease the mind, thinking "Go wherever you like to go," it will remain as it is, like a camel.... When you let the mind go, saying, "Do not return even for a while," even if it seems to have gone, it will return inwardly and remain as the self-dwelling emptiness. It is like a crow in a boat.... While the mind is being projected to the objects such as forms, since the objects are unreal, the mind will not continue to rely on them even for a moment. The mind will return and remain in the emptiness free from bonds of analysis. For example, a crow flying from a boat in the ocean will not land on other objects but will come down on the boat itself.

(d) WAY OF ARISING OF THE REALIZATION

115b/1 By gaining experience in the significance of not finding the thought of attachment to "I" and "self" by investigation, one realizes the non-existence of the apprehender "self of person" and thereby (one realizes) the non-existence of the apprehender [subject]. One has already realized (in the previous lessons) the non-existence of the "self of phenomena," since the apprehended (object) is non-existence in its essence. After realizing the two emptinesses of self, both the objects among which one takes *saṃsāric* birth and the subject who takes birth are established as non-existent. The liberation of *saṃsāra* as the non-existent in true nature (*'Khor-Ba Rang-bZhin Med-Pa*) is the attainment of the vision of *nirvāṇa*, because *saṃsāra* is nothing else than mind. . . . If one realizes thus, even if one could not attain liberation in this life, it is certain that one will do so in the next one. . . . It is like "the *karma* of definite effect," by which, if one has committed a grave evil or a virtuous act, it is impossible that one will not experience its effects in the next life.

(e) ATTAINMENT OF STABILITY (IN TRANQUILLITY AND INSIGHT)

[116a/1]When the reflection of the moon appears in a pond, the water and the reflection of the moon are inseparable. Likewise, when (things) appear (before the mind) and when they are being apprehended (by mind), the mind is inseparable (from the appearances). It should be understood that the appearances (before the mind) are the apprehended (phenomena) (*gZung-Ba*) and not the appearing objects (*sNang-Yul*). The object of appearances and its emptiness are inseparable like water and the (reflection) of the moon in water.

(f) HOW TO LEARN THE MEANING OF NON-DUALITY

[116a/4]By apprehending the non-existent object as self, one deludes (oneself) into *saṃsāra*, just as by perceiving water in a dream as fearful, fear is further aggravated. The creations of the stabilized habits of delusory perceptions are non-established (nothing but delusions). The basis of the arising of delusions, the mind, is naturally pure and its entity is non-existent. So it is never stained by defilements. . . . One should contemplate in the space-like unstained primordial wisdom, the core undefiled by extremes and the essence free from conceptualizations, without any search by examining or analyzing. If you search, the Mind will be defiled and thereby worldly thoughts (*Kun-rTog*) will increase. If you keep a poisonous snake in a cage by itself it won't harm (anyone), but if you harass it, it will. Likewise, the mind (itself) is free from efforts, acceptances, and abandonments.

(g) WAY OF REALIZING THE MIDDLE PATH, FREE FROM EXTREMES

116b/6(Thereby) one pacifies the defilements of emotions, and through the non-conceptualizing absorption of primordial wisdom, which is free from duality of apprehended and apprehender, one achieves the eyes and foreknowledges (etc.),the virtues of realization and liberation.

(h) THE FREEDOM FROM MEDITATION AND MEDITATOR IS THE REALIZATION OF THE BUDDHA.

117a/3While a person is in contemplation, although the appearing object (*sNang-Yul*) appears, there is nothing in his mind but remaining in the space-like absence of projections and withdrawals. So for him there is no concept of apprehender(*'Dzin-Pa*). That is the non-dual primordial wisdom, since the concept of dual nature has not been applied, and it is the liberation from creator and creation since there is no duality of meditator and meditation. At that time, one reaches the natural primordial sphere by dissolving the mind and mental events into the ultimate sphere, and one dwells in the realization of Mind, the absolute Buddha, the self-presence of the Ultimate Body. . . . At that time, the mind and mental events have dissolved in the natural purity of the Mind, like salt dissolving in water, and no more thoughts are flickering.

(i) WAY OF REALIZING THE ULTIMATE NATURE

117b/3By realizing the five external apprehended objects as reflections of the moon and as a mirage (*Mig-Yor*), there won't be the slightest tendency to cling by apprehended concepts to the (objects as) true. By realizing the internal apprehending senses as partless like space, the apprehender (subject) of them is emptiness in its entity. The sense which is natural, absence of apprehender and apprehended (object), and free from projections and withdrawal is the nectar-like perfection of wisdom. It is profound, peace, freedom, natural luminescence and self-discriminating primordial wisdom.... It is the perfection of wisdom in which there is no *saṃsāra* here, *nirvāṇa* there, or the path of training between.

(j) WAY OF COMPLETION OF THE VIEW

[118a/2]Dwelling in the boat-like state of realization of the meaning of the great vast view, one crosses the *saṃsāric* ocean of conceptualization, and then without conceptions unifies one's intellect with the ground which is primordially free from conceptualizations. Because the ultimate sphere and wisdom have become inseparable, it is called the state of Great Perfection, and so it is called the perfection of it (the Great Perfection). It is the arising of the realization of the total perfection of self-arisen and uncreated meaning.

(k) RECOGNITION OF THE PERFECT TRANQUILLITY AND INSIGHT

[118a/5]When one contemplates thus, the mind dwells naturally with no projections and withdrawals.The aspect of no-thought and emptiness due to abiding (in contemplation) is the tranquillity. It is the accomplishment of the accumulation of primordial wisdom and the perfection stage of wisdom, the cause of the Ultimate Body. The aspect of appearances due to clarity is the insight. It is the accomplishment of the accumulation of merits and the development stage of skillful means, the cause of the Form Body. At that time one completes the six absolute perfections, the freedom from conceptualization..... The training on giving, and so forth, is the abiding in them and it is not the perfection or going beyond them. When the *Bodhisattva* transcends them, it becomes the perfection of them. At that time, one perfects the absolute discipline. In *Ārya-susthitamatidevaputra-paripṛcchā-nāma-mahāyāna-sūtra* it is said: "In whom there is no concept of discipline nor stains of discipline (*Tshul-Khrims*), there is the perfection of discipline."

(l) THE FUNCTION OF TRANQUILLITY AND INSIGHT

119a/5 Gaining experience (*'Dris-Pa*) in the previously realized insight depends on tranquillity. So one should certainly make efforts to accomplish the union (of tranquillity and insight).

(m) THE TIME OF REALIZING NON-CONCEPTUALIZATION AFTER GAINING EXPERIENCE

119b/1 While practicing on the perfect meaning, to realize that the subjects and objects and the substances and non-substances (*dNgos Dang dNgos-Med*) are absence of inherent existence (*Rang-bZhin Med-Pa*) is the insight, which comes first. To remain in the state of that realization with no arising of forms in the intellect is the tranquillity, which comes later. When the sphere (*dByings*) and the primordial wisdom (*Ye-Shes*) become inseparable, their inseparability should be known as the attainment of the result of the union.

(iii) *Having gained experience, the way of perfecting the contemplation.*

(a) THE VIRTUES OF THE CONTEMPLATION

119b/4 In mind the virtues are present primordially, but while the mind has been covered by obscurations the virtues do not manifest. By meditating on tranquillity and insight, one purifies certain obscurations (such as adventitious concepts) and achieves temporary attainments. When the mental concepts are dissolved into the ultimate sphere (*dByings*), . . . because of having purified the mental concepts, for the time being one achieves many virtues, such as the absorptions (*sNyom-'Jug*).

(b) THE NINE ABSORPTIONS

[120a/3]The nine absorptions are the mind of cessation, four levels of absorptions (of the form realm), and four levels of the formless realm. They are the nine contemplations, the perfections of nine absorptions....

The one-pointed mind with the wisdom of bliss, clarity, and no-thought is achieved in the life of beings of the desire realm, such as human beings, through the training on tranquillity and insight, as explained earlier. It is achieved by means of precious human (*Dal-'Byor*) life, and that is why it is connected to human beings.... The mind of (four) absorptions (of the form realms): (1) First absorption: When one practices one-pointed contemplation, the preliminary (*Nyer-lDog*) is the ability (to contemplate). It will (start) with the (gross) thought that I should contemplate, and through the application (*sByor-Ba*) of analytic (subtle thoughts) recollections for contemplating in the state of no-thought, the wisdom free from conceptions, the actual (*dNgos-gZhi*) meditation arises. During the off-meditation period, one will have both (gross) thoughts and analysis (subtle thoughts). (2) Second absorption: Through the preliminaries of the mental (stage) of the first absorption and by the application of no-(gross) thoughts but analysis (subtle thoughts), the actual absorption of clarity and no-concepts arises. (3) Third absorption: Through the preliminaries of the mental (stage) of the second absorption and (by the application of) absence of (gross) thoughts and analysis (subtle thoughts), the extraordinary actual absorption of no-concepts arises directly. (4) Fourth absorption: Through the preliminaries of the mental (stage) of the third absorption (and by the application of the) contemplations, the extraordinary actual absorption of joy and bliss arises. *Yum-Bar-Ba* [*Middle Length Prajñāpāramitā-sūtra*] says:

> "An absorption with (gross) thoughts and analysis (subtle thoughts) is the first absorption. With analysis but no thoughts is the second absorption.With neither

thoughts nor analysis in the mind is the third absorption. Joyous mind is the fourth absorption.

(c) ATTAINMENT OF THE MIND OF THE ABSORPTIONS (OF THE FORMLESS REALMS)

121a/3By means of the mind of (the four) absorptions (of the form realms) the extraordinary minds of (the four) formless realms are generated. (1) The first is the (contemplative) state of space-like infinity. It is a stable conceptualization (*Yid-La Byed-Pa*) that the nature of all phenomena is pure and unstained like space (and the contemplating in it one-pointedly). (2) The state of infinity of consciousness. It conceptualizes that even the space-like infinity is mere mind and that mind (consciousness) is infinite, free from beginning and end. (3) The state of nothingness. It is the conception which does not observe even the infinity of consciousness and (in which) nothing is seen by the mind. (4) The state of the summit of existence (the world). It conceptualizes the transcendence of both extremes of existing and non-existing (non-predication).

The state of cessation: It is the cessation of all conceptualizations (*sPros-Pa*). . . . There are two cessations: the individual analytical cessation (*So-Sor brTags-Pa'i 'Gog-Pa*) (is attained through) discriminations and analysis by the mind. The non-analytical cessation (*brTags-Min 'Gog*) (is attained through) contemplating on the ultimate nature with no (mental) discriminations. In the case of the cessation (attained by the) *Bodhisattvas*, they (still) serve living beings through (the power of) their compassion. . . .

Question: (if he has compassion,) then how could he be free from conceptualizations?

Answer: There are no conceptualizations because he possesses the compassion of the wisdom of no-concepts.

(d) METHODS OF TRAINING IN THE NINE ABSORPTIONS

122a/3By meditating on the final contemplations, one discovers the (five) divine eyes and (six) foreknowledges which he did not possess. He will see different stages of Buddha-fields and Buddha-virtues as he advances in his attainment of the stages of the path. He receives teachings and perfects his accumulations.

(e) THE TIME OF ATTAINMENT OF THE THREE CONTEMPLATIONS

[123a/3]The single sun is known (by many names such as) "the illuminator" as it dispels darkness, "the thousand lights one" as it projects rays of brightness, and "the friend of the lotus" as it causes the lotus to open. Likewise, the contemplation is known (by the names) "the illusion-like contemplation," as it is the one-pointed contemplation on the realization of the appearances as illusions, "the moon-like unstained contemplation," as it dispels the darkness and pain of emotions, "the space-like unobscured contemplation," as it is the realization of all phenomena as space, and so on. The contemplation is of the same nature (*rDzas*), but in accordance with its progress, its virtues are increased and hundreds of thousands of more virtues will be obtained.

(f) ATTAINMENT OF THE UNITED CONTEMPLATION

[123b/1]The words and meanings of the Dharma are realized perfectly by discriminative insight, and they are maintained one-pointedly in the mind by tranquillity. So the insight is the recollection (*gZungs*, i.e., realization) and the tranquillity is the contemplation (*Ting-Nge 'Dzin*). In Ye-Shes rGyas-Pa it is said:

> Insight is the recollection (realization) of the Dharma,
> Tranquillity is the contemplation."

6. *Twenty-seven Courses of Training in Dzogpa Chenpo*

In *The Meaning Instructions on Three Virtues of Relaxation in the Natural State of The Mind* (BL), Longchen Rabjam presents a hundred and forty-one courses of training divided into three chapters. The first chapter is on outer common teachings of *Sūtra*, the second is on inner esoteric teachings of *Tantra*, and the third chapter is on the innermost resultant teachings of the Great Perfection (*rDzogs Pa Ch'en Po*). The following is an abridged translation of the third chapter, which has twenty-seven courses of training.

IDENTIFICATION (OF THE BASIS) THROUGH (UNDERSTANDING THE) VIEW.

The External Apprehended Objects Are Non-Existent Emptiness

(i) The appearances are unreal reflections like the eight examples of illusion. BL 44a/4Every aspect of the five objects, such as form, included in the phenomena of the world and beings, are mere appearances with no true existence. All the appearances which have appeared to both the pure perceptions of the Buddhas and the impure perceptions of deluded beings are the percepts of wisdom and the mind. While the appearances are appearing to both perceptions,they are appearing with no inherent existence(*Rang-bZhin*), like a reflection in a mirror and rainbow rays in the sky. To the pure perception of wisdom the (appearances) transcend the extremes of existing and

non-existing as there are no stains of apprehender and apprehended. As there is no creating, ceasing, and changing, all are free from the characteristics of compounded phenomena, the appearances of uncompounded emptiness-form, and are totally free from conceptualizations. To the perception of the deluded mind, (the appearances) merely appear as the object of apprehension of self (*bDag-'Dzin*), which have fallen into the extreme (concepts) of existing or non-existing, are detached from the characteristics of uncompounded (nature), and have strengthened the habituations of adventitious and circumstantial self-perceptions. So, here, one will understand that the objects, the delusory appearances of the mind, are unreal. Various external appearances, such as white and red, are merely the percepts of rigid habits, like a dream created by the drunkenness of ignorant sleep. There is not the slightest existence (in them) as the object in the (true) meaning. Also, those appearances are not mind from the very point of their arising, because their substantial characteristics, such as color, size, and distinctions, negate the character of the mind. At the same time, they are not other than the mind, because, in addition to their being merely the delusory perceptions (of the mind), no other object has ever been established as such. The appearances to the mind are just types of experience of rigid habits continuing from beginningless time. It is like dreaming last night about a magic show one has seen yesterday. Therefore, one should think that whatever appears are appearances of non-existence, and are without foundation, abiding place, natural existence, and recognizable (entity).They are merely a clear appearance of the empty nature like a dream, magical display, mirage, echo, shadowy view (*Mig-Yor*), water-moon (reflection), miracle, and the city of smell-eaters (a spirit world). Whatever appears, self or others, enemies or friends, countries or towns, places or houses, food or drink or wealth, and whatever one does, eating or sleeping, walking or sitting, one should train in seeing them as unreal. One should devote oneself to this training in all its aspects: the preliminary, actual, and concluding practices.

(ii) *The objects, if analyzed, are emptiness.* [45a/3]If the appearances are examined from gross to subtle down to atoms, they are partless and non-existent. So form is emptiness. (Likewise,) by examining color and recognition of sound, it (will be found to be) emptiness. By examining the form and essence of smell, it (will be found to be) emptiness. By examining the aspects of taste, they (will be found to be) emptiness. Especially, by examining the sources (sense-objects), the emptiness of touch will be reached. Although they are different in appearance, they are the same in their nature in being emptiness, so the emptiness of various objects are not separate categories. Their nature, like pure space, transcends being either separate or the same. So the nature of objective appearances is emptiness in its essence.

The Apprehender Has No Foundation and No Root

(i) *The consciousnesses are self-clarity without foundation.* [45b/1](There are eight consciousnesses.) The five sense-consciousnesses arise as the five objects such as form, the mind-consciousness cognizes the general impression (of the appearing objects) and designates them as the objects, the defiled-mind-consciousness is the sense of negating, accepting, hating and disliking (etc.), the mind-consciousness arises after the six consciousnesses (five senses and universal ground consciousness), . . .and the consciousness of universal ground is self-clarity (*Rang-gSal*) and no thought and is unrelated to the objects: these are the eight or six consciousnesses. At the (very) time of (functioning of any of) those consciousnesses themselves, whatever consciousness it is, it is clear, vivid, and self-clarity with no foundations. Although they appear clear, there is no substantial entity. They are appearing without existence, like clear space and a breeze with no dust. Their clarity is present naturally like the sky without clouds. Their movements are like wind, not in distinguishable substances. From the (very) time of appearing, (the consciousnesses) as the apprehenders are self-clarity and unrecognizable. Watch them when they are arising and when they are abiding. Relax naturally and watch the manner of appearing of the apprehender. Thereby one will realize the apprehenders as having the nature of merely an appearance of clarity with no existence, emptiness with no bias, and self-clarity with no foundation.

(ii) (*The subject*), *if analyzed, is emptiness without root.* [45b/6]By analyzing (whether) the self-clear, baseless mind (exists) in the external appearances, inner physical body, or intermediate movements, or if the entity of the self-dwelling mind itself (can be) recognized in (its) design, color, birth, cessation, and abiding, one will realize that its nature is non-existence, baseless and free from the extremes of either existence or non-existence. In this training the devotion to the Lama is the only important thing.

PROLONGING THE STATE OF (REALIZATION OF THE VIEW) BY CONTEMPLATION

Outline of the Contemplation (for the People) of Three Levels of Intellect

(i) *The level (of contemplation) for people of lesser intellect.*

(a) SEEKING TRANQUILLITY

(1) TAMING THE THOUGHTS

[46a/4]First one should practice *Guruyoga*. Then sit in the seven-fold *Vairocana* posture. In particular, the palms should cover the knees and the neck should be held straight. Visualize the three channels (in the body), and when you exhale, from the lower ends of the *Roma* and *Kyangma* channels send out the luminous air like a twisted smoky thread of (various colors and natures): white and clear, blue and spreading, red and deep, yellow and clear, green and rich, and blue and gray. When you inhale, count to five in your mind. Thus, by completing a rosary (108 cycles of breathing), the gross thoughts will be pacified.

(2) CONCENTRATION OF MIND

[46b/2]Keep an object such as an image, a book, a pebble, or a piece of wood in front of you. Remain watching the object without moving and concentrate on it without distractions. While concentrating, whatever animosity, smells, thoughts, or so on arise, cut them off and let them go. Watch the object of concentration with a blank mind. If the mind remains one-pointed, then meditate one-pointedly by closing the eyes, and concentrate on the form of the object of concentration (imprinted in the mind). If the mind becomes distracted, open your eyes and concentrate directly on the object itself. By practising in that way, develop tranquillity of mind, concentration on the appearances of the five objects of the five senses and phenomena (*Ch'os*), the object of mind.

(3) CONCENTRATION ON SOUND AND THE REST

46b/5 Likewise, one should train on sound.... Contemplate by concentrating one's ear one-pointedly on the sound of people, wind, or dogs, and so forth. Again, contemplate by turning inwardly, stop listening to the actual sound and listen to the imprinted sound. By repeating those (two) trainings (on sound) alternately, one will perfect the concentration on sound. In the same way, practice on smell, taste, and touch using the same techniques. By training in those practices, later, when one contemplates (on any meditation), the five objects will not be distractions but supports. So it is very important.

(4) TRAINING ON *DHARMA*

47a/1 Visualize oneself as a deity and contemplate in that state without wavering. When one becomes able to maintain the concentration one-pointedly, change the (way of) contemplation to such (subjects) as blessing beings by projection and withdrawal (*'Phro-'Du*) of rays of light, or the four boundless meditations, such as loving kindness (compassion, joy, and equanimity) towards beings, focusing on those meditations with clear and one-pointed mind without wavering. By repeating the two trainings (the mere concentration and the blessing of beings) alternately, one will develop tranquillity in maintaining the concentration on equalness in (circumstances of both) projecting and abiding (*'Phro gNas*) (of the mind).

(b) DEVELOPING INSIGHT

(1) CONTEMPLATING IN THE EQUAL STATE OF SPACE-LIKE ABSENCE OF EXTERNAL APPREHENDED OBJECTS

47a/4 Various appearing objects are manifesting as dreams and magic, but if analyzed down to partless atoms, they are (seen to be) emptiness, as they do not exist. So contemplate naturally in the state of self-clarity and emptiness (of the objects) as well as of the apprehending senses, which comprehend the percepts of the objects. This is an important point for realizing the no-self of the objects and perceptions (*gZung-Ba'i Shes-Pa*).

(2) THE INNER APPREHENDER IS ROOTLESS AND IS EMPTINESS

47b/1 When one searches for the nature of the mind, which comprehends (phenomena) as objects and subjects, one will not find that it has any extistence, past or present, material or immaterial, coming, abiding and going, or color and design, and so on. At that point, remain naturally in the state of baseless mind without apprehension. This will bring the realization of the emptiness of apprehending as "I" and "self."

(3) CONTEMPLATION ON THE UNION (OF TRANQUILLITY AND INSIGHT)

47b/3 This is the unified training of tranquillity and insight, whereas in the previous training they were practiced separately. . . . Whatever appears (in the mind), contemplate in the state that is naturally even, blissfully smooth, tracelessly clear, vastly free, and limitlessly open without any bounds of analysis. At that time the space-like realization arises, which has no (distinction of) outer, inner, or between. It is spontaneous accomplishment of tranquillity as it is abiding, of insight as it is clear, and of single union as it is inseparable.

(ii) *The way of meditation for people of mediocre intellect.*

(a) MEDITATION ON SPACE-LIKE EMPTINESS

47b/6 The body remains in the seven-fold Vairocana posture

without moving, like Mt. Meru. The senses remain clearly in self-clarity without ceasing, like the reflection of the moon in a pond. Whatever (appearance) arises (in the mind), do not focus (the mind) on the aspect of appearing but remain with the emptiness aspect of it, which is thorough clarity, floating and abundant without (differentiations and limitations of distinguishing) outer, inner, or between. Through that meditation one realizes all phenomena as emptiness with no break, like space.

(b) MEDITATION ON MIRROR-LIKE CLARITY.

[48a/2]The posture of the body and focus of the sense-faculties are similar to those in the previous meditation. Here one does not concentrate on the aspect of emptiness but contemplates on the state of self-clarity without apprehension of the percepts, clearly, vividly, and vigorously. Then the realization of undefining (perceptions or not defined appearances) (*Khral-Ma Khrol*) arises, in which all phenomena appear without being apprehended.

(c) MEDITATION ON WAVE-LIKE ARISINGS

[48a/3]The bodily postures and focus of the sense-faculties are the same as before. Here, one focuses especially on the arising of the thoughts of projecting and withdrawing, through the state of intrinsic awareness (*Rig-Pa*). Thereupon the realization of liberating (the thoughts) without basis and apprehension like waves dissolving in water arises (in oneself).

(iii) *The way of meditation for beings of higher intellect.* [48a/4]Here, (the state of meditation and realization) is a ceaseless continuum like the flow of a river. Because of one's realization of the awareness as the *Dharmakāya*, the (mental) projections and withdrawals arise and dissolve as the play of the ultimate nature. Hence, (everything) arises as the clarifying training for the realization, without abandonings or acceptances and deviations or obscurations. On an island of gold, ordinary stones and earth are hard to find even if they are searched for. Likewise, since whatever arises in the intellect has arisen as the spontaneously arisen wisdom, the subjective thoughts are nothing but the realization of the primordially liberated *Samantabhadra* (*Kun-Tu bZang-Po*). Whatever arises as the object has arisen as the emptiness-form. So, (for the *yogi*) the objective thoughts are nothing but the vast expanse of primordially liberated *Samantabhadrī (Kun-Tu bZang-Mo*). (For him) all the phenomenal aspects, which were apprehended separately as the mind and the object, cease in the sphere of non-dual Great Perfection. (At that time, all the phenomenal existents have) arisen in the expanse of the wisdom without (distinctions of) outer and inner, have become equalness without top or bottom, have arisen as the self-arisen primordial wisdom without (distinctions of) directions and cardinal points, have arisen as the play of the ultimate nature without partiality, have perfected (themselves) into the state of the natural way of dwelling without (distinction of) self and others, and have reached the primordial expanse without (distinction of) place and time. This is the time when the *yogi*, whose intellect has been exhausted, is happy in the state of exhaustion (of phenomena) in the ultimate nature. Here, having been introduced to the uninterrupted realization, and the awareness having become denuded, one maintains the pure meditationless natural mind, floating nakedly and completely without hindrance, and with confidence in it.

Explanation of the Skillful Means in Detail

(i) *Tranquillity.*

(a) ACQUIRING TRANQUILLITY

(1) CONTEMPLATION ON VISIBLE OBJECTS

48b/6 Contemplation on external visible objects such as a painted image is the same as discussed before. For the contemplation on inwardly appearing objects, when the senses are being distracted and are not remaining in concentration, visualize in the heart a white lotus or a crossed vajra and so on, and visualize that its root (or end) extends downwards and reaches the "majestic golden ground" and becomes stabilized. When the mind becomes capable of contemplation, withdraw (the root or end) into the heart and remain one-pointedly. By this practice (the realization of) "no-thought" arises.

(2) CONCENTRATION ON NON-APPEARING OBJECTS

49a/3 It is contemplation in the state of no thoughts in the mind. It is a training on contemplation in the state of emptiness (in which), having dissolved all the internal and external phenomena, or by visualizing the face or hands and so forth of the deities, one dissolves all the other thoughts into the visualization, and then one contemplates on that thought also in the non-visual state. Through these practices arise the tranquillity of non-conceptualization (*dMigs-Med*).

(b) PROGRESSION

49a/5 Take a little walk while focusing (the mind) on the previous contemplation (the tranquillity without conceptualization). By contemplating in the tranquillity, mixing it with little talking and thinking, the experience (of contemplation) will progress. If the contemplation becomes unclear, elevate it by letting the mind waver. Then the contemplation wil become very clear.

(ii) *Insight.*

(a) ACQUIRING INSIGHT

(i) TRAINING IN APPEARANCES

49b/1 It is to contemplate, thinking that whatever appears is unreal, as the appearances of the phenomenal objects are magical apparition and dreams. There is a big difference between the thoughts, "It is magical apparition" and "It is like magical apparition." In the previous trainings it was taught that phenomena are like a magical apparition, and here it is taught that they are the actual (magical apparition).

(2) TRAINING IN EMPTINESS

49b/2 At the very moment of the appearance of phenomena, whatever one watches, see them as emptiness nature without any traces and remain in the space-like nature without thinking anything. The previous trainings were on the emptiness arrived at by analysis and here it is on the emptiness (resulting from) the direct approach of self-clarity. So there is a great difference.

(b) PROGRESSION OF INSIGHT

[49b/4]Whatever one's activities, meditate by unifying them with the emptiness (resulting from) concentrating on dissolving the appearances into the emptiness. Afterwards, without for a moment becoming distracted toward the objects, such as form, train naturally in the clarity, emptiness and absence of apprehension.

(iii) *Union (of tranquillity and insight).*

(a) ACTUAL (UNION)

[49b/5]Sit in the proper physical posture. Whatever appears or arises, at that very moment, without discriminations, watch totally the intrinsic awareness, the very ground of arising. Contemplate here (in the awareness state) without analyzing over there (objects). This is the most profound point. Then, because of remaining always in the state of equality of projecting and abiding (of thoughts), the movements (of the mind) will not harm the abiding (in the intrinsic awareness state). This is the arrival at the essence of intrinsic awareness, the union of emptiness, clarity, and arising. It is the realization of the original state of the three bodies.

(b) PROGRESSION (OF THE UNION)

[50a/2]When the sky is clear of clouds, turn your back to the sun and stare into the depth of the sky in "watching positions" (*lTa-sTangs*). As the external sky is clear, the internal sense-sky becomes clear. Then there arises instantly the ultimate nature (*Ch'os-Nyid*) of clear sky of the secret luminous essence, transcending (the differences of) extremes or the center. This is the supremely profound instruction given by *Kāmaśrī* of Nepal. If the (experiences) are unclear (*lTings*), train in the skill (*rTsal*) of tranquillity and insight; if they are dull, elevate them, and if they are excited, calm them down. To apply this method to all the daily activities is a very important point for perfecting the skill.

(iv) *Perfecting* (*the skillful means of training*). 50a/5While meditating thus, all the experiences (*Nyams*), the abiding of mind in meditation, good thoughts, bad thoughts, pure perceptions, and impure perceptions, are of one taste in (being) baseless, great emptiness, the great exhaustion of phenomena, transcending the intellect, the great equalness without partiality and the great openess free from basis. So do not hold on to anything, do not think about anything, do not ask anybody anything, do not depend on anything, and cut off fear and clinging to hopes and doubts, but attain the state of great transcendence of the intellect and dissolution of phenomena (into the ultimate nature), reach the great actionless sphere, and never return. This is to develop confidence in "what it is."

THE RESULT, FREEDOM FROM EXPECTATIONS AND DOUBTS

The Self-Essence of the Ultimate Sphere of the Ultimate Nature

50b/2It is the absolute truth, the ultimate sphere, which exists neither as *saṃsāra* nor as *nirvāṇa*. It does not fall into the extremes of any dimensions, but is the basis of arising of everything. It is also called the final goal of the realization, source of the exhaustion, goal of the attainment, and ultimate sphere of the primordial state. It is not other than the spontaneously arisen wisdom. It is the self-awareness, free from conceptualizations and not having fallen into (the extremes of) dimensions, to which one has been introduced by the *Lama*. This will not be found in other (external) sources, even if it is searched for. . . . Since the ultimate sphere of the Buddha has been obscured (for us) by the adventitious defilements, although it is defined as "natural purity in nature," one should understand that in essence there is no (distinction of) good or bad in it. This is the attainment of confidence in the present (union of) awareness and emptiness as the great spontaneously accomplished ultimate sphere.

The Nature of the Bodies, the Appearances of the Ultimate Sphere

51a/1In that ultimate sphere is present the realization (*dGongs-*

Pa) of the union of the body and primordial wisdom. The aspect of the presence of the nature of that ultimate sphere, free from birth, cessation, and changes and beyond speech, conceptions, and expressions is the *Dharmakāya*. The aspect of the spontaneous arising of the major signs and minor marks, transcendent to the extremes of eternalism and nihilism, in the luminous sphere, is the *Saṃbhogakāya*. The aspect of projecting compassion (power) without partiality, as the sphere of ceaseless arising, is the *Nirmāṇakāya*. The aspect of spontanously possessing primordially pure virtues such as the ten powers and four fearlessnesses of the Buddha, as many as the sands of the river Ganges, in the ultimate sphere, is the *Sambodhikāya*. The aspect of the presence of the realization of the ultimate nature of the ultimate sphere without changes in the three times is the "Eternal *Vajrakāya*." Whether or not the adventitious defilements have been purified, from the very time of one's existence as an ordinary being, the essence of the awareness is emptiness, its nature is clarity, its way of arising is ceaseless, everything (all the virtues) is present and changeless from the nature of awareness. Those are the aspects of the five bodies which are present (in us) right now. So one should believe that the five bodies are spontanously present (in oneself) without need of seeking them from any other source. That is to realize that the (union of) intrinsic awareness and emptiness is the five bodies.

The Display of the Primordial Wisdoms from the (Buddha-)Bodies
[51b/1]The primordial wisdom of *Dharmakāya* is the great transcendence of speech, concepts, and expressions. The primordial wisdom of *Saṃbhogakāya* is possessed of five characteristics. The primordial wisdom of *Nirmāṇakāya* is the knowledge of absolute truth and relative truth. Whether or not the defilements have been purified, those (primordial wisdoms are) naturally present completely in the ultimate sphere. So they are present in the awareness at this moment. The intrinsic awareness-emptiness and the discriminative awareness (wisdom), the five poisons and self-liberation without traces, are

the essences and qualities or the phenomena and the nature of phenomena, and they are complete in the awareness as its aspects. Especially when a thought of desire flickers in one, although it is an ordinary emotional defilement, by recognizing it and contemplating on it, it arises as blissful without apprehensions. That is the Discriminative Primordial Wisdom. Hatred arising toward an object is ordinary anger. By recognizing it, it arises as clarity, free from concepts. It is the Mirror-like primordial Wisdom. The arising of unknowing is ignorance. By recognizing it, it arises as natural clarity with no concepts. It is the ultimate sphere primordial wisdom. Boasting that I am better than others is ordinary pride. By recognizing it, one realizes non-duality and equalness. It is the Primordial Wisdom of Equanimity. The arising of competitive thought is ordinary jealousy. By recognizing it, it is cleansed as free from partiality. It is the Primordial Wisdom of Accomplishment. In awareness, although the effect (*rTsal*) of not recognizing (the intrinsic awareness) itself arises as the five poisons, when it is recognized, the poisons arise as the power or the play of the five primordial wisdoms. So at this very moment the meaning of the inseparability of the (Buddha-) bodies and primordial wisdoms is naturally present (within oneself). Develop confidence. Do not have doubt or expectations. Decide and generate courage. This is the introduction.

1. Naturally Liberated Mind, the Great Perfection

Sanskrit: *Mahāsandhicittatāsvamutki-nāma*
Tibetan: *rDzogs-Pa Ch'en-Po Sems-Nyid Rang-Grol*

This section is a complete translation of *Naturally Liberated Mind* (SR). It is one of the *Three Cycles on Natural Liberation* (*Rang-Grol sKor-gSum*) in *Dzogpa Chenpo* by Longchen Rabjam. It consists of three chapters. The first chapter is on the views of the "basis," the second chapter is on the path of meditation, and the third chapter is on the perfection of result. In this section we tried to maintain the sequence of Tibetan lines in the translation, but in some places it was impossible to avoid shuffling the words from one line to another.

Homage to the Glorious Kuntu Zangpo[1]

From the utterly pure essence[2] which transcends objective thought
Arisen as the glow[3] of the essence of the spontaneously accomplished nature[4]
Pure from various characteristics of the duality of apprehended and apprehender,[5] the Mind[6]
Which is free from discriminations of dimensions and partiality: to you I pay homage.

Phenomenal existences are unborn, of equal nature;
In which the originally liberated appearances and mind[7] prevail evenly without apprehensions;
Concerning that marvelous sovereign, Naturally Liberated Mind,
Listen while I tell you what I have realized.

"LIBERATION BY REALIZING THE BASIS," the first chapter of NATURALLY LIBERATED MIND, THE GREAT PERFECTION

The utterly pure view has no extremes or center.
It cannot be indicated by saying "It is this," nor is there in it any distinctions of height or width.
It transcends eternalism and nihilism, and it is free from the stains of the four assertions of extremes.[8]
Sought, it will not be found; watched, it is not seen.
It is detached from directions and partiality, and it transcends all the objects of conception.
It has no standpoint, neither voidness nor non-voidness.
There is no realized and unrealized, no counting, nor objective aim.
All phenomena are primordially pure and enlightened, so
it is unborn and unceasing, inconceivable and inexpressible.
In the ultimate sphere[9] purity and impurity are naturally pure and
Phenomena are the great equal perfection, free from conception.
Since there is no bondage and liberation, there is no going, coming or dwelling.
Appearance and emptiness are conventions, apprehended and apprehender are like *māyā* (a magical apparition).
The happiness and suffering of *saṃsāra* and *nirvāṇa* are like good and bad dreams.
From the very moment of appearing, its nature is free from elaboration.

From it (the state of freedom from elaboration), the very interdependent causation of the great arising and cessation
Appears like a dream, *māyā*,[10] an optical illusion, a city of the *Gandharvas*,[11]
An echo, and a reflection, having no reality.
All the events such as arising, etc.,[12] are in their true nature unborn.
So they will never cease nor undergo any changes in the three periods of time.[13]
They did not come from anywhere and they did not go anywhere.
They will not stay anywhere: they are like a dream and *māyā*.
A foolish person is attached to phenomena as true,
And apprehends them as gross material phenomena, "I" and "self," whereas they are
Like a *māyā*-girl who disappears when touched.
They are not true because they are deceiving and act only in appearance.
The spheres of the six realms of beings and the Pure Lands of the Buddhas[14] also
Are not aggregations of atoms, but merely the self-appearances of beings' minds.
For example, in a dream Buddhas and sentient beings
Appear as real, endowed with inconceivable properties. However,
When one awakens, they were just a momentary object of the mind.
In the same way should be understood all the phenomena of *saṃsāra*[15] and *nirvāṇa*.[16]
There is no separate emptiness apart from apparent phenomena.
It is like fire and heat, the qualities of fire.
The notion of their distinctness is a division made by mind.
Water and the moon's reflection in water are indivisibly one in the pool.
Likewise, appearances[17] and emptiness[18] are one in the great *Dharmatā*.[19]

These appearances are unborn from the beginning, and they are the *Dharmakāya*.[20]
They are like reflections, naturally unstained and pure.
The mind's fabricating their existence or non-existence is an illusion,
So do not conceptualize whatever appearances arise;
Those appearing objects are also reflections of mind.
They are like a face and its reflection in a mirror.
While there is no duality, the perception of duality is
The natural characteristic of the experiences of beginningless habit.[21]
The mind and dreams are not separate,
Rather it is like the appearance of dreams to a person who is drunk[22] with sleep.
One should know that there is no essential distinction between (subject and object).
For example, like a baby seeing a mirror,
Ignorant people accept and reject external objects.
When a mother sees the mirror she cleans it; similarly
The *Yāna*[23] of Cause and Result[24] alters external objects.
A lady, seeing it, cleans her face; likewise
One who knows suchness[25] looks at the Mind within.
This is the immaterial, Essential *Yāna*.
In the mind which has no essence, various things
Arise because of the objective conditions,
Like reflections appearing in a mirror or in the ocean.
The emptiness essence, unceasing nature, and
Variously appearing characteristic, the magical display, is
The dual projection of *saṃsāra* and *nirvāṇa* within a single Mind.
It is like the color of a crystal altered by a black or white cloth.
The essence is without change, but because of conditional perceptions as the basis of arising,
Various perceptions seem to change at the time of their appearance;
But in reality it is unchanging like the purity of the crystal.
The primordially empty Mind, which has no root,

Is not defiled by the phenomenal appearances of *saṃsāra* and *nirvāṇa*.
Throughout the three times and timeless time, the state of *Kuntu Zangpo*,
The essence of the changeless perfection at the basis is
Undefiled by the appearances of the six objects,[26] like the water-moon [the moon's reflection in water].
For the non-existent appearances of *saṃsāra* and *nirvāṇa*, like a magic display,
Do not make efforts of acceptance and rejection,[27] negating and defending,[28] or hope and doubt.[29]
Attaining liberation by knowing the nature of the (world's) magical display:
It is as if, seeing the army of *māyā* one is taken in, but
By knowing the reality there is no fear. Likewise,
It is not necessary to renounce objective appearances in particular.
The nature of *saṃsāra* is the essence of the mind,
Which is primordially unborn and enlightened,
So by seeing the Mind, realization of the nature of existence is attained.
Then there is no other Peace to be accomplished.
(It is as if) being frightened of one's own forces (mistaking them for) others',
Later, by recognizing them, one is relieved.
Today by the blessing of the glorious Master,
Worldly thoughts are realized as *Dharmakāya*. So
The natural great bliss[30] arises within.
There is no need of acceptance and rejection since all existent phenomena arise as the *Lama*.
All the inexhaustible instructions are the support of enlightenment.
There is no end of satisfaction in happiness and peace.
All is happiness, prevailing in *Dharmatā*, from which
The play of unceasing varieties of phenomena is
The spontaneously accomplished *Rūpakāya*[31] and *Dharmakāya*, appearances and emptiness, the twofold accumulation,[32]

Skillful means[33] and wisdom,[34] meditation[35] and withdrawal from meditation.[36]
The unconstructed and natural Five Bodies[37] and Five Primordial Wisdoms[38]
Are perfected in the state of Intrinsic Awareness, free from grasping after perception and mind.
The stages, paths, recollection, and contemplation—
The qualities—are spontaneously perfected and are of the essence, the *Dharmatā*.
The great self-arisen impartial Intrinsic Awareness is
Unadulterated by an apprehended [object] and unbound by a subject.
It is like the nature of *māyā*, non-dual and pure. So
What is the use of pondering, discoursing, or contemplating?
There are no developing[39] and perfecting stages,[40] no duality, no union,
No standpoint or division of *Yānas*.
These are all conventions and drawings of the mind.
(All are of) the state of self-arising, just designated as self-liberation.
The Awareness has no objective and cannot be defined as "this is it,"
So do not make efforts to apprehend it, thinking "it is," for it transcends the mind.
The Mind is effortless and spontaneously perfected;
Do not adulterate it with antidotes of modification and transformation: let it go in ease.
If the *Dharmatā*, in which realization and non-realization are equal,
Is not adulterated by binding it with nets of contemplation,
Then in the ultimate meaning there is neither "is" nor "is not," neither phenomena nor emptiness.
It cannot be defined as "unity and multiplicity"[41] and the rest.
It transcends view and meditation, free from assertion and negation, no coming and going,
Free from extremes, non-dual, like *māyā* and a dream.
The purpose of [the teaching on the] Two Truths[42] is the

prevention of attachment to (phenomena) as real.
In the actual meaning there is no absolute and relative.
Things are not present as they are (mentally and conventionally) construed,
(But) one is bound in the net of apprehending them as "this is."[43]
Whatever one asserts, he will fall into the extremes of attachment;
And through efforts and achievements, *saṃsāra* will not cease.
Good and bad *karma* cause wandering in this world, and
The experiences of happiness and suffering, high and low, are like the revolving of an irrigation wheel.
In the *saṃsāra* of the three times, beings of the three spheres[44] wander in delusion;
They are tormented by the disease of ignorance, fabrications,[45] and efforts—
No beginning or end to it—oh, pity the living beings!
Kye Ho! All are just like dreams and *māyā*.
In the ultimate meaning there is no *saṃsāra* and no wanderers in it.
All are originally liberated in the state of *Kuntu Zangpo.*
There is no basis, root, or substance. How satisfying it is!
The unmodified, primordially pure Mind
Is unstained by the phenomena of existence: it is like a reflection.
In the appearing object nothing is conceptualized to be apprehended;
in the self-arisen mind, nothing is conceived for an apprehender.
That non-dual primordial wisdom arises from the dualistic perceptions.
Therefore, the ceaseless mind and its object are the great attributes.
The elephant of non-apprehending roves freely on the plain at the pace of Self-Liberation, ornamented by the trappings of non-duality.

He destroys the swamp of acceptance and rejection, hope and doubt, and
He possesses the strength of realization and enters into the ocean of non-duality.
He wanders freely without different phases between arising and liberation, and
Unbound by the ropes of the objects of abandonment and antidotes.
He freely maintains the standpoint of powerful accomplishment.
By fully perfecting the great power, phenomenal existence arises as *Dharmakāya*.
When perceptions of the six objects are unceasing and the perceiver is essentially empty,
And Mind free from extremes attains aimless liberation,
Then Intrinsic Awareness of the non-duality of *saṃsāra* and *nirvāṇa* reaches the (primordial) Ground.
It is called the achievement of the supreme attainment.[46]
Because of perfect accomplishment of the purpose of self and others,
It is the attainment of enlightenment in the unexcelled Pure Land.[47]
Alas! the animal-like contemplators
Stop the perceptions and remain without any thoughts.
They call this the absolute nature and become proud.
By gaining experience in that state (of concentration) they will be born in the animal realm.
Even if they do not gain experience [in it], it is certain [that they will be reborn in the realms of] Absorption[48] [Form] and the Formless.[49]
There will be no opportunity to get liberation from *saṃsāra*.
So, extremely proud ones,
Who are possessed by the harmful spirit of their own standpoint,
Follow mentally fabricated and deluded doctrines.
Because of their defiled fabrications, they will not see the *Dharmatā*.

Even if they analyze the Two Truths, they will fall into the extreme of eternalism or nihilism.
Even if they analyze the freedom from extremes, they will discover the view of [only] the summit of *saṃsāra*.
Whatever they do, because of bondage to their standpoint,
They will never actually see the natural Primordial Wisdom.
The actual meaning[50] is obscured by pondering, expression, and concepts.
By not understanding the proper (ways of) pondering, experiencing, and conceptualizing,
The error occurs by (turning) the meaning [object] of the search (into) the searcher [efforts].
Mind and primordial wisdom are like water and its moisture:
At all times there is no separation between them,
But they are adulterated by the discriminations of mental acceptance and rejection.
Mind and its object, whatever appears, is the essential nature,
But by apprehending partiality, its openness is restricted.
Now, if you wish for the meaning of the *Dharmakāya* free from conceptualization,[51]
Do not make efforts to search for the nature.[52]
The "sovereign of whatever arises"[53] suspends attachments and concepts,
Undiscriminated, and unrecognizable in terms of "this is it;"
(In it phenomena) do not exist in the way that they arise.
In their nature they do not exist as they appear.
Ordinary perception, unobstructed[54] and liberated from the beginning,
Is the view of the Natural Great Perfection.[55]
The nature of phenomena is exemplified by space,
But phenomena are not conceivable as the nature of space.
"The Mind is unborn and phenomena are like space."
We speak thus, but it is only indication and imputation.
It is free from (the aspects of) "is" and "is not," and it is beyond thought.
It cannot be indicated by saying "This is," and it is totally perfected from the beginning.

Kye Ho! In the pure nature of phenomenal existence[56]
Arises the sudden purity, non-apprehending Intrinsic Awareness.
From the very point of arising it does not exist anywhere.
The self-liberated Great Perfection—when will I be able to see that?
In the rootless Mind, pure from the beginning,
There is nothing to do and no one to do it—how satisfying!
The Intrinsic Awareness of aimless phenomena,
In which deliberate apprehension such as "this is it" has dissolved—what happiness!
In the view and meditation which have no discrimination,
There is no breadth or narrowness, height or depth—how pleasant!
In the action and result which have no acceptance and rejection, hope and doubt,
There is nothing to gain and nothing to lose—how warm!
In the equally perfected *māyā*-like nature,
There is no good to accept and no bad to reject—I feel like laughing!
In the perceptions which are blurred, evanescent, undefined,
Fragmentary, discontinuous, unobstructed and natural,
Whatever appears, there is no apprehension of "this is this" or "this is these appearances."
"Is" and "is not" are apprehending mind; and being detached from that mind is *Dharmakāya*.
When in the aimless[57] object the uncertain appearances arise,
The unapprehending cognition attains liberation without duality;
Then all the phenomena of perception are the great play of the Mind.
In the Mind which is free from ground, root, and substance,
The spontaneous uncreated qualities are fully perfected.
By liberating denial and assertion into *Dharmakāya*, happiness will be achieved.
All deliberate concepts are fabrications.

If whatever arises arises free from conceptualization, it is the real Primordial Wisdom.
By liberating acceptance and rejection in its own state, happiness will be achieved.
By liberating acceptance and rejection in its own state, the object of thought is transcended.
For the Buddhahood which is totally and naturally pure,
Do not search[58] anywhere but in your own mind.
Other than [in] the searcher[59] (itself) there is no separate place to search for.
It is like the caste of *māyā*-(people) and water in a mirage.
There is no duality of *saṃsāra* and *nirvāṇa* as apprehension of duality has
Ceased in the unadulterated self-arisen Intrinsic Awareness.
He who sees the meaning of the equality of all phenomena
And realizes the Mind as unborn like the sky
Is perfecting [realizing] the phenomena of the world and beings as the naturally pure Buddha-field,
The state of equanimity of unborn spontaneous accomplishment.
The essence of appearances and mind is emptiness, and that is the meaning of *Dharmakāya*;
Their nature is unceasing, and that is the appearance of *Saṃbhogakāya*;[60]
Their characteristics are various and that is the *Nirmāṇakāya*.[61]
By knowing this,
Everything is the three bodies, Primordial Wisdom, and Pure Land.
There is no [need of] modification, transformation, renunciation, and antidote, so it is completely satisfying.
E Ma! Living beings, by holding on to duality,[62]
When they dwell in this dream-like delusory *saṃsāra*,
Whatever efforts they make are causes and effects of *saṃsāra*.
By experiencing the non-conceptual universal ground,[63] they stray into the Formless Realm;
Experiencing the clear-empty consciousness of the universal ground, they stray into the Form realm;

Experiencing the six consciousnesses,[64] they stray into the Desire Realm.
The changes of the mind are the steps [to different realms] of *saṃsāra*.
For people who want enlightenment, the meaning of the unmodified absolute
Is to let the mind be at ease without effort.
The ordinary mind, unmodified and natural,
Unstained by apprehension of *saṃsāra* and *nirvāṇa*, attains liberation in its natural state.
By attaining liberation in that way, dwelling in the instantaneous nature
Without thought is the state of *Dharmakāya*;
The unceasing ground of arising, clarity, and emptiness is the *Saṃbhogakāya*, and
The emanation, liberation upon arising, is the *Nirmāṇakāya*. With confidence (in the foregoing)
It is certain that worldly thoughts will be enlightened.
Kye Ho! Since the character (*Rang-bZhin*) of appearances and mind is changing,
Watch the mirror of the aimless *Dharmakāya*.
The arising of non-apprehender in the aimless phenomena
Is the secret of mind; there is nothing else to be signified.
It is the natural character of spontaneously accomplished Intrinsic Awareness, the essential meaning of whatever arises;
Do not make modifications and adulterations.
Phenomena are the nature of substancelessness.
The sky of unapprehending mind has no center or end.
Although they arise naturally without creation or cessation,
Absence of denial, assertion, and of attachment to characteristics is the true meaning;
And they are changeless throughout the three times—this one should know.
The innate primordial wisdom free from the duality of percept and mind
Can [only] be signified by realizing, but there is nothing to be shown and nothing to see.

The absolute Mind is beautiful in its natural state.
By various [means]—unwavering contemplation, analytic wisdom, [and]
Precepts, intellectual knowledge and instructions—one will only gain theoretical understanding,
But one [will] never achieve the naked Primordial Wisdom.
For example, even if one indicates by pointing, saying "This is space,"
it is not an object that can be seen, so it is merely a way of differentiating.
The arising of realization through the kindness of the *Lama* is
Like the dispelling of darkness by the sun.
The moment one sees all (existents) as *Dharmakāya* by instantaneous Intrinsic Awareness,
Ignorance is turned into Primordial Wisdom and defilements into indications (of the Five Primordial Wisdoms).
One should devote oneself (to practice) by all means without wavering.
Common and uncommon attainments will be achieved in this life.
Fools hate *saṃsāra* and seek *nirvāṇa*.
It is like throwing away a very rare wishing-jewel,
Taking another wishing-jewel that needs cleaning,
And after cleaning it, looking around for a trinket.
The self-liberated Mind, the precious jewel,
By realizing its own nature cleanses the deluded stains.
Understanding that is the precious treasure of virtues
And the heart of the achievement of the benefit of self and others.
When the meaning realization of the Mind arises
Like the water and waves, the projections and dwelling are in the state of *Dharmakāya*.
(Then) whatever takes place, there is no need of rejection and acceptance.
There is never any need of practicing rejection and acceptance.
At all times for the joyous *yogi*
It is the great flowing-river *yoga*.[65]

In the state of all-equally perfected great nature.
Just upon the arising of the realization, [the mind] becomes naturally clear and luminescent.
Even when there is again projection, it will be in [the state of] *Dharmatā* as before.
As luminescent Intrinsic Awareness has no extremes and center,
There is no duality of defilements and antidotes.
So, things to be rejected, antidotes, detachment, attainment, hope and doubt, are liberated in their natural state.
People who do not know how to distinguish jewels from lamps
Think that the lamplight is the light of a jewel.
If one does not distinguish the absorption and experiences of self-liberation,
Then he will be bound by the attachment to liberation-upon-arising itself.
If one does not distinguish between experiences and realization,
He will be deluded by holding on to the experiences as realization.
After realization there are at all times no changes of good and bad.
By gaining experience of that, the virtuous experiences arise.
For example, space, by the changes within the four elements,
Will not undergo any alteration: the space will remain as before.
Likewise, for the *yogi* who has realized the Mind,
There is no good and bad realization due to the increasing and decreasing of experiences.
If there is a good and bad, it is experience, not realization.
Definite realization should be sought from a holy person.
Thereafter, in accordance (with his teachings) one should remain in contemplation (without wavering).
To meditate this is the definitive absolute view.
By seeing it [Mind], the person of superior intelligence[66] will attain liberation.
It will not depend on experiences, everything will arise as realization.
There is nothing to be rejected, so there is no antidote to meditate,

Just as for a healthy person there is no (need of) medicine.
Thus, you should learn the unapprehended view, free from partiality.

LIBERATION THROUGH EXPERIENCE OF THE PATH
for people of middle and lesser intellect
the second chapter of
NATURALLY LIBERATED MIND,
THE GREAT PERFECTION

In the meditation which is great natural self-perfection,
There is no need of modifications and transformations: whatever arises is the Great Perfection.
There is no need of accepting and renouncing, as in the primordial state itself
The world and beings of *saṃsāra* and *nirvāṇa* abide evenly.[67]
In the "whatever-arises Intrinsic Awareness,"[68] the spontaneous six consciousnesses,
Maintain the "unfabricated Intrinsic Awareness"[69] like an infant child.
If you reside in the groundless state through detachment from mind
You will accomplish, spontaneously and changelessly, the inconceivable sovereignty.
In the "ordinary mind,"[70] uncreated and spontaneous,
The "natural mind"[71] which is like water poured into water,
Maintain the "non-dual mind"[72] free from fabrications and adulterations;
[whereupon] the "effortless mind"[73] dwells in the great *Dharmatā*.
In the naturally free openness, peace of mind,
Remain naturally and gracefully like an old man.
Through the great state of self-arising, in which there is no observance of meditative periods,
The great, careless "self-liberated Intrinsic Awareness"[74] prevails.
In the "aimless Intrinsic Awareness"[75] which is great unhinderedness,

Maintain the "unapprehending Intrinsic Awareness"[76] like a madman.
Through "discipline Intrinsic Awareness"[77] which has no discriminations,
The various evil circumstances arise as the play of *Dharmatā*.
The various [perceptions] are one's own mind, the magic display of Intrinsic Awareness;
Remain fearlessly like a lion.
Through the great Primordial Wisdom, the suppressor of delusory perceptions,
The "spontaneously born Intrinsic Awareness"[78] arises as the great self-liberation.
Until one has fully attained the essence of realization,
Contemplate as with the eyes of jackals,[79] without differentiations of day and night.
By gaining experience and familiarity, if the mother [fully enlightened state] and son [realization of the path] are united,
Everything will arise simultaneously in the great carefreeness.
In the "impartial Intrinsic Awareness"[80] which has no middle and extremes,
Without indicating it as "this is it," remain like space.
Then the significance of "meditationless Intrinsic Awareness,"[81] unfabricated and unadulterated,
Which is "self-arisen Intrinsic Awareness,"[82] arises within naturally.
In the great natural cleansing, free from the pollution of defilements,
Maintain the "naturally clear Intrinsic Awareness"[83] like the ocean.
"Liberation-at-arising Intrinsic Awareness"[84] arises like big waves, as
A face in the mirror and the reflection of planets and stars.
In the unmoving and changeless Mind,
Maintain the unchanging *Dharmatā* like Mt. Meru.
The "simultaneously perfected Intrinsic Awareness,"[85] spontaneously perfected and uncompounded,

Neutrality [of good and bad] and non-duality of actions and efforts will be accomplished spontaneously.
In self-arising and self-liberating Innate Mind,[86]
Remain without interruption like a river.
Whatever thoughts arise will be the same taste as *Dharmakāya*:
No need of acceptance and renunciation, all are in total *nirvāṇa*.
Briefly, in whatever arises, the play of *Dharmatā*,
Freedom from conception and self-liberated contemplation is accomplished spontaneously.
By prolonged meditation without interruptions,
One should train in the exercises of realization without laziness.
For the "progress"[87] of that practice which is the support of the path,
With the "*māyā* actions," free from acceptance or rejection,
In order to turn unfavorable events into the path, and for uniting[88] the meditation and withdrawal from meditation,[89]
Go to mountaintops, charnel grounds, islets, and fairgrounds, etc.,—
Places which make the mind waver,
And let the body dance, the voice sing songs,
And the mind project various thoughts:
Fuse them with the view and meditation of instantaneous self-liberation.
Then all arises as the path.
Sometimes do the devotional practice of (perceiving) phenomenal existents as (the *maṇḍala* of) the *Lama*,
(And the practice of) accumulation of merits, purification of defilements, and (contemplation on) impermanence.
All existent phenomena are of the nature of a dream and *māyā*.
They are like an echo, a mirage, a reflection, and a miraculous display.[90]
And, as an optical illusion[91] and the moon's reflection in water, their nature is empty.
Train on the various appearances as untrue and blurred,
Instantaneously, without identifying them.
Having trained in the exercises of meditation and withdrawal from meditation day and night without straying,

In the state of bliss, clarity, and non-conceptuality, (which are) liberated-at-arising and are naturally present,
Self-dwelling meditation [progresses] without ceasing.
By dissolving illusory dreams into their unreal and luminescent (nature)
Day and night, *saṃsāra* and *nirvāṇa* are liberated in their true nature.
By the view[92] one expands the duration, by meditation[93] one prevents wavering,
By the activities[94] one copes with circumstances, and by the results[95] (one) protects oneself (from) falling into errors.
The nature of realization, nonconceptual Primordial Wisdom,
Dwells at all times without change.
At that time, there is the single nature, the primordial state;
In that "no-meditation-state"[96] one secures permanence.[97]
Thereafter, there will be no (further) result, Great Bliss, to seek for.
"Whatever-arises Intrinsic Awareness"[98] is the spontaneously accomplished *Trikāya*.
Without efforts the benefit of self and others will be achieved.
There will arise only the Intrinsic Awareness, which possesses the Qualities[99] and is free from discriminations.
Thus, a *yogi* who is attaining liberation in this very life,
Dissolves the earth-element into water, water into fire, fire into air, air into consciousness, and consciousness into luminescence;[100]
Then, uniting with Primordial Wisdom and the *Dharmadhātu*
Secures permanence in the state of primordiality.
For the benefit of others, like a dream, Primordial Wisdom and the two Bodies[101]
Appear to sentient beings, as the qualities for the purpose (of benefiting others).
This is the nature of Intrinsic Awareness, the secret of the mind,
And the supreme instantaneous self-liberation. By its realization,
The vast development of virtues is

(Comparable to) the waxing (of the moon) from the first of the month to the fifteenth (of the lunar calendar),
Which makes it appear to people that the moon is increasing, whereas
There is really no increase or decrease. Likewise,
Even if one sees the face of the realization and increases the power of the meditation,
The realization has no change, and yet the virtues of the experience arise.
Because of the brightness of the moon, the shadow on the moon (seems) small,
Or because of the smallness of the shadow, the moon (seems to) grow. Likewise,
Because of detachment from dualistic apprehension, experience and realization (seem) to be increasing. Or,
Because of the increase of realization, the defilements (seem to) be decreasing.
Even if one perfects the virtues of renunciation and realization,
The essence does not change and the nature does not cease,
(As) the *Dharmatā* is pure and liberated from any conditions.
Briefly, if the defilements have not arisen as realization,
Then after renouncing the five poisons[102] there isn't any excellent alternative path (to pursue).
If you do not know the secret of the self-liberation (of all into a) single Body,
Then you will be deceived by apprehending the duality of defilements and antidotes.
If the apprehender and the apprehended were not liberated in their own place at the crucial point,
Even if one spoke about a high standpoint, it would just be the secret words of *māra* [devil], and
Even if one had good contemplation, the result would merely be the happiness of the higher realms.
Whatever efforts were made would just be the causes of *saṃsāra*.
Broad view, aimless[103] meditation,
Tamed behavior, and freedom from deliberate apprehension are important.

When, in whomever, the vast non-duality of liberation-at-arising
In the aimless phenomenal existents occurs without wavering,
It is the sign of a *yogi* who has crossed the ocean of *saṃsāra*.
(Then there is) no tight bondage by the apprehended [object] and no attachment of the apprehender [subject],
All existents dwell in the blissful expanse of the simultaneously perfected *Dharmakāya*.
There is no fear in crossing the mountain passes, valleys, and narrow defiles (encountered along the path of practice).
It is the arrival at one's own native land [the final result], which transcends all hopes and fears.
By gaining experience in that way, the [signs of] four elements as
The degrees of attainment of the path of non-apprehension will arise.
[a.] Previously accumulated (virtuous) *karma*,[104] the kindness of the *Lama*,
Time and skill in means: when these interdependent causes[105] come together,
Then unhindered, free, simple "self-arisen Intrinsic Awareness,"
Which is non-apprehending-at-arising, is directly realized,
It is the great vision of "Direct Realization of *Dharmatā*."[106]
[b.] By having confidence that [all the] external and internal imputations are *Dharmakāya*,
Whatever arises, there will be nothing to be accepted or rejected, modifed or transformed.
Everything will arise solely as exercise of realization.
Then, when those experiences are increased,
One will be able to turn unfavorable circumstances of affirming and negating inner and outer existents into the path.
By the arising [of realization] liberation will be attained, and by dwelling [in it], bliss will be achieved.
By gaining experience, "eyes," foreknowledges, miracles, and so on,
The various virtues of Intrinsic Awareness arise.

Then it should be known as "The Vision of the Development of Experience."[107]

[c.] By further expanding the experience,

The Intrinsic Awareness [becomes] clarity, emptiness and naked Primordial Wisdom,

In which there are no torpor[108] and elation,[109] no wavering and unwavering,

There is no difference between meditation and withdrawal from meditation, but it is always (unceasing) like a river.

When such an extraordinary degree of virtues is achieved,

It is the attainment of the "Vision of the Perfection of Intrinsic Awareness."[110]

[d.] When one never moves from that state,

One becomes free from conceptualizations[111] of apprehending characteristics,[112] and transcends the objects of attachment, the (objects of) abandonment and their antidotes, and

Everything is simultaneously perfected and free from deliberate apprehensions and

The attachment to external and internal existents are exhausted,

Then that is the realization of the "Vision of the Dissolution into *Dharmatā*."[113]

Then, by bringing the Intrinsic Awareness to perfection in the four visions,[114]

The Form Bodies[115] dissolve into the *Dharmakāya*,

And one attains liberation by transcending the empty appearances and apprehensions—

That is the attainment of permanence in the primordial state.

When one practices in that way, since one is not diverted from the (right) path,

There are also [signs of] the three levels[116] of dreams:

First, by getting training in the liberation of appearances (to the) mind at their arising,

When bad dreams are transformed into good dreams,

It is a sign of the one-tasteness of one's merit[117] because of the purification of bad *karma*.

It is like smoke coming from fire and crops from seeds.

Secondly, by gaining experience, the recognition[118] of dreams

And instantaneous liberation of them take place simultaneously.
It is the sign of the liberation even of the antidote (recognition) itself into its own [natural] state.
[Thirdly], through complete insight the total experience is gained,
Dreams cease, and one dwells day and night in luminescence.
It is a sign of having dissolved worldly thoughts into their nature.
Then one is close to attaining ultimate *nirvāṇa*, and simultaneously
The attainment of permanence in the primordial state of cessation.
Having the three realms and the three doors[119] liberated in the state of *Trikāya*,[120]
One attains the *nirvāṇa* which does not remain in the extremes of the peaceful state.
In the Mind which has no establishings and abandonings from the beginning,
There is no need of modifying and transforming antidotes (because) it is in the innate nature.
It is free from all discriminative apprehensions, so
It is spontaneous accomplishment with neither meditation nor anything to be meditated upon.
Thus in the Self-liberated Ordinary Mind
There is no inner and outer, and it has gone beyond the extremes of apprehender and apprehended.
Affirmation and denial are self-liberated, and the defilements and antidotes have arisen as innate nature.
Liberation will be attained without any objective aim (such as) "what is" or "this is."
There is no need of acceptance or renunciation. The omnipresent Primordial Wisdom[121] is
Free from discriminations, [and is] great bliss, unsought for, and spontaneously accomplished.
It is the "great total liberation," free from the beginning and natural,[122]

(In which) there is nothing to be recognized as "who" [subject], "this is" [action], or "they are" [objects].
It is aimless, free from apprehension, and it transcends the extremes of existence and non-existence.
Kye Ho! Because of its total liberation from the beginning,
The effortless Awareness attains liberation in the state of equalness.[123]
The spontaneously accomplished sovereign[124] is unborn and will not cease.
So it is non-dwelling and imperceptible, and its nature is inexplicable.
Everything is in the state of actionlessness and of the true nature.
Ah Ho! In the perception which is natural and pure from the beginning,
Arises the wonderful Intrinsic Awareness that makes one laugh.
There is no duality of mind and its object, and the perceiver[125] is void in essence.
It cannot be indicated by saying "this is it"—it is freedom in the great aimlessness.
It is a single state of simultaneously perfected skillfull means[126] and wisdom.[127]
Everything is changeless and dwells equally as it is.
(In it the differentiations of) planets, stars, dates of the calendar, are not conceived of;
It transcends time and its calculation.[128]
The four continents do not exist, Mt. Meru and the sun and moon are empty;
No *maṇḍala* is conceived of, and there is neither recitation nor practice of austerities.
No objects are conceived; they are empty [pure] in the form of channels,[129] essence,[130] and *cakras*.[131]
Although the external objects themselves appear, they are not conceptualized.
So the entire sphere of the world, the five objects,[132] are empty in essence.

Everything is non-arisen, (as they are) the self-arisen mansion.[133]
There is no creator,[134] (as they are) the deity of absolute meaning.[135]
The projection and withdrawal of thoughts[136] are the great play of Primordial Wisdom.
The objects are offering clouds; by offering them to the Primordial Wisdom-deities
The great accumulations are perfected; sounds and words are Great *Mantra*.[137]
Defilements spontaneously arise as primordial wisdom; this is the self-born Stage of Perfection.[138]
There is no need of actions and efforts, as it is spontaneous and naturally accomplished.
It is the state of gone beyond,[139] the perfection of the stages and paths.
It does not dwell as the middle, as it is pure union.[140]
There is not even an atom of defilement, antidote, or obscuring error.
So, the "meditation of whatever arises" is spontaneously accomplished without effort.
The phenomena of differentiations and non-differentiations and
karmic causation of white virtues and black evils just function as interdependence:
They are empty in essence but they do not cease (to appear) as reflections.
So one should know the total transcending self-liberation.
Because of good and bad *karma* the higher and lower worlds are established.
If *karma* is transcended, natural *nirvāṇa* will be attained.
If one practices acceptance and rejection, one will certainly be liberated from unvirtuousness.
But even if one practices virtue, one should not be bound by attachment (to virtue).
Later one should search for the meaning of freedom from acceptance and rejection.

One should take the examples of holy persons[141] and do practice.
Renounce the meaningless and deceptive, the childish activities.
Always be together with holy persons.
Follow the inerrant preliminary practices[142] of realization, (namely) hearing and pondering.
Steadfastly tolerate (harsh conditions) alone in remote mountain places,
With determination get the real essence.
Shorten your mental (plans[143] by reflecting upon) impermanence and revulsion.[144]
To practice Dharma with efforts from the heart is essential.
If in this life one cannot proceed along the path of liberation,
Later on it will be difficult to find free[145] and endowed[146] human life and the Dharma.
Hoist the victory-banner of practice in a solitary place,
And check what one has achieved if one dies now.
If in that way one spends day and night in (the practice of) Dharma,
Even if one loses the *māyā*-like body, Mind has no birth and death.
One will secure the reign of the changeless *Dharmakāya*.
This life will be meaningful and the supreme attainment will be achieved.
Even people of middling and lesser intelligence [respectively]
Will attain liberation in the intermediate state[147] or will achieve the result in the next life.
They will find the path of liberation from the causation of *saṃsāra*
And attain the fortress of Mind in the land of Great Bliss.
This is the heart of absolute meaning.
If a path of error is taken, there are many obscurations of deviation;
(So) one will never achieve the suchness of the essence.[148]
They are tiring for this life and fruitless for the next.
Therefore one should seek the unerring view and meditation.

If (one's training) has no thoughts of kindness, compassion and the mind of enlightenment,[149]
Then it is certain to be another path than the *Mahāyāna*.[150]
If to the extent that one practices, one's mind becomes more rigid,
It is certain that Dharma practice and the person have gone separate ways.
If one is attached to the external, inner or middle meditations,
It is certain that one has no opportunity to realize non-duality.
If one does not remember the urge to escape and revulsion[151] (towards *saṃsāra*),
One is certainly deceived by the devil[152] of attachment to this life.
If one does not gain any new attainment even if one meditates,
It is certain that deviations and obscurations have occurred, such as torpor and elation.
If the "moisture" of the tranquillity meditation[153] does not permeate the insight meditation,[154]
It is not insight meditation but only a picture of realization.
If one talks about non-duality from an intellectual understanding,
But cannot face unfavorable circumstances, then it is (just) a support for the growth of the five poisons.
If the power of insight meditation does not support the tranquillity meditation,
It is not tranquillity meditation but just the dwelling[155] of the ignorant mind, and
Even if the absorption[156] is stable, it is a cause of the upper realms.
To the absorption with torpor, elation, and dullness, the meditation of animals,
Never be attached. The power of the Primordial Wisdom of insight,
When realized without stains through the discourses of holy persons,
Turns all kinds of meditation into the supports of Enlightenment.

Uncreated bliss, clarity, and absence of thought will arise from within.
Otherwise, it is not the absolute essence.
If one does not understand the secret of Intrinsic Awareness now,
Then one becomes attached to meditation, and will be bound by the chains of acceptance and rejection.
Few favorable things will occur, and unfavorable ones will come like rain.
One's expectations will not be achieved and one will always be harassed by fears.
Even the bliss, clarity, and nonconceptuality invented by the body, speech, and mind
Are, like a vase in a child's hands, without benefit since they will be broken.
The uncreated, indestructible source of attainments,
The realization of the natural essence, to seek this is important.
Even by posing the body, silencing speech, activating the mind, preventing thoughts,
And piercing[157] with the spear of vivid and clear awareness,
It seems that by preventing concepts and feelings in the state of apprehension,
One achieves the *saṃsāra* of Form and Formless realms.
The apparent object of the senses, the nonconceptual and clear perceptions;
The state of great Primordial Wisdom, self-liberation of the five poisons, and
The subtle Intrinsic Awareness pure from elation and torpor
Are regarded (by some people) as objects of abandonment, being called "very coarse, coarse, and subtle (abandonments)."
Those asses try to find ways of rejecting them.
One recollects the earlier thoughts by the succeeding thoughts, and
By just experiencing that, says that one saw the innate meaning.
(Thus) one counts the arisings and cessations (of thoughts) and continues the thoughts,

And accepts them as the meaning of non-duality: this meditator is deluded.
However much (meditative) effort one makes, if from the nets of thoughts
Later (thoughts) arise upon the cessation of the earlier ones,
Although one considers that (cessation) as liberation, it is (just) thoughts coming in succession, not self-liberation.
In the path of "skill in means,"[158] indulging in the bliss of the sense (-organs),
Is attachment to sensuality; so in most cases it is the cause of birth in the inferior realms.
Even if one reaches happy realms, one will be reborn in inferior births.
"Skill in means" is the path of only a very few *yogis*.
(In this path) there are great dangers of deviative obscurations, and it is very difficult to see the meaning of realization.
To alternate [but not to unite] the two accumulations or the development and perfecting stages, with (observations)[159] and without (observations)
Is claimed by some to be the true meaning [way], and they adhere to it; but there will be little benefit.
Only higher realms will be reached; it will not be possible to end *saṃsāra*.
Briefly, people who have little previously accumulated good fortune,
And who have entered lower, diverted, and deviated paths, how pitiable they are.
At some time may all beings find excellent unerring paths
And accordingly reach liberation !
Whoever possesses the unerring emptiness and compassion
And instantaneous liberation is on the path to self-dwelling *Dharmakāya*.
The arising of it is the denuded insight-wisdom, and
As it is the dwelling, it is the means of the equal state of tranquillity.
It is natural, united, and free from all fabrications and adulterations.

Changing creates wavering and steadiness overcomes them.
In the state where there is no torpor or elation, free from the root of defilements,
Whatever arises is the self-liberated *Dharmakāya*.
However it presents itself, it is in the state of equal non-duality.
There is no need of acceptance and rejection, it is the meaning of true mind.
In the innate essence, the Primordial Wisdom of *Dharmatā*,
Please do the exercise of practice without interruption.
This is the self-liberation of the absolute innate nature.
It is the excellent, deep supreme meditation,
The essence of the heart, condensed again and again.
It is the essence of all the summits of supreme truth.[160]

THE GREAT SPONTANEOUSLY ACCOMPLISHED RESULT
the third chapter of
NATURALLY LIBERATED MIND, THE GREAT PERFECTION

Spontaneously accomplished result has two aspects: the immediate[161] (or temporary) and the ultimate[1262] (result).
For the immediate, by meditating on the view, one will achieve virtues.
Defilements and dualizing mind will be liberated in their own natural state.
Stability in relation to internal and external phenomena will be achieved.
One will achieve "eyes," foreknowledges, and miracles.
Realization will develop, compassion for the sake of others will arise.
At that time, within the instantaneous Primordial Wisdom of Intrinsic Awareness,
If it is classified into its various aspects, the following virtues are present:
Appearances as the skillful means, and the stage of development (as) the accumulation of merits.

(Through it one attains) renunciation of the emotional concepts and apprehended [or perceptual] thoughts.
Emptiness (as) the wisdom, and the stage of perfection (as) the accumulation of Primordial Wisdom.
(Through it one attains) liberation of innate intellectual defilements and the apprehending thoughts.
Avarice, immorality, anger, laziness, distraction,
Faulty intellect, unskillfulness, weakness, lack of inspiration, and ignorance;
The pure states of those ten aspects are
The accomplishment of generosity, moral discipline, patience, diligence, contemplation, wisdom, skillful means,
Power, aspiration, and primordial wisdom, the Ten Perfections.
When the realizations arise through the kindness of the *Lama*,
The developing of supreme joy is the stage of "the Joyous."
The self-liberation of the defilements is the stage of "the Pure."
Blissful, clear, and thoughtless Primordial Wisdom is "the Light-maker."
Self-liberation of the projected thoughts is "the Radiant."
The object of none but the Excellent Ones is "the Invincible."
Actualization of the realization is the stage of "the Actualization."
Liberation from *saṃsāra* is "the Far-ranging."
Unmoving realization like Mt. Meru is "the Unshakeable."
The supreme of all is "the Excellent Wisdom."
Pervading the sky of Mind, the Tenth Stage is "the Cloud of Dharma."
The perfection of the accumulation of merits and of Primordial Wisdom are (the paths of) "accumulation"[163] and "application,"[164]
Seeing and experiencing the meaning of realization are (the paths of) "seeing"[165] and "meditation,"[166]
The liberation is called the stage of "the Result."
Freedom from the three poisons[167] (in intrinsic awareness) is the (meaning of the) "Three Scriptures."[168]
(Likewise, intrinsic awareness's) purification of the three doors is the perfection of the "Three Trainings."[169]

Liberation from everything (in intrinsic awareness) is *Kriyā Yoga*, and that is (also) *Carya Yoga*.
To reach the realized insight is the *Yoga Tantra* and *Anuttara Yoga*.
So these four *tantras*[170] are completed in (intrinsic awareness).
The benefit of self (in intrinsic awareness) is (the *yānas* of) *Śrāvakas* and *Pratyekabuddhas*,
The benefit of others is the *Mahāyāna*, and realization is *Kriyā Tantra*,
Experience (of meditation) is *Upatantra*, and enjoyment of it is *Yoga Tantra*;
And skillful means and wisdom are *Mahā Yoga* and *Anu Yoga*;
All the nine *yānas* corresponds to the self-perfection of *Ati Yoga*:[171]
The recollection and contemplation with the essence of Primordial Wisdom
Present (in intrinsic awareness) as the divisions of "instantaneous self-liberation"
Signifies that the stages, paths, and Enlightenment are the same (in intrinsic awareness).
The innate Primordial Wisdom, enlightened mind, the Great Seal,[172]
Are equally perfected (in intrinsic awareness) as the great spontaneous accomplishment.
[a. *Dharmakāya*]: In the ultimate result, the primordial state which does not dwell in extremes,
Is the Buddha-Field of the *Dharmakāya*, which is inconceivable and inexpressible.
When the Dharma-space and Primordial Wisdom have become inseparable,[173]
Full Enlightenment is attained and the Three *Kāyas* are spontaneously accomplished.
In Subtle Primordial Wisdom[174] which dwells in the sky-like sphere,
The omniscient nature dwells (in the state of) arising.
It is without accomplishments and renunciations, so it is the spontaneously accomplished *Dharmatā*,

Unborn, unceasing, of the nature of Space.
[b. *Saṃbhogakāya*]: from that state appears [1] the pure and "beautifully arrayed Buddha-Land,"[175]
The luminescently self-apparent and spontaneously accomplished *maṇḍala*,
(Along with) (2) the Teachers of the Five Classes[176] with fully perfected signs of excellence, radiating light,
Each of whom enjoy the nature of Ultimate Sphere, Mirror-like, Equanimity, Discriminating
And Accomplishing Primordial Wisdom, the Five Primordial Wisdoms,
(3) With the self-percept retinues of disciples of the ten directions[177] and four times,[178]
The *maṇḍalas* of the Teachers of the Five Classes, numerous as a vessel filled with sesame seeds,
Who dwell, pervading all the zenith and nadir, the quarters and cardinal points of space.
Doors, embrasures, pediments and railings [of the mansions], are
Resplendently beautiful in accordance with each distinct class [of teachers].
Everything is spontaneously accomplished in the nature of a single *maṇḍala*.
(4) Everywhere, without limits or center, is pervaded by the equally perfected teachings.
(5) The three times and timeless time is *Kuntu Zangpo* time,
And it is the originally accomplished and changeless state.
[c. *Nirmāṇakāya*]: From that state (are manifested) (1) the Five Classes of Pure Lands of the "Natural[179] *Nirmāṇakāya Buddhas*":
Ogmin, Ngon-ga, Rinchen Yongkang,
Pematseg, and *Lerabtrub*,
In which the Teachers of the Five Classes, to the Disciples of the Ten Stages
In all the three times, display the Excellent Mirror-(like) Form.
By their rays the disciples are purified of the obscurations to the Tenth Stage,

And are enabled to attain the (eleventh) stage of "the All-Radiant."
These Pure Lands appear for the pure Sons of the Victor (Buddha).
From the rays emitted from the mouths of the *Saṃbhogakāya* forms
In the six realms of gods, demi-gods, men, animals,
Hungry spirits, and hell
Are manifested the forms of [the six Buddhas:] *Gyachin, Thegzang, Shākyamuni,*
Seng-ge Rabten, Khabar Deva, and
Awa Lang-go.
They act for the benefit of impure beings, and are based on the peaceful ultimate sphere.
The "Various *Nirmāṇakāyas*"[180] such as forms of art, birth (as beings),
Ponds, bridges, lotuses, wish-fulfilling trees,
Medicine, jewels, and lamps
Provide the source of happiness and joy for beings and
Bring about the ultimate good [enlightenment] as the final result.
After exhausting the (population of) disciples, the Teachers will dissolve into the Dharma-sphere.
This should be understood in terms of three aspects:
(a.) the dissolution of "Various *Nirmāṇakāyas*" and the "Subduer-of-Beings *Nirmāṇakāyas*"[181] is
As when there is no water vessel [disciple], the reflections dissolve.
The projection and withdrawal of the play of the Natural[182] (*Nirmāṇakāya*) is just play.
(b.) When those who are in the position of disciples have attained peace,
The Teacher, the five classes of "Natural *Nirmāṇakāya*"
Automatically dissolves into the self-manifested *Saṃbhogakāya*[183] without separation,
Just like the dissappearance of the new moon into space.

(c.) The "Self-manifesting *Saṃbhogakāya*" dissolves into the sphere of *Dharmakāya*.
Then it does not appear externally, but in its essential nature it is the great *maṇḍala*.
It dwells without before or after, increase or decrease, or change;
Just as in spite of the apparent wax and wane, the moon remains the same.
Again, if there is a disciple,[184] they will appear again as before.
These are the results of the fully perfected Liberation.

[COLOPHON]

Thus this teaching, the essence of the sun,
illuminated by the rising of Immaculate Radiance[185]
Today in the struggling age[186] (when people) are enveloped in the darkness of wrong views,
In order to dispel (those conditions), this absolute path[187] is composed.
By the virtue of writing this, may all living beings, who are like myself,
Attain Liberation in the primordial state simultaneously, without any remaining.
May they fully perfect the qualities of abandoning and realization,
And become the Sovereigns of the Dharma[188] who spontaneously accomplish the benefit of others.

This *Dzogpa Chenpo* teaching on the Naturally Liberated Mind written by Yogi Trimed Odzer (i.e., Longchen Rabjam, 1308-1363), who was blessed by the glorious great Ācārya Padmasambhava of Orgyen, for the benefit of future generations at the excellent holy place, the Fortress of Orgyan, at the crest of Kangri Thodkar is completed. Virtue!

NOTES TO SECTION VII

1 *Kun-Tu bZang-Po,* S. *Samantabhadra.* Name of the Primordial Buddha: the union of the ultimate sphere and the primordial wisdom of the absolute truth.

2 *Ngo-Bo,* S. *bhāva.* Nature, the identity and nature of existents. In the text we have mostly translated it merely as "essence.".

3 *gDangs* (or *mDangs*): Inner or natural glow, ultimate or subtle clarity, luminous nature; inner ultimate or subtle force, profundity.

4 *Rang-bZhin,* S. *svabhāva.* Signifies the character of existents. In the text it is mostly translated merely as "nature.".

5 *gZung-'Dzin*: grasping and grasper, apprehended and apprehender, subjective and objective perception or apprehension.

6 *Sems-Nyid,* S. *cittatā.* It is the absolute nature of the mind; mindness; mind as such; the true nature of the mind; intrinsic awareness; essence of mind. In the text it is simply translated as "Mind.".

7 *sNang-Sems*: appearances and mind, "percept and mind," objective appearances and subjective perception. In this text mostly translated as "perception.".

8 Is, is not, both, and neither.

9 *dByings* (*Ch'os-Byings*), S. *dharmadhātu*; the ultimate sphere.

10 *sGyu-Ma,* S. *māyā.* An apparition created by a magician who with meditative power utters a mantra over certain specific materials such as sandalwood, etc. It is one of the eight examples of the illusory nature of phenomena.

11 *Dri-Za'i Grong*: a city of a class of spirits who live on odors.

12 cessation, coming, and going.

13 past, present, and future.

14 *Sangs-rGyas,* S. *Buddha.* The Fully Enlightened or Awakened One.

15 *'Khor-Ba,* S. *saṃsāra.* The world; the cycle of birth and death; cyclic existence.

16 *Myang-'Das.* S. *nirvāṇa.* The cessation or transcendence of suffering, the liberation from *saṃsāra*; the three goals of attainment of the *yānas* of *śrāvaka*, *pratyekabuddha*, and *bodhisattva*; Buddhahood.

17 *sNang* (*-Ba*), S. *avabhāsa.* The appearances; percept; apparent or delusory phenomena, the relative truth.

18 *sTong* (*-Nyid*), S. *śūnyatā.* The emptiness; true nature; openess; the absolute truth.

19 *Ch'os-Nyid,* S. *dharmatā.* The absolute nature of existents; suchness.

20 *Ch'os-sKu,* S. *dharmakāya.* The ultimate or Truth-Body or Absolute Body of the Buddha, the formless Body of the Three Bodies.

21 *Bag-Ch'ags,* S. *vāsanā.* The traces or the habituation caused by past actions and experiences.

22 *Myos*: madness, intoxication.

23 *Theg-pa,* S. *yāna.* Vehicle; path of spiritual training.

24 *rGyu-'Bras* (*Kyi*) *Theg-pa*: the vehicles of cause and result. The vehicle of cause is the common path of Buddhist training, *Hīnayāna* and *Mahāyāna.* The vehicle of result is the path of *tantric* or *vajrayāna* training, including *ati yoga*, or *Dzogpa Chenpo* .

25 *De-Nyid,* S. *tathatā*; thatness; true nature.

26 *Yul-Drug*: the six objects of the senses: form, sound, smell, taste, touch, and mental events.

27 *Blang-Dor*: discrimination; accepting and rejecting.
28 *dGag-sDrub*: discrimination; refuting and defending, negating and proving.
29 *Re-Dogs*: hope and fear; expectations and doubt.
30 *bDe-Ch'en*, S. *mahāsukha*: Great Bliss; Great Joy.
31 *gZhugs-sKu*, S. *rūpakāya*. The form-body of the Buddha, which is the *saṃbhogakāya* and the *nirmāṇakāya*.
32 *Tshogs-gNyis*: the accumulations of primordial wisdom and merit.
33 *Thabs*, S. *upāya*.
34 *Shes-Rab*, S. *prajñā*.
35 *mNyam (-bZhag)*: absorption.
36 *rJes (-Thob)*.
37 *bDe-Ba Ch'en-Po'i-sKu, Ngo-Bo-Nyid sKu, Ch'os-sKu, Longs-sKu*, and *sPrul-sKu*. S. *mahāsukhakāya, svabhāvikakāya, dharmakāya, saṃbhogakāya*, and *nirmāṇakāya*.
38 *Ch'os-dByings Ye-Shes, Me-Long lTa-Bu'i Ye-Shes, mNyam-Nyid Ye-Shes, Sor-rTogs Ye-Shes* and *Bya-Grub Ye-Shes*: The Primordial Wisdoms of Ultimate Sphere, Mirror-like Primordial Wisdom, the Primordial Wisdom of Equanimity, Discriminative Primordial Wisdom, and Action-accomplishing Primordial Wisdom.
39 *bKyed (-Rim)*, S. *utpannakrama*.
40 *rDzogs (-Rim)*, S. *sampannakrama*.
41 *gChig-Dang Du Bral*, S. *ekatvaviyuktaviniścayamarma* and *anekatvaviyuktaviniscayamarma*: lack of being one or many. .
42 Absolute Truth and Relative Truth.
43 *'Di-Zhes*.
44 *Khams-gSum*: the realms of desire, forms and the formless.
45 *Kun-bTags (brTags)*, S. *parikalpanā*.
46 *mCh'og-Gi dNgos-Grub*: Buddhahood.
47 *A'og-Min*, S. *akaniṣṭha*.
48 *bSam-gTan*, S. *dhyāna*.
49 *gZugs-Med*, S. *ārūpadhātu*.
50 *rNal-Ma'i Don* .
51 *dMigs-Med*, S. *niravalamba*: unobservability, aimlessness.
52 *gNyug-Ma*: absolute, essential, and innate nature.
53 *Gang-Shar rGyal-Po*.
54 *Zang-Ka-Ma*.
55 *Rang-bZhin rDzogs-Pa Ch'en-Po* .
56 *sNang-Srid*.
57 *gTad-Med*.
58 *rTsal*: manifestative power.
59 *Tshol-mKhan*.
60 *Longs-sKu*: the Buddha-body of Enjoyment, one of the two Form-Bodies of the Buddha.
61 *sPrul-sKu*: the Created or Manifested Body, one of the two Form-Bodies of the Buddha.
62 Perceiving from the subject-object standpoint.
63 *Kun-gZhi*, S. *ālaya*.
64 The six senses (*rNam-Shes*, S. *vijñāna*) of the eye, ear, nose, tongue, body, and mind.
65 *Ch'u-Bo rGyun-Gyi rNal-'Byor*.
66 *Yang-Rab dBang-Po*.
67 *Phyam-brDal*.
68 *Gang-Byung Rig-Pa*.

69 *Ma-bChos Rig-Pa.*
70 *Tha-Mal Shes-Pa.*
71 *Rang-Bab Shes-Pa.*
72 *gNyis-Med Shes-Pa.*
73 *Byar-Med Shes-Pa.*
74 *Rang-Grol Rig-Pa.*
75 *gTad-Med Rig-Pa.*
76 *'Dzin-Med Rig-Pa.*
77 *brTul-Zhug Rig-Pa.*
78 *Shugs-'Byung Rig-Pa.*
79 *lChe-sPyang Mig.*
80 *Phyogs-Bral Rig-Pa.*
81 *bsGom-Med Rig-Pa.*
82 *Rang-Byung Rig-Pa.*
83 *sNang-Dangs Rig-Pa.*
84 *Shar-Grol Rig-Pa.*
85 *mNyam-rDzogs Rig-Pa.*
86 *gNyug-Ma'i Sems-Nyid.*
87 *Bogs-'Byin.*
88 *bSre-Ba.*
89 *mNyam-rJes.*
90 *sPrul-Pa*: a miraculous creation by powerful gods, spirits, or human beings.
91 *Mig-Yor.*
92 *lTa-Ba*, S. *darśana.*
93 *sGom-Pa*, S. *bhāvanā.*
94 *sPyod-Pa*, S. *caryā.*
95 *'Bras-Bu*, S. *phala.*
96 *sGom-Med Don.*
97 *gTan-Srid.*
98 *Gang-Shar Rig-Pa.*
99 *Yon-Tan*, S.*guṇa.*
100 *A'od-gSal*, S. *ābhāsvarā*, *prabhāsvara*: clarity, clear light, luminous absorption.
101 *sKu-gNyis*: the two Bodies of the Buddha, the formless absolute body (*S. dharmakāya*), and the form body (*S. rūpakāya*).
102 *Dug-lNga*: the five passions or defilements are ignorance, lust, anger or hatred, jealousy or envy, and pride.
103 *sGom-Pa Kha-Zlum.*
104 *Las*, S. *karma*: the dynamic pattern of cause and effect, the causation which always conditions every good and bad action, linking past, present, and future lives of all individual beings.
105 *rTen-'Brel*, S. *pratītyasamutpāda*: dependent arising.
106 *Ch'os-Nyid mNgon-Sum sNang-Ba.*
107 *Nyams-sNang Gong-'Phel sNang-Ba.*
108 *Bying*: dullness, depression, laxity. .
109 *rGod*: excitement, distractedness, lethargy, discursiveness.
110 *Rig-Pa Tshad-Phebs sNang-Ba.*
111 *Mi-dMigs.*
112 *mTshan-'Dzin.*
113 *Ch'os-Nyid Zad-Pa'i sNang-Ba.*
114 *bZhi*: In the text it is spelled *gZhi* (basis), but according to Khyentse Rinpoche it should read as *bZhi*, i.e., Four Visions of *Dzogpa Chenpo.*
115 *gZugs-sKu*, S. *rūpakāya.*

116 *Tshad.*
117 Meaning that there is only the taste of merit in one's character.
118 *Zin-Pa.*
119 *sGo-gSum*: body, speech, and mind.
120 *sKu-gSum*, S.*trikāya: dharmakāya, saṃbhogakāya*, and *nirmāṇakyāna.*
121 *Kun-Khyab Ye-Shes.*
122 *Sor-bZhag.*
123 *mNyam-Pa'i Ngang.*
124 *Lhun-rDzogs rGyal-Po.*
125 *sNang-mKhan.*
126 *gZa', rGyu-sKar, Tshes-Grangs.*
127 *Dus.*
128 *sByor-Ba.*
129 *rTsa*, S. *nāḍī.*
130 *Khams.*
131 *'Khor-Lo.*
132 *Yul-lNga*: form, sound, smell, taste, and touch.
133 *gZhal-Yas Khang.*
134 *Byed-Po.*
135 *sNying-Po Don-Gyi Lha.*
136 *rNam-rTog 'Phro-'Du.*
137 *gSang-sNgags.*
138 *rDzogs-Rim*, S. *sampannakrama.*
139 *Pha-Rol Phyin-Pa*, S. *pāramitā.*
140 *Zung-'Jug*, S. *yuganaddha.*
141 *Dam-Pa*, S. *parama.*
142 *sNgon-'Gro.*
143 *Blo-sNa bsTung.*
144 *sKyo-Shes.*
145 *Dal (-Ba)*: Free human life has eight aspects: freedom from taking birth in the realms of hell, hungry ghosts, animals, long-lived gods, barbarous people, people with wrong views, in a world in which no Buddha has appeared, and as a stupid person.
146 *'Byor (-Ba)*: A fortunate human life has ten endowments: being born as a human being, possessing all the faculties, born in a land that is central in relation to the Dharma, not reverting to wrong living, having faith in the Buddha's doctrine, the Buddha having appeared and having expounded the Dharma, the Dharma is remaining, one has entered into it, and one has been accepted by a holy teacher.
147 *Bar-Do*: the intermediate state between death and rebirth.
148 *sNying-Po'i De-Nyid.*
149 *Byang-Ch'ub Sems*: the intention to benefit others, to attain Enlightenment for all sentient beings, and to practice accordingly.
150 *Theg-Chen*: the Great Vehicle, one of the two main paths and schools of Buddhism, the other being the *Hīnayāna.*
151 *Nges-'Byung*, S. *niḥsaraṇa.*
152 *bDud*, S. *māra*: it is the personification of the forces obstructing the practice of Dharma and realization.
153 *Zhi-gNas*, S. *śamatha.*
154 *Lhag-mThong*, S. *vipaśyāna.*
155 *gNas (-Pa).*
156 *bSam-gTan*, S. *samādhi*: contemplation, deep meditative absorption.
157 *bTsug.*

158 *Thabs-Lam*, S. *upāyamārga*: esoteric training involving the *vajra*-bodies of oneself and others.
159 *dMigs-Pa*.
160 *rDo-rJe*, S. *vajra*: diamond, symbolizing the supreme and indestructible.
161 *gNas-sKab*.
162 *mThar-Thug*.
163 *Tshogs (-Lam)*, S. *sambhāramārga*.
164 *sByor (-Lam)*, S. *prayogamārga*.
165 *mThong (-Lam)*, S. *darśanamārga*.
166 *sGom (-Lam)*, S. *bhāvanāmārga*.
167 *Dug-gSum*: ignorance, lust, and hatred.
168 *sDe-sNod gSum*, S. *tripiṭaka*: *vinaya* (the monastic discipline), *sūtra* (discourses), and *abhidharma* (psycho-metaphysics).
169 *bSlab-gSum*, S. *triśiksā*: *śīla* (discipline), *samādhi* (contemplation), and *prajñā* (transcendental wisdom).
170 *rGyud-sDe bZhi*: the four levels of *tantra*: *kriyātantra*, *caryātantra*, *yogatantra*, and *anuttārāyogatantra*.
171 *rDzogs-Pa Ch'en-Po*, S. *mahāsandhi*.
172 *Phyag-rGya-Ch'e*, S. *mahāmudrā*.
173 *Ro-gChig*.
174 *Pra-Ba'i Ye-Shes*.
175 *sTug-Po bKod-Pa'i Zhing*.
176 *Rigs-lNga'i sTon-Pa*: S. *akṣobhya*, *amoghasiddhi*, *ratnasambhava*, *amitābha*, and *vairocana*.
177 *Phyogs-bChu*: east, south, west, north, northeast, northwest, southeast, southwest, zenith and nadir.
178 *Dus-bZhi: past, present, future, and timeless time.*
179 *Rang-bZhin sPrul-sKu*.
180 *sNa-Tshogs sPrul-sKu*.
181 *'Gro-'Dul (sPrul-sKu)*.
182 *Rang-bZhin Rol-Ba*.
183 *Longs-sKu*: one of the two form bodies of the Buddha.
184 *gDul-Bya*: literally one who is capable of being trained in the path of enlightenment.
185 *Dri-Med A'od-Zer*: one of the names of Kunkhyen Longchen Rabjam.
186 *rTsod-Dus*.
187 *Nges-Pa'i Lam*.
188 *Ch'os-Kyi rGyal-Po*.

8. *Instructions on the Meditation on Naturally Liberated Mind, the Great Perfection*

This is a translation of a complete short text by Longchen Rabjam entitled *The Quintessential Meaning—Instructions on the Stages of the Path of Naturally Liberated Mind, the Great Perfection*. (NDK). It is a summary of *Naturally Liberated Mind* (SR), arranging the teachings into courses of training, starting from preliminaries to the highest level of *Thregchod* meditation. As it is very brief and compact, in many places it is hard to comprehend. Although it explains the means of training, it is appropriate to engage in this practice only after having full instructions and proper transmissions from a well qualified master.

QUINTESSENTIAL MEANING-INSTRUCTIONS ON THE STAGES OF THE PATH OF NATURALLY LIBERATED MIND, THE GREAT PERFECTION

Homage to the Glorious *Vajrasattva*,
Whose nature from the beginning is unborn,
Inexpressible, inconceivable, non-dual, the Ultimate Body,
The compassionate Mind, spontaneously present *Kuntu Zangpo*,
(Who is) the Perfection at the basis without changes: to you I pay homage.

The teachings to *yogis* for their certain attainment in this very lifetime,
The direct blessings of the holy beings,
The meaning of the self-liberation of whatever arises without accepting or rejecting,
I shall teach (here) in writing.

The fully enlightened Buddha has discoursed upon inconceivable doors of vehicles and kinds of teachings with his great compassion and skillful means appropriate to the natures and intellects of beings. The meaning of all these teachings is encompassed in the intrinsic awareness, the enlightened mind. Although there are many teachings (that are supposed to be) practices on it, there are very few paths which (actually) lead to liberation in a single lifetime, because those (other paths) are bound by attachments to apprehending the extremes. This instruction on Naturally Liberated Mind of Great Perfection is the most secret method of instant realization of the acceptances and rejections as the liberation at the basis. This teaching transcends all the (other) *yānas*. To learn it, there are three parts: (a) the lineage of teachers, (b) the teaching transmitted through them, and (c) the command to entrust the teaching (to protectors) because of its importance.

The Lineage of Teachers

This teaching is transmitted through:

1. Samantabhadra, the Ultimate Body of the Unexcelled Buddha field
2. Amitābha, the Enjoyment Body
3. Padmasambhava, the Manifested Body
4. *Ḍākinī* Yeshey Tshogyal
5. Guru Silamati
6. Khedrub Geleg Gyatsho
7. Choje Monlam Odzer
8. Myself (Longchen Rabjam)

The Teaching Transmitted through Them

(i) *Teaching of practice for self-liberation in this very lifetime.*

(a) PRELIMINARIES

(1) UNIFICATION WITH THE *GURU* FOR RECEIVING THE BLESSINGS

Sit on a comfortable seat. Take refuge (in the triple gem) and generate the mind of enlightenment. Then visualize (the following) instantly: Above the crown of one's head is the great master Padmasambhava, inseparable from one's root *Guru*, sitting on a lotus, sun and moon seat. He is in the *Heruka* costume, blazing with major and minor auspicious signs and marks. His complexion is blue. He holds a *vajra* and bell in his hands and embraces his consort. He is ornamented with precious jewels and bone ornaments. In his lap is the Lady of the Kharchen family(i.e., *Yeshey Tshogyal*). She has a reddish complexion. She holds a curved blade and a skull and embraces her consort. They are surrounded by all the teachers of the lineage and inconceivable (numbers and immensity of) Buddhas, *Bodhisattvas*, *Ḍākas*, and *Ḍākinīs*. Before them, in one's mind: pay homage, make offerings, purify (by confessing) one's evil deeds, rejoice (in others' virtuous deeds), pray (to the teachers) to turn the wheel of Dharma and request (them) to remain without entering into the cessation of sorrow. Then supplicate them saying:

> O precious Guru (the embodiment of all the enlightened ones)! Please bestow your blessings upon me (and all beings) (to) purify the obscurations of my (our) body, speech, and mind, to obtain the accomplishments of the body, speech, and mind (of the enlightened ones) and to be able to attain Buddhahood in this very lifetime.

Then think, "Lights are emitted from the body of the *Guru* (and the rest). (Just by being touched by the lights), the obscurations of body, speech, and mind of all living beings are purified and the whole universe is transformed into the nature of the *Guru*. Then lights are emitted from the body, speech, and mind of all (the objects of devotion) and they enter the crown of one's head and generate the primordial wisdom of bliss, clarity, and no-concept, which is the extraordinary realization, the instantaneous self-liberation." Hold one's breath for a while. Practice by expanding the meditation (gradually). At the end, dedicate the merits by (understanding) the state of magical apparition (*Māyā*). If one trains thus for seven days, the extraordinary blessings and signs of accomplishment of the *Guru* will suddenly be received.

(2) TRAINING ON THE MAṆḌALA OFFERING TO PERFECT THE TWO GREAT ACCUMULATIONS

Visualize hosts of *Gurus* and the *maṇḍalas* of tutelary deities in the sky in front of oneself. Arrange the heaps of *Maṇḍala* offering (materials). Think, "All the (world and the Buddha-)fields of the ten directions are symbolized by the world system of four continents and are made of various precious gems. They are filled with various human and celestial objects of enjoyment." Then offer them to the guests of offering with one's own body, wealth, and merits, and think that they are all pleased. Continue the *maṇḍala* offering for seven days. The purpose, by performing the two accumulations, the accumulation of merits and of primordial wisdom, is to generate the extraordinary realization in one's mind.

(3) TRAINING ON THE HUNDRED SYLLABLE MANTRA FOR PURIFICATION OF THE TWO-FOLD OBSCURATION

From the (meditative) state of emptiness, visualize instantly *Vajrasattva* with white complexion and one face. He has two hands holding *vajra* and bell. He is ornamented with precious jewels and sits with crossed legs. At his heart, in the middle of a lotus and moon disc, is a "HŪṂ" letter surrounded by a hundred syllables. Rays of light are emitted (in all directions from the syllables) and the obscurations of all beings are purified (at the mere touch of the rays). Recite the hundred syllable *mantra* as much as one can for seven days. The purpose of this training is to purify the obscurations of evil deeds and to realize the ultimate nature swiftly.

(4) PRACTICE ON IMPERMANANCE OF LIFE (TO) GENERATE DEFINITE EMERGENCE (FROM) AND REVULSION (FROM *SAṂSĀRA*)

Think, "Human life is adorned by the precious freedoms and endowments, but its nature is certain impermanence and swift destruction. The externally appearing objects are impermanence since they change with the times of days, months, and years. No living being has ever transcended death." Think about "the occurence of death to one's relatives and friends." Think about "the certainty of one's own death since life is impermanent. One's body is going to disintegrate and be dispersed like a bubble breaking, and there is no certainty that one will not die even today." Think, "Today is my last day in this world, and the elements (one's body) are dissolving and the mind and the body are being separated." Meditate on this from the heart for seven days. The purpose of this meditation is to induce (awareness of) impermanence in one's mind, reduce mental planning, and enable one to enter into and exert oneself in Dharma training.

(5) THE PRACTICE OF GOING FOR REFUGE, WHICH INITIATES THE PATH OF TRAINING

Visualize in the sky in front of oneself the triple gem, such as the Buddhas of the three times and ten directions with *Bodhisattvas*, hosts of *maṇḍalas* of tutelary deities, and the *Arhats* of the *Śrāvakas* and *Pratyeka-buddhas*. With the intention of taking them as the refuges until one attains enlightenment, recite the (prayers of) going for refuge to the *Guru* and the rest. Doing so, think, "As parents are loving and kind to their children, the (refuges) are looking (at beings) with a compassionate mind." Reciting the (prayers of) refuge from the depth of the heart's core, think, "All living beings are loudly repeating the refuge prayer after me." Dedicate oneself to this practice for seven days. The purpose is to pacify the obstructions of Dharma training and to develop realization.

(6) THE PRACTICE OF DEVELOPING THE MIND OF ENLIGHTENMENT, WHICH IS ADVANCEMENT ON THE PATH OF *DHARMA*

Think of the suffering of freezing and burning torments of the hell realm, the hunger and thirst of the hungry ghost realm, the servitude of the animal realm, birth, old age, sickness, and death of the human realm, the combat of the demi-gods' realm and the death and fall of the gods' realm, and so on, in front of oneself. Thus, beings are suffering all the time, and the nature of *saṃsāra* is nothing but suffering. So think, "May all living beings, who are worn out by the sufferings of *saṃsāra*, by means of my merits, body and wealth, and so on, remain in the four measureless experiences of enjoying happiness, freedom from suffering, (not being separated from happiness free from suffering and the equanimity of) having neither hatred nor attachment. Ultimately, may they attain the state of Buddhahood." Vocally take (the vow of) developing the mind of enlightenment with a simple ritual and recite:

> O lords, with your (spiritual) children, please pay attention to me!
> As the Buddhas of the three times
> Developed the mind of enlightenment,
> Likewise, for the sake of living beings,
> I generate the mind of enlightenment in myself.
> In the disciplines as they are taught (in the scriptures),
> I properly train myself gradually.
> May I be able to destroy the sufferings of living beings,
> And whatever I do, may it cause the benefit of others to be fulfilled.

Also meditate on the training of taking others' sufferings upon oneself and giving away one's happiness to them. Meditate on heartfelt compassion for seven days. Its purpose is that whatever one does physically and vocally may become solely for the benefit of others, and thereby become the training in the path of *Mahāyāna*.

(7) TRAINING ON THE ESSENTIAL PATH OF ASCERTAINED MEANING TO GENERATE THE REALIZATION OF THE ULTIMATE NATURE

(a) SEEKING TRANQUILLITY

Sit in the cross-legged posture. Contemplate in the state in which thoughts of the past have ceased, thoughts of the future have not arisen, and for the present there are no conceptualizations in any of the senses. Contemplate on this for seven days. The purpose is to suppress the ordinary evil thoughts, the obscurations, and to make it easier to recognize whatever adventitious thoughts arise by distinguishing the aspects of clarity and the impurities in the intrinsic awareness.

(b) GENERATING INSIGHT

At a time when the thoughts are projecting more grossly then before, one should analyze them. When the thoughts are scattering, search for where they arise. Search the body from top to bottom and the phenomena inside, outside, and in between. Search for the color, design, and identity of the thoughts. As they arise from nowhere, (they lead) one to realize the state of unborn Mind, free from roots. When a thought is present, analyze what is its color, design and identity and whether it dwells inside, outside, or in between (phenomena). (This analysis will lead) one to realize the great ceaseless clarity and emptiness Mind, the great presence at the basis. The thoughts arise suddenly and then disappear without trace of where they go. At the time of cessation (of the thoughts), by analyzing where they go, one will realize the meaning of the intrinsic awareness, the liberation in its own state, without any traces, by transcending any recognitions.

(c) RECOGNITION OF THE UNION (OF TRANQUILLITY AND INSIGHT)

Having relaxed the body and mind naturally, remain in equalness, peace, clarity, and distinctiveness, in the state of mind which transcends thoughts and recollections. (As a result,) the aspect of pacifying the movement of the thoughts and recollections is "tranquillity" and seeing it clearly and vividly is "insight." Experiencing both aspects simultaneously is the "union." The purpose of this training is to recognize the absorption with skillful means. Meditate for one day on each of them.

(ii) *The actual path, introduction (to the realization).* Place both mind and body in total relaxation. The recognition takes place at the point of the present instant mind. All the external and internal world and beings are the modes of arising of one's own mind. They are like dreams. The mind itself is also emptiness in its essence, clarity in its nature and variously arising in its character, like the appearances of forms in an unstained mirror. They are free from all the elaborations of extremes of existents and non-existents as they appear, but at the same time they are free from being recognizable. It means that there is no separate ultimate nature (*Ch'os-Nyid*) other than the present mind projecting in various forms.

The Great Master (*Padmasambhava*) said:

> If one understands that the very mind is the ultimate nature,
> Then there is no other ultimate sphere to meditate (upon).
> (Merely) knowing the methods for realization and liberation is enough,
> As the very mind is the Ultimate Body.
> This excellent path is uniqely superior (to others).
> This is the universal *Yāna* of *Samantabhadra*.
> Whoever performs the so-called renunciation of thoughts, meditation on no-thoughts,

And sees the universe as the enemies of liberation and as
delusion, falls (into the extremes).

So relax naturally and spontaneously in the present mind itself without any efforts and imputations. Whatever thoughts arise, contemplate in it (the present mind) by relaxing ordinarily, as it is, and nakedly without rejections and acceptances. Being in the essence which is liberation upon seeing; in the nature which is liberating upon realizing; and in the characteristic which is self-liberating is the natural state of the mind. Whatever arises (in the mind), treat it without paying much attention, then the mind remains in the naturalness of the intrinsic awareness and the self-completion arises naturally. At that time, without the influence of any attachments either to rejecting or accepting, remain in the state of changeless intrinsic awareness,the instantly liberated primordial wisdom, (the union) of bliss, clarity and no-concepts. When not apprehending the present mind with assertions of "this is this," the intrinsic awareness itself becomes self-liberated, and simultaneously it dissolves. When the intrinsic awareness is dissolved, remain in the state of no imputations and pollutions until the next intrinsic awareness arises. When it arises again do not prolong the unrecognizable intrinsic awareness but remain in it freely (*Yan-sTabs*), maintain it openly (*Yengs-sTabs*), and let it go without holding on to it (*'Dzin-Med*). Like putting things in a bottomless vessel, gain experience in the intrinsic awareness which is transparent (*Zang-Thal*), instantaneous (*sKad-Chig*), self-liberated (*Rang-Grol*), unhindered (*Thal-Grol*), and having no objective point of "this is this." In brief, as the view and meditation of liberation-upon-arising happen in (the manner of) self-arising and bursting forth from the depth (*Klong-rDol*), both the object of abandonments and the antidotes are liberated through self-dissolution. Then, as all phenomenal existents have arisen as the ultimate nature, the meditation has no interruption. As the intrinsic awareness and emptiness are liberated without apprehensions, the defilements are purified as primordial wisdom. As the virtues are present as the spontaneous perfection, one transcends efforts and accomplishments. As all have arisen as the nature, it is the self-attainment of the ultimate nature, pure from all errors and obscurations. Therefore, all the present ordinary thoughts and recollections are the state of self-nature of the Ultimate Body. The Great Master (*Padmasambhava*) said:

> In the Mind free from concepts:
> Remain in equalness (*Phyam-Me*) with no meditation.
> Even (if you) meditate, remain naturally (*Khril-Le*) with no negating.
> Remain in instantness (*Tsen-Ne*) with no wavering,
> Even (if you) waver, remain freely (*Khril-Le*) with no negating.
> Remain in suspension (*Chog-Ge*) with no watching.
> Even (if you) watch, remain blank (*Che-Re*) with no negating.
> Remain in instinctiveness (*Hrig-Ge*) with no projecting.
> Even (if you) project, remain "herely" (*'Di-Gar*) with no negating.
> Remain in distinctiveness (*Wal-Le*) without withdrawing.
> Even (if you) withdraw, remain clearly (*Ting-Nge*) with no negating.
> Remain in openess (*Khrol-Le*) with no exertions.
> Even (if you) exert, remain restrained (*dTud-De*) with no negating.
> Remain in lucidness (*Sa-Le*) with no modifications.
> Even (if you) modify, remain purely (*Sang-Nge*) with no negating.
> Remain in effortlessness (*rTsol-Med*) with no acquiring.
> Even (if you) acquire, remain spontaneously (*Lhun-Gyis*) with no negating.
> Remain in spontaneity (*Rang-Byung*) with no rejecting.
> Even (if you) reject, remain in the unborn (*sKye-Med*) with no negating.
> Remain in alertness (*Hu-Re*) with no limits.
> Even (if you) are limited,remain naturally (*Lhan-Ne*) with

no negating.
Remain in relaxation (*'Bol-Le*) with no efforts.
Even (if you) make efforts, remain spontaneously (*Shugs-'Byung*) with no negating.
Remain in no-basis (*gZhi-Bral*) with no contemplation.
Even (if you) contemplate, remain spontaneouly (*Lhug-Par*) with no negating.

The present mind having been released freely into the state of naturalness, the unmodified spontaneous perfection of whatever arises, there is no attachment toward external and internal phenomena. (In the present mind,) as there are no thoughts of rejecting or accepting, the state of non-duality of the mind remains ceaselessly. As there are no gross thoughts, the wildly roaming mind has been liberated from the thoughts of the desire (realm). As the projecting thoughts have arisen in naturalness, the mind has transcended all diversion to the form and formless realms. Having no apprehension as "this," the tranquillity has been accomplished spontaneously. As the naturalness (*So-Ma*) (of the mind) has arisen spontaneously, the insight has been accomplished spontaneously. As there is no separate projecting and dwelling, their union has been accomplished spontaneously. As it has been liberated in the instantaneous state itself (or instantaneously in its own state), the wisdom has been accomplished spontaneously. As there is no dwelling, the absorption has been accomplished. As there is no apprehension of liberation-upon-arising (of intrinsic awareness), the primordial wisdom has been accomplished spontaneously. As all the faults are present through the aspect of apprehension, they are liberated in freedom from apprehension and hindrances. As all the virtues arise in the awareness wisdom, they are progressing. It is the mind perfected in its own naturalness, and it is the attainment of supreme accomplishment of the Great Seal (*Mahāmudrā*), in this very lifetime.

Remain in the uncreated, natural, and unobstructed awareness,

The state of whatever arises, through great self-arisen (realization).
The supportlessness king (-mind) is content with no apprehensions
And has attained the unborn Ultimate Body, the eternal state.

(iii) *Conclusion.*

(a) THE MEDITATIVE EXCERCISES

In the off-meditation periods—of training on actual contemplation, the naturalness of the present mind of whatever arises—train clearly in the power of exercises of (seeing that) all the external appearances and internal awareness, as well as the training experiences, are non-existent at the very point of their arising, like a dream, illusion, mirage, water-moon (reflection), and apparition. These exercises liberate the attachment to all existents as real. Even in sleep one remains in *Dharmakāya*, the absence of apprehensions.

(b) DISPELLING THE OBSCURATIONS, SUCH AS SICKNESS AND HARMFUL EFFECTS

If sickness and harmful effects, the manifestations of the thoughts, are examined, it is certain that they do not exist anywhere outside, inside, or in between. So, with a joyful attitude because of (the opportunity of) turning the obstructions into the means of practice on the path of the unborn, meditate (by thinking and visualizing): on piercing into and relieving the pains of sickness, and on the power of exercises of compassion and of (realization of) the non-existence in their true nature (of the obstructions) causing the harmful effects. It will certainly pacify them.

(c) PROGRESSING IN THE EXERCISES

If the virtuous training becomes slow, or if there is no progress, pray strongly to the Guru, generate strong emergence and revulsion (from *saṃsāra*) in the mind, accumulate merits by feasts of offering (*Tshogs*) and meditate on loving kindness, compassion, and the mind of enlightenment. Go to a totally solitary place such as a cemetery, an empty valley, or mountain peaks. Visualize the *Guru* on the crown of the head, and run and jump (around spontaneously), utter words (whatever comes out), and mentally project various experiences of happiness or suffering and rejecting or accepting. Then unite the experiences naturally with the instantaneous self-liberation. Training thus for many days produces various extraordinary realizations. These are the very crucial points of training.

A trainee who has gained such experiences attains confidence in having no fear of death and liberates apprehender (subjective) and apprehended (objective perception) in their natural state. He realizes directly the common and uncommon attainments in this very lifetime. This is a brief condensation as it would be endless to explain this training in detail. The teachings for the attainment of liberation in this lifetime are completed.

The Teaching on Clarity, the Arising-Basis of the Intermediate State

Because of experiences in the crucial points of instant liberation of birth and death (through meditation) in the past, also at the time of the dream intermediate state (*rMi-Lam Bar-Do*), the natural state (*gNas-Lugs*) of primordial liberation, free from apprehensions, arises. At the time of a *yogi's* death, by dissolving (or transferring the focus of the energy of) earth (element of the body) into water, he loses the physical energy, by dissolving water into fire the liquid of the water dries up, by dissolving fire into air heat withdraws (starting) from the extremities, and by dissolving air into consciousness he ceases breathing. By dissolving (or transferring the focus of energy of) form into sound he won't see forms with his eyes, by dissolving sound into smell he won't hear any sound, by dissolving smell into taste he won't feel smell with his nose, by dissolving taste into touch he won't feel taste with his tongue, by dissolving taste into phenomena he won't feel touch, and by dissolving phenomena into mind his gross subjective and objective thoughts cease. This is similar to becoming unconscious. It is the dissolution of the eight consciousnesses into the universal ground. At the very point of contemplating in the absorption, one liberates oneself as the bodies of the five families (of Buddhas) and attains the primordial state. It is the state which endows the five (Buddha-families) and the great perfection.

At the very moment of contemplating naturally without support on the blue light as the Primordial Wisdom of the Ultimate Sphere, he liberates his self-awareness as the body of *Vairocana Buddha*. Likewise, contemplation on the white light as Mirror-Like Primordial Wisdom liberates him as *Akṣobhya*, the yellow light as Primordial Wisdom of Equanimity liberates him as *Ratnasambhava*, the red light as Discriminative Primordial Wisdom liberates him as *Amitābha*, and the green light as Primordial Wisdom of Accomplishment liberates him as *Amoghasiddhi Buddha*. Then through the manifested body he serves living beings. This is the attainment of full enlightenment at the primordial ground. This is the (method of) instant liberation by unifying (the primordial wisdom) with the clarity of the intermediate state by recognizing the spontaneously present and unsearched for primordial wisdom of bliss, clarity, and no-thought, which has naturally arisen and has been naturally recognized when one gained experiences in this crucial point of instant self-liberation in the past. As the essence of intrinsic awareness is emptiness, it dwells nowhere. As the nature of intrinsic awareness is clarity, the basis of arising is unceasing. As the character of intrinsic awareness is various, it is present in the state of all-arising, free from discriminations. These are (called) the three endowments (of intrinsic awareness). Then four separate visions of the dissolution of the four elements (appear and they) are the four endowments. Then (one attains) liberation as the five bodies (of the five Buddha families) by realizing the clarity as the primordial wisdoms. They are the five endowments (of intrinsic awareness). Then one acts for the benefit of beings through manifestations. It is the endowment of total perfection. Then, by dissolving the Enjoyment body into the Ultimate Body and securing the state of changeless ultimate nature, one dwells in the great equalness perfection. It is the endowment of great total perfection. That is the instruction on liberation in the intermediate state for trainees of mediocre (intellect).

Supplementary (Instructions) for Continuing the Karmic Process in the Intermediate State of Existence (Srid-Pa Bar-Do)

If one cannot recognize or maintain the clarity at death, then (one will take the subtle or) mental body which appears for the first half of the duration (of the life in the intermediate state) in the form of one's previous birth and for the last half in the form of the next birth. This body possesses all the sense faculties, and it reaches anywhere (in *saṃsāra*) by thinking because of its *karmic* force. The possessor passes without hindrance thorough (everything) except his mother's womb and the *Vajra*-seat (Enlightened State). He goes through many happy and unhappy experiences like appearances in a dream. The duration of this is uncertain. Some take rebirth faster while others remain as long as 49 days. When they realize they are dead, they experience sorrow. At that time, if they remember the previously received instructions and train in the great apprehensionlessness of the appearances and the mind, and if they pray to the *Guru*, then there are trainees among them who attain liberation. At that juncture, it is also very important to reflect upon pure lands with the mind, to understand that the perceptions of the intermediate state are unreal, and to remember devotion and veneration (toward enlightened ones). It is said (in scriptures) that such trainees then take rebirth in pure lands and there attain enlightenment.

The best way (of training to turn the intermediate state into the means of higher attainments) is the (understanding) that (phenomena) do not truly exist. The second best way is (to perceive the appearances as) the development stage, perfection stage, and pure lands like a magical apparition (*Māyā*). The least good way is to train in sealing the doors of (inferior) wombs. For sealing the doors of birth (one should recognize their symbolic images). The (door of birth) of the gods' realm appears as a garden or a mansion, of the demi-gods' realm as a wheel of light, of the human realm as a house, either a house of enjoyment or one full of people, of the animal realm as a cave or hut, of the hungry ghosts' realm as a dry ravine, a cave or filth, and of the hell realm as darkness and a rainstorm and so on. At that time, do not be attached to any of those doors of birth. Perceive a special birth door, either of the gods' realm or the human realm, as a celestial mansion and in it visualize a letter such as "HŪṂ." Then make one's consciousness enter the letter. Then thinking, "I will meet Dharma and attain the supreme accomplishment in the next life," visualize oneself as one's tutelary deity. By this method one takes rebirth in a precious birth in the human or gods' realm, possessing the qualities of freedom and endowments, one meets holy, virtuous friends as spiritual masters and attains the supreme accomplishment in that lifetime. The instruction on the intermediate state is completed.

The Instructions on the Result, the Perfection

Whether one attains liberation in this lifetime, in the intermediate state, or in the next life, the result is certain (to be) unexcelled Buddhahood. By making one's mind become totally pure by being self-liberated, and by realizing the meaning of the clarity directly, one will secure the stronghold in the state of the unstained Ultimate Body (*Ch'os-sKu*). At that time, as the sun and moon arise in the sky, from the state of the Ultimate Body the Enjoyment Body (*Longs-sKu*) appears with five certainties and serves the beings who have attained (any of) the ten stages. Through various forms of Manifested Bodies (*sPrul-sKu*), one accomplishes the benefits of various beings spontaneously. Particularly, (a) if one realizes the self-appearances of the intermediate state as clarity of the basis, one secures the state of the Ultimate Body. Then, from that state, the benefits for living beings take place through Enjoyment Bodies and Manifested Bodies. (b) If one realizes the self-appearances as the appearances of the fivefold primordial wisdom, one secures the state of the Enjoyment Body and fulfills the welfare of beings by Manifested Bodies. And then the Manifested Bodies dissolve into the Enjoyment Bodies, which dissolve into the Ultimate Body, and there one remains in the primordial basis. (Again) from that (primordial) state, one serves beings through the appearances of the two Form Bodies. (c) If one realizes the self-appearances as the pure bodies and Buddha-fields of Manifested Bodies, (one secures the state of the Manifested Body and) the apparances of the Enjoyment Bodies and Manifested Bodies dissolve into the Ultimate Body, and (from it) one accomplishes benefits of beings (through the two form bodies).

In this very present intrinsic awareness, both *saṃsāra* and *nirvāṇa* are completed. So, if one could not realize it, various kinds of happiness and suffering arise (for one) in the dream-like appearances of the *saṃsāra* of ignorant sleep, and one wanders in the three realms and six classes of beings. If one gains experiences of the realization, the visions of *nirvāṇa*, like dreams, appear as the various pure lands of the Enjoyment Body and serve beings as in dreams. Whatever colors appear, at the very moment of their appearance (by realizing that they) do not exist in reality, they disappear just as dreams disappear when one awakens and then become one taste within the Ultimate Body, free from elaborations, like appearances in daytime.

So if one does not realize the emptiness, the essence of the present intrinsic awareness, then because of ignorance, one becomes deluded into mind and the formless realm. These are of the no-thought (nature). (Likewise, if one does not realize) the clarity [luminescence], the nature (of the present intrinsic awareness), then because of anger one becomes deluded into speech and the form realm. (These are of the clarity nature.) (If one does not realize) the varieties, the character (of the present intrinsic awareness), because of desire one becomes deluded into the body and the desire realm. These are of the bliss nature.

Subsequently, from unvirtuous deeds one will suffer in the hell realms, from contaminated virtuous deeds unrelated to contemplations (one will suffer) in the human and gods' migrations, from clarity of contemplation (one will suffer) in the form realms and from dwelling in stable contemplations (one will suffer) in the formless realm.

When one sees and realizes the present awareness, then its emptiness essence is the Ultimate Body free from elaborations, its clear nature is the Enjoyment Body with five certainties, and its character, appearing in various forms, is the Manifested Body appropriately appearing to perfect the welfare of beings spontaneously. The Ultimate Body is the freedom from all elaborations, like space, and from that state (appears) the "unexcelled Buddha-field' of the Enjoyment Body, with the teachers of Peaceful and Wrathful Buddhas of the Enjoyment Body adorned with major and minor marks. They please endless self-appearing Buddhas and Bodhisattvas of the ten stages with the teachings of the Great Vehicle until *saṃsāra* is emptied. From that (Enjoyment Body) state, through inconceivable Manifested Bodies of inexhaustible body, speech, and mind with the (two) wisdoms of knowing the absolute truth and conventional variations, one performs enlightened deeds for the beings in all six classes of beings of the ten directions, in accordance with their different perceptions. This is the great compassion of the immeasurable enlightened actions.

(In) the manifesting aspect of Buddha's primordial wisdom there are (two categories:) the five greatnesses of the Enjoyment Body (*Saṃbhogakāya*), which is the essence appearing inwardly; and the two greatnesses of the Manifested Body (*Nirmāṇakāya*), which are the forms appearing outwardly. The five inner (primordial wisdoms) are: the primordial wisdoms of the ultimate sphere, mirror-like, equanimity, discriminative, and accomplishment. The two outer (primordial wisdoms) are: the primordial wisdom of knowing every detail of conventional phenomena separately without confusing them, and the primordial wisdom of knowing the one-taste ultimate nature as it is. The explanation of the stages of arising of the result, the perfection of the path, is completed.

The excellent path and the great chariot of fortunate beings:
The nondual self-liberated innate primordial wisdom
Is the self-liberated and instant present mind.
It is liberated simultaneously at-the-arising and is liberated naturally without (distinction of) earlier or later.
It is uncontaminated by being apprehended and unstained by apprehenders.
It is the arising of all the emotional defilements as the very primordial wisdom.
As (this teaching was) transmitted to me by the grace of the Guru,
For the sake of future followers, I have put it together as written instructions.
People who wish to be liberated from this existence should rely on this.
In any case, whoever makes assertions of rejecting and accepting
Does not have the good fortune of non-dual teachings.
On this path, as all experience is the very wisdom,
One attains the eternal state of the Ultimate Body, the perfection at the basis.
O friends! In this quintessential mansion free from extremes,
Get the wealth of ultimate Mind.
It is certain that one will attain the great blissful result in this lifetime.
And later, the benefits of others will be accomplished naturally.
Our life is changing like clouds,
The body is essenceless like a bubble.
It is hard to hear teachings and it is harder to practice what one has heard.
So quickly generate the energy of exertion (for practice).
By ripening the fruits and flowers of virtuous efforts in time,

May all beings attain the state of the Buddha.
At Kangri Thodkar (White Peaked Snow Mountain), the fortress of the Ogyen (Oḍḍiyāna, i.e., Padmasambhava),
This is written by Trimed Odzer (Immaculate Radiance, i.e., Longchen Rabjam).
By the merits, may the three realms together without remainder
Achieve the state of All Goodness (*Kun-Tu bZang-Po*).

The quintessential meaning instruction of the path of stages of the Naturally Liberated Mind of Great Perfection, written by Longchen Rabjam (Infinite Vast Expanse), is completed.

The Command of Entrusting the Teaching Because of Its Importance

As this teaching is an extraction of the most secret instructions, if it is taught to more than three fortunate people, it will bring the *Ḍākinīs*' punishments. So keep it strictly (secret). O glorious protector Legden Nagpo (*Legs-lDan Nag-Po*), the protectress of the *tantras* Ekajati (*E-Ka Dza-Ti*) and Rahula, the sage of the Za (class), please protect this teaching strictly. May it be virtuous!

9. *The Training and Attainments of Five Paths of Mahāyāna*

In the *Sūtric* (exoteric) teachings of *Mahāyāna* the levels of spiritual attainment in the process of training are categorized as the ten stages and five paths. In the *sūtras* the Ten Stages and Five Paths with Thirty-seven Aspects of Enlightenment are discussed in detail and that structure is the common basis for *tantric* teaching and for *Dzogpa Chenpo*. In *Shingta Chenpo* (SC) Longchen Rabjam summarizes the training on "thirty-seven aspects of enlightenment" for perfecting five paths.

THE PATH OF ACCUMULATION (*Tshogs-Lam*)

SC-II, 123b/6 The contemplation on and the realizations of, for example, hearing, pondering and meditation with (their) hosts of virtues, which start from the developing of the mind of enlightenment in *Mahāyāna* (and proceed) until the development of heat (of the path of application) in ones' mind, which leads to the island of liberation, is the path of accumulation.

Cause: The awakening of the lineage (*Rigs*), which is the basis (*rTen*) for developing the mind of enlightenment.

Result: The four following paths.

Etymology: The path of accumulations, as it mainly accumulates the hearing (study), pondering and merits.

Division: There are three:

Small (Sub-Division of the Path of Accumulation)

[124a/2]In this practice one meditates on the fourfold awareness (*Dran-Pa Nye-Bar bZhag-Pa bZhi*) in both meditation and post-meditation periods. These are the contemplations on: (i) (Seeing) the bodies (*Phung-Po*) of oneself and others as space during the meditation period. During the post-meditation period seeing the body as *Māyā* (*sGyu-Ma*). One also meditates on the filthiness (of the body) as the antidote to attachment. (ii) (Seeing) feeling (*Tshor-Ba*) without conceptions in the meditation period, and during the post-meditation period as (unstable) like a water-tree. One also meditates on seeing them as mere sufferings. (iii) (Seeing) the mind (*Sems*) as unborn (during the meditation) and as impermanent (during the post-meditation). (iv) (Seeing) that phenomena (*Ch'os*) are merely nominal (during the meditation) and that they are mere *Māyā* (during the post-meditation period).

Mediocre (Sub-Division of the) Path of Accumulation

[124b/1]It is the meditation on the four perfect purifications [efforts] (*Yang-Dag sPongs-Pa bZhi*), which are the highest degree of progress of experiences achieved through the previous (contemplations). They are (i) not to generate any unwholesomeness which has not been generated (in the past), (ii) removing any unwholesomeness which has been generated, (iii) generating virtues which have not arisen, and (iv) developing virtues which have arisen in oneself through the four means: admiration (*'Dun-Pa*), exertion (*'Bad-Pa*), efforts (*rTsol-Ba*), and diligence (*brTson-'Grus*).

Great (Sub-Division of the) Path of Accumulation

[124b/5]It is the contemplation on the four miraculous feet (*rDzu-'Phrul Gyi rKang-Pa bZhi*): (i) Admiration (*'Dun-Pa*), (ii) investigation (*dPyod-Pa*), (iii) concentration (*Sems-Pa*), and mindfulness (*Dran-Pa/brTson-'Grus*). . . .

Meditation: During the training in the Path of Accumulation, with the intention of achieving enlightenment, one makes efforts in the disciplines of sealing the doors of the sense-faculties, eating modestly, and not sleeping during the early and later parts of the night. The meditator is joyous because of being mindful in the efforts of accepting and rejecting. He advances on the path which leads to the Path of Application with no regrets about virtuous deeds but with joy, faith and admiration (*Mos-Pa*), and so on, with all the other virtues, which are the cause of liberation. He devotes (his life to) study, pondering, and meditation.

Time: The Small (sub-division of the) Path of Accumulation is the beginning of the three countless eons of training (in the path of enlightenment). At the time of the practice on the fourfold awareness (*Dran-Pa Nyer-bZhag*), the time of attainment of the Path of Application is uncertain. At the time of practice on the four perfect efforts (*Yang-Dag sPong-Pa bZhi*), it is certain that the attainment of the Path of Application will take place in the next life. At the time of training on the four miraculous feet, it is certain that one will attain the Path of Application in this very lifetime.

Antidote: In the Path of Accumulation, one trains on the antidote of assaulting (the defilements) (*Sun-'Byin*) by seeing the compositional factors (*'Du-Byed*) as faults.

Abandonment: One renounces all the direct attachments by seeing the contaminated phenomena (*Zag-bChas Kyi Ch'os*) as faults.

Realization: One realizes generally (*Don-sPyi*) the twofold no-self mainly by study and pondering and in some cases by meditation.

Virtues: One attains the virtues of eyes and foreknowledges and so on.

Meditation: One meditates on the (following) trainings: disciplining oneself in concentration on entering and withdrawing from (proper and improper) physical and vocal (activities); wisdom of studies, pondering and meditation concerning the words and meanings of the scriptures and the recollections of the triple gem. One meditates on the four Dharma seals, seeing that all compounded things are impermanent, that everything with flaws (*Zag-bChas*) is suffering, that all phenomena are emptiness and all beings are no-self. Meditate on the five liberative virtues: confidence, diligence, recollection, contemplation, and wisdom, which are not yet developed in the form of (five) faculties (*dBang-Po*). One contemplates on disciplines, generosity and recollections on precious human life, death, birth, inhaling and exhaling.

Activities: While acting one meditates on (nine) impurities and eight concepts of great beings. One meditates on them beginning with going for refuge and developing the mind of enlightenment and dedication of the merits. The meditations on the nine impurities are seeing one's own and others' bodies as decaying, eaten by worms, reddish, bluish, dark, scattered, burnt, and putrid. As (the antidote) to desire one meditates on filthiness, for hatred on loving-kindness and for ignorance on interdependent causation.

[126a/5]The eight conceptions (*rNam-Par rTog-Pa*) of the great beings: In Nyi-Khri gZhung-'Grel it is said:

> They are the thoughts, (1) When may I dispel the sufferings of living beings? (2) When may I lead people who are in danger of poverty to great wealth? (3) When may I fulfill the needs of living beings with my body of flesh and blood? (4) When may I benefit living beings by living in hell for a long time? (5) When may I fulfill the wishes of beings through the great prosperities both of the world and the transcendence of the world? (6) When may I become a Buddha and uproot the sufferings of beings? (7) When may I never have rebirths which are not beneficial to beings, in which I exclusively analyze the taste of absolute truth, speak words that are uncaring of (the benefit of) beings, have life, body, intellect, wealth or majesty that are not beneficial to others and am eager to harm others? (8) When may I experience the results of others' non-virtuous deeds and may others experience the results of my virtuous deeds?

THE PATH OF APPLICATION [ENDEAVOR] (*sByor-Lam*)

127a/1The basis (of life): It is the beings in any of the six realms in whom the final stages of the great (sub-division of the) Path of Accumulation has been generated. In the *sūtras* it is said that in numerous beings among the gods, *nāgas*, and demi-gods (the Path of Application) has been generated.

Basis of intention: It is the (mind) of the desire realms or of the six stages of absorption.

Cause: It is the final stage of the great level of the Path of Accumulation.

Essence (*Ngo-Bo*): It is the worldly wisdom generated by meditation.

Division: There are four: heat (*Drod*), climax(*rTse-Mo*), forbearance (*bZod-Pa*), and supreme (mundane) realization (*Ch'os-mCh'og*).

Meditation: In heat and climax one practices on the five faculties (*dBang-Po*): confidence(*Dad-Pa*), diligence (*brTson-'Grus*), awareness (*Dran-Pa*), contemplation (*Ting-Nge 'Dzin*), and wisdom (*Shes-Rab*). They are called faculties as they directly enforce the generating of enlightenment.... (In forbearance and supreme (mundane) realization one practices on the five powers (*sTobs*): confidence, diligence, awareness, contemplation, and wisdom.)

Primordial Wisdom: In the four divisions of the Path of Application there are four primordial wisdoms: (1) The attainment of light of primordial wisdom of "heat" (*Drod sNang-Ba Thob-Pa'i Ye-Shes*) of *Mahāyāna* is the antidote to apprehending the objects as real, by seeing all phenomena as merely the lights of the mind, a little light generated by mundane meditation.... Here, light means the forbearance of definite concentration on Dharma....

(2) The increase of the light of primordial wisdom of "climax" (*rTse-Mo sNang-Ba mCh'ed-Pa'i Ye-Shes*) is the attainment of the mediocre light generated by mundane meditation through the efforts of meditation on no-self for the purpose of increasing the light of the Dharma itself....

(3) The primordial wisdom of entering partially into the suchness of the "forbearance" (*bZod-Pa De Kho-Na-Nyid Kyi Phyogs-gChig-La Zhugs-Pa'i Ye-Shes*) is the antidote of distractions toward external phenomena (viewing them) as the objects, through the attainment of the great light generated by meditation on abiding in mere mind....

(4) The primordial wisdom of supreme (mundane) realization (is achieved) "immediately before" (*Ch'os-mCh'og De-Ma Thag-Pa'i Ye-Shes*) (the attainment of the Path of Seeing without interruption (of any other attainments). This primordial wisdom is the completion of the visions generated by mundane contemplations, as there is no distraction by apprehension of the objects.

(Sub-division): Each of the four aspects of the Path of Application (*Nges-'Byed*) has three sub-divisions, classified as small, mediocre, and great....

Antidote: It is the renunciation (*sPong-Ba*) of the defilements by suppressing (*mGo-gNon-Pa*) them. Generally there are four kinds of antidotes: the antidote of assault (*Sun-'Byin-Pa*), renunciation (*sPong-Pa*), the basis (*rTen*), and the uprooting (*rTsa-Ba Nas sPong-Pa*), like the uninterrupted path which uproots from the root....

Abandonment: It diminishes the seed and the direct obscurations, and liberates from the decline and poverty of ordinary beings (*So-So'i sKye-Bo*).

Realization: General realization (*Don-sPyi*) of the two noselves through the primordial wisdom generated by mundane meditations.

Virtues: In *Ratnamegha-sūtra* many virtues such as contemplations, recollections (*gZungs*), and foreknowledges are mentioned.

Supreme over the Path of Accumulation: There is no difference (between this and the Path of Accumulation) generated by meditation (*bsGom-Byung*), but in this the primordial wisdom of no-thought is clearer, and it is closer to the Path of Seeing.

THE PATH OF SEEING (*mThong-Lam*)

128b/2The primordial wisdom of the Path of Seeing arises at the end of the great supreme (mundane) realization (of the Path of Application) and it is in sixteen moments (*sKad-Chig*). They are the forbearance of knowledge of the attributes (*dharmas*), the knowledge of the attributes, the forbearances of subsequent knowledge, and the subsequent knowledge of each of the four truths: suffering, source of suffering, cessation (of suffering), and the path (of cessation)....

The basis (of life): The basis of arising of primordial wisdom is the same as in the case of great highest (mundane) realization (of the Path of Application) and it could be any being from any of the six realms.

The basis of mind: It is the fourth absorption.

Cause: The highest (mundane) realization (of the Path of Application) is the direct cause and other aspects of the Paths of Accumulation and Application are the indirect causes.

Result: It is the development of the two later paths.

Essence: There are sixteen moments related to the (levels of) purification of the defilements of the nature by the divisions of the four truths.

Abandonments: There are ten defilements: five defilements related to view and five defilements unrelated to view. The five related to view are: views of transitory collections (I and mine as real)(*'Jigs-Tshogs-La lTa-ba*), view holding to extremes (*mThar-'Dzin*), wrong view (*Log-lTa*), viewing (a wrong view) as supreme (*lTa-Ba mCh'og-'Dzin*) and view that ethics and asceticism are supreme (*Tshul-Khrims brTul-Zhugs mCh'og-'Dzin*). The five unrelated to view are: desire, hatred, pride, ignorance, and doubt.

In the desire realm, the ten abandonments become 40 by multiplying each of them by the four truths. For the two upper realms (the form and formless realms), excluding hatred, there are nine defilements, and by multiplying them (by the four truths) they become 72. So in total there are 112 defilements (of the three realms) to be abandoned in the Path of Seeing....

In the four absorptions (form realms) and four formless realms, hatred is not applied, as the beings' minds are moistened by tranquillity, because they do not possess the nine bases of hatred, the thought of harming. The nine are: (thinking that this person) harmed me in the past, is harming me at present, and will harm me in the future. In the same way, three towards one's friends and three towards one's enemies, (thinking that he) benefited my enemy and so on. These (ten) emotional defilements lead the wrong way. For example, in the case of the truth of suffering (*saṃsāra*): (1) by the view of transitory collection one apprehends the truth of suffering as "I" and "my." (2) By the view of holding to extremes one apprehends the truth of suffering as existent or non-existent and eternal or nil. (3) By wrong view one apprehends that the truth of suffering is non-existent. (4) By ignorance one enters into it without knowing its characteristics. (5) By doubt one enters into it. . .with doubt that there is a truth of suffering. There are those five ways of relating to the truth of suffering. (6) Desire generates attachment. (7) Pride generates haughtiness and boasting. (8) Apprehending (wrong views) as the supreme view generates apprehending them as supreme. (9) The view of apprehending ethics and asceticism as supreme generates apprehending them as the way of purity and liberation. (10) Hatred creates ill will toward whatever is not in accord with those five ways of relating. As they (the ten defilements) are applied to the truth of suffering, they are applied to the other three truths as well. In the case of the truth of cessation, the nominal (aspect) is related to, but is not the meaning. . . .

Antidote: All the emotional defilements (*Nyon-Mongs-Pa*) of the three realms, which are the abandonments of the Path of Seeing, are to be purified together. The four forbearances of the knowledge of the attributes (*Ch'os Shes-Pa'i bZod-Pa*) of the fourfold truth, namely, suffering [*saṃsāra*], source of suffering [emotions], cessation of suffering [*nirvāṇa*], and the path of cessation are one in their being mental phenomena (*Blo-sDzas*), but they are four in their isolated factors (*lDog-Pa*).

When it (the antidote) arises, in a single (instant of a) moment,it becomes the uninterrupted path (*Bar-Ch'ad Med-Lam*), the antidote of renouncing the abandonment of the Path of Seeing from the root. It renounces the 112 abandonments of the Path of Seeing in a moment. (The process of abandonment: In the first instant,) the secondary cause (*Nye-rGyu*) of the forbearances and the knowledge of the attribute (*Ch'os-bZod*) of each of the four truths and their respective active (*Nus-lDan*) abandonments encounter (each other). In the second instant, the actual cause (*dNgos-rGyu*) (of the forbearances of the knowledge of the attribute of the four truths) and their respective (*Ngo-sKal*) inactive (*Nus-Med*) abandonments encounter (each other). In the third instant, the four forbearances of the attributes (*Ch'os-bZod*) arise and the cessation of the entirety (up to the) subtle abandonments takes place spontaneously. . . .

The four attributes (*Ch'os*) of the individual four truths are the same mental phenomena. So the liberation from defilements of the forms (*rNam-Pa*) of the four truths of the three realms is the path of liberation (*rNam-Grol Lam*, i.e., the Path of Seeing), the antidotes. Likewise, the four subsequent forbearances (*rJes-bZod*) and four subsequent knowledges (*rJes Shes*) are the distinguishing path, the far-abandoning antidote. . . . Those abandonments are (included in) the two obscurations, and the (antidotes) liberate (one) from them. . . .

The distinction of the two (obscurations) is: The nature (*Ngo-Bo*) of misery and so forth, of unvirtuous or neutral obscurations (*bsGrib-Pa Lung-Ma-bsTan*) which make the mind very unpeaceful are the "emotional obscurations" (*Nyon-bsGrib*). The subject and object of the concept of apprehender and apprehended with the nature (*Ngo-Bo*) of contaminated (*Zag-bChas*) virtues or unobscuring neutrality, which is not free from the attachment to the truth of the three cycles (subject, object, and action), is the "intellectual obscuration" (*Shes-brGrib*). Among them the imaginary obscurations of emotions are the abandonments of the Path of Seeing, and the innate emotions (*lHan-sKyes*) are the abandonments of the Path of Meditation.

The gross concept of apprehender and apprehended, the intellectual obscurations, are the abandonments of the Path of Seeing, and the subtle ones are the abandonments of the Path of Meditation. . . .

Realization: It is the direct realization of the two no-selfs through the transmundane primordial wisdom.

Virtues: The twelve hundred, and so on, of the first stage, which have been mentioned earlier.

Time: First, the four forbearances of the attributes of the four truths arise simultaneously. After that, the four knowledges of the attributes arise simultaneously. After that, the four subsequent forbearances arise simultaneously. After that, the four subsequent knowledges arise simultaneously. So, in four sets of "instants in which an action can be completed" (*Bya-rDzogs Kyi sKad-Chig-Ma*) arise all four kinds of entities (*Ngo-Bo*) with their sixteen isolated factors (*lDog-Pa*), because the realization of the four truths arises instantly and their (two sets of) four forbearances and (two sets of) four knowledges are developed successively (*Rim-Pas*). The abandonments of the Path of Seeing are renounced in a moment by the forbearances of the attributes (*Ch'os-bZod*), and the Path of Seeing arises in four parts successively. . . .

Meditation: During the first stage, one meditates on the seven branches of enlightenment (*Byang-Ch'ub Kyi Yan-Lag bDun*). . . .

The Aryabodhipakṣanirdeśa-sūtra says:

> (1) O *Mañjuśrī*, whoever sees all phenomena as no-thing (*dNgos-Med*), because there are no concepts and recollection is the awareness (*Dran-Pa*) branch of enlightenment. (2) O *Mañjuśrī*, whoever remains isolated from all phenomena without conceptualizations, as he never establishes either virtuous, unvirtuous or neutral (deeds), is the discriminative (*Ch'os rNam-Par 'Byed-Pa*) branch of enlightenment. (3) O *Mañjuśrī*, whoever neither abandons nor accepts the three realms (*Khams-gSum*), as he has destroyed the perception (*'Du-Shes*) of the body (*Lus*), is the

diligence (*brTson-'Grus*) branch of enlightenment. (4) O *Mañjuśrī*, whoever does not generate joy in the formations (*'Du-Byed*), as he has destroyed joy and distress, is the joy (*dGa'-Ba*) branch of enlightenment. (5) O *Mañjuśrī*, whoever has total pliancy of mind in all phenomena, as there are no conceptualizations of non-conceptualized things, is the pliancy (*Shin-sByang*) branch of enlightenment. (6) O *Mañjuśrī*, he whose mind is not conceptualizing, as he subsequently conceives the destruction of phenomena, is the contemplation (*Ting-Nge-'Dzin*) branch of enlightenment. (7) O *Mañjuśrī*, whoever does not abide in, rely on, is not attached to and not bound to any phenomena and remains neutral about not subsequently seeing any phenomena perfectly and acquiring joy is the equanimity (*bTang-sNyoms*) branch of enlightenment.

THE PATH OF MEDITATION (*bsGom-Lam*)

131b/6It is (the meditation which) advances the experiences of the meanings of the (trainings and realizations) of the aspects which are concordant with the "definite differentiations" (*Nges-'Byed Ch'a-mThun*) (i.e., Application) and of the Path of Seeing, which has already been realized....

There are nine levels in this path; small, mediocre, and great, each of which are sub-divided into small, mediocre, and great (levels)....

(Objects of) Abandonments: In the Path of Meditation there are great, mediocre, and small (objects of) abandonment and they are divided into nine sub-divisions; the great of great, mediocre of great, small of great, great of mediocre, mediocre of mediocre, small of mediocre, great of small, mediocre of small, and small of small (objects of) abandonment. These (objects of) abandonment are abandoned in the nine levels of stages, such as the "immaculate" (*Dri-Ma Med-Pa*, the second) stage. By the small of the small level of the Meditation Path, the immaculate stage, are abandoned the (objects of) abandonment of the great of the great level of the Meditation Path, and the (objects of) abandonment of the small of the small level of the Meditation Path are renounced by the great of the great level of the Meditation Path, the tenth stage. Here, the gross defilements are called the great (objects of) abandonment and the subtle ones are called the small....

The basis of birth: The basis of birth for the arising of the Path of Meditation is similar to the Path of Seeing. Most of the births are of the men and women of the three continents, but they are also possible among (the births of) other (realms). Any (life) is appropriate if it maintains the attainments which have already been generated in oneself....

Basis of mind: Mostly (the attainments of the path of meditation) are based on the fourth absorption, but they could also be based on other absorptions.

Cause: The first three paths are its cause.

Result: It is the path of "no more training...."

Essence(*Ngo-Bo*): From the point of view of abandoning the defilements of the individual nine stages there are four levels; the preliminary (*sByor-Ba*), the uninterrupted path (*Bar-Ch'ad-Med Lam*), the liberation path (*rNam-Grol Lam*), and the special path (*Khyad-Par Gyi Lam*). The preliminary and uninterrupted paths are the antidotes of renouncing (the objects of abandonment) (*sPong-Ba'i gNyen-Po*). The path of liberation is the basis of the antidote (*rTen-Gyi gNyen-Po*). The special path is the far-abandoning antidote (*Thag-bSring Gi gNyen-Po*). For example, (1) by the end of the first stage ("the preliminary path"), which is the last moment (before) the arising of the wisdom of the second stage, "one suppresses (*mGo-gNon*) the manifesting emotions," which obscure the arising of the second stage, (2) by the "uninterrupted path," which is the arising of the second stage, one "abandons the faults of discipline" (*Tshul-'Cha'l*) of its stage "from the root," (3) the "path of liberation," which starts from the second moment (of the arising of the second stage), is the "basis of the antidote," and (4) the "special path," the final one of the stage, is the "far-abandoning antidote." Thus all the respective defilements of this stage are abandoned by starting from the first moment till the completion of the stage. All the defilements of those (respective) stages are abandoned at the time the (particular) stage ends.

These days some coarse scholars of the *Prajñāpāramitā* say:

> The (objects of) abandonment (i.e., the defilements) of the Path of Insight are to be abandoned by the path which is to be developed. The (objects of) abandonment of the Path of Meditation are to be abandoned by the path which is to be ended.

It is clear that they are very ignorant of the subject of antidotes.

Virtues: Explained before. . . .

Way of Abandoning the Nine Defilements of the Nine Stages: There are six innate (*Lhan-Chig sKyes-Pa*) defilements; desire, hatred, pride, ignorance (lack of knowledge), the view of the transitory collection (I and mine as real), and the view of holding to extremes. They can be subdivided in two different ways. (a) According to the point of view of realms, there are sixteen defilements. They are the six defilements of the desire realm, and for the absorptions (form realms) and formless realms there are five defilements each, excluding hatred. (b) According to the levels (*Sa*), there are forty-six defilements. Six are for the desire realm, five each for the four absorptions and four formless realms. If each of them are subdivided again into nine degrees of great, mediocre and small, then the six defilements of the desire realm become fifty-four and the five defilements, excluding hatred, of the four absorptions become four sets of forty-five (=180) abandonments. Likewise, in the formless realm there are four sets of forty-five (=180) defilements. So in total there are four hundred and fourteen (objects of) abandonment in the Path of Meditation.

The "(path of) preliminaries" subdues the abandonments, the "uninterrupted path" abandons them directly, the "liberation path" creates the basis of the antidote and the "special path" abandons the antidotes to a far distance. . . .

In these stages they practice on the Eightfold Noble Path

(*'Phags- Lam brGyad*).... In *Aryabodhipakṣanirdeśa-sūtra* it is said:

> (1) O *Mañjuśrī*, whoever sees all phenomena (*Ch'os*) without lack of equanimity and with non-duality has the right view (*lTa-Ba*). (2) O *Mañjuśrī*, whoever sees that all phenomena are never existing, very never existing and totally never existing through the way of not-seeing has right thought (*rTog-Pa*). (3) O *Mañjuśrī*, seeing all phenomena as inexpressible is right speech (*Ngag*). (4) O *Mañjuśrī*, seeing all phenomena as free from creator and creation is right action (*Las Kyi mTha'*). (5) O *Mañjuśrī*, seeing all phenomena as free from increase or decrease is right livelihood (*'Tsho-Ba*). (6) O *Mañjuśrī*, accomplishing all phenomena in the manner free from efforts and creating is right effort (*rTsol-Ba*). (7) O *Mañjuśrī*, seeing all phenomena with no concepts and recollections is right recollection (*Dran-Pa*). (8) O *Mañjuśrī*, seeing all phenomena in natural contemplation without commotion and conceptualizations because they are free from conceptualizations is right contemplation (*Ting-Nge Dzin*). These stages are, according to their nature (*Ngo-Bo*), free from concepts and thinking.... But (they are designated) separately because the realization of enlightenment, which is the transformation into (*gNas Gyur-Pa*) the ultimate nature (*Khams*), depends on the purification of the degrees of obscurations of the nature (*Khams*). At the time of ultimate purity (*Dag-Pa mThar-Thug*), one sees the self-clarity of the primordial sphere or the Luminous Buddha, (like) seeing the (fullness of the) moon because of the day (of the full moon).

THE PATH OF NO MORE TRAINING (*Mi-Slob-Lam*)

[135a/2](Objects of) Abandonment: It renounces the twofold obscurations with their traces.

Special Relization: It realizes the complete *Dharmakāya* directly.

Virtues: They complete the endless qualities of both mundane and transmundane virtues.

Purpose of the Paths and Stages

135b/2 The unexcelled Buddhahood is impossible to attain until one completes the paths and stages....

Whether Buddhahood is attained in sixteen lives, etc., or very fast as in one life time, one has to proceed through the levels of the paths and stages as they are, because it is necessary that the defilements (of the different levels) be abandoned, and the virtues need to be achieved. Today there are people who say that even without relying on the paths and stages, Buddhahood will be attained, and that without completion of accumulations and purification of the obscurations, the paths and stages and enlightenment will be achieved. It is clear that they are possessed by someone else [*Māra*]. Because they contradict the scholars, adepts, great *sūtras*, *tantras* and the great scriptures. Therefore, one should endeavor in the training of the pure stages and paths.

10. The Training and Attainments of Paths and Stages of Tantra

In *tantra* the attainment of paths and stages, which were mentioned in Section IX in relation to the *sūtric* training, are achieved through extraordinary skill in means of training. In *tantra*, through the practices on the two stages, the development stage and perfection stage, one attains the results. In the twenty-first chapter of *Pema Karpo* (PK Vol-II), Longchen Rabjam explains that by releasing the knots of the central channel by maturing the mind and air/energy of the four wheels, gradually one attains the ten stages and five paths.

PK II,175a/5 Here, I am explaining by combining the inner (*tantric*) and outer (*sūtric*) ways of training. The *tantras* expound the "thirty-seven aspects of enlightenment" as the means of transformation (*rNam-Dag*) (of the perceptions) as the *maṇḍalas*; and this means is in some ways similar to the inerrant teachings of the characteristic (*sūtric*) approach....

Both the old and new (translated) *tantric* traditions (of Tibet) agree that by gradually maturing(*Las-Su Rung-Ba*) the air and mind in the four *cakras* of channels (of the body), the virtues of the perfection of the "four paths" arise. They are the paths of accumulation, application, seeing, and meditation. Upon releasing two of the twenty-one knots of *Roma* and *Kyangma* channels around the central channel for each of the "ten stages," one attains the virtues of the "ten stages" in succession; and by releasing the last knot, one attains the state of Buddhahood. This is the view of scholars and adepts such as the masters, Vimalamitra and Padmasambhava....

This training has two categories: maturation of the air/energy and mind (*rLung-Sems Las-Su Rung-Ba*) and the perfection (*'Byong-Ba*) of them. The admission (of the air and mind) into them (the respective *cakras* of channels) is the maturation, and the releasing of their knots, including the knots of their branches, is the perfection.

With the maturing of the air and mind in the petals (or spokes) of the "*cakra* of creation" at the navel (*lTe-Ba sPrul-Pa'i 'Khor-Lo*) arise the heats (*Drod*), the signs of small, mediocre and great levels of the "path of accumulation." Then one sees the faces of the Buddhas in *Nirmāṇakāya* form and becomes able to exhibit manifestations, and miracles because one has achieved minor (divine) eyes, foreknowledges and miracles as the result of one's meditation and by gaining control over (*dBang Thob-Pa*) admiration (*'Dun-Pa*) and the rest, the "four miraculous feet" of contemplation. Some people of gross intellect assert that in the "path of application" one achieves miracles but not on the great level of the "path of accumulation." That is not correct.

PATH OF ACCUMULATION (*Tshogs-Lam*)

[175b/6]By maturing (*Las-Su Rung-Ba*) the air and mind in the "*cakra* of creation" at the navel, there arise signs of heat [experience] of small, mediocre and great levels of the Path of Accumulation. One possesses the power of creating manifestations as one has achieved the attainment of minor "eyes," foreknowledge, and miracles.

Small Level of the Path of Accumulation

[176a/5]On the small level of "(the Path of) Accumulation," one perfects the fourfold awareness (*Dran-Pa Nye-Bar bZhag-Pa*):

(a) Visualizing the body as the divinity is the awareness of the body (and it is the development stage).

(b) Transformation of the thoughts of feeling as primordial wisdom
Is the awareness of feeling.
(c) Contemplation on the total pacification of elaborations of the mind and mental events
Is the awareness of the mind; and they (b and c) are the perfection stage.
(d) Realizing that the phenomena of perceptions and imputations are like *māyā*
Is the awareness of phenomena. Thus it is said in the *tantras.*

In *(Guhyagarbha)māyājāla-tantra* it is said:

> By a trainee of *tantra*: (a) to bless his (body) is the "awareness of the body," as he peceives (himself) in the form of the deity, like a reflection, (b) (to transform) his thoughts into the state of great primordial wisdom is the nature of the "(awareness of) feeling," the great bliss, (c) victory over the elaborations is the "(awareness of) mind," freedom from conceptualizations, and (d) realization of (phenomena as unreal) as reflections is "(awareness of) phenomena."

Mediocre Level of the Path of Accumulation
One practices on the "four perfect purifications" (*Yang-Dag sPong-Ba bZhi*).

[176b/5]By remaining in (the training and perfection of) the "development" and "perfection stages," one purifies the attachments to the "four (objects of) abandonments" and their four antidotes as real. One contemplates the following in one-pointed mind with physical, vocal, and mental joyful efforts: (a) not to generate any unvirtuousness which has not arisen, (b) to purify the unvirtuousness which has already arisen, (c) to develop virtues which have not arisen, and (d) to develop the virtues which have already arisen.

Great Level of the Path of Accumulation

One practices on the "four miraculous feet" (*rDzu-'Phrul Gyi rKang-Pa bZhi*).

177a/3While making exertions in the practice on the developing and perfection stages day and night, one (a) apprehends the trainings by awareness without losing their meaning, (b) contemplates with "admiration," (c) distinguishes by analysis which is erroneous and which is correct training, and (d) contemplates one-pointedly without waverings of mind. Thereby, having perfected the contemplation, and through the "miracles," which one has achieved by the maturing of air and mind, one goes to the manifested Buddha-fields such as *Pema Chen*, receives teachings from the Buddhas, purifies the defilements of the nature (*Khams-Kyi Dri-Ma*), and receives prophecies from the tutelary deities in pure visions.

PATH OF APPLICATION (*sByor-Lam*)

177a/5By maturing the air and mind in the *Cakra* of Dharma
(*Ch'os-Kyi 'Khor-Lo*) (at the heart),
The virtues of the "path of application" arise....

With the "five faculties" one meditates on the meaning of the previous training of union of the development and perfection stages: the faculties of (a) faith, (b) diligence, (c) awareness, (d) contemplation, and (e) wisdom. One achieves control over (one's training) and (the faculties) become capable of destroying the abandonments.

Through the training on the faculties, one attains (the first two of the four levels of the "path of application"): (a) No-thought, the light of primordial wisdom (*sNang-Ba'i Ye-Shes*) is the "heat" (*Drod*) levels with the signifying characteristics of exhaustion of doubts and lack of freedom and so on, and (b) stability of the virtues, the "increase of primordial wisdom" (*mCh'ed-Pa'i Y e-Shes*) is the "climax" (*rTse-Mo*) level (with the characteristic of) realizing all phenomena as a dream....

(As the sign of perfection,) whatever word of truth one utters becomes accomplished and one always lives in the twelve virtuous trainings (*sByang-Ba'i Yon-Tan bCh'u-gNyis*)....

When the effects of faith and so forth (diligence, awareness, contemplation and primordial wisdom) become very powerful and capable of destroying the abandonments, they are the "five powers" (*sTobs-lNga*) (and one attains the last two of the four levels of the "path of application"): (a) The "realized primordial wisdom" (*Thob-Pa'i Ye-Shes*), and partial attainment of the primordial wisdom of suchness, is the "forbearances" (*bZod-Pa*) level (with the characteristic that) birth in inferior realms has ceased. The "thoroughly realized primordial wisdom" (*Nye-Bar Thob-Pa'i Ye-Shes*), the contemplation of the immediate moment (before the insight), is the "supreme (mundane) realization" (*Ch'os-mCh'og*) level (with the characteristics that) one's virtues do not change from being the cause of enlightenment, and one attains contemplations and miracles and so forth superior to previous ones.

PATH OF SEEING (*mThong-Lam*)

[178a/3]By maturation of mind and air in the "*cakra* of enjoyment" at the throat (*mGrin-Pa Longs-sPyod Kyi 'Khor-Lo*), one realizes the "path of seeing" and attains the first (of the ten) noble stages with twelve hundred virtues. (As a result) one is able to go and listen to the teachings in the pure lands of the Buddhas of five classes of the enjoyment body. The twelve hundred virtues are: the simultaneous achivements of 100 contemplations, seeing 100 Buddhas, knowing the receiving of 100 blessings, going to 100 world systems, going to 100 pure lands, projecting lights to 100 worlds, maturing 100 beings, remaining for 100 kalpas, applying one's primordial wisdom to 100 (events of) the past and future, expounding100 teachings, manifesting 100 forms, each one accompanied by the auspiciousness of 100 virtues....

In this path one (trains in and) perfects the "seven branches of enlightenment": faith, diligence, awareness, contemplation, equanimity, joy, and pliancy.

PATH OF MEDITATION (*bsGom-Lam*)

[178b/4]By maturation of air and mind in the "*cakra* of great bliss" at the crown of the head (*sPyi-Bo bDe-Ch'en 'Khor-Lo*), one attains the nine stages (in the nine levels) of the path of meditation. (In this path one trains in and perfects the "noble eightfold path of enlightenment." From the first to the tenth stage, one also mainly perfects each of the ten perfections (S. *pāramitā*) in succession and the other perfections secondarily. The ten perfections are the perfections of generosity, moral discipline, patience, diligence, contemplation, wisdom, skillful means, power, aspiration, and wisdom. . . .

In those (ten) different stages, once the subtle knots of the petals of the channels are liberated, the primordial wisdom air is admitted into the channels and it dries up or cripples the worldly defiled mind and air with their basis, the channels. . . .

The question of going to other pure lands and remaining in contemplation simultaneously is not contradictory, because in the three pure stages (eigth through tenth) one has the power of control over the contemplation of no-thought. . . . In the eighth stage one also attains control over no-thought as the mind-consciousness has been transformed, in the ninth stage one attains control over pure lands as the consciousnesses of the five doors have been transformed, and in the tenth stage one attains control over the prosperous enlightened actions as the consciousness of the universal ground has been transformed. . . .

(Out of the twenty-one knots of the channels,) by the releasing of the first two knots of the three channels (central, *Roma*, and *Kyangma*) one attains the first stage (and likewise by the releasing of the rest of the knots one attains the stages) through the tenth. By releasing the last (the twenty-first) knot one attains the stage of *Vajradhara*, the "supreme stage of the crown of the head" (*gTsug-Tor rTse-Mo'i Sa*). . . .

As when the sun rises the rays appear simultaneously, when

one attains realizations of the paths and stages, it is natural that one obtains without fail the (divine) eyes and fore-knowledges, the virtues of abandonment and realization.

(CONCLUSION)

[182b/5]As one moves up to the advanced stages and paths, the virtues increase like green grass, plants, forests, and crops (growing) in summer. When one attains Buddhahood like wish-fullfilling gems, vases, and trees, although there are no concepts, the spontaneously accomplished bodies, primordial wisdoms, and enlightened actions appear for the sake of beings, filling the expanse of space. These are examples (of the appearing aspect of the enlightened manifestations of actions for beings), but not (indicating that Buddhahood does) not possess the ten powers, compassion, and loving kindness without concepts. Therefore, although the mind and mental events are dissolved into the ultimate sphere, the realization of the bodies and discriminative wisdoms are eternally and spontaneously present in the nature of luminescence like the sun and moon.

11. Attainment of the Paths, Stages and Visions of Dzogpa Chenpo

Dzogpa Chenpo training perfects the paths and stages of attainment of the *sūtric* and common *tantric* trainings outlined earlier in sections 9 and 10. The following are excerpts from *Choying Rinpoche'i Dzod* (CD), *Namkha Longchen* (NKC), *Tshigdon Dzod* (TD), *Semnyid Rangtrol* (SR), and *Namkha Longsal* (NKS). In these passages Longchen Rabjam explains the attainments of the realization of "the enlightened mind" (*Byang-Ch'ub Sems*) and the "four visions or realizations" (*sNang-Ba*) attained by the practice of Thregchod and Thodgal. "Four visions" are a technical term for the levels of attainment in *Dzogpa Chenpo*. Longchen Rabjam compares the "enlightened mind" and "the four visions" of *Dzogpa Chenpo* with the attainments of the five paths and with the perfections of the 'thirty-seven aspects of enlightenment' and the Buddha-bodies as they are explained in the common Buddhist scriptures.

ALL THE YĀNAS ARE ENCOMPASSED IN THE ENLIGHTENED MIND OF *DZOGPA CHENPO*

In *Choying Rinpoche'i Dzod* (CD) Longchen Rabjam states that the meaning of the teachings and attainments of all the nine *yānas* are encompassed in the Enlightened Mind (*Byang-Ch'ub Sems*), the realization of *Dzogpa Chenpo* meaning:CD 10a/5

The teachings of (the *Yānas* of) Hearers, Self-Buddhas, and
Bodhisattvas are the same in that
By ascertaining the non-existence of "self (of person)" and
"self of (phenomena),"

One realizes the space-like freedom from elaborations.
According to the teachings of the supremely secret and great *yoga*, the *Ati*,
In the space-like vastness free from distinctions of self and others
One naturally maintains the self-awareness wisdom, as it is. So
All the realizations of those (*Yānas*) are encompassed in this supreme essence (the Enlightened Mind).
The three classes (of the outer *tantra*), *kriyā*, *Upa* (or *Caryā*), and *Yoga* are the same in that
By the means of suchness, deity, and offering clouds of contemplation
One attains the accomplishment of the purifications of the three doors.
In this secret, vajra-summit, king of the teachings,
The percepts, sounds, and thoughts are pure; they are deities from the origin and
It is the accomplishment of the perfection of the three doors. So
The realization of those (*yānas*) is encompassed in this supreme essence.
Mahā, *Anu*, and *Ati* also agree
That by (realizing) the world and beings of phenomenal existence as the male and female deities and their pure lands,
And by (training in) the indivisibility of primordial wisdom and the ultimate sphere,
One attains the changeless ultimate nature, the self-arisen primordial wisdom.
In this most supreme secret, everything is (primordially) perfected as
The uncreated mansion, the pure land of blissful primordial expanse,
Which has no outer or inner divisions and is omnipresent and omnipervading.
There are no characteristic elements to be accepted or rejected.
All are liberated in the infinite origin in the expanse of *Dharmakāya*.

So all the realizations of these (*yānas*) are encompassed in this great secret essence.

THE ATTAINMENTS OF THE FOUR VISIONS, PATHS AND STAGES OF THODGAL

Longchen Rabjam writes:[NKC 109b/2]

By progressing in the experiences of that (meditation), one attains the four (levels of) visions (*sNang-Ba*).
(1) First, in the vision of) "direct (realization of) the ultimate nature" (*Ch'os-Nyid mNgon-Sum*),
One achieves the experiences of realization equivalent to (that of) the "path of accumulations."
One becomes naturally free from the attachments to the body, feelings, mind, and phenomena (i.e., *Dran-Pa Nyer-bZhag-bZhi*),
The virtues increase in one and so the non-virtues will spontaneously decrease (i.e., *Yang-Dag sPong-Ba bZhi*), and
By perfecting contemplations one achieves foreknowledges and miracles (i.e., *rDzu-'Phrul rKang-bZhi*).
(2) Then in the (vision of) the "increase of experiences" (i.e., *Nyams-sNang Gong-'Phel*),
Which is similar to the "path of application," one achieves the (five) faculties (*dBang-Po lNga*): faith, diligence,
Awareness, contemplation and wisdom.
And one also achieves the great (five) powers (*sTobs-lNga*), the antidotes which eliminate the aspects of defilements.
One does not have lice and eggs of lice and one's dreams are pure.
Rebirth in inferior realms ceases and one's words of truth become actualized.
(3) Then in the vision of "perfection of the intrinsic awareness" (*Rig-Pa Tshad-Phebs*),
In the first, middle, and final stages (of it),
One realizes (the paths of) "Seeing" and "Meditation" (up to the eighth stage). The vision of pure lands, contemplations, miracles, and the rest

Increases and one realizes the virtues of the essential nature (*Khams*).
(One perfects the "seven branches of enlightenment," i.e., *Byang-Ch'ub Kyi Lam Yan-Lag bDun*)....
(4) Then (one attains) the vision of "cessation (into the) ultimate nature" (*Ch'os-Nyid Zad-Pa*).
Because in the "three pure stages" (eighth through tenth), the hosts of conceptual defilements
Are manifestly exhausted and the gross bodies are exhausted,
And the delusory perceptions are exhausted, this vision is called the dissolution.
This vision is the great luminous intrinsic wisdom,
(In which) the mind (consciousness), apprehensions (consciousnesses of the five sense doors), and concepts (the consciousness of the universal ground) are dissolved.
One attains control over the wisdom (of no thought), pure lands, (the illusory body of) primordial wisdom and the virtuous elements (of enlightened activities).

THE ATTAINMENTS OF THE FOUR VISIONS AND THE TEN STAGES

Basing himself on *tantras*, in *Tshigdon Dzod* (TD) Longchen Rabjam writes that in the "four visions" the attainments of the ten stages are embodied. TD 169b/1

The ten stages embody (the attainment of the "four visions" of *Dzogpa Chenpo*).... When the person who has been introduced (to the realization) first realizes the truth, the arising of joy in him is the attainment of "the Joyous," the first stage. Recognizing (the realization of the truth) as self-visions is the attainment of "the Pure," the second stage. Gaining experiences in it is the attainment of "the Light Maker," the third stage. Having the visions of lights is the attainment of "the Radiant," the fourth stage. Having gained experiences in the seeing of the light of primordial wisdom and having purified all the emotional defilements naturally, to see the primordial wisdom is the attainment of "the Invincible," the fifth stage. Actualizing (or seeing) the light-bodies directly is the attainment of "Actualization," the sixth stage. Having perfected the experiences, going far away from emotional defilements is the attainment of "the Far-ranging," the seventh stage. After fully perfecting the virtues of the visions, no movement of thoughts is the attainment of "the Unshakable," the eighth stage. Seeing the complete *maṇḍala* (the Buddhas and Buddha-fields) is the attainment of "the Excellent Wisdom," the ninth stage. Having maintained one's senses in the visions of primordial wisdom, the visions arise naturally; then, seeing all the phenomenal existents as clouds is the attainment of "the Cloud of Dharma," the tenth stage.

THE ATTAINMENTS OF THE PATH OF FOUR VISIONS IN *THREGCHOD*

Generally, the four visions are the attainments resulting from *Thodgal* training. But *Thregchod* also provides a system for attaining the four visions according to Longchen Rabjam. So, through the training in *Thregchod*, too, one perfects the "four visions" as well as the attainments of five paths and ten stages.

Longchen Rabjam summarizes:[SR 11a/4]

(1) Previously accumulated (virtuous) *karma*, the kindness of the *Guru*,
And skill in means: when these interdependent causes come together,
Then unhindered, free, simple "self-arisen awareness"
Which is non-apprehending-at-arising, is directly realized.
It is the great vision of "direct realization of *Dharmatā*."
(2) By having confidence that all the external and internal imputations are *Dharmatā*,
Whatever arises, there will be nothing to be rejected or accepted and modified or transformed,
Everything will arise solely as exercise of realization.
Then, when those (experiences are) increased,
One will be able to turn unfavorable circumstances of affirming and negating inner and outer existents into the path.
By the arising (of realization) liberation will be attained, and by dwelling (in it), bliss will be achieved.

By gaining experiences, "eyes," foreknowledge, miracles and the rest,
The various virtues of intrinsic awareness arise.
Then it should be known as the vision of "increase of the experiences."
(3) By further expanding the experience,
The intrinsic awareness (becomes) clarity, emptiness and naked primordial wisdom,
In which there are no torpor and elation, no wavering and unwavering,
(There is) no (difference) between meditation and withdrawal from meditation, but it is always (unceasing) like a river.
When such an extraordinary degree of virtues is achieved,
It is the attainment of the vision of the "perfection of intrinsic awareness."
(4) When one ever moves from that state,
One becomes free from the conceptualizations of apprehending characteristics, and transcends the objects of attachment, the (objects of) abandonment and their antidotes, and
Everything is simultanously perfected and free from deliberate apprehensions,
The attachment to external and internal existents exhausted,
Then that is the realization of the vision of the "dissolution (into) *Dharmatā*."
Then, by bringing the intrinsic awareness to perfection in the four visions,
The form bodies dissolve into the *Dharmatā*,
And one attains liberation by transcending the empty appearances and apprehensions—
That is the attainment of permanence in the primordial state.

ATTAINMENT OF *THREGCHOD* AND *THODGAL*

As the practice on the union of the ultimate sphere and intrinsic awareness through the training of *Thregchod* and *Thodgal* without separation is the *Dzogpa Chenpo*, the "four visions" are the attainments of *Dzogpa Chenpo*, both *Thregchod* and *Thodgal*.

Lonchen Rabjam writes:[NKS 102a/1]

The appearances of clarity are the primordial wisdom of *Thodgal*, and
The self-present peace (free) from projection and withdrawal
Is the spontaneously accomplished emptiness of *Thregchod*.
The aspect of cessation of mind is the *Thregchod*.
The spontaneously accomplished self-clarity is the *Thodgal*.
The union of (both), which is the self-arisen intrinsic wisdom,
Is the secret path of *Nyingthig* (*Innermost Essence*).
When all the elaborations are completely pacified,
At that time the self-awareness intrinsic wisdom will naturally arise. . . .
People who cling to *Thregchod* and *Thodgal*
Separately and practice accordingly
Are similar to a blind person examining forms.
They have not understood the (meaning of) the ultimate sphere and intrinsic awareness.
They are the friends of donkeys.
By gaining the experiences of the ultimate nature, the supreme luminous absorption,
The attainment of the universal supreme (*rNam-Kun mCh'og-lDan*),
One perfects the (*Four Visions:*) the Direct (realization of the Ultimate Nature), Increase (of experiences), Perfection (of intrinsic awareness)
And Dissolution (into *Dharmatā*),
And one actualizes the primordial nature.

ATTAINMENT OF THE FINAL RESULT

Having perfected the *Dzogpa Chenpo* path, one attains the ultimate sphere and obtains the three bodies.

Longchen writes:[NKC 112a/5]

This is the way of liberation, the perfection of the result:
When one has exhausted the path (of training) and the objects of abandonments,
One's mind, mental events with their basis,
Is exhausted totally into the ultimate sphere.

(Then) like clouds uncovering the sun in the sky,
From the sphere of the ultimate body, one manifests the *maṇḍala* of form bodies
In the nature of luminosity.
At that time, in the sky of the ultimate sphere, which is emptiness free from conceptualizations,
Shines the luminescent Enjoyment Body with major signs and minor marks.
It is the attainment of enlightenment, the enlightened nature.
It is the perfection of (the virtues of the Ultimate Body): the ten powers, (four) fearlessnesses, and (eighteen) uncommon virtues,
(The virtues of the Manifested Body:) the inconceivable compassion, spontaneously completed virtues,
And the knowledges of seeing the absolute and relative truths.
Hence, it is the perfection of ocean(-like) virtues of the Buddha.
From that state, the projections for the world of trainable beings,
The inexhaustible manifestations in various forms,
Appear for all, as the reflection of the moon in water.
Because of the interdependent causation of *Karma* of the trainees and the blessing-power of the enlightened ones,
They appear as it is appropriate.

RESULT

12. Attainment of the Result, the Buddha-Bodies and Primordial Wisdoms of Buddhahood in Mahāyāna Sūtras and Tantras

This is an abridged translation of the twenty-second chapter of the *Pema Karpo* (PK) and a quotation from *Shingta Chenpo* (SC) on the result of the path of training. It describes the five Buddha-bodies and the five Primordial Wisdoms, the final result of training according to general Buddhist *sūtras* and *tantras*.

PK II-183a/6 Buddhas of the ten directions confer the empowerment of the Great Light (*A'od-Zer Ch'en-Po*) on the *Bodhisattvas* who have (reached) the end of the tenth stage. Immediately, (the *Bodhisattvas*) achieve numerous absorptions such as *Vajra*-like Absorption (*rDo-rJe lTa-Bu'i Ting-Nge 'Dzin*), which they have not obtained previously.

Thereby, they attain Buddhahood and spontaneously achieve the (state of the) Universal Dharma King. At that time, the universal ground with its traces ceases, as well as the process of mind and mental events. When the stains are cleansed, simultaneously all the spontaneously accomplished virtues, the nature of luminous essence (which is present) within oneself, develop, like the fully developed disc of the sun in the cloudless sky....

At that time, the *Bodhisattvas* attain the accomplishment of the Ultimate Body, the cessation of elaborations and the wish-fulfilling jewel-like Enjoyment Body, which is spontaneously accomplished or arisen (from the state of the Ultimate Body) and is free from concepts. Their Buddha activities, the inexhaustible manifestations, pervade all the realms of trainable beings and appear before every individual being....

By having liberated the obscuration of appearances of the bodies of the three realms, the *Bodhisattvas* appear in the form of five *Vajra*-bodies. By having liberated the subjects, the eight consciousnesses, the *Bodhisattvas* appear in the essence of the five Primordial Wisdoms....

Concerning the result (of the path of training), there are three aspects: the Buddha-bodies, (which are) the basis; the Primordial Wisdoms (which are) based (on the bodies) and the Buddha activities.

THE FIVE BODIES

[185b/1]There are many ways to classify (the Buddha-bodies); for example, into three, four, and five bodies. Here, following *Māyājāla*, the non-dual (class of) *tantra*, they are classified into five classes. In *Mañjuśrīnāmasaṅgīti* it is said:

> Buddha is the nature of the five bodies.
> Universal Lord is the nature of the five Primordial Wisdoms....

(a) Ultimate Body: It is the freedom from elaboration and it is the supreme source, the vast (open) sphere like the sky for (the arising of various Buddha-) virtues. (b) Enjoyment Body: From the state (of the Ultimate Body), it appears as the five classes of Buddhas, like the sun and moon shining (in the sky). For the *Bodhisattvas* who are in the tenth stage, it appears as a (duplicate of the) five classes (of Buddhas) and their Buddha-fields, similar (to the actual ones). (c) Manifested Body: For impure beings it appears in three categories (of display); for example, as the Manifestation of the Supreme Enlightened One, like the arising of the reflections of the sun and moon in clear water.... The three categories of Manifested Body are: The Manifested Body of Art, the forms (*rTen*) of body, speech, and mind (of the Buddhas) such as paintings, which are made or which arise spontaneously as the object of generation of merits for beings.... The Manifested Body of Birth, the manifestation as a noble person (*Des-Pa*: i.e., *Bodhisattva*) and so on, to protect beings from such things as famine and sickness. The Manifestation as the Supreme Enlightened One, the manifestation (as sages) who display the twelve (Buddha-) deeds....

The next two bodies are the same as the first three bodies in essence, but from the point of view of virtues (they are categorized as two separate bodies). The uncontaminated Great Blissful Body is the (aspect of) omnipresence or the essence of the (three) bodies. The Bodies of Great Bliss and Essence are synonymous. The Vajra-body is the (aspect of) the indestructible nature of the fully enlightened state.... (d) Great Blissful Body: It is the nature of the Three Bodies, the essence of non-existence as singular or plural, and it is the inconceivable Great Bliss, the uncontaminated essence which pervades and (remains) inseparably in all the Buddha-bodies and Primordial Wisdoms. So it is nothing else than the Great Bliss.... (e) Vajra-body: As it has abandoned all the dual obscurations and has developed all the virtues, it is the Body of Full Enlightenment. As it never diminishes from (being) totally liberated, and as it is changeless, it is the Vajra-body....

The five bodies are not present as separate substances. They are the discriminating self-primordial wisdom of the Buddha and are one ultimate sphere.... The aspect of the emptiness-essence of the luminous absorption, which has been realized (upon the attainment of enlightenment), is called the Ultimate Body. Its clarity-nature is called the Enjoyment Body. Appearing in various (forms and activities), it is called the Manifested Body. The inseparability of the (defilements which) are to be purified and the realization of it is called the *Vajra* Body. The one-tasteness of its great bliss is called the Great Blissful Essence Body. . . .

THE FIVE PRIMORDIAL WISDOMS

The five Primordial Wisdoms are based (on the five Bodies). . . . The Primordial Wisdom of the Ultimate Sphere is the wisdom of the Ultimate Body. The Mirror-like Primordial Wisdom is the wisdom of the Enjoyment Body. The Primordial Wisdom of Equanimity is the wisdom of the Blissful Body. The Primordial Wisdoms of Discriminative and Accomplishment Wisdom are the wisdoms of the Manifested Body. They are all in the form of Full Enlightenment (or the *Vajra-*) Body. The five Primordial Wisdoms are present in the intrinsic awareness, the spontaneously accomplished essence (in all beings). But they do not manifest as they are obscured (for people who are still) on the path of training. There are two ways for the Primordial Wisdoms to manifest: to be (self-arising) upon the purification (*Dag-Pa*) of the five obscurations, and by dispelling (the obscurations to the primordial wisdoms) with five means:

(a) The dissolution of the universal ground and so on. In *Kāyatrayā* [*vatāra*]-*sūtra* it is said:

> The dissolution of the universal ground into the ultimate sphere is the Primordial Wisdom of the Ultimate Sphere. The dissolution of the consciousness of the universal ground into the ultimate sphere is the Mirror-like Primordial Wisdom. The dissolution of the mind-consciousness into the ultimate sphere is the Primordial Wisdom of Equanimity. The dissolution of the defiled mind into the ultimate sphere is the Discriminative Primordial Wisdom.The dissolution of the consciousnesses of the five doors into the ultimate sphere is the Primordial Wisdom of Accomplishment.

Also, upon the purification of the five emotional defilements, the five Primordial Wisdoms arise. . . . The purification of desire is the Discriminative Primordial Wisdom. The purification of hatred is the Mirror-like Primordial Wisdom. The purification of ignorance is the Primordial Wisdom of the Ultimate Sphere. The purification of pride is the Primordial Wisdom of Equanimity. The purification of jealousy is the Primordial Wisdom of Accomplishment. The aspect of (defilements) which are to be purified and transformed is like clouds.

(b) The five means of dispelling the (obscurations) are: . . . By learning the words and meaning of the dharma one dispels the obscurations to seeing the Mirror-like Primordial Wisdom. Likewise, meditation on the mind of enlightenment, equanimity toward all beings, is for the Primordial Wisdom of Equanimity. Giving teachings to others is for the Discriminative Primordial Wisdom. Serving others' needs is for the Primordial Wisdom of Accomplishment. By contemplating on suchness one dispels the obscurations to seeing the Primordial Wisdom of the Ultimate Sphere.

The Essence (*Ngo-Bo*) of the Primordial Wisdoms: The knowledge of the essence of the ultimate nature, the cessation of elaborations, is the Primordial Wisdom of the Ultimate Sphere. Knowledge of the nature of phenomena as luminous absorption is the Mirror-like Primordial Wisdom. Knowledge of everything as equalness and of one taste is the Primordial Wisdom of Equanimity. Knowledge of all the details of phenomena without confusion is the Discriminative Primordial Wisdom. Knowledge of all knowable phenomena without obscurations is the Primordial Wisdom of Accomplishment. . . .

(The five Primordial Wisdoms can be included in two Primordial Wisdoms of Knowledge:) The Primordial Wisdoms of the Ultimate Sphere and of Equanimity are included in the Primordial Wisdom of the Knowledge of Suchness (as it is). It does not conceptualize the phenomena of *saṃsāra* and *nirvāṇa* as one or separate. It dwells indivisibly in the Ultimate Body, which is like space free from elaborations. The Mirror-like, Accomplishment and Discriminative Primordial Wisdoms are encompassed in the Primordial Wisdom of the Knowledge of (all) Varieties. It sees and knows all the endless knowable phenomena. As the compassion of the Buddha) has no limits, it sees the whole universe. Even in something the size of a mustard seed, a system of immeasurable worlds and beings appears and the Buddha serves their needs. . . .

THE BUDDHA ACTIONS

[191a/5]The Buddha activities are the manifestative play of the Primordial Wisdom of Accomplishment. They instantly appear everywhere, wherever there are beings, in the form of Buddha-bodies, teachings, and so on for whomever is trainable.

DISSOLUTION OF FORM BODIES

[SC-II,185a/2]When there is a vessel filled with water, the reflections of the moon dissolve spontaneously into the moon itself. Likewise, if there is no water-vessel of receptive beings, the moon-reflection of manifested bodies of the Buddhas, which has appeared in beings' perceptions, will not exist any more. There is nothing but the state of self-appearing *Saṃbhogakāya*. The dissolution (of the *Nirmāṇakāya*) into the *Saṃbhogakāya* is just a nominal (process) and it is not like something dissolving into something else. The moon also dissolves into its own inner clarity (*Nang-gSal*) during the days of the new moon. Likewise, the self-appearing present *Saṃbhogakāya* dissolves into the inner clarity of the sphere of *Saṃbhogakāya*, and that is called remaining (*'Khyil-Ba*) in the sphere of primordial wisdom. At this point the discriminative self-awareness wisdom (*So-So Rang Rig-Pa'i Ye-Shes*) reaches the most subtle primordial wisdom, and this is the time of the utmost contemplative state.

13. *The Buddha-Bodies and Primordial Wisdoms in Dzogpa Chenpo*

This section is an abridged translation explaining the Buddhahood presented in the 11th chapter, entitled The Stages of Perfection of Results, from *Tshigdon Dzod* (TD). In this section Longchen Rabjam explains the division of three Buddha-bodies and the Primordial Wisdoms of the three Buddha-bodies according to *Dzogpa Chenpo*.

TD 227b/3 When the Intrinsic Awareness becomes free from all the adventitious defilements, one attains the naturally pure Ultimate Body (*Dharmakāya*) and achieves the ultimate sphere, the union of the Buddha-bodies and Primordial Wisdoms. Then, without moving from the Ultimate Body, one manifests (as) lamps for all existence, extending in all directions, and fulfills the dual benefits through the (form Buddha-bodies,) the Enjoyment Body (*Saṃbhogakāya*), and the Manifested Body (*Nirmāṇakāya*) through the mind of enlightenment (compassion). This is the ultimate result (of this path of training). This (enlightenment) endows one with infinite qualities, but in brief it can be explained in two categories: (a) the essence (*Ngo-Bo*) of the Buddha-bodies, the abode of ocean-like attainment of enlightenment, and (b) the nature (*Rang-bZhin*) of Awareness Wisdom, the victory banner of wish-fulfilling gems....

THE THREE BUDDHA-BODIES

228a/2The essence (of the Buddha-bodies) is their being the basis or the bodies of the virtues of the Buddhas. The essence of the Ultimate Body is the great purity from its origin, because of its being free from conceptions and expressions. The essence of the Enjoyment Body is the great spontaneity because of its being self-clarity free from extremes of concepts. The essence of the Manifested Body is the compassion (power) (as it is) the basis of the arising of appropriate (manifestations). . . .

Characteristics (*mTshan-Nyid*): The two ultimate purities (*Dag-Pa*), functioning as the bodies of the Buddhas, are the general characteristics of the (Buddha-bodies). For the characteristics of the individual Buddha-bodies, in *Senge Tsaldzog* (*Seng-Ge rTsal-rDzogs*)*tantra* it is said:

> The inconceivable is the characteristic of the Ultimate Body.
> The clarity without concepts is the characteristic of the Enjoyment Body.
> The manifestation in various forms is the characteristic of the Manifested Body. . . .

Their way of being present (*bZhugs-Tshul*): The Ultimate Body is present free from characteristics, like space. The Enjoyment Body is present free from mortal form, like a rainbow. The Manifested Body is present in indefinite and various forms, like the play of illusions. . . .

The Buddha-field (*Zhing-Khams*): The Buddha-field of the Ultimate Body is purity from the origin, freedom from concepts. The Buddha-field of the Enjoyment Body is the clarity of the five Buddha-bodies and Primordial Wisdoms. The Buddha-field of the Manifested Body is the trainable beings appearing as the world and beings throughout the extent of space. . . .

Trainable Beings (or Disciples) (*gDul-Bya*): The disciple of the Ultimate Body, the pure self-essence, is the Intrinsic Awareness which transcends movements and efforts. The disciple of the Enjoyment Body is the self-appearances of the assemblies of masters and disciples. The disciple of the Manifested Body is ordinary beings of the six realms. . . .

Activities (*Byed-Las*): Having perfected the goal for oneself in the Ultimate Body, without moving from it, and remaining in the state of the ultimate sphere, one arises in the form Buddha-bodies for others, and provides the accomplishment of the dual benefits till the end of *saṃsāra* by leading beings forward (or towards the goal). . . . The benefits of others are brought forth without one's moving from the ultimate sphere, like the water-moon (the reflection of the moon in water). . . .

Perfection of Confidence (*gDengs-Tshad*): It is the attainment of the three Buddha-bodies by perfecting the virtues of both abandonings and realizations. Similarly, the fulfillment of wishes is the perfection of a wish-fulfilling gem. The (quality of being) unmoving and free from conceptualizations is the perfection of the Ultimate Body. The self-clarity, the completion of major and minor marks, is the perfection of the Enjoyment Body. Causing the accomplishment of the dual purposes is the perfection of the Manifested Body.

THE NATURE OF THE INTRINSIC AWARENESS PRIMORDIAL WISDOM

232b/3 There are three aspects: (a) The Essence (*Ngo-Bo*) of Intrinsic Awareness Primordial Wisdom (*Rig-Pa Ye-Shes*): The sun-like Intrinsic Awareness dwells as the Omniscient Intrinsic Awareness (*mKhyen-Rig*) primordially, and it is free from all the cloud(-like) adventitious obscurations. So it is the vision of undefiled Primordial Wisdom and is present as the essence of the Buddha-bodies. . . . (b) The aspect of primordial (*Ye*) awareness knowledge (*mKhyen-Rig*) is spontaneously luminescent. Realizing (*Shes*) this awareness knowledge directly liberates (one) from all the obscurations and makes the *maṇḍala* of all the virtues blossom. So the Buddha-bodies and the primordial wisdoms are present in union in the expanse of bliss. (c) Division (*dBye-Ba*): There are two divisions of Primordial

Wisdom, the general and specific.

The General Primordial Wisdom

There are three aspects, the "Primordial Wisdom-at-the-basis" of the Ultimate Body (*Ch'os-sKu gZhi gNas Kyi Ye-Shes*), the "Primordial Wisdom Endowed with Characteristics" of the Enjoyment Body (*Longs-sKu mTshan-Nyid 'Dzin-Pa'i Ye-Shes*), and the "Primordial Wisdom of Omnipresence" of the Manifested Body (*sPrul-sKu Kun-Khyab Kyi Ye-Shes*). The Primordial Wisdom of the Ultimate Body is like the disc of the sun, and it provides the basis of arising for the Enjoyment Body and Manifested Body, like the sun and its rays. The Primordial Wisdom of the Enjoyment Body is like a mirror and it displays the reflections of the complete "Primordial Wisdom Endowed with Characteristics," clearly without confusion. The Primordial Wisdom of the Manifested Body is like a water-moon (or reflection), and it appears appropriately for the receptive vessels (i.e., disciples)....

Of the Ultimate Body, "the Primordial Wisdom at-the-basis" dwells in (the nature of) emptiness and clarity, the ground of arising (of the form Buddha-bodies), and it is like a crystal ball which is present as it is (without external influences). From the state (of "the Primordial Wisdom at-the-basis") nothing manifests directly, except the aspect of providing the sphere of arising of the "Primordial Wisdom Endowed with Characteristics" (of the Enjoyment Body) and the "the Primordial Wisdom of Omnipresence" (of the Manifested Body).

In the (state of "the Primordial Wisdom) Endowed with Characteristics" (of the Enjoyment Body), the "Primordial Wisdom at-the-basis" is merely present as the basis of arising (of the form Buddha-bodies), and the "Primordial Wisdom of Omnipresence" merely radiates as the rays. So they are present directly. The nature of "the Primordial Wisdom Endowed with Characteristics" is present as the five (colored) lights appearing from the crystal ball.

In the state of the Primordial Wisdom of the Manifested Body, "the Primordial Wisdom at-the-basis" is unmoved from the ultimate sphere like the disc of the sun, and the "Primordial Wisdom Endowed with Characteristics" dwells in the Buddha-field of the Enjoyment Body like rays and rainbow colors. So they are not manifestatively present. The "Omnipresent Primordial Wisdom," like a reflection of the moon appearing (in vessels), appears (directly) for the disciples individually.

These divisions of Primordial Wisdom are made (merely) in respect to phenomenal existents (*Ch'os*) according to how they appear. In respect to the nature of phenomena (*Ch'os-Nyid*), all are of the sameness essence, which transcends being one or separate.

The Specific Primordial Wisdoms of the Buddha-Bodies

234a/4 There are three: (the Primordial Wisdoms) at the basis of the Ultimate Body, endowed with characteristics of the Enjoyment Body, and of omnipresence of the Manifested Body.

The primordial wisdom of the ultimate body. The Ultimate Body, which is the liberation in the liberated state, is pure from the origin and of one taste, like space. In it are present three Primordial Wisdoms: (i) the "Primordial Wisdom of Originally Pure Essence" (*Ngo-Bo Ka-Dag*), which transcends all concepts and expressions like a transparent crystal ball, (ii) the "Primordial Wisdom of Spontaneously Accomplished Nature" (*Rang-bZhin Lhun-Grub*), which is merely the basis of the arising of the virtues of appearances, a subtle clarity, and has no substance, and (iii) the "Primordial Wisdom of Omnipresent Compassion" (*Thugs-rJe Kun-Khyab*), which is the aspect of the mere power (*rTsal*) of the essence, which unceasingly (is present) as the basis of arising (of the two form Buddha-bodies), and is the aspect of the Awareness Wisdom (*Shes-Rig*) which doesn't analyze the objects directly.

If the Ultimate Body has gross aspects, it falls into (the extremes) of substances(*dNgos-Po*) and characteristics (*mTshan-Ma*) and it won't be peace from conceptualizations. If there is not the (presence of) a subtle aspect of profound clarity as the basis of arising (in the Ultimate Body), it falls into (the extreme of) nihilism like space. So the Ultimate Body, contrary to both these extremes, is a subtle Primordial Wisdom, (the union) of emptiness and clarity, which is present as the basis of arising.

The Primordial Wisdom of the Enjoyment Body. [235b/4]It is the Primordial Wisdom Endowed with Characteristics and it has five divisions:

(i) Primordial Wisdom of the Ultimate Sphere (*Ch'os-dByings*):

Essence (*Ngo-Bo*): It is the inseparability of the three aspects: (a) the emptiness, the primordially pure sphere, which is the ground of liberation, (b) the self-clarity of Primordial Wisdom, which is the basis of the self-light, and (c) the ultimate sphere of Awareness Wisdom....

(ii) Mirror(-like) (*Me-Long lTa-Bu*) Primordial Wisdom:

Essence: It is the clarity, which is the unobstructed sphere for the arising (of the Buddha-qualities) in (the union of) the emptiness and clarity of Intrinsic Awareness....

(iii) Primordial Wisdom of Equanimity (*mNyam-Nyid*):

Essence: It is (the state of equalness) without falling into (the extremes of) partiality and dimensions. The cause of equanimity is the primordially liberated great equanimity in the (ultimate) sphere of *saṃsāra* and *nirvāṇa*. The condition of equanimity is the dwelling in the great equanimity of the three doors, the (enlightened) body, speech, and mind (of the Buddhas), and the essence, nature, and compassion (power) (of the Ultimate Body)....

(iv) Discriminative (*Sor-rTog*) Primordial Wisdom:

Essence: (It is the Primordial Wisdom of) discriminating all the phenomenal existents directly without confusion....

(v) Primordial Wisdom of Accomplishment of Actions (*Bya-Grub*):

Essence: Having achieved the goal for self in the state of intrinsic awareness, it fulfills the needs of others as wish-fulfilling gems, without effort.

Primordial Wisdom of the Manifested Body. [238b/6]It is the "Primordial Wisdom of Omnipresence" of the Manifested Body, and it has two aspects. The manifested bodies (which appear) for others, the trainable beings, are not like mere inanimate beings or reflections, but are spontaneously (manifested) through the twofold Primordial Wisdom for the spontaneous fulfillment of the goals of beings.

(i) The Primordial Wisdom of the Knowledge of Suchness of (phenomena as they are) (*Ji-lTa-Ba*) is the knowledge of the absolute truth, the essence of phenomena without error. Through this, the Buddha teaches (the disciples) the absolute nature free from elaboration of arising and cessation, like space. (ii) The (Primordial Wisdom of the) Knowledge of Varieties (of phenomena) (*Ji-sNyed-Pa*) is the knowledge of the relative truth, the details of all phenomena without confusion. Through these (knowledges), the Buddha teaches the faculties (*dBang-Po*), elements (*Ch'os*), *karma*, and the path of training, and so forth (to trainable beings), (in the manner of) the eight examples of illusion. . . .

(i) Primordial Wisdom of the Knowledge of Suchness (Absolute Truth):

Essence: It is the knowledge without error of how phenomena are present (in their true nature). . . .

Division: It has two divisions: They are the (Primordial Wisdom of) the knowledge of suchness, the nature of phenomenal appearances, and the (Primordial Wisdom of) the knowledge of suchness, the empty nature of the absolute nature. Does it know the varieties of appearances (also)? In the appearances there are two aspects, the essence and the form. (This knowledge) knows both the essence, the suchness, and the forms, the varieties. It is like (perceiving) the blue lily (*utpala*) and its (details such as) its blue color etc. . . .

(ii) Primordial Wisdom of Knowledge of Varieties (Relative Truth):

Essence: It is the knowledge of all the details of phenomenal appearances, such as dispositions (*khams*) and dormancies (*Bag-La-Nyal*), of the habits of trainable beings. . . .

Division: (There are two aspects:) The knowledge of all the aspects of pure qualities of the Buddhas that are perceivable by the Manifested Body and (the knowledge of) the entire aspect of impure elements of mundane beings: (the Manifested Body) fulfills the dual goals spontaneously like a wish-fulfilling gem, until *saṃsāra* is emptied....

Therefore, through the inseparable union of the Buddha-bodies and Primordial Wisdoms, the Buddhas perfect their goal of self in the (ultimate) sphere and fulfill the benefits of others, and it is the result. In *Longtrugpa* (*Klong-Drug-Pa*) it is said:

> From the space-like Ultimate Body arise spontaneously the Enjoyment Body like the hosts of stars and the cloud-like Manifested Body. They gather spontaneously and provide (light and rain-like) benefits for living beings without ceasing.

Appendix

The following are some passages on *Karma* from the Commentary on Khejug (LNA) by Khenpo Nuden of Khathog monastery.

CAUSE OF *SAṂSĀRA*

LNA 100a/5 The cause which produces birth in *saṃsāra* is the truth of the source (of suffering) (*Kun-'Byung bDen-Pa*). The contaminated forms of *saṃsāra* do not develop without any cause as the *Lokāyata* (school of Hinduism) asserts. They do not develop from any other improper cause such as from self, time, and god as the *Vaiśeṣika* (school of Hinduism) and other schools assert. They arise from the cause of contaminated *karmic* and emotional defilements. So (the defilements) are the truth of the source (of suffering i.e., *saṃsāra*).

KARMA AND EMOTIONAL DEFILEMENTS

100b/1 There are two aspects of the truth of the source (of suffering): *Karma* and emotional defilements.... First, beings of the three realms (*Khams-gSum*) develop through the cause of accumulation of *karmas* in the past. The pure and impure external world has developed through the cause of common *karma* of similar types of beings. The bodies, and the happy and unhappy experiences of individual beings based on them, which are not common to other beings, develop through the *karmic* causes which are not common to other (beings).

212b/4 Second, the *karmas* which produce the *saṃsāra* of beings of the three realms are generated first by the emotional defilements; then, if one does not maintain (the *karmas*) by defilements such as clinging, no rebirths will take place in this world as the effect. Similarly, water is necessary for the *Nāgas* to live, and roots for trees, seeds for shoots, trees for fruit and flowers. Emotional defilements are the cause of generating *saṃsāra*.

SOME DIFFERENT CATEGORIES OF *KARMA*

Virtuous, Non-Virtuous, and Neutral Karma

101a/3 What kinds of *karmas* are there? There are three. (a) Virtuous *karmas* with stains (*Zag-bChas Kyi dGe-Ba*), which generate rebirths in higher realms (of *saṃsāra*), such as the god and human migrations (*'Gro-Ba*), and so forth, and (worldly) happy experiences. (b) Non-virtuous *karmas*, which generate rebirths in inferior migrations, such as hell, and all unhappy experiences. (3) Neutral *karmas* are neutral with respect both to virtuous and non-virtuous *karmas*, and they do not create the basis (i.e., rebirth) or happy or unhappy experiences.

Virtuous Karmas

(Nāgārjuna said: "Non-attachment, absence of hatred and ignorance, the *karmas* generated by these are virtues.")

109b/5 The actual virtues are the "eleven (virtuous) mental events" such as faith (shame, embarassment, non-attachment, non-hatred, non-deludedness, diligence, pliancy, conscientiousness, equanimity and nonviolence).. The related (*'Brel-Ba*) virtues are the mind and mental events associated (*mTshungs-lDan*) with the eleven (virtuous) mental events. The follow-up (*rJes-'Brel*) virtues are habits of that virtuous mind and those mental events which are planted in the universal ground. The generated (*Slong-Ba*) virtues are the visible and invisible deeds of the body and speech produced by them (the virtuous mind and mental events). The absolute (*Don-Dam-Pa*) virtue is suchness, the nature of phenomena, and the result, *nirvāṇa*.

Non-Virtuous Karmas

(Nāgārjuna said: "Attachment, hatred and ignorance, the *karmas* generated by these are non-virtues.")

111a/4The actual non-virtuous *karmas* are the (six) roots (i.e., desire, anger, arrogance, unenlightenment, doubt, (defiled view) and (twenty) subordinate emotional defilements (i.e., hatred, resentment, spite, violence, lack of compassion, jealousy, dishonesty, deceit, shamelessness, slyness or concealment, avarice, pride, lack of confidence, laziness, lack of conscientiousness, forgetfulness, inattentiveness, gloominess, wildness, and desultoriness), which create all the misdeeds. The related unvirtuous *karmas* are the mind and mental events associated with these root and subordinate emotional defilements. The follow-up non-virtuous *karmas* are the habits of these emotional defilements planted on the universal ground. The generated non-virtuous *karmas* are all the (non-virtuous) deeds committed by the body and speech, such as killing, generated by them (the non-virtuous mind and mental events and habits).

Neutral Karmas

112a/5All the deeds which are caused by the mind neither by the three poisons, such as attachment, nor by (the three non-poisons), such as non-attachment, are neutral in respect to both virtuous and non-virtuous deeds.

MENTAL AND PHYSICAL KARMAS

(As it is said in *Abhidharmakoṣa*: "Thinking is the *karma* of mind, (there are two *karmas*) created by it: the *karma* of body and speech.")

101a/5*Karmas* first are thought in the mind and then acted by the body and speech. So there are two *karmas*, the *karmas* thought by the mind and the *karmas* of body and speech which have been generated by thought.

Contaminated and Uncontaminated Karmas
[101b/2]Virtuous and non-virtuous *karmas* which generate worldly happiness and unhappiness are the contaminated *karmas* (*Zag-bChas*). The *karmas* which belong to the truth of the path and generate any of the three *nirvāṇas* (cessations) as the result are the uncontaminated *karmas*, (*Zag-Med*) and these are the antidotes which exhaust the contaminated *karmas*. Although they do not belong to the category of the truth of the source of suffering, they are mentioned here to explain the different categories of *karma*. The uncontaminated *karma* is for transcending *karmic* effects through the *karmic* law of the truth of the path, and it is not for producing a chain of *saṃsāric karmas*. So it does not belong to the truth of the source.

Meritorious, Demeritorious, and Changeless Karmas
[101b/6]Meritorious *karma* is the virtuous deeds which produce happy experiences in the god and human migrations of the desire realm (*'Dod-Khams*). Unmeritorious *karma* is the unvirtuous deeds which produce the experiences of suffering in the three inferior migrations of the desire realm. Changeless (*Mi-gYo-Ba*) *karma* is the virtuous deeds associated with contemplation in tranquillity, which produce (the births) in the two upper realms (*Khams*), the contemplative (or form) realm and the formless realm. It is called changeless *karma* because a particular contemplation will only lead to birth in that particular realm and there will be no change to others.

Four Aspects of Karmas According to the Time of Experiencing
[107a/5](a) Very strong *karmas* which have result in the same lifetime (*mThong-Ch'os mNgon-gSum*).... (b) *Karmas* of which the effect will be experienced in the next life without any interruption by any other lives (*sKyes-Nas Myong-'Gyur*). It is the effect of *karmas* such as the five uninterruptable *karmas* (*mTsham-Med-Pa'i-Las*).... (c) *Karmas* the effect of which will be experienced during any lives after the next one (*Lan-Grangs gZhan-La Myong-'Gyur*).... (d) *Karmas* the effect of which are uncertain ever to be experienced (*Myong-Bar Ma-Nges-Pa'i*

Las). Even if one has committed certain *karmas*, because of training in the antidotes such as purification it becomes uncertain that the effect will ever be experienced.

Bibliography of Works Cited

BGT Bla-Ma rGyang-'Bod Tshig-'Grel (f. 16a-59b, Upadeśa Rin-Po-Ch'e'i Za-Ma-Tog) by Ah-Bu Hral-Po (alias dPal-sPrul Rin-Po-Ch'e, 1808-1887). Publisher unknown.

BL rDzogs-Pa Ch'en-Po Sems-Nyid Ngal-gSo'i gNas-gSum dGe-Ba gSum Gyi Don-Khrid Byang-Ch'ub Lam-bZang (f. 53) by Dri-Med A'od-Zer (Klong-Ch'en Rab-'Byams, 1308-1363). Published by (the 4th) Dodrup Chen Rinpoche.

BN gNyug-Sems A'od-gSal Gyi Don-La dPyad-Pa rDzogs-Pa Ch'en-Po gZhi-Lam 'Bras-Bu'i Shan-'Byed Blo-Gros sNang-Ba (f. 76) by rDo-rJe dBang-mCh'og dGyes-Pa rTsal (Zhe-Ch'en rGyal-Tshabs).

BP Byang-Ch'ub Sems-dPa'i sPyod-Pa-La 'Jug-Pa (f. 140) by Śāntideva. A xylographic copy from Dodrup Chen Monastery.

BZ bTsan-Po Khri-Srong lDe-bTsan Dang mKhan-Po Slob-dPon Padma'i Dus...mDzad-Pa'i sBa-bZhed ZhabsbTags-Ma. Published by Shes-Rig Par-Khang, Dharamsala, India (1968).

CD Ch'os-dByings Rin-Po-Ch'e'i mDzod (f.26) by Klong Ch'en Rab-'Byams. Published by Dodrup Chen Rinpoche.

DC rDzogs-Ch'en (f 58) by 'Jigs-Med bsTan-Pa'i Nyi-Ma (1865-1926). Published by Dodrup Sangye Lama.

DCT rDzogs-Ch'en Thor-Bu (f. 7) by 'Jigs-Med bsTan-Pa'i Nyi-Ma. Published by Dodrup Sangye Lama.

DL Dris-Lan (f. 1-11, Vol. Kha, rDo-Grub Ch'en gSung-'Bum) by 'Jigs-Med bsTan-Pa'i Nyi-Ma. Published by Dodrup Chen Rinpoche.

DM Bar-Do sPyi'i Don Thams-Chad rNam-Par gSal-Bar Byed-Pa Dran-Pa'i Me-Long (f.40) by sNa-Tshogs Rang-Grol (1608?-?) of rTse-Le. A xylographic copy from rGyal-Gyi Sri sNeu-sTeng.

DNM rDo-rJe Sems-dPa' sNying-Gi Me-Long Gi rGyud (f.265b-291a, Vol. 10, rGyud bChu-bDun of rNying-Ma rGyud-'Bum). Published by Jamyang (Dilgo) Khyentse, 1974.

DNN Rang-bZhin rDzogs-Pa Ch'en-Po'i Lam-Gyi Ch'a-Lag sDom-gSum rNam-Par Nges-Pa (f.16) by Padma dBang-Gi rGyal-Po (1487-1542), Published by Khamtul Rinpoche.

DO Zhal-Ch'em Dri-Ma Med-Pa'i-A'od (f.132-140, Vol. Hung, mKha'-'Gro Yang-Tig, Ya-bZhi collection) by Dri-Med A'od-Zer. Published by Sherab Gyaltsen Lama.

DRT Byang-Ch'ub Kyi Sems Kun-Byed rGyal-Po'i Don-

Khrid Rin-Ch'en Gru-Bo (f. 71-89, Don-Khrid) by Klong-Ch'en Rab-'Byams. Published by Dodrup Chen Rinpoche.

DTG De-bZhin gShegs-Pas Legs-Par gSung-Pa'i gSung-Rab rGya-mTsho'i sNying-Por Gyur-Pa Rig-Pa 'Dzin-Pa'i sDe-sNod Dam-Pa sNga-'Gyur rGyud-'Bum Rin-Po-Ch'e'i rTogs-Pa brJod-Pa 'Dzam-Gling Tha-Gru Khyab-Pa'i rGyan (f.336) by 'Jigs-Med Gling-Pa (1729-1798). Published by Jamyang Khyentse.

DTM Deb-Ther dMar-Po by Tshal-Pa Situ Kan-dGa' rDo-rJe (1309-1364) Published by Mi-Rigs dPe-bsKrun-Khang, Peking, 1981.

DTN Deb-Ther sNgon-Po (Vol. I & II) by 'Gos-Lo gZhon-Nu dPal (1392-1481). Published by Si-Khron Mi-Rigs dPe-bsKrun Khang, 1984.

DZ mTshungs-Bral rGyal-Ba'i Myu-Gu O-rGyan 'Jigs-Med Ch'os-Kyi dBang-Po'i rTogs-brJod Phyogs-Tsam Gleng-Ba bDud-rTsi'i Zil-Thig (f.101-136, Vol. Nga, rDo-Grub-Ch'en gSung-'Bum Collection) by 'Jigs-Med bsTan-Pa'i Nyi-Ma. Published by Dodrup Chen Rinpoche.

GB rJe-bTsun Mi-La Ras-Pa'i rNam-Par Thar-Pa rGyas-Par Phye-Ba mGur-'Bum (f. 319) by Mi-La Ras-Pa. A zylographic copy from Chitra monastery, India.

GC Yon-Tan Rin-Po-Ch'e'i mDzod dGa'-Ba'i Ch'ar by 'Jigs-Med Gling-Pa. Published by Sonam T. Kazi.

GCD Klong-Ch'en Nam-mKha'i rNal-'Byor Gyi gSung-'Bum Thor-Bu Las, bsKyed-rDzogs bsGom-Phyogs Dris-Lan Dang Zhal-gDams rNams Phyogs-Su sDeb-Pa (f. 174) by 'Jigs-Med Gling-Pa. Published by Sonam T. Kazi.

GCG Thegs-Pa Ch'en-Po rGyud Bla-Ma'i bsTan-bChos Zhes-Bya-Ba'i mCh'an-'Grel (f. 53) by Zhan-Phan (Ch'os-Kyi sNang-Ba, 1800?-?). Published by Ven. D. G. Khoch-hen Tulku, India.

GD Theg-Pa Tham-Chad Kyi Don gSal-Bar Byed-Pa Grub-Pa'i mTha' Rin-Po-Ch'e'i mDzod (f. 206) by Dri-Med A'od-Zer. Published by Dodrup Chen Rinpoche.

GN rDzogs-Pa Ch'en-Po sGyu-Ma Ngal-gSo (f. 23) by Dri-Med A'od-Zer. Published by Dodrup Chen Rinpoche.

GNE *Guide to Nyingma Edition* (Vol. I & II), edited by Tarthang Tulku. Published by Dharma Publishing.

GP Klong-Ch'en sNying-Gi Thig-Le-Las, rDzogs-Pa Ch'en-Po'i rGyud Phyi-Ma (f. 5, Vol. Hung, Klong-Ch'en sNying-Thig Collection) discovered by 'Jigs-Med Gling-Pa. Published by Jamyang Khyentse.

GPK rDo-rJe Thegs-Pa'i sMin-Grol Lam-Kyi Rim-Pa-Las 'Phros-Pa'i rGyab-brTen Padma dKar-Po (f. 27, Vol. Hung, Klong-Ch'en sNying-Thig Collection) by mKhyen-brTse'i A'od-Zer (alias 'Jigs-Med Gling-Pa). Published by Jamyang Khyentse.

GT Rin-Po-Ch'e 'Byung-Bar Byed-Pa sGra Thal-'Gyur Ch'en-Po'i rGyud. (f. 193b-265b, Vol. Tha, rGyud bChu-bDun, rNying-Ma rGyud-'Bum). Published by Jamyang Khyentse, 1974.

HZB *History of Zen Buddhism* by Heinrich Dumoulin. Boston: Beacon Press.

JG lTa-Grub Shan-'Byed gNad-Gyi sGron-Me Yi Tshig-Don eNam-bShad 'Jam-dByangs dGongs-rGyan (f.105) by mDo-sNgags bsTan-Pa'i Nyi-Ma (Bod-Pa sPrul-sKu).

KBG Ch'os Tham-Chad rDzogs-Pa Ch'en-Po Byang-Ch'ub Kyi Sems Kun-Byed rGyal-Po (f. 1-110, Vol. Ka, rNying-Ma rGyud-'Bum). Published by Jamyang Khyentse, 1974.

KG Klong-Ch'en sNying-Gi Thig-Le-Las, Kun-Tu bZang-Po'i dGongs-Nyams (f. 5, Vol. Hung, Klong-Ch'en sNying-Thig Collection) discovered by 'Jigs-Med Gling-Pa. Published by Jamyang Khyentse.

KGT Dam-Pa'i Ch'os-Kyi 'Khor-Lo bsGyur-Ba rNams-Kyi Byung-Ba gSal-Bar Byed-Pa mKhas-Pa'i dGa'-sTon (part 1-5, Vol. I & II) by dPa'-Bo gTsug-Lag Phreng-Ba. Published by Mi-Rigs dPe-bsKrun-Khang. China. 1986.

KRD rDo-rJe bKod-Pa Kun-'Dus Rig-Pa'i mDo (f. 1-138, Vol. Na, rNying-Ma rGyud-'Bum). Published by Jamyang Khyentse.

KRG Klong-Ch'en Rab-'Byams rGyal-Po'i rGyud (f. 128-197, Vol. Ga, rNying-Ma rGyud-'Bum). Published by Jamyang Khyentse, 1974.

KS Yid-bZhin mDzod-Kyi dKa'-gNad Chi-Rigs gSal-Bar Byed-Pa (f. 38) by Mi-Pham rNam-Par rGyal-Ba, 1846-1912). Published by Dodrup Chen Rinpoche.

KT rDzoga-Pa Ch'en-Po Ye-Shes Bla-Ma'i sPyi-Don, sNying-Thig Ma-Bu'i lDeu-Mig Kun-bZang Thugs-Kyi Tikka (f. 271) by Padma Las-'Brel-rTsal (alias mKhan-Po Ngag-Ch'ung, 1879-1941).

KTT Shin-Tu gSang-Ba Ch'en-Po Thod-rGal sNyan-brGyud Kyi Zin-Bris Kun-Tu bZang-Po'i dGongs-rGyan Yig-Med Upadesa mKha'-'Gro'i Thugs-Kyi Tikka (f. 40) by Padma Las-'Brel-rTsal.

KYL Klong-Ch'en sNying-Gi Thig-Le-Las, rDzogs-Pa Ch'en-Po Kun-Tu bZang-Po Ye-Shes Klong-Gi rGyud (f. 12, Vol. Hung, Klong-Ch'en sNying-Thig Collection). Published by Jamyang Khyentse.

KZ Rig-'Dzin 'Jigs-Med Gling-Pa'i Yang-Srid sNgags-'Ch'ang 'Ja'-Lus rDo-rJe'i rNam-Thar mKha'-'Gro'i Zhal-Lung (Autobiography of mDo mKhyen-brTse, Ye-Shes rDo-rJe, 1800-?) (f.199). Published by Dodrup Chen Rinpoche.

KZD Kun-mKhyen Zhal-Lung bDud-rTsi'i Thig-Pa (f 14, Vol. Hung, Klong-Ch'en sNying-Thig Collection) discoverd by 'Jigs-Med Gling-Pa. Published by Jamyang Khyentse.

KZG sMin-Byed Kyi dBang Dang Grol-Lam Phyag-rGya Ch'en-Po'i gNad-Don Gyi Dri-Ba Lan-Du Phul-Ba sKal-bZang dGa'-Byed bDud-rTsi'i 'Dod-'Jo (f. 101) by sNa-Tshogs Rang-Grol (1608-?). A xylographic copy from rGyal-Gyi Sri sNeu-sTeng.

KZZ rDzogs-Pa Ch'en-Po Klong-Ch'en sNying-Thig Gi sNgon-'Gro'i Khrid-Yig Kun-bZang Bla-Ma'i Zhal-Lung Gi Zin-Bris (f. 205) by Pema Ledrel Tsal.

LC rDzogs-Pa Ch'en-Po sNying-Thig Gi Lo-rGyus Ch'en-Mo (f. 90, Vol. Ma, Vima sNying-Thig, Ya-bZhi). Published by Sherab Gyaltsen Lama.

LG Ngal-gSo sKor-gSum Gyi sPyi-Don Legs-bShad rGya-mTsho (f. 60) by Ngag-Gi dBang-Po (alias Klong-Ch'en Rab-'Byams). Published by Dodrup Chen Rinpoche.

LGY Lo-rGyus (of sNying-Thig) by rGyal-Ba gYung (f 203-211, Vol. Wam, from mKha'-'Gro sNying-Thig of Ya-bZhi). Published by Sherab Gyaltsen Lama.

LN sNga-'Gyur rDo-rJe Theg-Pa'i bsTan-Pa Rin-Po-Ch'e Ji-lTar Byung-Ba'i Tshul Dag-Ching gSal-Bar brJod-Pa Lha-dBang gYul-Las rGyal-Ba'i rNga-Bo-Ch'e (f. 410) by 'Jigs-Bral Ye-Shes rDo-rJe (1903-1987). Published by Dudjom Rinpoche.

LNA mKhas-Pa'i Tshul-La 'Jug-Pa'i msGo'i mCh'an-'Grel Legs-bShad bNang-Ba'i A'od-Zer (f. 351) by Nus-lDan. Published by Lama Gyurtrag.

LNG gSang-sNgags sNga-'Gyur rNying-Ma-Pa'i bsTan-Pa'i rNam-bZhag mDo-Tsam bJod-Pa Legs-bShad sNang-Ba'i dGa'-sTon (f. 232) by 'Jigs-Bral Ye-Shes rDo-rJe. A xylographic copy from Zangdog Palri monastery, Kalimpong, India.

LNT bDe-Bar gShegs-Pa'i bsTan-Pa Thams-Chad Kyi sNying-Po Rig-Pa 'Dzin-Pa'i sDe-sNod rDo-rJe Theg-Pa sNga-'Gyur rGyud-'Bum Rin-Po-Ch'e'i rTogs-Pa brJod-Pa Lha'i rNga-Bo-Ch'e lTa-Bu'i gTam (Vol. I & II) by 'Gyur-Med Tshe-dBang mCh'og-Grub (1764?-?). Published by Jamyang Khyentse.

LNTT Blo-gSal Ri-Bong Gi rTogs-Pa brJod-Pa'i Dris-Lan Lha'i rNga-Bo-Ch'e lTa-Bu'i gTam (f. 45, Vol. I, gSung-Thor-Bu) by Ngag-Gi dBang-Po (alias Klong-Ch'en Rab-'Byams). Published by Sanje Dorje.

LRT Lo-rGyus Rin-Po-Ch'e'i Phreng-Ba (f. 5-30, Vol. E, Lo-rGyus, Bla-Ma Yang-Tig, Ya-bZhi) by Klong-Ch'en Rab-'Byams. Published by Sherab Gyaltsen Lama.

LSM Grub-mTha' Thams-Chad Kyi Khung-Dang 'Dod-Tshul sTon-Pa Legs-bShad Shel-Gyi Me-Long by (Thos-kvan) Ch'os-Kyi Nyi-Ma (1737-1802). Published by Ngawang Gelek Demo.

LT Ch'os-dByings Rin-Po-Ch'e'i mDzod Kyi 'Grel-Ba Lung-Gi gTer-mDzod (f. 212) by Klong-Ch'en Rab-'Byams. Published by Dodrup Chen Rinpoche.

MC Ch'os-Tshul sNa-Tshogs Las brTsams-Te 'Bel-gTam-Tu bGyis-Pa'i Rabs Me-Tog Ch'un-'Phyang (f. 75) by sNa-Tshogs Rang-Grol. A zylographic copy from rGyal-Gyi Sri sNeu-sTeng.

MD Man-Ngag Rin-Po-Ch'e'i mDzod (f. 78) by Klong-Ch'en Rab-'Byams. Published by Dodrup Chen Rinpoche.

MK bsKyed-Rim Zin-Bris *Yoga* sPyi-'Gros lTar bKod-Pa Man-Ngag Kun-bsTus (f. 80) by mKhar-sPrul bsTan-Pa'i Nyi-Ma. A xylographic copy.

MN Mi-La Ras-Pa'i rNam-Thar by rNal-'Byor-Pa Rus-Pa'i rGyan-Chan. Published in China.

MT Mu-Tig Gi 'Phreng-Ba Zhes-Bya-Ba'i rGyud (f. 234-289, Vol. Ta, rNying-Ma rGyud-'Bum). Published by Jamyang Khyentse 1974.

NCC gZhi Khregs-Ch'od sKabs-Kyi Zin-Bris bsTan-Pa'i Nyi-Ma'i Zhal-Lung sNyan-brGyud Ch'u-Bo'i bChud-'Dus (f. 67) by Padma Las-'Brel-rTsal. Publisher unknown.

ND gNas-Lugs Rin-Po-Ch'e'i mDzod (f. 16) by Klong-Ch'en Rab-'Byams. Published by Dodrup Chen Rinpoche.

NDG sDe-gSum sNying-Po'i Don-'Grel gNas-Lugs Rin-Po-Ch'e'i mDzod Ches-Bya-Ba'i 'Grel-Ba (f. 93) by Klong-Ch'en Rab-'Byams. Published by Dodrup Chen Rinpoche.

NDK rDzogs-Pa Ch'en-Po Sems-Nyid Rang-Grol Gyi Lam-

Rim sNying-Po'i Don-Khrid (f. 17-28, Don-Khrid) by Dri-Med A'od-Zer. Published by Dodrup Chen Rinpoche.

NK Nyi-Ma Dang Zla-Ba Kha-sByor-Ba Ch'en-Po gSang-Ba'i rGyud (f. 192-218, Vol. Ta, rNying-Ma rGyud-'Bum). Published by Jamyang Khyentse, 1974.

NKC gNyis-Ka'i Yang-Yig Nam-mKha' Klong-Ch'en (f. 105-116, Vol. E, Bla-Ma Yang-Tig, Ya-bZhi) by Klong-Ch'en Rab-'Byams. Published by Sherab Gyaltsen Lama.

NKT Nags-Tshal Kun-Tu dGa'-Ba'i gTam (f. 66-72, Vol. I, gSung Thor-Bu) by Ngag-Gi dBang-Po. Published by Sangje Dorje.

NKS Thod-rGal Gyi Yang-Yig Nam-mKha' Klong-gSal (f. 98-105, Vol. E, Bla-Ma Yang-Tig, Ya-bZhi) by Klong-Ch'en Rab-'Byams. Pub by Sherab Gyaltsen Lama.

NM gDams-Ngag Sangs-rGyas Lag-bChang-Ma'i sByong-Thabs gNad-Kyi Man-Ngag (f. 71-84, Upadeśa) by Mi-Pham. Publisher unknown.

NMT bChing-Grol Med-Pa gShis-Kyi gNad-brTags-Pa Sems-Nyid Nam-mKha'i Me-Long blTa-Ba (f. 119-123, Upadesa) by 'Jam-dPal rDo-rJe (alias Mi-Pham rNam-rGyal). Publisher unknown.

NN rDzogs-Pa Ch'en Po Bla-Ma Yang-Tig Las, gNyis-Ka'i Yang-Yig Nam-mKha' Klong-Ch'en Gyi rNam-Par bShad-Pa Nyi-Ma'i sNang-Ba (f.114) by Padma Las-'Brel rTsal. Publisher unknown.

NS Yon-Tan Rin-Po-Ch'e'i mDzod-Las, 'Bras-Bu'i Theg-Pa'i rGya-Ch'er 'Grel rNam-mKhyen Shing-rTa (f. 440) by mKhyen-brTse'i Lha (alias 'Jigs-Med Gling-Pa). Published by Pema Thrinley for Ven. Dodrup Chen Rinpoche, Sikkim National Press, Gangtok, Sikkim, India. 1985

NTG rGyal-Ba gNyis-Pa Kun-mKhyen Ngag-Gi dBang-Po'i gSung-Rab-Las, mDzod-bDun Ngal-gSo gSang-Tik rNams rMad-Byung 'Phrul-Gyi Phyi-Ch'os Ji-lTar bsGrub-Pa'i-Tshul Las mTshams-Pa'i Ngo-mTshar gTam-Gyi Gling-Bu sKal-bZang rNa-Ba'i dGa'-sTon (f. 79) by 'Gyur-Med Kun-bZang rNam-rGyal (1713-1769). Published by Dodrup Sangyey Lama, 1976.

NGR A'od-gSal Rin-Po-Ch'e'i sNying-Po Padma Las-'Brel rTsal Gyi rTogs-brJod Ngo-mTshar sGyu-Ma'i Rol-Gar (f. 147) (Autobiography of mKhan-Po Ngag-Ch'ung, 1879-1941). Published by Sonam T. Kazi.

NTD Kun-mKhyen Dri-Med A'od-Zer Gyi rNam-Thar mThong-Ba Don-lDan (f. 46, Vol. Ya, Vima sNying-Thig, Ya-bZhi) by Ch'os-Grags bZang-Po (14th century). Published by Sherab Gyaltsen Lama.

OT mThong-sNang Rin-Po-Ch'e A'od-Kyi Drva-Ba (f.101-132, Vol. Hung, mKha-'Gro Yang-Tig, Ya-bZhi) by Padma Las-'Brel rTsal (alias Klong-Ch'en Rab-'Byams). Published by Sherab Gyaltsen Lama.

PK Theg-Pa Ch'en-Po'i Man-Ngag-Gi bsTan-bChos Yid-bZhin Rin-Po-Ch'e'i mDzod Kyi 'Grel-Ba Pama dKar-Po (Vol. I & II) by Tshul-Khrims Blo-Gros (alias KLong-Ch'en Rab-'Byams). Published by Dodrup Chen Rinpoche.

PKD sNga-'Gyur rDo-rJe Theg-Pa gTso-Bor Gyur-Pa'i sGrub-brGyud Shing-rTa brGyad-Kyi Byung-Ba brJod-Pa'i gTam mDor-bsDus Legs-bShad Padma dKar-Po'i rDzing-Bu (f. 284) by Zhe-Ch'en rGyal-Tshab Padma rNam-rGyal (19th cent.). Published by T. Y. Tashigangpa.

PS *The Platform Sūtra of the Sixth Patriarch.* The Text of the TUN-HUANG manuscript, translated, with notes, by Philip B. Yampolsky. Published by Columbia University Press.

PZ Klong-Ch'en sNying-Gi Thig-Le-Las, *Yoga* gSum-Gyi sPyi-Ch'ings dPal-Ch'en Zhal-Lung (f. 6, Vol. Om, KLong-Ch'en sNying-Thig Collection) by 'Jigs-Med Gling-Pa. Published by Jamyang Khyentse.

RDD dPal-gSang-Ba sNying-Po'i rGyud-Kyi sPyi-Don Nyung-Ngu'i Ngag-Gis gSal-Bar 'Byed-Pa Rin-Po-Ch'e'i mDzod-Kyi lDeu-Mig (f. 107) by 'Jigs-Med bsTan-Pa'i Nyi-Ma. Published by Dodrup Chen Rinpoche.

RG Byang-Ch'ub Kyi Sems Kun-Byed rGyal-Po'i Don-Khrid Rin-Ch'en Gru-Bo (f. 71-89, Don-Khrid) by Klong-Ch'en Rab-'Byams. Published by Dodrup Chen Rinpoche.

RK Byang-Ch'ub Kyi Sems Rig-Pa Khu-Byug (f.109, Vol. Ka, rNying-Ma rGyud-'Bum). Published by Jamyang (Dilgo) Khyentse, 1974.

RR Rig-Pa Rang-Shar Ch'en-Po'i rGyud (Pp. 1-167, rNying-rGyud, Vol. 10). Published by Jamyang khyentse, 1974.

RT De Kho-Na Nyid Rin-Po-Ch'e'i Phreng-Ba by Avadhutipa gNyis-Su Med-Pa'i rDo-rJe. rGyud,, Vol. VI, page 115 A/6-120 A/1, Dege Edition.

SC rDzogs-Pa Ch'en-Po Sems-Nyid Ngal-gSo'i 'Grel-Ba

Shing-rTa Ch'en-Po (Vols. I & II) by Dri-Med A'od-Zer. Published by Dodrup Chen Rinpoche.

SD Sems-Don gDams-Ngag (f. 129-131, Upadeśa) by 'Jam-dPal rDo-rJe.

SDN gSang-Ba'i sNying-Po De-Kho-Na-Nyid Nges-Pa (f. 1-31, Vol. Pha, rNying-Ma rGyud-'Bum). Published by Jamyang Khyentse, 1974.

SKG Shes-Bya Kun-Khyab 'Grel-Ba (Vols. I-IV) by Kong-sPrul Yon-Tan rGya-mTsho. Published by Jamyang Khyentse.

SM gNubs-Ch'en Sangs-rGyas Ye-Shes Rin-Po-Ch'es mDzad-Pa'i sGom-Gyi gNad gSal-Bar Phye-Ba bSam-gTan Mig-sGron (f. 253) by gNubs-Ch'en Sang-rGyas Ye-Shes (9th cent.). Published by 'Khor-gdon Gter-sprul 'Chi-med-rig-dzin, India.

SN rDzogs-Pa Ch'en-Po Sems-Nyid Ngal-gSo (f. 56) by Dri-Med A'od-Zer. Published by Dodrup Chen Rinpoche.

SND bSam-gTan Ngal-gSo'i 'Grel-Ba Shing-rTa rNam-Dag (f. 46) by Klong-Ch'en Rab-'Byams. Published by Dodrup Chen Rinpoche.

SR rDzogs-Pa Ch'en-Po Sems-Nyid Rang-Grol (f. 17) by Dri-Med A'od-Zer. Published by Dodrup Chen Rinpoche.

ST Yon-Tan Rin-Po-Che'i mDzod-Kyi dKa'-gNad rDo-rJe'i rGya-mDud 'Grol-Byed Legs-bShad gSer-Gyi Thur-Ma (f. 306) by Sog-Po bsTan-Dar (1759-?). Published by Jamyang Khyentse.

STN rDzogs-Pa Ch'en-Po bSam-gTan Ngal-gSo (f. 13) by Dri-Med A'od-Zer. Published by Dodrup Chen Rinpoche.

SYD Sems-Dang Ye-Shes Kyi Dris-Lan (f. 66-74, Vol. I, gSung-Thor-Bu), by Tshul-Khrims Blo-Gros. Published by Sange Dorje.

SZ rDzogs-Pa Ch'en-Po sGyu-Ma Ngal-gSo'i 'Grel-Ba Shing-rTa bZang-Po (f. 87) by Dri-Med A'od-Zer. Published by Dodrup Chen Rinpoche.

TCD Theg-mCh'og Rin-Po-Ch'e'i mDzod (Vol. I & II) by Ngag-Gi dBang-Po. Published by Dodrup Chen Rinpoche.

TD gSang-Ba Bla-Na Med-Pa A'od-gSal rDo-rJe'i gNas-gSum gSal-Bar Byed-Pa Tshig-Don Rin-Po-Ch'e'i mDzod (f. 243) by Ngag-Gi dBang-Po. Published By Dodrup Chen Rinpoche.

TRG Zab-Pa Dang rGya-Ch'e-Ba'i Dam-Pa'i Ch'os-Kyi Thob-Yig Rin-Ch'en sGron-Me (bKa'-'Gyur and rNying-rGyud Thob-Yig) by 'Jigs-Bral Ye-Shes rDo-rJe.

TRL gTer-'Byung Rin-Po-Ch'e'i Lo-rGyus (f. 53, Vol. Om, Mkha'-'Gro Yang-Tig, Ya-bZhi) by Dri-Med A'od-Zer. Published by Sherab Gyaltsen Lama.

TSC dBu-Ma rTsa-Ba'i Tshig-Leur Byas-Pa Zhes-Bya-Ba'i mCh'an-'Grel (f. 63) by gZhan-Phan (Ch'os-Kyi sNang-Ba). Published by Ven. D. G. Khochhen Tulku, India.

TT Gangs-Chan Du Byon-Pa'i Lo-Pan rNams-Kyi mTshan-Tho Rags-Rim Tshig-bChad-Du bsDebs-Pa Mahāpandita Silaratna'i gSung (or mTshan-Tho) (f. 238) by mKhyen-brTse'i dBang-Po (1820-1892). Published by Jamyang (Dzongsar) Khyentse, India.

TTN *The Tantric Tradition of the Nyingmapa* by Tulku Thondup. Published by Buddhayāna, U.S.A.

YB rDzogs-Pa Ch'en-Po Klong-Ch'en sNying-Thig-Gi gDod-Ma'i mGon-Po'i Lam-Gyi Rim-Pa'i Khrid-Yig Ye-Shes Bla-Ma (f. 83, Vol. Hung, Klong-Ch'en sNying-Thig Collection) by 'Jigs-Med Gling-Pa. Published by Jamyang (Dilgo) Khyentse.

YD Theg-Pa Ch'en-Po'i Man-Ngag-Gi bsTan-bChos Yid-bZhin Rin-Po-Ch'e'i mDzod (f. 78) by Tshul-Khrims Blo-Gros. Published by Dodrup Chen Rinpoche.

YDGD Yid-bZhin Rin-Po-Ch'e'i mDzod-Kyi Grub-mTha' bsDus-Pa (f. 38) by Mi-Pham rNam-rGyal. Published by Dodrup Chen Rinpoche.

YM Slob-dPon Sangs-rGyas gNyis-Pa Padma 'Byung-gNas Kyi rNam-Par Thar-Pa Yid-Kyi Mun-Sel Zhes-Bya-Ba bZhugs (f. 128) by Sog-bZlog-Pa Blo-Gros rGyal-mTshan. Published by Ogyen Tshering, India.

YTD Yon-Tan Rin-Po-Ch'e'i mDzod dGa'-Ba'i Ch'ar Zhes-Bya-Ba bZhugs. (f. 51) by 'Jigs-Med Gling-Pa. Published by Pema Thrinley for Ven. Dodrup Chen Rinpoche, Sikkim National Press, Gangtok, Sikkim, India. 1985.

ZDS Zhus-Lan bDud-rTsi gSer-Phreng (f. 203-211, Vol. Wam, mKha'-'Gro sNying-Thig, Ya-bZhi). Published by Jamyang Khyentse.

ZL dPal gSang-Ba'i sNying-Po De-Kho-Na-Nyid Nges-Pa'i rGyud-Kyi rGyal-Po sGyu-'Phrul-Dra-Ba sPyi-Don Gyi sGo-Nas gTan-La 'Bebs-Par Byed-Pa'i Legs-bShad gSang-bDag Zhal-Lung (f.419) by Lo-Ch'en Dharmashri (1654-1717). Published by Ven. D. G. Khochhen Tulku, Nyingmapa Lama's College. Clement Town, Dehra Dun, India.

ZM Klong-Ch'en sNying-Gi Thig-Le-Las. gZhi-Lam 'Bras-Bu'i sMon-Lam (f. 2) by 'Jigs-mEd Gling-Pa. Published by Ven. Dodrup Chen Rinpoche, Sikkim, India.

ZYD gZhi-sNang Ye-Shes sGron-Me (f. 1-10, Vol. Wam, Bla-Ma Yang-Tig, Ya-bZhi). Published by Sherab Gyaltsen Lama.

Index

1. TECHNICAL TERMS IN ENGLISH

phenomena), 411, 419
of omnipresence (Kun-Khyab Kyi Ye-Shes), 202, 416, 418
of supreme (mundane) realization "immediately before" (Ch'os-mCh'og De-Ma-Thag Pa'i Ye-Shes). *See also* thoroughly realized primordial wisdom (Nye-Bar Thob-Pa'i Ye-Shes), 380
of the three Bodies; 416, 417, 440
-at-the basis of Ultimate Body, 416
endowed with characteristics of Enjoyment Body, 416
of omnipresence of Manifested Body, 416
of the Ultimate Body (Dharmakāya), three; 417
of omnipresent compassion, 417
or originally pure essence, 417
of spontaneously accomplished nature, 417
'property of the subject' (Phyogs-Ch'os), 267
pure or white substances, 21
purification, basis of; result of, 8
purity, primordial (Ka-Dag), 9, 42, 83, 205
realm, 79, 80, 223, 224, 228, 231, 255, 300, 323, 326, 327, 360, 370-372, 381, 387, 424
realms, 17, 36, 55, 68, 75, 115, 118, 183, 184, 209, 210, 213, 224, 231, 253, 255, 256, 283, 300, 301, 318, 323, 327, 334, 337, 341-343, 348, 351, 353, 365, 371, 372, 374, 379, 381-384, 386, 387, 394, 399, 408, 415, 421, 422, 424
desire realm, 223, 224, 231, 300, 327, 371, 381, 387, 424
desire realms, 379
form, 224
formless, 212, 223, 224, 255, 300, 326, 371, 372, 387, 424
reasoning, 11, 12, 37, 101, 110, 162, 267
Relaxation in the Natural State of the mind, posture of, 137
renunciation (Rab-Byung), 77, 147, 326, 332, 337, 380
renunciations, 346
result, 7, 10, 17, 18, 20, 21, 28, 38, 41, 49, 65, 66, 70, 72, 82, 86, 87, 90, 92, 97, 156, 179, 193, 198-200, 202, 207, 233, 234, 236, 241, 242, 259, 313, 316, 333, 344, 346, 348, 350, 362, 370, 372, 403, 407, 408, 413, 420, 423
of unmodified Natural Contemplation, 71
resultant yāna (tantra), 91
ritual (Ch'o-Ga), 17
rituals, 26, 101, 108, 146
Samye debate, 114
Schools, 3, 22, 89, 90, 112, 118-120, 245, 353, 421
Gelug, 3
Kagyud, 3
major, 3
Nyingma, 3, 9
oldest, 3
Sakya, 3, 148
scriptures, 3, 9, 11, 21, 22, 28-31, 35, 37, 43, 81, 82, 89, 107, 108, 111, 112 114, 115, 121, 122, 125, 131, 138, 148, 151, 164, 165, 173, 175, 179, 187, 188, 198, 200, 201, 217, 228, 236, 237, 242, 262, 263, 267, 268, 345, 360, 369, 377, 389, 397
Atiyoga, 43
Three, 345
seats (gDan-gSum), 9, 16, 24
self, 22, 28, 36, 39, 41-45, 48-56, 58-63, 68, 70-72, 78, 79, 83, 87, 93, 99, 101, 103-105, 110, 117, 120-122, 132, 157, 173, 179-183, 186, 192, 194, 197, 206-208, 210, 227, 242, 245-248, 250-254, 258, 264, 272, 282, 283, 286, 289, 295-298, 304-306, 308-310, 312-314, 318, 321, 322, 323, 325, 326, 328-335, 337, 339, 342-349, 356-358, 363, 364, 366, 367, 368, 370-373, 377-379, 388, 397, 398, 400, 401, 403, 409, 410, 412, 414,

2. SELECTED TECHNICAL TERMS IN SANSKIRT AND TIBETAN

five major tantras, 30
four cakras, 40, 390
gathering of luck, 111
gDangs, 51, 52, 58, 60, 75, 207, 350
Gelug, 3, 22
golden stupa, 137
Guhyagarbhamāyājāla-tantra, 11, 30, 200
Guhyasamāja, 28
Guru, 3, 30, 34, 35, 75, 108-111, 118, 125, 145, 146, 151, 153-155, 159, 160, 356, 357-359, 366, 367, 369, 373
Guruyoga, 306
gZung-Ba, 222, 296, 308
Heruka, 30, 134, 357
H!nayāna, 3, 350, 353
Kagyud, 3, 22
Kagyur, 108
Kālacakra, 28
Karma, 8, 18, 20, 30, 85, 108, 115, 165, 170, 183, 184, 192-194, 209, 211, 212, 214-216, 221-223, 227, 228, 231-235, 251-253, 255, 257, 258, 265, 271, 296, 322, 335, 336, 339, 352, 401, 404, 419, 421-424
karma of liberative virtues, 193
karma of samsaric deeds, 193, 214
karma of virtuous deeds, 235
kāya, 42
Kriyā, 11, 16, 17, 95, 96, 98, 179, 346, 398
Kriyā tantra, 346
Kriyāyoga, 3, 11, 15-18, 95, 102
Lamdre, 90
Latrang, 141
Lhun-Grub Kyi 'Ch'ar-Tshul brGyad, 53, 191
lokāyata, 246, 421
Longde, 32, 33, 43-45, 49-52, 68, 101, 155
lower yānas, 4, 42, 95, 97-99, 101
Madhyamaka, 9, 90, 101, 104, 105, 111, 147, 194, 245
Mahā, 11, 26-28, 98, 180, 346, 398
Mahāmudrā, 13, 20, 90, 111, 116, 354, 365
Mahāparinirvāṇa, 29, 114, 193, 237, 239, 245, 247
Mahāsandhiyoga, 11
Mahāsukhakāya, 351
Mahāyāna, 3, 5, 7, 8, 23, 79, 89, 91, 93, 112, 114-120, 122, 155, 181, 193, 194, 195, 198, 200-202, 231, 243, 261, 299, 341, 346, 350, 361, 375, 379
Mahāyoga, 3, 9, 11, 22-26, 28-30, 36, 37, 96, 100, 102, 121
maṇḍala, 9, 19-21, 24, 25, 27, 28, 38-40, 42, 96, 97, 99, 100, 102, 152, 218, 332, 338, 347, 349, 358, 401, 404, 415
maṇḍala of primordial suchness, 24, 39
maṇḍala of the deities, 25, 39, 40
mantra, 40, 339, 350, 358, 359
Matṛtantra, 22
Māyā, 6, 185, 248, 263, 317, 318, 320-322, 325, 326, 332, 340, 350, 358, 369, 376, 392
Mengagde, 32, 34, 35, 43-46, 50-52, 57, 60, 64, 66-68, 79, 155-158
meritorious karma, 424
nāgas, 379, 422
Namkha Sumthrug, 128
Natural Nirmāṇakāya, 348
neutral karma, 223, 422
New tantra, 147
Ngo-Bo, 13, 41, 46, 48, 49, 52, 57, 58, 60, 64, 71, 103, 191, 200, 205, 207, 208, 214, 217, 219, 226, 239, 251, 253, 267, 276, 277, 350, 351, 379, 383, 384, 386, 411, 413, 415, 417, 418
Ngulchu, 150
nine yānas, 3, 179, 180, 346, 397
Nirmāṇakāya, 42, 74, 153, 314, 326, 327, 347, 348, 351, 372, 391, 412, 413
nirvāṇa, 10, 28, 36, 42, 47, 48, 53, 57, 64, 87, 98, 101, 134, 163, 166, 180, 183, 191, 192, 202, 205-207, 210-212, 214, 216, 217, 220, 225, 226, 232, 238, 250, 251, 255, 262, 265, 274, 277, 286, 296, 298, 313,

3. SELECTED NAMES OF PERSONS, PLACES AND TEXTS

T: text, P: persons, Buddhas, PL: places, countries or institutions